# ENRICHMENT AT THE CLAIMANT'S EXPENSE

This book presents an account of attribution in unjust enrichment. Attribution refers to how and when two parties—a claimant and a defendant—are relevantly connected to each other for unjust enrichment purposes. It is reflected in the familiar expression that a defendant be 'enriched at the claimant's expense'. This book presents a structured account of attribution, consisting of two requirements: first, the identification of an enrichment to the defendant and a loss to the claimant; and, secondly, the identification of a connection between that enrichment and that loss. These two requirements must be kept separate from other considerations often subsumed within the expression 'enrichment at the claimant's expense' which in truth have nothing to do with attribution, and which instead qualify unjust enrichment liability for reasons that should be analysed in their own terms. The structure of attribution so presented fits a normative account of unjust enrichment based upon each party's exchange capacities. A defendant is enriched when he receives something that he has not paid for under prevailing market conditions, while a claimant suffers a loss when he loses the opportunity to charge for something under the same conditions. A counterfactual test—asking whether enrichment and loss arise 'but for' each other—provides the best generalisation for testing whether enrichment and loss are connected, thereby satisfying the requirements of attribution in unjust enrichment.

The law is stated as at 25 January 2016.

**Volume 18 in the series Hart Studies in Private Law**

# Enrichment at the Claimant's Expense

## Attribution Rules in Unjust Enrichment

Eli Ball

•HART•

OXFORD • LONDON • NEW YORK • NEW DELHI • SYDNEY

HART PUBLISHING
Bloomsbury Publishing Plc
Kemp House, Chawley Park, Cumnor Hill, Oxford, OX2 9PH, UK

HART PUBLISHING, the Hart/Stag logo, BLOOMSBURY and the Diana logo are trademarks of Bloomsbury Publishing Plc
First published in Great Britain 2016

First published in hardback, 2016
Paperback edition, 2019



A catalogue record for this book is available from the British Library.

**Library of Congress Cataloging-in-Publication Data**

Names: Ball, E. B. S. (Eli Byron Stuart), 1984– author.

Title: Enrichment at the claimant's expense : attribution rules in unjust enrichment / Eli Ball.

Description: Oxford ; Portland, Oregon : Hart Publishing, an imprint of Bloomsbury Publishing Plc, 2016. | Series: Hart studies in private law ; volume 18 | Based on author's thesis (doctoral - University of Oxford, 2014). | Includes bibliographical references and index.

Identifiers: LCCN 2016034341 (print) | LCCN 2016035220 (ebook) | ISBN 9781782258391 (hardback : alk. paper) | ISBN 9781782258407 (Epub)

Subjects: LCSH: Unjust enrichment—English-speaking countries.

Classification: LCC K920 .B348 2016 (print) | LCC K920 (ebook) | DDC 346.02/9—dc23

LC record available at https://lccn.loc.gov/2016034341

ISBN: HB: 978-1-78225-839-1
PB: 978-1-50992-888-0
ePDF: 978-1-78225-841-4
ePub: 978-1-78225-840-7

Series: Hart Studies in Private Law, volume 18

Typeset by Compuscript Ltd, Shannon

For Mum and Dad.

# FOREWORD

JAMES EDELMAN
JUSTICE OF THE FEDERAL COURT OF AUSTRALIA

The immediate impression of doctrinal private law in most countries outside the United States is of an intensely conservative, highly technical tradition bound by rules. This private law tradition dates back two millennia. At that time, one of the greatest Roman jurists noticed the existence of obligations outside contract and tort. This jurist, about whom we know little more than his (common) name Gaius, wrote that 'Obligations arise either from contract or from wrongdoing or by some special right from various types of causes' (D 44.7.1.pr). Gaius settled on the label 'quasi contract' to describe a large group of those other special rights.

In 1888, writing in the same tradition in the second edition of the *Harvard Law Review*, JB Ames said, without a trace, of irony that 'nothing impresses the student of the Common Law more than its extraordinary conservatism'. Ames described 'quasi contract' as including 'the fundamental principle of justice that no one ought unjustly to enrich himself at the expense of another'. This principle, like the notion that contractual obligations should be respected, conceals a vast morass of detailed rules which were yet to be explicated.

130 years later, both the common law and the civil law are far advanced in the development of the detail of rules concerning liability for the unjust enrichment of a defendant at the expense of a claimant. A huge contribution has come from the work of English academic scholars. Some of those are in a direct line of academic teaching and learning from Goff and Jones to Birks and to Burrows. The line of teaching and learning has been heavily reductionist. Rules have been collected by reference to criteria such as 'injustice', 'enrichment', and 'at the expense of the claimant'. Although the rules concerning unjust enrichment at the expense of another are now well developed there are still many difficult questions which remain. In Australia, question marks even surround the very existence of the subject.

Against this background, Dr Ball's book, *Enrichment at the Claimant's Expense: Attribution Rules in Unjust Enrichment*, is notable in three respects. First, Dr Ball is Australian. He writes for an audience who are, in part, Australian and likely to be sceptical. To borrow a metaphor from one of the forefathers of the subject, he publishes in Australia from a Sherman tank. His book, the manuscript of which was submitted on the eve of Australia Day 2016, commences with a powerful and compelling methodological defence of his approach focusing upon the labels 'top down' and 'bottom up'. In Australia the former label is a term of extreme derision. But although Dr Ball's thesis is powerfully anchored in case law, he notices, as did the progenitor of those labels (Judge Posner), that no coherent theory of law can ever be truly 'bottom up' or 'top down'.

Secondly, Dr Ball writes as a scholar of the fifth generation in the direct line of English teaching and learning that commenced with Goff and Jones. Each step in that English learning has become increasingly more sophisticated without losing the clarity needed to communicate conceptual ideas. In England, I supervised the very early stages of the thesis upon which Dr Ball's book is based. It was written at a time when the sophistication of legal scholarship in this area owed much to the tango between the academy and the practising profession, and judiciary. Scenarios from cases, usually where billions of pounds are at stake, immediately expose the difficulty with generalised rules forged upon a limited mass of case law.

Thirdly, Dr Ball has tackled directly the most difficult set of rules in the law of unjust enrichment. These are the rules concerning attribution. Perhaps the most sophisticated systemic attempt at these rules is the German approach. German law divides restitutionary claims into those based upon performance, *leistungkondiktion*, and those that are not based upon performance, *eingriffskondiktion*. Further and further subdivisions then occur. The complexity of the German approach contrasts with the simplicity seen in many of the English and Australian cases. But English and Australian law has been less successful. In the Court of Appeal in England it was claimed that the notion that an enrichment is at the claimant's expense does 'no more than point to the requirement that the immediate source of the unjust enrichment must be the plaintiff'. In Australia, it was said in the High Court that the 'subtraction from the plaintiff's wealth enables one to say that the defendant's unjust enrichment has been at the expense of the plaintiff'. Neither of these approaches can be applied directly as a means of deciding cases. The first is simply wrong.

Dr Ball's thesis presents a deep intellectual challenge to anyone seeking to understand the law of unjust enrichment. Some strong academic voices will object to Dr Ball's advocacy for a counterfactual test which, in areas such as the law of torts, has sometimes been abandoned in favour of tests such as whether an event was a contributing factor or exceptions where proof of causation is impossible. But those who object on this ground should bear in mind the subsequent English lament by Lord Sumption (judicially) and Lord Hoffmann (extrajudicially) that the abandonment of causation where proof is impossible is an exception that could not 'be justified by reference to any general principle and depended on a distinction which had no rational factual or legal justification'.

Dr Ball's thesis is written for the future. It has one eye on normative concerns and the other on the descriptive analytical tradition of the common law. It is written to develop rules in an important and developing area of private law. It is conservative and highly technical. In short, it has all the hallmarks of outstanding scholarship.

# ACKNOWLEDGEMENTS

In the preface to his opus, *The Structure of Property Law* (Hart, Oxford 2008), Professor Ben McFarlane proposed: 'Law, unlike life, must have structure.' Few sentences have caused as much perturbation in me as this. In 2009, when I embarked on my studies of restitution and unjust enrichment in Oxford, it was axiomatic. Today, seven years and half a world away, I am unsure. Structure in both law and life seems to have its relative advantages and disadvantages—but there is still so much more of each left to consider.

This book is based upon the thesis I submitted for the degree of Doctor of Philosophy in Law at the University of Oxford in 2014. I am indebted to many people for its success. The first is my supervisor, Professor Charles Mitchell. Charles's patience, guidance, and wisdom not only made my research possible, but also immensely enjoyable. Second are my examiners: Professor Andrew Burrows and Dr Stephen Watterson, who examined the final thesis; Professor Robert Stevens, who with Professor Burrows, oversaw my confirmation of status in 2013; and Professor Graham Virgo, who (again) with Professor Burrows examined my embryonic Master of Philosophy thesis in 2011. Justice James Edelman, who was my supervisor in Oxford for a time before returning to the warmer climate of the Australian judiciary, not only stoked the early research fires of my mind, but has now also done me the great honour of writing the Foreword to this book. It is truly humbling to have had the input of so many giants of law in what seems such a small and insignificant handful of pages.

I am extremely grateful to Hart Publishing and its staff for the opportunity to publish my work as part of the wonderful Studies in Private Law series, and for the professional support they have provided in making this happen. I am also grateful for the assistance of Anna Glen and Valiant Warzecha (both of the excellent institution, Macquarie Law School, Sydney) in preparing the manuscript for final submission.

During my time at Oxford I received invaluable support from the members and staff of Magdalen College and the Faculty of Law. My college supervisor, Professor Katharine Grevling, was particularly supportive of my efforts, as were Professors Simon Whittaker and Richard Ekins of St John's College, where I was fortunate to work as a Lecturer in Law.

My work and I have benefited tremendously from the assistance, enthusiasm, and friendship of Tatiana Cutts, Andrew Dyson, Jodie Gardner (with Sebastian, Eleanor and now Margaret), Sebastian Hartford-Davis, Olivia Hatton,

James Hillis, Nikolas Kirby, Lauren Kreamer, Andrew Lodder, Ayowande McCunn, Jeremias Prassl, Jaani Riordan, Benjamin Spagnolo, Anna Stelle, Frederick Wilmot-Smith, David Winterton, and Rebecca Zaman—to name but a few. I also could not have completed my work without the counsel and friendship of my cousin, Rebecca Silberberg. My sister, Hannah, has settled and inspired me. And Elizabeth's love has now put everything into a much wider perspective.

Above all, however, I must thank my parents, Jim and Judy. Without their love and support none of this (like so much of my life) would have been possible, and so it is only fitting that I dedicate this book to them.

*Narrabeen, Australia*
*April 2016*

# CONTENTS

## Part III Qualifying Liability

# LIST OF ABBREVIATIONS

| | |
|---|---|
| BCCA | British Columbia Court of Appeal |
| CA | Court of Appeal of England and Wales |
| CA Kent | Court of Appeal of Kentucky |
| Ch | Chancery Division |
| CP | Court of Common Pleas |
| DC | Divisional Court |
| ECJ | Court of Justice of the European Union |
| Exch | Exchequer |
| FCA | Federal Court of Australia |
| FCAFC | Full Court of the Federal Court of Australia |
| HCA | High Court of Australia |
| HL | House of Lords |
| KB | King's Bench |
| NSWCA | Court of Appeal of the Supreme Court of New South Wales |
| NZCA | Court of Appeal of New Zealand |
| Ont SC | Ontario Superior Court of Justice |
| PC | Privy Council |
| QB | Queen's Bench |
| SC Calif | Supreme Court of California |
| SC Minn | Supreme Court of Minnesota |
| SC Mont | Supreme Court of Montana |
| SC NJ | Supreme Court of Judicature of New Jersey |
| SCC | Supreme Court of Canada |
| UKSC | Supreme Court of the United Kingdom |
| USDC | United States District Court |
| VSC | Supreme Court of Victoria |

# TABLE OF CASES

**United Kingdom**
(including appeals from other jurisdictions to the Privy Council)

**Court of Justice of the European Union**



**Australia**

**Canada**



**New Zealand**



**United States of America**

# TABLE OF LEGISLATION

**United Kingdom**



**Australia**

# Introduction

## (A) Aim

This book presents an account of attribution in unjust enrichment. Attribution refers to how and when two parties—a claimant and a defendant—are relevantly connected to each other for unjust enrichment purposes. It is reflected in the familiar expression that a defendant be 'enriched at the claimant's expense'. The point has been made that this is not a statutory expression, and should not be interpreted as if it were.[1] The real issue, it is said, is not what those words mean, but what constitutes a sufficient connection between a claimant and defendant in an unjust enrichment claim.[2]

This book aims to unpack 'enrichment at the claimant's expense' so as to present a structured account of attribution in unjust enrichment. The account presented consists of two requirements: first, the identification of an enrichment to the defendant and a loss to the claimant; and, secondly, the identification of a connection between that enrichment and that loss. These two requirements must be kept separate from other considerations often subsumed within the 'enrichment at the claimant's expense' requirement, which in truth have nothing to do with attribution, but instead qualify unjust enrichment liability for different reasons.

## (B) Methodology

Every work of scholarship must have a purpose. In legal scholarship, purpose is coextensive with an appreciation of the character of the legal concepts under scrutiny, and the significance of those concepts within a given legal system. This is a deceptively simple task in the case of unjust enrichment, a term that may be employed to denote, variously, 'a unifying theme', 'a claim', 'a cause of action', 'an event', 'a principle' or even a 'law of unjust enrichment'.[3] This variety can confuse analysis and generate substantial debate. The American Law Institute's *Restatement*

[1] *Kleinwort Benson Ltd v Birmingham City Council* [1997] QB 380 (CA) 400 (Morritt LJ).
[2] P Birks, *Unjust Enrichment*, 2nd edn (Oxford, Oxford University Press, 2005) 73–74.
[3] See generally K Barker, 'Understanding the Unjust Enrichment Principle in Private Law: A Study of the Concept and its Reasons' in J Neyers, M McInnes, and S Pitel (eds), *Understanding Unjust Enrichment* (Oxford, Hart, 2004).

*of the Law Third: Restitution and Unjust Enrichment* ('*Third Restatement*') makes the point:[4]

> It is by no means obvious, as a theoretical matter, how 'unjust enrichment' should best be defined; whether it constitutes a rule of decision, a unifying theme, or something in between; or what role the principle should ideally play in our legal system. Such questions preoccupy much academic writing on the subject.

The *Third Restatement* itself proceeds on the assumption that the law can be usefully described without insisting on answers to any of these questions.[5] That may be true to an extent, but as Mr Leeming (as his Honour then was) has observed, the status afforded 'unjust enrichment' impacts upon how legal arguments proceed and are adjudicated, as well as upon the precedential force and fit of earlier authorities within the unjust enrichment paradigm.[6] At the very least, any work purporting to be about unjust enrichment must explain just what it means for a work to be *about* unjust enrichment. In short, this requires the adoption of a particular framework for understanding the subject. In English law, for example, 'unjust enrichment' is commonly analysed according to five questions: (1) Was the defendant enriched? (2) Was it at the expense of the claimant? (3) Was there an unjust factor? (4) Is the remedy personal or specific restitution? (5) Are there any defences?[7] There is nothing inherently wrong with this approach,[8] provided that we understand what we intend each of these questions to convey and achieve.

This is not a purely academic question: it is alive within the adjudication of actual cases. Much has been written, for example, about the High Court of Australia's applied methodological approach to unjust enrichment, and a comparison of it to that of other jurisdictions, including that of English courts.[9] But within English courts too there appears a degree of methodological uncertainty.[10]

[4] American Law Institute, *Restatement of the Law Third: Restitution and Unjust Enrichment* (2012) § 1 comment a.

[5] ibid.

[6] M Leeming, 'Subrogation, Equity and Unjust Enrichment' in J Glister and P Ridge (eds), *Fault Lines in Equity* (Oxford, Hart, 2012) 28.

[7] P Birks, *Unjust Enrichment* (n 2) 39. Cf the four-question analysis advanced in Professor Birks's earlier work and later adopted by the courts. See, eg, P Birks, *An Introduction to the Law of Restitution*, revised edn (Oxford, Clarendon Press, 1989) 21; *Banque Financière de la Cité SA v Parc (Battersea) Ltd* [1999] 1 AC 221 (HL) 227 (Lord Steyn), 234 (Lord Hoffmann, with whom Lords Griffiths, Steyn, Clyde, and Hutton generally agreed). In *Unjust Enrichment*, Birks introduced what is now the fourth question of the five. See further *Sempra Metals Ltd (formerly Metallgesellschaft Ltd) v Inland Revenue Commissioners* [2007] UKHL 34, [2008] 1 AC 561 [29] (Lord Hope).

[8] Cf *Third Restatement* (n 4) § 1, Comment d and Reporter's Notes.

[9] See, eg, J Dietrich, 'Unjust Enrichment versus Equitable Principles in England and Australia' in J Glister and P Ridge (eds), *Fault Lines in Equity* (n 6); Leeming (n 6); A Burrows, 'The Australian Law of Restitution: Has the High Court lost its way?' in E Bant and M Harding (eds), *Exploring Private Law* (Oxford, Hart, 2010) 84; K Mason, JW Carter, and G J Tolhurst, *Mason & Carter's Restitution Law in Australia*, 2nd edn (Sydney, LexisNexis Butterworths, 2008) Ch 1; M Bryan, 'Unjust Enrichment and Unconscionability in Australia: A False Dichotomy?' in J Neyers, M McInnes, and S Pitel (eds), *Understanding Unjust Enrichment* (Oxford, Hart, 2004).

[10] See further Dietrich (n 9) 18–21.

In *Foskett v McKeown*,[11] for example, the House of Lords considered the relationship between tracing and unjust enrichment where a rogue trustee had used trust monies to pay premiums on a life insurance policy that was paid out to his children. Lord Millett stated that the correct classification of the case was more than just academic,[12] and that the transmission of property rights from one asset to its traceable proceeds 'is part of our law of property, not of the law of unjust enrichment'.[13] This begs several questions. What does 'the law of unjust enrichment' mean in this context? And how does it differ from analysis according to 'the law of property'? The answers will depend upon the methodology adopted.

This book does not purport to definitively answer these questions: it would be naïve to attempt to do so without dedicating a whole work to them. Instead, the aim here in this Introduction is to provide a framework for understanding the relevance of this book to legal problems, and to foster an awareness of the underlying methodological complexity that influences substantial differences in the resolution of those problems. This requires both recognition of the inherent complexities of the common law system, and characterisation of unjust enrichment in a manner capable of transcending those complexities so as to provide purpose to this work.

## (1) Common Law Reasoning

An important initial step is to appreciate the nature of 'common law' reasoning. Among its several meanings,[14] this describes a legal culture and epistemology: 'an attitude towards the law and the resolution of legal problems'.[15] Lord Goff, writing extra-judicially, has observed that common lawyers tend to proceed by analogy, moving gradually from case to case:[16]

> We tend to avoid large, abstract, generalisations, preferring limited, temporary, formulations, the principles gradually emerging from concrete cases as they are decided. In other words, we tend to reason *upwards* from the facts of the cases before us, whereas our continental colleagues tend to reason *downwards* from abstract principles embodied in a code.

The meanings of what Lord Goff here terms 'upwards' and 'downwards' reasoning tend to cause significant difficulty and confusion, especially within the context of unjust enrichment. The High Court of Australia has expressed particularly stinging criticism of so-called 'top-down legal reasoning' in unjust enrichment

[11] *Foskett v McKeown* [2001] 1 AC 102 (HL).

[12] ibid 129 (Lord Millett).

[13] ibid 127.

[14] See generally J Bell, 'Sources of Law' in A Burrows (ed), *English Private Law*, 3rd edn (Oxford, Oxford University Press, 2013) [1.21]–[1.23].

[15] ibid [1.23].

[16] R Goff, 'The Future of the Common Law' (1997) 46 *International & Comparative Law Quarterly* 745, 753.

scholarship.[17] By this, the Court has intended to convey a dichotomy explained by Judge Richard Posner.[18] On the one hand, in top-down reasoning, the judge (or other legal analyst) starts with a theory of law. Such a theory need not be articulated in cases or existing 'legal jargon'. The theory is then used to organise, criticise, accept or reject, explain or explain away, distinguish or amplify existing decisions to make them conform to the theory, and to generate an outcome in each new case as it arises that will be consistent with the theory and existing cases. On the other hand, in bottom-up reasoning, one relies on techniques such as the 'plain meaning' approach to statutory material and 'reasoning by analogy' within a case or a mass of cases. One moves from there 'but doesn't move far'.[19]

One reason why the 'top-down' versus 'bottom-up' dichotomy tends to create tension between different camps of legal analysts is that it is often assumed that the top-down description cannot apply to a theory that relies upon case law. Professor Burrows, for example, has described the High Court of Australia's top-down reasoning objection as 'most surprising', and has defended 'the modern unjust enrichment movement' as 'the very antithesis of top-down reasoning'.[20] He argues that leading academic works on unjust enrichment work bottom-up from the raw material of the case law and are crammed with details of cases.[21] Leading unjust enrichment scholars, he adds, are sometimes derided precisely for their so-called 'black-letter' analysis, including painstaking analysis of the rules, principles, and doctrine laid down by the judges.[22] This may well be true, but it misses the substance of the top-down accusation. Fit with, and reliance upon, decided cases is not the hallmark of bottom-up reasoning, nor is it the antithesis of top-down reasoning. Reliance on case law does not provide an impenetrable defence to accusations of top-down reasoning because reliance upon cases is a feature of *both* bottom-up and top-down reasoning. The difference is more subtle. It does not lie in the question of whether cases are relied upon, but in the question of *how* they are relied upon. Leeming has thus described the High Court of Australia's criticisms of certain unjust enrichment scholarship as directed 'to a profoundly

[17] See, eg, *Roxborough v Rothmans of Pall Mall Australia Ltd* [2001] HCA 68, (2001) 208 CLR 516, [72]–[74] (Gummow J). See also *Farah Constructions Pty Ltd v Say-Dee Pty Ltd* [2007] HCA 22, (2007), 230 CLR 89 [151] (Gleeson CJ, Gummow, Callinan, Heydon, and Crennan JJ); *Bofinger v Kingsway Group Ltd* [2009] HCA 44, (2009) 239 CLR 269 [90] (Gummow, Hayne, Heydon, Kiefel, and Bell JJ). Cf K Mason, 'What is Wrong with Top-Down Legal Reasoning?' (2004) 78 *Australian Law Journal* 574.

[18] RA Posner, 'Legal Reasoning from the Top Down and from the Bottom Up: The Question of Unenumerated Constitutional Rights' (1992) 59 *University of Chicago Law Review* 433.

[19] ibid. A similar (though not necessarily identical) way of expressing the dichotomy of approach—at the point of legal classification—is to distinguish between *expository classification* (where the aim is to describe the present state of the law and so enable its communication to others) and *dispositive classification* (where the aim is to shape or influence the law and future legal developments). See further C Webb, 'Treating Like Cases Alike: Principle and Classification in Private Law' in A Robertson and TH Wu (eds), *The Goals of Private Law* (Oxford, Hart, 2009) 216–21.

[20] A Burrows, *The Law of Restitution*, 3rd edn (Oxford, Oxford University Press, 2011) 36.

[21] ibid. See also Birks, *An Introduction to the Law of Restitution* (n 7) 19.

[22] Burrows, *The Law of Restitution* (n 20) 36.

different methodological approach in resolving hard cases and developing the law' from that of the so-called modern unjust enrichment movement:[23]

> The approach sanctioned and applied by the High Court remains historical, seeking to identify and extrapolate principle from the reasoning contained in the body of the case law. The 'unjust enrichment' approach is essentially interpretive; it seeks to focus on the *outcomes* of case law, and to reinterpret the reasons for them so as to fit, as best they may, within a more recently identified conceptual framework or 'taxonomical dogma'.

Whether the distinction between these two approaches is truly as 'profound' as Leeming suggests is debatable. First, it is by no means self-evident which approach is superior in producing transparent, certain and coherent results.[24] Indeed, these and other measures for the qualitative assessment of a given legal approach, including 'logicality' or 'rationality', are deeply subjective and do not necessarily provide a definitive basis for assessment.[25] Secondly, the differences in approach may not always arise sharply in practice. In a given case for decision, the possibility of identifying and extrapolating principle from the reasoning of previous cases may be limited by the extent to which those previous cases have had to consider and express an opinion on relevant issues. Judges cannot cover the field of every possible future case in the course of deciding the actual case before them.[26] Indeed, the content of judicial decisions is necessarily limited by facts, pleadings and submissions by the parties.[27] There is also the very real problem that, to the extent that a particular issue has arisen for consideration in the past, a survey of existing judicial pronouncements and reasoning will reveal disagreement and inconsistencies in how that issue has been resolved. And all of this has a tendency to become severe as litigation (and, with it, the resolution of legal issues and problems) grows in complexity, cost, and time consumption.

These things being so, it seems that a degree of 'top-down reasoning' may be necessary and inevitable to navigate the thicket of legal precedent. Robert Goff J (as his Lordship then was) observed the reality of this essentially complementary approach when he described the ideal interaction between judge and jurist as co-operative, not competitive.[28] It also means that it is probably naïve to classify a

[23] Leeming (n 6) 32. See also W Gummow, 'Moses v Macferlan: 250 Years On' (2010) 84 *Australian Law Journal* 756, 757.

[24] Cf *Roxborough* (n 17) [74] (Gummow J).

[25] See further Leeming (n 6) 42; Barker (n 3) 6.

[26] See further Bell (n 14) para 1.26.

[27] A good example is the case of *Ford (by his Tutor Beatrice Ann Watkinson) v Perpetual Trustees Victoria Ltd* [2009] NSWCA 186, (2009) 75 NSWLR 42, where the defendant, Mr Ford, was held not liable to make restitution in respect of loan monies he had received as the 'mentally incapable dupe' of his son. Though Mr Ford had been used as a mere conduit for the funds in question, he did not plead a defence based upon change of position. The Court instead adopted a pragmatic approach to the question of his enrichment, finding Mr Ford had not, in any real or substantive sense, received and retained benefits such that it would be unjust for him not to repay the loan. It is worthwhile considering whether the Court would have approached the case in that way had a change of position defence actually been pleaded.

[28] R Goff, '1983 Maccabaean Lecture in Jurisprudence: The Search for Principle' (1983) *LXIX Proceedings of the British Academcy* 169.

particular approach (be it contained in a judicial decision, academic monograph, legal text, or treatise) in as black and white terms as 'top-down' versus 'bottom-up' reasoning.[29] A comparison of different reactions to the *Third Restatement* is illuminating in this respect. Professor Lionel Smith, on the one hand, has described it in terms that resonate with the 'top-down' approach explained above.[30] Dr Kremer, on the other hand, has described it as an example of the 'bottom-up' approach.[31] The reality is that a work as long and as complex as the *Third Restatement* is likely to comprise a mixture of both approaches, and a strict 'top-down/bottom-up' dichotomy is an oversimplification of reality.

## (2) A Unifying Legal Concept

In *Pavey & Matthews Pty Ltd v Paul*,[32] Deane J said that unjust enrichment:

> [C]onstitutes a unifying legal concept which explains why the law recognizes, in a variety of distinct categories of case, an obligation on the part of a defendant to make fair and just restitution for a benefit derived at the expense of a plaintiff and which assists in the determination, by the ordinary processes of legal reasoning, of the question whether the law should, in justice, recognize such an obligation in a new or developing category of case.

The High Court of Australia has subsequently and consistently endorsed this view,[33] and coloured Deane J's reference to 'ordinary processes of legal reasoning'. In *Bofinger v Kingsway Group Ltd*, for example, the Court compared unjust enrichment to the fate of 'proximity' as the 'unifying theme' for recognising a duty of care in negligence,[34] before explaining that unjust enrichment 'provides

[29] See further S Waddams, *Dimensions of Private Law: Categories and Concepts in Anglo-American Legal Reasoning* (Cambridge, Cambridge University Press, 2003) 222.

[30] L Smith, 'Legal Epistemology in the Restatement (Third) of Restitution And Unjust Enrichment' (2012) 92 *Boston University Law Review* 899, 900: 'It situates itself in the interpretive tradition that has been a hallmark of the development, not only of the common law, but of the civil law as well … The enterprise is a justificatory one: in addition to explanatory comments and illustrations, the Reporter provides notes whose purpose is to show that the black letter of the Restatement reflects the best interpretation of the collected decisions of the courts. The voice, in other words, is the voice of doctrinal law, which is also backwards-looking and justificatory.'

[31] B Kremer, 'Book Review: Restatement (Third) of Restitution and Unjust Enrichment' (2012) 35 *Melbourne University Law Review* 1197, 1204.

[32] *Pavey & Matthews Pty Ltd v Paul* [1987] HCA 5, (1987) 162 CLR 221, 256–57.

[33] *David Securities Pty Ltd v Commonwealth Bank of Australia* [1992] HCA 48, (1992) 175 CLR 353, 378–379 (Mason CJ, Deane, Toohey, Gaudron, and McHugh JJ), 389 (Brennan J), 406 (Dawson J); *Roxborough* (n 17) [70] (Gummow J); *Farah Constructions Pty Ltd v Say-Dee Pty Ltd* (n 17) [151] (Gleeson CJ, Gummow, Callinan, Heydon, and Crennan JJ); *Lumbers v W Cook Builders Pty Ltd (In Liquidation)* [2008] HCA 27, (2008) 232 CLR 635, [83]–[85] (Gummow, Hayne, Crennan, and Kiefel JJ); *Friend v Brooker* [2009] HCA 21, (2009) 239 CLR 129, [7] (French CJ, Gummow, Hayne, and Bell JJ); *Bofinger v Kingsway Group Ltd* (n 17) [85]–[91] (the Court); *Equuscorp Pty Ltd v Haxton* [2012] HCA 7 [29]–[30] (French CJ, Crennan, and Kiefel JJ); *Australian Financial Services and Leasing Pty Ltd v Hills Industries Ltd* [2014] HCA 14 [20] (French CJ) [73]–[76] (Hayne, Crennan, Kiefel, Bell, and Keane JJ), [105] (Gageler J).

[34] *Bofinger v Kingsway Group Ltd* (n 17) [87].

a means for comparing and contrasting various categories of liability' and 'also may assist in … recognition of obligations in a new or developing category of case'.[35] This 'ordinary process of legal reasoning' is not a nebulous concept; nor is it an unfamiliar one. In *Dorset Yacht Co Ltd v Home Office*, for example, Lord Diplock observed that judicial development rightly proceeds by identifying the relevant characteristics common to the kinds of conduct and relationship between the parties that are involved in the case for decision, and the kinds of conduct and relationships that have been held in previous judicial decisions to engage the legal principle in question.[36]

There is much to commend to this approach. It resonates with the methodology underlying common law reasoning described above: proceeding by analogy, and moving gradually from case to case. In doing so, it recognises and adapts to the complications attending the resolution of real cases, including the difficulties inherent in the exercise of deciphering what the law actually is in a system based upon a combination of facts, logic, principle, and history. It is unsurprising, therefore, to find that the editors of one of the leading English texts subscribe to this conception of unjust enrichment.[37]

A related benefit of the 'unifying legal concept' view is that it pitches unjust enrichment at approximately the same level of conceptual generality and utility as tort and contract. 'Tort', for example, is often described as a miscellaneous grouping of civil wrongs. There is, however, no single 'principle of tort'. For convenience, we commonly refer to the existence of a 'law of tort' to group a variety of different bases of liability. 'Tort' thus has an adjectival and taxonomical utility, but it does not function as a source of liability in its own right, save at a high level of generality. No lawyer simply pleads 'tort' to sustain a claim; instead, he pleads particular facts capable of matching those that have sustained particular liability in previous cases (or under a code or statute where necessary). Work is then done within that matching exercise: facts and bases of liability in past cases are compared and contrasted with those of the instant case, and a decision so made as to whether liability is appropriate. In many cases the exercise is so straightforward and mundane that it passes by almost unnoticed. So, for example, the conclusion that a driver of a vehicle owes a duty of care to his or her passenger is probably so uncontroversial at this time that little or no work is necessary to show it in a simple case. Other cases, however, may require more work, such as that of the driver of a vehicle in which all participants are engaged in a joint illegal enterprise.[38] Cases that resonate as 'like' the case in question must be drawn together and analysed; and this is done by grouping them under unified themes (such as tort, negligence, and the duty of care) and thereafter drawing appropriate comparisons and explaining

[35] ibid [88]–[89].

[36] *Dorset Yacht Co Ltd v Home Office* [1970] AC 1004 (HL) 1058 (Lord Diplock).

[37] C Mitchell, P Mitchell, and S Watterson (eds), *Goff & Jones: The Law of Unjust Enrichment*, 8th edn (London, Sweet & Maxwell, 2011) para 1.08.

[38] See, eg, *Miller v Miller* [2011] HCA 9, (2011) 242 CLR 446; *Hall v Hebert* [1993] 2 SCR 159 (SCC); *Pitts v Hunt* [1991] 1 QB 24 (CA).

their application to the facts at hand. Indeed, this is why comparisons between unjust enrichment and the law of negligence, such as those made by the High Court of Australia in *Bofinger v Kingsway Group Ltd* are particularly insightful. The law of negligence does not provide a single test for the existence of a duty of care in novel cases located on the so-called 'periphery' of established 'core' cases, but instead provides a uniform framework for the discussion and grouping of arguments that may be deployed in the course of developing the law to cover those novel cases.[39] Negligence thus operates as a unifying legal concept but not a definitive legal principle.[40]

The same point can be made in respect of contract. The factual bases, dimensions, and content of contractual liability will differ in every case—making contract, in some respects, more miscellaneous than tort. The law does not generally lay down any comprehensive set of contractual rights, duties and liabilities. Instead, it sets out the common parameters within which liability arises, organised around common and unifying themes such as the concept of agreement; comprising offer, acceptance, certainty, and so on. In this way it is possible to reason outwards by analogy from the most mundane of cases, such as a written, signed, and bilateral contract, to less intuitive and more complex situations, such as a unilateral offer made to the world at large, or the intricate and lengthy exchange of electronic communications over a period of time.

So it is with unjust enrichment. In the simple case of money paid under mistake of fact, for example, the exercise of establishing a claim will require little more than a recitation of the relevant facts. But if the move is to be made from that simple case to a more complex one, such as a claim for the use value of money paid as tax earlier than necessary under invalid legislation,[41] then more work based upon comparison will be necessary: how does one progress from the straightforward benefit of money and the uncontroversial injustice of mistake recognised in previous cases, to the incorporeal benefit of use value and the injustice of invalid legislation in a novel case? The answer does not lie in treating unjust enrichment as a freestanding principle detached from decided cases. Rather, the answer starts with grouping previous cases under a single heading—unjust enrichment—and thereafter comparing, applying and distinguishing those cases as necessary from the particular controversy at hand,[42] possibly with the aid of further, subsidiary, and principled subdivisions. This is the exercise

[39] See D Nolan and J Davies, 'Torts and Equitable Wrongs' in A Burrows (ed), *English Private Law*, 3rd edn (Oxford, Oxford University Press, 2013) [17.45].

[40] Cf A Burrows, *The Law of Restitution* (n 20) 37.

[41] See, eg, *Sempra Metals* (n 7).

[42] See also *Bofinger v Kingsway Group Ltd* (n 17) [89] (the Court) where the earlier case of *David Securities Pty Ltd v Commonwealth Bank of Australia* (n 33) was described as one in which unjust enrichment was relied for the purpose of deriving the conclusion that the unjust factors that enliven restitution include mistakes of fact or law. See further *Australian Financial Services and Leasing Pty* (n 33) and also Gummow (n 23) where unjust enrichment assisted the consideration and delineation of the 'change of position' defence to restitutionary claims.

described by Lord Diplock in *Dorset Yacht Co Ltd v Home Office*.[43] It is as much an 'art' as it is a 'science'.[44]

An important consequence of conceiving of unjust enrichment in this way is that it provides methodological substance to what otherwise appear as formulaic concepts within a particular scheme of analysis, such as the five-question approach outlined earlier.[45] The identification and articulation of these concepts is a commendable achievement of what might be described as top-down legal reasoning. They do not, however, exist in abstract. Instead, they provide the means for initiating and engaging the processes of legal reasoning with respect to particular controversies as they arise. The complementary relationship between 'top-down' and 'bottom-up' legal reasoning envisioned by Lord Goff is thus achieved in practice. As Henderson J observed in *Investment Trust Companies (In Liquidation) v Revenue and Customs Commissioners*:[46]

> I have no quarrel with this basic conceptual structure. It needs to be remembered, however, that the four questions are no more than broad headings for ease of exposition. They should not be approached as if they had statutory force. There may also be a considerable degree of overlap between the first three questions.

As was observed earlier, much of the competition between top-down and bottom-up legal reasoning is, in reality, a matter of balance and of degree.[47] Though it is one thing to say, for example, that enrichment, attribution, and unjust factors are underpinned by similar considerations, it is quite another to say that they are the same inquiry. They are not, and Henderson J's point is *not* that they are. Rather, his point is that the structure of unjust enrichment is a conceptual tool for the resolution of controversies as they arise, and so that structure should not be applied in an unnecessarily rigid or dogmatic fashion.

It was observed above that the 'enrichment' and 'unjust factor' inquiries within the five-question approach to unjust enrichment can provide the unifying themes against which one can assess restitution in contexts different from those in which it has previously been allowed. The same is true of the 'at the expense of the claimant' inquiry, the unpacking of which is the central aim of this book. That inquiry uniformly addresses an issue that arises whenever a claimant seeks restitution from a defendant: how, if at all, is the enrichment of *that* defendant attributable to *that* claimant? The solution lies in studying different cases, ranging from the

[43] *Dorset Yacht Co Ltd v Home Office* (n 36) 580. See above p 8.

[44] See generally G Watt, *Equity Stirring: The Story of Justice Beyond Law* (Oxford, Hart, 2009) 10–14. See also Leeming (n 6) 43.

[45] (1) Was the defendant enriched? (2) Was it at the expense of the claimant? (3) Was there an unjust factor? (4) Is the response personal or proprietary restitution? (5) Are there any defences? See above p 2.

[46] *Investment Trust Companies (In Liquidation) v Revenue and Customs Commissioners* [2012] EWHC 458 (Ch), [2012] STC 1150 [39] (Henderson J). Reference to only four questions (rather than five) was to the exclusion of the remedy question. See also *Bank of Cyprus UK Ltd v Menelaou* [2015] UKSC 66 [19] (Lord Clarke).

[47] See above pp 5–6.

mundane to the complex, searching for points of commonality and distinction, and then drawing from that descriptive analysis a prescription for the resolution of future and yet-to-be-decided cases. This is what it means to say that this book is *about* attribution in unjust enrichment.

There are two final benefits that follow from the 'unifying legal concept' view of unjust enrichment that are particularly relevant to this book. The first is coherence. This point lies at the heart of much of the High Court of Australia's jurisprudence on unjust enrichment. In *Lumbers v W Cook Builders Pty Ltd (In Liquidation)*,[48] for example, the plurality emphasised that the application of a framework for analysis expressed at too high a level of abstraction created 'a serious risk of producing a result that is discordant with accepted principle, thus creating a lack of coherence with other branches of the law'—including, in that case, the relevant contractual arrangements existing between the parties.[49] And in *Farah Constructions Pty Ltd v Say-Dee Pty Ltd*, the Court was critical of the NSW Court of Appeal's application of unjust enrichment analysis in the face of the established principles relevant to determining recipient liability for breach of trust or fiduciary duty, observing the resultant precedent and confusion of principle arising following the intermediate court's decision.[50] Unjust enrichment is not unique in this respect.[51] The outlook of this book is much the same. In particular, the concern for the relationship between unjust enrichment and other established principles is evident in the separation of attribution from the qualifications imposed upon liability that arise independently (and regardless) of attribution, and which are therefore considered separately in Part III of this book.

Finally, and when all of the foregoing points are kept in mind, the 'unifying legal concept' view of unjust enrichment brings with it a flexibility of approach that is commendable for its adaptability. It was observed, at the start of this Introduction, that 'unjust enrichment' has been relied upon and described in various ways, including 'a principle', 'an event', 'a claim', and 'a cause of action'. This can lead to unnecessary confusion and considerable debate as different stakeholders argue at cross-purposes. Conceiving of unjust enrichment as a unifying legal concept, and therefore nothing more than an instance of ordinary legal reasoning, avoids over-fixation upon taxonomy, in favour of explaining and resolving cases as the need arises. In simple cases, for example, such resolution may be possible without recourse to the distinct stages of an unjust enrichment 'claim', but instead by reference to the old forms of action such as money had and received or *quantum meruit*. Though the necessity of pleading the old forms of action has been abolished by statute,[52]

[48] *Lumbers* (n 33).

[49] ibid [75]–[80] (Gummow, Hayne, Crennan, and Kiefel JJ).

[50] *Farah Constructions Pty Ltd v Say-Dee Pty Ltd* (n 17) [134]–[135].

[51] The genesis of the High Court's caution in this respect (at least during the late 20th and early 21st centuries) can be traced to decisions on negligence, the 'duty of care', and 'proximity' concepts. See especially *Sullivan v Moody* [2001] HCA 59, 207 CLR 562, cited in *Lumbers* (n 33) at fn 33. See also *Bofinger v Kingsway Group Ltd* (n 17) [87] (the Court).

[52] Common Law Procedure Act 1852.

they may still be used as a 'convenient and succinct description of a particular category of factual situation which entitles one person to obtain from the court a remedy against another person'.[53] The unifying legal concept of unjust enrichment then has a role to play in moving from these to novel factual situations. In time, unjust enrichment and its elemental components may too become a 'convenient and succinct description'. Indeed, this may have already occurred in some jurisdictions. But that does not mean that unjust enrichment should be permitted to rule in the rigid fashion denied to the old forms of action,[54] especially in novel cases. It is for this reason that this book does not adopt a single descriptive object of unjust enrichment beyond the unifying legal concept idea. References throughout to 'unjust enrichment' should be read as appropriate to the particular context. In certain situations, unjust enrichment may well fit the paradigm of a 'claim' dictating a remedy as between two parties. In other situations, it may be more appropriate to conceive of it as a guiding and useful 'principle' underlying established claims or modes of legal reasoning. The unifying legal concept is a flexible idea capable of accommodating a range of purposes.

## (C) Normativity

Flexibility, however, cannot be limitless. If unjust enrichment is a unifying legal concept, then it must be a manageable one, and so the basis of the unity it purports to achieve must be identified. In other words, the idea around which cases are organised as 'like' or 'unlike' for the purposes of legal development must be articulated. This necessitates the adoption of a particular normative outlook. Dr Webb has neatly explained the extra-legal quality of this task:[55]

> A classificatory scheme which seeks to influence future legal developments cannot be value-neutral. Instead, it must address the question of what differences and similarities matter, what makes cases alike or unlike. To answer these questions requires the application of standards which are in a sense external to or independent of the law, in that they are sourced not (only) in the legal rules we may currently have but in some theory of what law exists to do, what its goals and functions are, and just as importantly, how best to achieve them.

He observes that these issues have no means of authoritative resolution, 'and for that reason will always be contestable'.[56] But, he rightly concludes, this does not mean that lawyers should abandon attempts to answer (or at least speculate upon) them. The most difficult (and perhaps impossible) question in private law generally is why *ought* the law—be it of unjust enrichment, contract, tort, or

[53] *Letang v Cooper* [1965] 1 QB 232 (CA) 243 (Diplock LJ).
[54] ibid.
[55] Webb (n 19) 237.
[56] ibid.

other—exist in the first place. One might say, for example, that the law of contract exists to uphold the sanctity of promises and agreement, or that the law of tort exists to protect bodily and proprietary integrity, but doing so immediately exposes us to the follow up question: why do *those* things matter? And even if we can answer *that* question, then the process of questioning repeats over (and over) again, producing a seemingly endless series of 'Why?' questions that spiral ever downwards (or, upwards) to the point where all law is completely disassembled, and so revealed to be nothing more than an artificial construct built by the human mind upon imponderables and unprovables.

And well it may be. This book does not, however, attempt to answer such 'Why?' questions; nor does it need to. Within every work of legal scholarship, the downward spiral must be arrested at some point by basal assumptions about why the law exists—even if those assumptions are, in reality, open to deeper and ever more philosophical inquiry, that being beyond the purpose and scope of the particular work. And the exact point at which the downward spiral is arrested will depend, ultimately, upon the particular legal theory one adopts.[57] At one extreme, the particular work of legal scholarship may eschew all normative inquiry and present nothing more than an historical account of decided cases. At another extreme, the particular work of legal scholarship may undertake normative inquiry with gusto in an attempt to answer the most fundamental of questions so as to present a theory of what the law *ought* to be rather than what it actually *is* based upon existing authorities. And between the different extremes there is a diverse middle ground.

This book exists within that middle ground. The view of unjust enrichment as a 'unifying legal concept' described above is concerned both with what the law *is* insofar as it appreciates and justifies the existing authorities, and what the law *ought* to be insofar as it provides a means for deciding future cases by comparison to existing ones. Unjust enrichment is not a freestanding principle that exists in abstract: its origins are in the cases and so the development and expansion of the law it purports to achieve must necessarily be tied to those cases.

The normative basis for understanding and organising unjust enrichment is explained, in chapter one, according to Aristotelian and Weinribean corrective justice and what this book terms 'the exchange capacity'. The exchange capacity satisfies the need (explained by Webb above) to decide 'what differences and similarities matter, what makes cases alike or unlike'.[58] The exchange capacity is the normative backbone of unjust enrichment; external from the law insofar as it reflects a theory of why the law exists, but also internal to the law insofar as it can be derived from the analysis of existing cases.

The normative account provided by the exchange capacity is limited insofar as the inevitable 'Why?' questions behind it are left unanswered. The most that can be said of the exchange capacity, in this respect, is that its existence and

[57] See generally C Webb, 'Property, Unjust Enrichment, and Defective Transfers' in R Chambers, C Mitchell, and J Penner (eds), *Philosophical Foundations of the Law of Unjust Enrichment* (Oxford, Oxford University Press, 2009) 336–39.

[58] Webb (n 19) 237. See above p 12.

theoretical importance is supported by the decided cases, and that it provides a means for advancing the law of unjust enrichment to undecided cases. One objection to this outlook is that it does not really amount to a normative account of the law at all, because it still relies upon a description of the cases for its content. That objection, however, is itself premised upon a particular view of what a normative account of law should look like; namely, that it should exist independently of the prevailing methodology within a given legal system—in this case, the common law methodology of case-based reasoning. But even that is not an unshakeable proposition. Questions of what the law *ought* to be may inevitably be tied to what the law *is* precisely because our answer to the normative question is subjective insofar as it reflects our experiences of and within a given legal system. The interrelation between normative and positive accounts of the law is thus a form of 'model-dependent realism' similar to that encountered in scientific inquiry.[59]

## (D) Structure

This book is divided into three parts that follow the account of attribution in unjust enrichment described at the start of this Introduction. Part I examines the concepts of enrichment and loss, as they are relevant to unjust enrichment, and Part II examines the connection that must exist between enrichment and loss to sustain a claim of unjust enrichment. Together, these two parts cover the topic of attribution in unjust enrichment. Part III then examines certain qualifications on unjust enrichment that arise independently (and regardless) of attribution.

Part I consists of three chapters: one, two, and three. It explains 'enrichment' and 'loss' as the two 'sides' of unjust enrichment requiring connection, and situates them within the single normative framework of corrective justice and the 'exchange capacity'.

Chapter one proposes the exchange capacity as the normative basis of unjust enrichment. The exchange capacity reflects the freedom that individuals have to participate in systems for exchanging things that are capable of being exchanged. It is an aspect of a wider 'freedom of will' interest that underlies the internal structure of private law according to corrective justice generally. Furthermore, and looking past that internal structure, the exchange capacity directs attention to the instrumental considerations that define the ambit of unjust enrichment. So understood, the exchange capacity explains both the formal structure of unjust enrichment as well as its substantive scope.

Chapter two provides a framework for understanding the 'enrichment' requirement within unjust enrichment that fits the exchange capacity. It explains that every enrichment within the scope of unjust enrichment can be expressed in 'saved necessary expenditure' terms: the receipt of something valuable enriches

[59] See S Hawking and L Mlodinow, *The Grand Design* (New York, Bantam Books, 2010) 61–70.

the defendant because and insofar as he does not have to pay for it. The chapter also includes analysis of difficult issues of subsequent exchangeability and subjectivity of value within the enrichment inquiry. Understanding these issues benefits greatly from the adoption of the exchange capacity analysis proposed by this book.

Chapter three explains that loss is a necessary feature of unjust enrichment and provides a framework for understanding that requirement that fits the exchange capacity. Loss is the lost opportunity to exercise the exchange capacity. This aligns with the view that enrichment is expressible in saved expenditure terms—expenditure being 'necessary' insofar as it reflects what ought to have been (but was not in fact) exchanged by the defendant *vis-à-vis* the claimant for what was received. The chapter also includes analysis of the issue of loss correspondence and an explanation as to why, within a framework of unjust enrichment based upon the exchange capacity, it is a mistake to conceptualise enrichment and loss in separate terms.

Part II consists of three chapters: four, five, and six. It sets about the task of mapping the different kinds of connection that may exist between enrichment and loss in unjust enrichment revealed by the cases, and proposes a single generalisation of that connection that is consistent with the exchange capacity.

Chapter four explains that the parties to an unjust enrichment claim may be connected by single or multiple connections. Single connections include the acquisition of a right, the discharge of (or release from) an obligation, the use of property, the performance of a service, and the satisfaction of a request. Multiple connections may be sequential, concurrent, or interceptive combinations of single connections.

Chapter five generalises the connection between loss and enrichment into a single test. It considers two generalisations—'transfer' and 'causation'—and explains why neither is satisfactory. The chapter then proposes a third generalisation as a superior basis for understanding the cases: a 'but for' counterfactual connection between loss and enrichment. The chapter explains why this is not the same as a causal test, and how it relates back to the underlying exchange capacity analysis of unjust enrichment.

Chapter six explains the relationship between the counterfactual connection and another type of connection that has been suggested (both in decided cases and academic literature) as forming the basis of attribution in unjust enrichment and, specifically, cases involving multiple parties. That connection is a transactional one based upon the processes of following and tracing. Chapter six explains what these processes are, and argues that transactions add nothing to our understanding of attribution in unjust enrichment because transactions do not form part of the law of unjust enrichment in the first place.

Part III comprises only one chapter, chapter seven. It sets about explaining how liability in unjust enrichment may be qualified by considerations of legal policy that operate in much the same way as the rules of remoteness operate to limit liability based upon factual causation in the law of tort and of breach of contract. Liability in unjust enrichment is limited insofar as it cannot undermine or disturb pre-existing contractual and proprietary rights, equitable regimes of fault-based liability, or statutory schemes such as that governing insolvency. Previous analysis of these and other qualifications has tended to be muddled, and often entangled with the separate issue of whether there is a connection between enrichment and loss. That is the main reason why they appear in this book: having presented a model of attribution in unjust enrichment that consists of a counterfactual connection between enrichment and loss, the book must then explain why a number of considerations that have tended to make their way into the attribution inquiry do not properly belong there. The truth is that the matters presented in chapter seven need to be considered in their own right and separately from attribution.

## (E) Limits

As has already been observed, the English law of unjust enrichment is commonly analysed according to five questions: (1) Was the defendant enriched? (2) Was it at the expense of the claimant? (3) Was there an unjust factor? (4) Is the remedy personal or specific? (5) Are there any defences? These questions do not constitute a rigid formula in the abstract, but instead provide a means for initiating and engaging the process of legal reasoning with respect to particular controversies as they arise. Their utility lies in reducing the complexity of real-world transactions and events into manageable components susceptible to legal analysis and discourse. That being so, a degree of overlap and interrelation between the five questions is inescapable, and any work that purports to be about one question inevitably raises issues and concepts relevant to another, other, or all questions within the analysis.[60] Only the longest and most detailed of treatises can cover the subject as a whole with the detail necessary to gain a complete insight into the workings of unjust enrichment. Otherwise, limits must be imposed upon the reach of analysis that any one work can purport to achieve.

That is true of this book as much as it is of any other work. This book is about attribution in unjust enrichment. That 'attribution' does not feature explicitly within the above five-question analysis is not a source of difficulty precisely because the five questions are not an exact formula. Rather, the necessity of attribution is reflected in the requirement that a defendant's enrichment must have come at the claimant's expense. This requires knowledge of what must happen to each of the defendant and claimant for an unjust enrichment claim to be possible, as well as an appreciation of how, if at all, what has happened to one is connected to what has happened to the other. Unpacking those matters is the aim of this book, though in the course of doing so several tangential matters relevant to the larger picture of unjust enrichment as a whole arise, which this book does not aim to resolve.

[60] See above pp 8–9.

First, this book is not about the 'unjust factor' element of unjust enrichment. Part I of this book advances the exchange capacity as defining the scope of unjust enrichment so that the connection between defendant and claimant can be understood. This is different from the question of injustice, the analysis of which has occasionally been expressed in similar terms.[61] That similarity in terminology should not, however, be allowed to obscure these distinct inquiries. There is certainly a relationship between the two: the unjustness of a particular relationship cannot be adjudged without understanding that relationship and the qualities to which it *ought* to conform.[62] But an eagerness to understand and answer *all* aspects of unjust enrichment should not surpass the necessity of understanding unjust enrichment in a manageable form. This book is about attribution, not injustice. This is not to deny the relationship between the two issues, it is to say that they cannot both be addressed within the limited space of a single work such as this book.

Secondly, and similar to injustice, this book is not about the possible defences to unjust enrichment. Though the normative framework of the exchange capacity outlined and examined throughout Part I of this book may be capable of explaining a variety of defences, this book stops short of elaborating upon them beyond observing their relationship to the requirements of enrichment and loss that are central to this book. Furthermore, though the qualifications upon unjust enrichment outlined in chaper seven may appear to operate in much the same way as established defences, an elaboration of the relationship between them and such defences is necessarily beyond the scope of this book.

Finally, this book is not about the nature of the remedy following unjust enrichment. Again, the exchange capacity framework examined in Part I may be relevant to this issue; indeed, it is suggested that a natural limit of that analysis is the restriction of remedies for unjust enrichment to personal restitution only. But the book stops short of dismissing the possibility of specific restitution for unjust enrichment completely.

[61] A notable example is to be found in JM Nadler, 'What Right Does Unjust Enrichment Law Protect?' (2008) 28 *Oxford Journal of Legal Studies* 245. In that article, Dr Nadler argues that unjust enrichment 'vindicates the claimant's right of self-determination'. Nadler's point is directed to the issue of injustice; that is, how and why the law determines that a particular connection between claimant and defendant is *defective* and therefore subject to reversal. What it does not seek to do is explain *which* connections are relevant or *what* interests of the parties form the basis of that connection. See further EJ Weinrib, 'The Structure of Unjustness' (2012) 92 *Boston University Law Review* 1067.

[62] See, eg, EJ Weinrib, *Corrective Justice* (Oxford, Oxford University Press, 2012) 200.

# Part I

# Defining Enrichment and Loss

It is the essence of unjust enrichment that some connection should exist between two parties. Were matters otherwise, a defendant could be liable to make restitution to any person who simply identified the fact that the defendant had been enriched in circumstances that were unjust.[1] Before we can understand that connection, however, we must first understand what it is that is being connected. That is the aim of this Part: to explain 'enrichment' and 'loss' as the two sides of unjust enrichment requiring connection and, moreover, to situate them within a single normative framework based upon the 'exchange capacity'. The exchange capacity is the freedom to engage in systems of exchange, and is derived from wider considerations of free will and self-determination. It is the exchange capacity that brings substance to the scope of unjust enrichment, and uniformity to the concepts of enrichment and loss, by situating analysis of the subject within the real-world setting of value and exchange systems.

[1] *Chase Manhattan NA v Israel-British Bank (London) Ltd* [1981] Ch 105 (Ch) 125 (Goulding J).

# 1

# The Exchange Capacity

Unjust enrichment has been described by Professor Burrows as resting upon a disruption to each of two parties' positions requiring correction.[1] This is a neat conceptual summary, but it lacks explanatory force if we do not first understand the meaning of 'position' in this context. Human beings are multifaceted, and a given legal system may be concerned with any one of several aspects of their condition, including the physical, emotional, psychological, cultural, religious, intellectual, and so forth. If all of these were relevant to unjust enrichment, then it could bite in many areas where most people would agree it should not. The good vibes of a nightclub, the cultural enlightenment of a museum visit, and the affectionate embrace of a friendly animal at a zoo may each be considered 'enriching' in a colloquial sense, but no one would say that they are within the scope of unjust enrichment. They are not the kind of enrichments that the law is concerned with. Similarly, if I happen to enjoy a good (albeit inappropriate) laugh at a man clumsily falling over in the street, then he has no claim in unjust enrichment against me, even though I have gained a beneficial experience from his misfortune.

The challenge is to understand why these things are so, and to understand where (if at all) such extraneous matters fit within an account of the law.[2] To understand the meaning and scope of 'enrichment' and 'loss' as they appear in the decided cases, we must first equip ourselves with a theoretical definition of what interests are relevantly within the law of unjust enrichment, and explain why they are so.

That is the aim of this chapter: to explain, from a theoretical standpoint, the interest that engages unjust enrichment. According to this book, the solution lies in the 'exchange capacity'; that is, the capacity we each have to participate in systems for exchanging things that are capable of being exchanged. The exchange capacity is, in turn, one aspect of a wider 'free will' that underlies the internal structure of private law generally. Furthermore, and looking past that internal structure, the exchange capacity directs attention to instrumental considerations

[1] See, eg, A Burrows, *The Law of Restitution*, 3rd edn (Oxford, Oxford University Press, 2011) 36.

[2] See also EJ Weinrib, 'The Structure of Unjustness' (2012) 92 *Boston University Law Review* 1067, 1071, where the 'enrichment at the expense of the claimant' requirement is described as having 'aspects' relating to the defendant and claimant.

that define the ambit of unjust enrichment.[3] So understood, the exchange capacity explains both the formal structure of unjust enrichment and its substantive scope.

# (A) Corrective Justice

In *Kingstreet Investments Ltd v New Brunswick (Finance)* the Supreme Court of Canada observed:[4]

> Restitution is a tool of corrective justice. When a transfer of value between two parties is normatively defective, restitution functions to correct that transfer by restoring parties to their pre-transfer positions.

Corrective justice, so framed, is traceable to the work of Aristotle.[5] In time, it has come to provide a normative account of the private law of obligations, including unjust enrichment. But corrective justice, in itself, cannot provide a complete account of the subject. It only explains why unjust enrichment bites in situations that are within its scope. It does not explain what that scope is in the first place, nor does it purport to do so.

## (1) Corrective Justice and Unjust Enrichment

In *Nicomachean Ethics*, Aristotle advanced a theory of corrective justice that immediately seems to provide a blueprint for unjust enrichment:[6]

> [W]hen something is subtracted from one of two equals and added to the other, the other is in excess by these two; since if what was taken from the one had not been added to the other, the latter would have been in excess by one only. It therefore exceeds the intermediate by one, and the intermediate exceeds by one that from which something was taken. By this, then, we shall recognize both what we must subtract from that which has more, and what we must add to that which has less; we must add to the latter that by which the intermediate exceeds it, and subtract from the greatest that by which it exceeds the intermediate. … Therefore the just is intermediate between a sort of gain and a sort

[3] See further H Dagan, 'The Limited Autonomy of Private Law' (2008) 56 *American Journal of Comparative Law* 809, 811: 'The normative infrastructure of any private law doctrine should be responsive both to … bipolarity constraints on the one hand, and to social values appropriate to the pertinent category of human interaction on the other.'

[4] *Kingstreet Investments Ltd v New Brunswick (Finance)* [2007] SCC 1, [2007] 1 SCR 3, [32] (Bastarache J, the rest of the Court concurring).

[5] See, eg, Aristotle, *Nicomachean Ethics* (Lesley Brown ed, David Ross tr, Oxford, Oxford University Press, 2009).

[6] ibid 87. See further M Rush, *The Defence of Passing On* (Oxford, Hart, 2006) 144–46; M McInnes, 'The Measure of Restitution' (2002) 52 *University of Toronto Law Journal* 163, 186–96; L Smith, 'Restitution: The Heart of Corrective Justice' (2001) 79 *Texas Law Review* 2115, 2135.

> of loss, namely, those which are involuntary; it consists in having an equal amount before and after the transaction.

This theory is a tidy one of essentially arithmetical equality. As Professor Weinrib observes, however, it does not explain 'what the equality is an equality of', and so leaves corrective justice 'opaque to the extent that the equality that lies at its heart is unexplained'.[7] In *The Idea of Private Law*, Weinrib sought to provide the missing explanation by situating corrective justice theory within Kant's philosophy of right. The equality of corrective justice, according to Weinrib, is 'the equality of free wills in their impingements on one another'.[8] Accordingly, the bilateral equality of corrective justice is of a normative character; a reflection, according to Weinrib, of the normativity extrinsic to all self-determining activity within Kant's philosophy of right.[9] Corrective justice is therefore about normative gains and losses:[10]

> This equality is not itself factual: ... it does not refer to an equality in the amount or condition of the parties' holdings. Rather, equality is a formal representation of the norm that ought to obtain between doer and sufferer. Action that conforms to this norm, whatever it is, maintains the equality between the parties, so that no complaint is justified. Action that breaches this norm produces a gain to the injurer and a loss to the person injured. Then the court ... restores the parties to the equality that would have prevailed had the norm been observed. The normative nature of the equality indicates that the variations from that equality are also normative.

Weinrib explained unjust enrichment in these terms.[11] As Professor Lionel Smith later observed, however, this explanation jars with corrective justice insofar as it presupposes some form of wrongdoing.[12] Private law liability, according to Weinrib, requires the violation of a norm of equality that exists between claimant and defendant; the correlativity of normative gains and losses justifying legal intervention is founded upon the violation of a duty.[13] This sounds like a requirement of

[7] EJ Weinrib, *The Idea of Private Law* (Cambridge, Harvard University Press, 1995) 57. See also JM Nadler, 'What Right Does Unjust Enrichment Law Protect?' (2008) 28 *Oxford Journal of Legal Studies* 245, 247–49.

[8] Weinrib, *The Idea of Private Law* (n 7) 84.

[9] ibid.

[10] ibid 117. To be clear, and despite its heavy influence upon this book (as well as upon other scholarly works on unjust enrichment), it should be noted that Weinrib's theories do not occupy a monopoly position over corrective justice. Several other key jurists have worked on and contributed to the theory and its application within private law; perhaps most notably, Professor Jules Coleman and Professor John Gardner. See, eg, J Coleman, *Risks and Wrongs* (Oxford, Oxford University Press, 2002); J Gardner, 'What is Tort Law For? Part 1. The Place of Corrective Justice' (2011) 30 *Law and Philosophy* 1; J Gardner, 'Corrective Justice, Corrected' (2012) 12 *Diritto & Questioni Pubbliche* 9. To the extent that there are differences between the theories, their exploration is beyond the scope of this book. 'Weinribean' corrective justice is, in this sense, one of the basal assumptions about law for the purposes of this book. See above pp 11–12.

[11] Weinrib, *The Idea of Private Law* (n 7) 141. See further EJ Weinrib, *Corrective Justice* (Oxford, Oxford University Press, 2012) 200, Ch 6.

[12] Smith, 'Restitution: The Heart of Corrective Justice' (n 6) 2132–34.

[13] ibid 2125–26.

wrongdoing. It is now widely accepted, however, that unjust enrichment does not depend upon wrongdoing. Weinrib's account seems to conflict with this view. The problem therefore arises that unjust enrichment appears oddly beyond the scope of Weinrib's theory of corrective justice, despite it seemingly lying at the very base of Aristotelian corrective justice.[14]

The solution to this problem, according to Smith, lies in an elucidation of Kant's theory of right as not requiring wrongdoing:[15]

> We still need to get from material to normative gains and losses to have liability under corrective justice. However, it appears, to put it crudely, that less normative work is required. Less is required in exactly this sense: when a single transaction, necessarily some kind of transfer, gives rise to both a material gain on the part of the defendant and a material loss on the part of the plaintiff, it is not necessary to find that the defendant did anything wrong to characterize that gain and loss as normative. It is enough to find that the plaintiff did not fully consent to the transfer. It may also be enough to find that the defendant's conduct was in some way unconscientious, even if it does not rise to the level of wrongdoing.

On this view, the normative gains and losses in unjust enrichment claims are not the product of wrongdoing. Instead, they represent the violation of a norm of equality based on the parties' wills. This view appears to have been subsequently adopted by Weinrib and expressed in his own terms.[16]

Mr Doyle, however, has argued that even this strict liability account of unjust enrichment does not work because it is inconsistent with Weinrib's own theory of corrective justice.[17] First, he alleges that the strict liability account treats the claimant's normative loss as arising in abstract isolation and so without the bilateral quality *vis-à-vis* the defendant's enrichment necessary to explain unjust enrichment.[18] Secondly, he argues that the strict liability account fails to treat the defendant as a Kantian self-determining agent in cases where a defendant does not know (and does not take the risk) that a benefit is being conferred non-gratuitously.[19] As he explains:[20]

> Kantian responsibility is premised upon free choice as the condition that implicates the defendant's autonomy, rendering the imposition of liability consistent with his free will. If the defendant is oblivious to the non-gratuitous nature of the transfer, however, his acceptance of the enrichment does not constitute any choice at all because the possibility of returning the benefit to the plaintiff simply does not arise.

[14] ibid 2135.

[15] ibid 2139–40.

[16] EJ Weinrib, 'Correctively Unjust Enrichment' in R Chambers, C Mitchell, and J Penner (eds), *Philosophical Foundations of the Law of Unjust Enrichment* (Oxford, Oxford University Press, 2009) 52. See also EJ Weinrib, 'The Normative Structure of Unjust Enrichment' in C Rickett and R Grantham (eds), *Structure and Justification in Private Law* (Oxford, Hart, 2008) 44.

[17] M Doyle, 'Corrective Justice and Unjust Enrichment' (2012) 62 *University of Toronto Law Journal* 229.

[18] ibid 240.

[19] ibid 244.

[20] ibid 245.

There are two problems with these arguments. First, they overlook the fact that a defendant's free will is accommodated elsewhere within the scheme of unjust enrichment. As we shall see later,[21] the defence of change of position is also supported by considerations of corrective justice. Secondly, Doyle's argument is compelling only if Weinribean corrective justice is viewed in abstract isolation; that is, without regard to the necessity of a particular real-world relationship between two parties. For example, Doyle relies upon the example raised by Professor Stephen Smith of someone dropping a bag of money down a deep hole where he cannot retrieve it: he was entitled to the money, but that entitlement was not violated when he dropped it, and so he suffered no normative loss.[22] The suggestion, however, is that on a Weinribean account of corrective justice, there is a normative loss. That is incorrect: as Lionel Smith makes clear,[23] the normative loss is premised upon the existence of a 'single transaction'. Precisely what that 'single transaction' is requires unpacking, and it is the aim of this chapter to do precisely that. But at least two points follow from the recognition of its necessity at this stage. First, neither the normative loss nor the normative gain arises in abstract. Secondly, the manner in which the defendant is treated as a Kantian self-determining agent depends upon how that real-world transaction is understood. As Weinrib has explained, the point is that defendant's participation (what he terms 'acceptance of the benefit as non-gratuitously given')[24] is a relational notion:[25]

> It refers to what is to be imputed to the defendant in the light of the plaintiff's non-gratuitous transfer of value. Although it is defendant-oriented, it does not treat the defendant in isolation from what the plaintiff did … [A]s a member of the conceptual sequence that unites the transferor and transferee of value within an obligation-creating relationship, it is a structural feature of liability for unjust enrichment.

He adds that the defendant's 'acceptance is imputed when the law can reasonably regard the beneficial transfer as something that forwards or accords with the defendant's projects' and that such accordance is a juridical, not a subjective or psychological notion: 'what matters is the purpose … as externally pertinent to the relationship of plaintiff and defendant'.[26]

As we shall see in the sections that follow, the requisite conceptual unity between claimant and defendant, including the external pertinence of the latter's participation within that system, should be understood in terms of systems of exchange, and each party's exchange capacity.

[21] See below pp 60–62.

[22] Doyle (n 17) 240. See further S Smith, 'Justifying the Law of Unjust Enrichment' (2001) 29 *Texas Law Review* 2177, 2190. See also D Klimchuk, 'Unjust Enrichment and Corrective Justice' in J Neyers, M McInnes, and S Pitel (eds), *Understanding Unjust Enrichment* (Oxford, Hart, 2004) 130.

[23] Smith (n 15) and accompanying text.

[24] Weinrib, *Corrective Justice* (n 11) 203–04.

[25] ibid 203.

[26] ibid 208.

## (2) The Limits of Corrective Justice

If we adhere to the theory of corrective justice outlined in the previous section, then the interest that engages unjust enrichment appears to be the parties' 'free will'. That, however, is pitched at too high a level of abstraction and generality to be of any real use. Many aspects of human life can be related back to free will, but seem to fall outside unjust enrichment. The man clumsily falling over in the street no doubt does so against his free will, but that does not mean he has a claim in unjust enrichment against the bystander who has enjoyed watching his tumble—even if the bystander is responsible for his fall. We face the same underlying question, albeit expressed slightly differently: what particular aspects of free will engage unjust enrichment?

This difficulty stems from the very purpose of corrective justice. Corrective justice is an exercise in legal formalism and so creates problems of substantive indeterminacy. It merely provides an internally consistent structure to private law, including unjust enrichment,[27] and is not a panacea capable of explaining the scope or substance of particular claims. Nor does it purport to do so.[28] As Weinrib explains, the so-called 'indeterminacy critique' of corrective justice is really beside the point:[29]

> [T]he autonomy of private law depends not on the determinacy of the rules laid down but on the immanence of corrective justice in private law conceived as justificatory—and thus as a normatively coherent—enterprise. The function of the posited private law is to express corrective justice through its doctrines and institutions, rather than to predetermine every case.

Such limitations are evident throughout a formalist analysis of private law. A good example, arising outside the context of unjust enrichment, is the gradual demise of tort claims for interference with domestic relations over the past century. Torts such as enticement and seduction were historically dominated by paternalistic concepts of family life, and were essentially based upon the notion that a husband or father had something approaching a proprietary interest in his wife or child.[30] Such claims, though socially archaic, do not conflict with a corrective justice view of private law; instead, corrective justice is silent about their social

[27] Weinrib, *The Idea of Private Law* (n 7) 4, 19, 117.

[28] ibid 222–27. So, in the particular context of unjust enrichment, corrective justice does not, for example, dictate that the quantum of a defendant's liability in restitution is capped by the quantum of the loss actually sustained by the claimant: ibid 119. See further below pp 89–96. See also, C Mitchell, P Mitchell, and S Watterson (eds), *Goff & Jones: The Law of Unjust Enrichment*, 8th edn (London, Sweet & Maxwell, 2011), para 6-24: 'Theories of corrective justice are ultimately too abstract … to generate clear cut answers to the sorts of concrete questions that the courts must face, when identifying the boundaries of the law of unjust enrichment'.

[29] Weinrib, *The Idea of Private Law* (n 7) 222. See further C Webb, 'Property, Unjust Enrichment, and Defective Transfers' in R Chambers, C Mitchell, and J Penner (eds), *Philosophical Foundations of the Law of Unjust Enrichment* (Oxford, Oxford University Press, 2009) 336–39, 363–65.

[30] See generally JG Fleming, *The Law of Torts*, 9th edn (Sydney, Lawbook Company, 1998) 718–29.

appropriateness. In the case of the tort of enticement, for example, the point that corrective justice makes is not as to the rightness of the underlying assumption made about a husband's interest in his wife, but whether, given the acceptance of that underlying assumption as a protected norm, the husband should be able to maintain an action against the suitor who entices the wife away from the marriage. The answer that corrective justice provides is that he should: once the husband's interest is accepted as a norm that ought to be protected, the suitor is liable to him because his actions have interfered with that norm, producing a normative gain to the suitor and a normative loss to the husband that must be corrected. But the ambit of tort liability—that is, whether the husband's interest is a norm that *ought* to be protected—is not a matter for corrective justice. It is a matter of judgement that is made with regard to prevailing social norms and values. In the particular context of tort claims for interference with domestic relations, the relevant social attitudes are those of sexual equality and the progressive shift away from a paternalistic conception of family life.[31]

The challenge that arises in the context of unjust enrichment is to identify where relevant matters of judgement arise in determining the scope of liability; that is, how and where in our account of unjust enrichment do we shift from a formal description of its structure to a substantive description of its scope? The answer—according to Weinrib and others[32]—lies within the concept of a 'transfer of value'.

## (B) Debunking Transfer of Value

One of the aims of this book is to demonstrate the limited utility of the concept of 'transfer of value' in understanding unjust enrichment in clear and practical terms. That aim, however, is not quickly achievable. The language of 'transfer of value' pervades much of the judicial and academic literature on unjust enrichment, and the explanation of its shortcomings must proceed in stages. This is because 'transfer of value' is a composite concept, which takes in two ideas: 'transfer' on the one hand, and 'value' on the other.

With this point in mind, we must not allow ourselves to be distracted from the present inquiry: to understand the interest that engages unjust enrichment. That such claims are concerned with reversing defective 'transfers' between two parties may be true at a very high level of generalisation. As we shall see later in this book, however, describing a relationship between two parties as one of 'transfer'

[31] ibid 719–20.

[32] Weinrib, 'Correctively Unjust Enrichment' (n 16) 37; Weinrib, 'The Normative Structure of Unjust Enrichment' (n 16) 29–30. See also Smith, 'Restitution: The Heart of Corrective Justice' (n 6); Burrows, *The Law of Restitution* (n 1) 66; J Edelman, 'The Meaning of Loss and Enrichment' in R Chambers, C Mitchell, and J Penner (eds), *Philosophical Foundations of The Law of Unjust Enrichment* (Oxford, Oxford University Press, 2009) 224; Rush, *The Defence of Passing On* (n 6) 100, 109–11.

from one party to the other is really expressive of a conclusion rather than of underlying reasoning: many unjust enrichment claims do not neatly fit the concept of a 'transfer'.[33] But that is beside the point at this stage of this book. 'Transfer' describes the connection between the parties' interests. The concern here is to explain *what* those interests are. The answer lies, not in the concept of 'transfer', but in the elucidation of concept of 'value' and of the concept of 'exchange' underlying it.

## (C) Value and Exchange

'Value' is an important concept within unjust enrichment which, until relatively recently, was under-explained and imperfectly understood. Significant advances have, however, recently been made towards understanding the nature of value and the function it performs in unjust enrichment.[34] Weinrib, for example, has defined value as the treatment of different things in equivalent terms:[35]

> A judgement of value takes the form that such-and-such a quantity of one thing is equivalent to such-and-such a quantity of another thing. Value thereby relates different persons through the exchange of different things. Because value exists only in and through exchange with another, it is intrinsically relational.

Value is thus an abstract standard for the comparison and exchange of qualitatively heterogeneous things in quantitatively comparable and equivalent terms.[36] This 'relational' concept—according to which particular things are reducible to some single dimension or substance, notwithstanding their diversity—is different from 'idiosyncratic' value, which refers to the subjective valuation afforded by a given individual to an object in the light of his (or her) particular preferences, utilities, and choices.[37] It has been said that the latter is not relevant to unjust

[33] See below pp 120–124.

[34] See, eg, R Chambers, 'Two Kinds of Enrichment' in R Chambers, C Mitchell, and J Penner (eds), *Philosophical Foundations of the Law of Unjust Enrichment* (Oxford, Oxford University Press, 2009); J Penner, 'Value, Property and Unjust Enrichment' in R Chambers, C Mitchell, and J Penner (eds), *Philosophical Foundations of The Law of Unjust Enrichment* (Oxford, Oxford University Press, 2009); AVM Lodder, *Enrichment in the Law of Unjust Enrichment and Restitution* (Oxford, Hart, 2012).

[35] Weinrib, 'The Normative Structure of Unjust Enrichment' (n 16) 27. See also Lodder, *Enrichment in the Law of Unjust Enrichment and Restitution* (n 34) 14–23; P Benson, 'The Unity of Contract Law' in P Benson (ed), *The Theory of Contract Law: New Essays* (Cambridge, Cambridge University Press, 2001) 188.

[36] See further Lodder, *Enrichment in the Law of Unjust Enrichment and Restitution* (n 34) 16.

[37] Benson (n 35) 195; Lodder, *Enrichment in the Law of Unjust Enrichment and Restitution* (n 34) 16–19. For the relationship between matters of preference, utility, choice, and budgetary constraints to the determination of consumer demand and value in economic theory, see, eg, HR Varian, *Intermediate Microeconomics: A Modern Approach* (New York, W W Norton & Company, 2009) Chs 2–5.

enrichment.[38] As Birks explains, the law 'does not pretend to attempt the impossible task of finding out at what price the particular recipient of an unrequested benefit would have bought it'.[39]

The two concepts—idiosyncratic value and relational value—may not, however, be so easily separable. Dr Lodder has observed that idiosyncratic value is a feature of relational value insofar as the latter represents an aggregation of the former: market price abstracts from the qualitative reasons underpinning the subjective judgements of multiple individuals a quantitatively heterogenous and comparable value for exchange.[40] Within this observation there is a further important point about the relational quality of idiosyncratic value itself: an individual's subjective judgement of value reflects that individual's application of an abstract standard for the comparison of one thing for another thing in equivalent terms. For example, I may own a painting from which I derive personal pleasure and utility through its hanging on my living-room wall. If pressed, I may be able to assign that personal benefit a monetary figure (say, £1000). This is the idiosyncratic value of the painting to me, expressed in relational terms: one thing (the painting) is compared to another thing (money). Strictly speaking, this is a kind of relational value. But it is a *subjective* relational value, not an *objective* relational value. When we say that relational value matters in unjust enrichment, and idiosyncratic value does not, what we really mean is that what matters is objective value determined by the market, rather than our own subjective determinations of value. Birks's remark above, to the effect that the law does not pretend to find the price that a particular recipient of a benefit would have bought it, is thus slightly misleading in this respect. The very process of asking what one person would have paid for a benefit presupposes the existence of a second person willing and able to sell that benefit. That is, it presupposes the existence of a market and, by necessity, the observation and application of market conditions to the process of price determination.

Similarly, to exalt relational value (be it subjective or objective) within unjust enrichment is not to ignore the reality that people can and do desire things in their own right and for reasons of utility unrelated to exchange. Because idiosyncratic value reflects an amalgam of individual preference, utility, and choice,[41] a concern for relational value (as an aggregation of idiosyncratic value) is capable of promoting and protecting these idiosyncrasies, albeit indirectly and to the limited extent that they are manifested within systems of exchange. To completely understand this point requires some knowledge and appreciation of economic

[38] See, eg, *Benedetti v Sawiris* [2010] EWCA Civ 1427 [145] (Etherton LJ); *Benedetti v Sawiris* [2013] UKSC 50, [2013] 3 WLR 351, [17] (Lord Clarke), [101] (Lord Reed). See also Lodder, *Enrichment in the Law of Unjust Enrichment and Restitution* (n 34) 18–43. This is not, however, to deny the significance of a defendant's own 'freedom of choice' within unjust enrichment. See generally Lodder Ch 5. See further below pp 62–66.

[39] P Birks, *Unjust Enrichment*, 2nd edn (Oxford, Oxford University Press, 2005) 54.

[40] Lodder, *Enrichment in the Law of Unjust Enrichment and Restitution* (n 34) 17.

[41] See generally Varian, *Intermediate Microeconomics: A Modern Approach* (n 37) Chs 2–5.

theory, the detailed description of which is beyond the scope of this book. In essence, though, the key point to appreciate is that, in microeconomic theory, an individual's demand for something is derived from his utility function as a representation of preference subject to budgetary constraint. So while individual preference, utility, and choice are not susceptible to market analysis in their own right, they do feature within the determination of demand and price of those things that are susceptible to market analysis. This is particularly important in understanding the scope of unjust enrichment because it explains how the matters outlined at the start of this chapter should be treated. The pursuit of things like good vibes, cultural enlightenment, affection, and laughter may influence our individual preference, utility, and choice: we want things that will deliver us these sort of idiosyncratic benefits, and so their existence influences our individual demand for such things which, in aggregate, shapes the operation of systems of exchange.

Returning to the example of the painting, the sources of my pleasure and utility in respect of it may be many and varied: it may have sentimental value to me as a gift from an old friend; it may remind me of scene from my childhood, or; I may simply like the contrasting colours and brush-strokes. Whatever their source, these benefits are reflected in the idiosyncratic value of the painting to me, and not in its relational value. When I assign them a subjective relational value (again, say £1000) I am taking the position that I am prepared to forgo those benefits in exchange for £1000. I do not, however, derive pleasure and utility from the £1000 in its own right,[42] but rather from the use to which that money can be put in acquiring something else from which I can derive pleasure and utility. The same logic applies to objective relational values determined by the market: if the market value of the painting is merely £500, then my idiosyncratic value is promoted and protected to the extent that this sum will enable me, as closely as possible, to enter the market and purchase a substitute painting and so derive equivalent pleasure and utility. Clearly there is a margin for imbalance and imperfection. If, on the one hand, the painting is the work of a master, then its market value will greatly exceed my own idiosyncratic value, in which case I will have the benefit of a surplus. If, on the other hand, the painting is a cheap copy, the market value will not necessarily reflect the utility and pleasure I derive from its sentimental character. The point about such imbalances and imperfections, however, is that they are not rooted in strict, abstract, or legal logic, but in the pragmatic operation of markets as systems of exchange operating in a real social context.

[42] This is assumed to be generally true: people do not possess money for its own sake, but for the purpose of using money to acquire goods, services, and experiences that will advance their pleasure and utility. Of course, there are always possible exceptions in both reality and fiction. For example, the fictional Disney character, 'Scrooge McDuck', derived pleasure from the act of swimming in his money in a large enclosed 'money bin'. See further B Rudden, 'Things as Thing and Things as Wealth' (1994) 14 *Oxford Journal of Legal Studies* 81, 93–94.

## (1) The Necessity of Exchange

The existence of some mechanism of exchange is therefore critically important to the relational concept of value. This is because value is an abstract concept, rather than something that is capable of being possessed in its own right: value must be realised.[43] And for it to be realised, one thing with value must be exchanged for another thing; the value of such-and-such a quantity of one thing is realised by exchanging it for such-and-such a quantity of another thing. Value is, in this sense, a progressive concept based upon exchange: I realise the value of one thing by exchanging it for another thing, and I realise the value of that thing by exchanging it, and so on.[44]

Not everyone agrees with this exchange-centred concept of value. Lodder, for example, argues that exchange value is 'simply one relational measure of the monetary value of a thing' and that 'it is perfectly possible to place a relative value on something for which there is no market'.[45] He explains:[46]

> For example, the value of a non-transferable asset, such as an unassignable lease, may be measured by the present future value of the income that will be generated from its use, ie rent. Alternatively, a thing may be valued by the capital value of its component parts. The difference between these valuation approaches can be demonstrated by the valuation of share capital, which can be measured by its exchange value, the present value of its future dividend income or the capital value of the asset-share on dissolution of the company.

Lodder is correct that there are many things that cannot be exchanged in and of themselves, and that we must therefore look at their products or components to assign them a relational value. But this does make exchange irrelevant in these situations. It merely shifts the focus of what is being exchanged. In the case of shares, for example, their exchange value on the share market, the present value of their future dividend income, and the capital value of their asset-share on dissolution of the company are each the result of a comparison between those products and money. When we say, for example, that a company share is worth ten pounds because that is the present value of future dividend income, we mean that we are prepared to exchange our entitlement to dividends in the future, for money in our pockets today. All relational values depend upon exchange.

It is worth observing that, in the majority of cases, exchange is expressed in monetary terms. This is because money is 'a universal medium of exchange'[47] and therefore has a homogeneous quality that satisfies the abstract standard in clear

[43] Penner, 'Value, Property and Unjust Enrichment' (n 34) 309.

[44] See further ibid (n 34) 309: 'One owns the property, not its exchange value. When one realises the exchange value, what one must *relinquish* is one's property. One never has the two of them at the same time.'

[45] Lodder, *Enrichment in the Law of Unjust Enrichment and Restitution* (n 34) 17.

[46] ibid 17–18. See also Mitchell, Mitchell, and Watterson, *Goff & Jones* (n 28) para 4.04.

[47] *BP Exploration Co (Libya) Ltd v Hunt (No 2)* [1979] 1 WLR 783 (QB) 799 (Robert Goff J). See also Birks, *Unjust Enrichment* (n 39) 53.

and uniform terms. This does not mean money is value; merely that it acts as both a measure and store of value.[48] It is certainly plausible to conceive of exchanges (and, therefore, relational values) arising without reference to money.[49] For example, I may have an arrangement with my mechanic according to which he services my car in exchange for my legal services. Neither of us need have gone through the exact process of considering how much our services are worth in money terms and matching that precisely to the measure of the other's services. Money is the universal medium of exchange, but that does not mean it is the sole and necessary medium.

## (2) Formal to Substantial

Corrective justice, as we have observed above, is concerned with the distinct aim of presenting private law as a 'justificatory—and thus as a normatively coherent—enterprise'.[50] It addresses what Weinrib has described as 'the central theoretical question for any liability regime': 'Why is it that the law connects a particular plaintiff with a particular defendant?'[51] While this is an important theoretical question for unjust enrichment, it is certainly not the *only* theoretical question. Matters of actual substance and scope are also important, and necessarily require consideration of matters external to the structure of unjust enrichment. The external account of unjust enrichment is therefore just as important as the internal account.[52]

Professor Dagan's position exemplifies this reality. He admits that private law should be able to justify the structure of claims, including the identity of the parties, and the type and degree of the liability that is imposed.[53] But, he insists, this does not mean that private law has an inner intelligibility decipherable without recourse to social values:[54]

> Quite the contrary: the pivotal role of private law in defining our mutual legitimate claims and expectations in our daily interactions undermines the legitimacy of a private law regime that ignores these values. For this reason, the parties' *ex ante* entitlements, from which this correlativity must be measured, are best analysed by reference to our social values.

[48] Lodder, *Enrichment in the Law of Unjust Enrichment and Restitution* (n 34) 19.

[49] ibid.

[50] See above Weinrib, *The Idea of Private Law* (n 29) and accompanying text.

[51] EJ Weinrib, 'Restoring Restitution' (2005) 91 *Virginia Law Review* 861, 868.

[52] See generally, S Hedley, 'Looking Outward or Looking Inward? Obligations Scholarship in the Early 21st Century' in A Robertson and TH Wu (eds), *The Goals of Private Law* (Oxford, Hart, 2009) 195.

[53] H Dagan, 'Restitution's Realism' in R Chambers, C Mitchell, and J Penner (eds), *Philosophical Foundations of The Law of Unjust Enrichment* (Oxford, Oxford University Press, 2009) 65. See also Dagan (n 3) 813.

[54] Dagan (n 53) 65–66. See further H Dagan, *The Law and Ethics of Restitution* (Cambridge, Cambridge University Press, 2004) 6–9.

Dagan's realism (or, 'value instrumentalism'[55]) is not irreconcilable with Weinrib's corrective justice, precisely because each is ultimately concerned with a different theoretical question: corrective justice with the justificatory internal structure of private law, and realism with its external social context. Indeed, Dagan does not dismiss corrective justice from his account of private law, but instead presents his theory as a middle ground operating between two extremes: a private law scheme completely devoid of social values on the one hand, and the 'full-blown instrumentalisation of private law'—according to which civil suits are just a mechanism whereby the state authorises private parties to enforce the law—on the other.[56]

The reason why this matters in the present context is that reliance upon 'value' within a corrective justice account of unjust enrichment achieves precisely this middle ground. It transforms the formal, structural, and internal account of unjust enrichment based upon corrective justice into a substantive description of its scope based upon external criteria. This is because value presupposes exchange[57] and exchange presupposes a system in which exchanges can occur: what we commonly refer to as a 'market'.[58] Many definitions of market are possible, ranging in purpose and degree of complexity[59]—reflecting the diversity of exchanges that are possible. The number of participants in a market may range from many millions to only a handful, or even just two: a possibility of exchange limited to just one other person is still a possibility of exchange. Adopting a precise and exhaustive definition of markets, however, is not important. What matters is the underlying and common feature that markets embody legitimate exchange. That legitimacy is a product of social, moral, and legal considerations beyond the internal structure of private law and of unjust enrichment.[60] The key point is that exchange is not internally explicable from within unjust enrichment. It is external to it.

[55] D Klimchuk, 'The Normative Foundations of Unjust Enrichment' in R Chambers, C Mitchell, and J Penner (eds), *Philosophical Foundations of the Law of Unjust Enrichment* (Oxford, Oxford University Press, 2009) 93–94.

[56] Dagan, 'The Limited Autonomy of Private Law' (n 3) 812–13.

[57] Weinrib, 'Correctively Unjust Enrichment' (n 16) 35.

[58] ibid 38: 'Whether a person who gives another something of value has in return received something of equivalent value is an objective question, the answer to which is systemically determined by exchanges within a competitive market.'

[59] See, eg, D Satz, *Why Some Things Should Not Be for Sale: The Moral Limits of Markets* (Oxford, Oxford University Press, 2010) 3. Dr Satz sets out a functional description of markets as important forms of social and economic organisation, allowing people who are otherwise completely unknown to one another to cooperate together in a system of voluntary exchange. Cf G Hodgson, 'Markets' in TB Veblen and E Mandel (eds), *New Palgrave Dictionary of Economics*, 2nd edn (Basingstoke, Macmillan, 2008): 'A market is defined as an institution through which multiple buyers or multiple sellers recurrently exchange a substantial number of similar commodities of a particular type. Exchanges themselves take place in a framework of law and contract enforceability. Markets involve legal and other rules that help to structure, organize and legitimize exchange transactions.'

[60] See generally Satz, *Why Some Things Should Not Be for Sale* (n 59); M Sandel, *What Money Can't Buy: The Moral Limits of Markets* (New York, Farrar, Straus and Giroux, 2012).

## (3) Adjustment to Money

That the external quality of exchange explains the scope of the law of unjust enrichment is evident from repeated insistence that unjust enrichment is concerned with monetary value. Birks, for example, defined unjust enrichment as 'the law of all events materially identical to the mistaken payment of a non-existent debt'.[61] He then explained that the logic of such liability could not stretch beyond acquisitions measureable in money,[62] or to the point 'where adjustment in money is unthinkable'.[63] The Supreme Court of Canada has similarly observed, on several occasions, that the law of unjust enrichment takes a 'straightforward economic approach' to questions of enrichment and corresponding deprivation,[64] and that 'without a benefit … which can be restored to the donor *in specie* or by money, no recovery lies for unjust enrichment'.[65]

These qualifications to money are important because, money being a universal medium of exchange, adjustment into money provides a yardstick by which we can determine the acceptability of treating claims as part of unjust enrichment. That adjustment in money is 'unthinkable' is not a conclusion derived from within unjust enrichment, but is instead derived from external considerations.

Consider again the possible arrangement I might have with my mechanic: if we agree that he will service my car in exchange for me drafting his will, then he may have a claim in unjust enrichment for the value of his services if I fail to perform my side of the bargain. But he will not have a claim (at least in unjust enrichment) if our agreement is for the possession of his child, and I reneged on my side of the bargain after taking receipt. As Birks bluntly put it:[66]

> [P]arents turn to courts to recover abducted children … Although contrary practices obtain in a particularly unpleasant sector of the underworld, there is no situation whatever in which the law allows an individual or a court to turn them into money.

Unjust enrichment does not include the recovery of children because it does not permit their translation into money, and it does not permit their translation into

[61] Birks, *Unjust Enrichment* (n 39) 3.

[62] ibid 51.

[63] ibid 52.

[64] See, eg, *Kerr v Baranow, Vanasse v Seguin* [2011] SCC 10, [2011] 1 SCR 269 [37] (Cromwell J); *Garland v Consumers' Gas Co* [2004] SCC 25, [2004] 1 SCR 629 [31] (Iacobucci J); *Peter v Beblow* [1993] 1 SCR 980 (SCC) 990 (McLachlin J).

[65] *Peel (Regional Municipality) v Canada* [1992] 3 SCR 762 (SCC) 790 (McLachlin J). See further M McInnes, '*Hambly v Trott* and the Claimant's Expense: Professor Birks' Challenge' in S Degeling and J Edelman (eds), *Unjust Enrichment in Commercial Law* (Sydney, Thomson Reuters, 2008) 128–129. It is worthwhile observing that this was also essentially the position adopted by Lord Reed in *Benedetti (UKSC)* (n 38) at [96]–[119], and that his Lordship relied upon the Canadian authorities in support (at [118]).

[66] Birks, *Unjust Enrichment* (n 39) 51.

money because that entails acceptance of markets that are socially, morally, and legally reprehensible (among other things).[67]

Many things can and do influence the legitimacy of exchange, markets, and so the recognition of value. And they can do so in different ways. Consider, for example, the illegitimacy of a purported market for illegal goods and services—such as that for assassins and assassinations. No doubt there are (in darker sectors of society) persons willing and able to offer and obtain such services and so carry out exchanges. But no claim by an assassin (in unjust enrichment or otherwise) could ever succeed against his employer. Unjust enrichment does not recognise value in those situations because they raise deeper social, moral, ethical, and legal concerns. Lord Mansfield's classic statement in *Holman v Johnson* captures this relationship neatly:[68]

> No Court will lend its aid to a man who founds his cause of action upon an immoral or an illegal act. If, from the plaintiff's own stating or otherwise, the cause of action appears to arise *ex turpi causâ*, or the transgression of a positive law of this country, there the Court says he has no right to be assisted. It is upon that ground the Court goes; not for the sake of the defendant, but because they will not lend their aid to such a plaintiff. So if the plaintiff and defendant were to change sides, and the defendant was to bring his action against the plaintiff, the latter would then have the advantage of it; for where both are equally in fault, *potior est conditio defendentis.*

Interesting distinctions arise in this context. First, the application of Lord Mansfield's point to unjust enrichment varies depending upon which side of the illegal or immoral act one stands. In *Chapman v Haley*,[69] for example, the plaintiff had paid the defendant $300 for ten-fold that amount in counterfeit currency. The defendant failed to deliver. The court held that the $300 paid to the defendant could not be recovered: the law would not aid the recovery of money paid for an illegal purpose. The $300 clearly enriched the defendant; the recovery of money is the archetypal unjust enrichment claim. But overriding policy considerations defeated it. If the facts had been reversed, however, and a claim brought by the defendant for the plaintiff's failure to pay upon delivery of the counterfeit currency, dismissal of the claim could also have been on the basis that receipt of the counterfeit money was not enriching in the sense required by law. The policy against illegal and immoral conduct would bite at the point of recognising value: counterfeit currency, assassinations, illicit substances, slave labour, and other immoral and illegal enterprises may all have value within black markets that exist within the underworld, but recognising the existence of these markets within the context of legal claims is repugnant to social, moral, and legal concerns. Without

[67] In this respect it is noteworthy that, with different social norms, comes a different ambit of private law claims. Roman law, for example, treated ownership of slaves (including children) as acceptable. Restitutionary claims in respect of slaves and the value of slave labour were therefore possible. See, eg, *The Digest of Justinian* (Alan Watson tr, Pennsylvania, University of Pennsylvania Press, 1998) 12.6.65.8.

[68] *Holman v Johnson* (1775) 1 Cowp 341, 98 ER 1120 (KB) 343.

[69] *Chapman v Haley* 117 Ky 1004, 80 SW 190 (1904) (CA Kent).

a recognised market, there can be no exchange, without exchange there can be no value, and without value there can be no unjust enrichment.

A second distinction lies in the reasons why a market may be considered repugnant. On the one hand, it may be that the particular object of exchange is reprehensible or offensive, as in the case of counterfeit currency, assassinations, illicit substances, and slave labour. On the other hand, the object of exchange may be inherently good, but its marketability and exchange reprehensible. No one denies that children are cherished in society, but the idea of a market for them attracts significant disapprobation. And each of us is familiar with the utility of our kidneys, but their trade under market conditions remains a social and ethical taboo. Indeed, the underlying complexity of the policies that inhibit markets can be illustrated well by private law claims involving human tissues.[70] In *Moore v Regents of the University of California*,[71] for example, doctors developed a multi-million dollar cell line obtained from Mr Moore's tissue without his informed consent. A majority of the court held that liability of the doctors in conversion could not extend to the gains embodied in the cell line because that would hinder socially important medical research, implicating policy concerns far removed from the traditional private disputes in which the law of conversion had developed.[72] The same policies would apply, *mutatis mutandis* it seems, to a claim in unjust enrichment.[73] The point is not that human tissue is inherently objectionable, but that there are strong social and ethical objections to the legal recognition of markets for its exchange.

This is not to suggest that reprehensibility and illegality are the only bases for denying the existence of markets. A further possibility is that the particular thing in question may be so subjective in nature that any attempt to conceive of a market in respect of it is simply confounding or nonsensical.[74] Love and other emotions are one example: they are so personal that they cannot be reliably measured, detected, or understood so as to be susceptible to exchange, markets, and market analysis. The most that can be said of love and other emotions is that they influence individual preference, utility, and choice that drive demand for things that are susceptible to exchange. They are not, however, susceptible to exchange in and of

[70] For more detailed discussion see, eg, Satz, *Why Some Things Should Not Be for Sale* (n 59) Ch 9; R Hardcastle, *Law and the Human Body* (Oxford, Hart, 2007); L Skene, 'Proprietary Rights in Human Bodies, Body Parts and Tissue' (2002) 22 *Legal Studies* 102. See further MJ Radin, *Contested Commodities* (Cambridge, Harvard University Press, 1996).

[71] *Moore v Regents of University of California* 51 Cal 3d 120, 793 P 2d 479 (1990) (SC Calif).

[72] ibid 135–36, 143–45 (Panelli J; Lucas CJ, Eagleson and Kennard JJ concurring).

[73] See further Dagan, *The Law and Ethics of Restitution* (n 54) 240–45; M Traynor, 'The Unjust Enrichment Claim in *Moore v Regents*' (1990) 9 *Biotechnology Law Report* 240. Cf *Greenberg v Miami Children's Hospital Research Institute Inc* 264 F Supp 2d 1064 (2003) (USDC, Southern District of Florida) where the Court declined a motion to dismiss a claim in unjust enrichment brought by the donors of human tissue and fluids against the doctors who had received those materials and used them to isolate a gene causing disease, and then obtained a patent and attempted to license it. For criticism and comment, see American Law Institute, *Restatement of Law Third: Restitution and Unjust Enrichment* (2012) ('*Third Restatement*') § 11 comment (b).

[74] See further the examples considered above at p 19 and below at pp 50–51.

themselves. It may even be the case that, being so personal in nature, attempts to market something like love would be met with disapprobation similar to attempts to market children and body parts. Irrespective of how one reaches the conclusion, however, the ultimate point is the same: without a market, there can be no exchange, without exchange there can be no value, and without value there can be no unjust enrichment.

## (D) What Interest Engages Unjust Enrichment?

The aim of this chapter is to explain the interest that engages unjust enrichment: why does unjust enrichment bite in some cases, but not in others? Equipped with an understanding of the corrective justice foundations of unjust enrichment, and the important roles played by value and exchange within that scheme, we are now in a better position to confront this issue. As a penultimate step, however, it is useful to explain why certain other concepts do not provide the right answer. Three of these are considered below.

First, though it is a linchpin concept within unjust enrichment, the relevant interest is not 'value'. This is because value is an attribute of things, not of people. People do not 'own' or 'have' value: at most, they have the ability to realise the value of things through the mechanism of exchange.[75]

Secondly, it is unhelpful to describe the relevant interest as 'wealth'. Wealth is an abstract conception of someone's net worth, taking into account both their assets and liabilities.[76] It is 'an abstract fund netting tangible and intangible assets held against valuable obligations owed to others'.[77] So, unlike value, wealth *is* an attribute of people and so we can sensibly speak of unjust enrichment as interested by wealth. The problem, however, is that 'wealth' does not go far enough. If unjust enrichment were concerned only with the protection of a person's wealth, then the performance and receipt of services could not form the subject matter of claims. That is not the law.[78] Nor is it conceptually or theoretically consistent for claims in respect of services to be so excluded from unjust enrichment. Services have value because they are capable of being compared and exchanged in a market, but they do not comprise a person's wealth. Lodder gives the example of the receipt of a valuable haircut which, of itself, does not alter the defendant's stock of rights or assets.[79] Nor, on the other side of the barber's chair, is it sensible to talk of the barber as 'wealthy' by virtue of his ability to cut hair. The mere ability to perform a service is not part of a person's wealth: nothing accrues to the

[75] Penner, 'Value, Property and Unjust Enrichment' (n 34) 308–09.
[76] Birks, *Unjust Enrichment* (n 39) 69; Chambers, 'Two Kinds of Enrichment' (n 34) 250–52.
[77] Lodder, *Enrichment in the Law of Unjust Enrichment and Restitution* (n 34) 32.
[78] See, eg, *Cobbe v Yeoman's Row Management Ltd* [2008] UKHL 55, [2008] 1 WLR 1752.
[79] Lodder, *Enrichment in the Law of Unjust Enrichment and Restitution* (n 34) 33.

barber until he actually performs and either has money in his hands, or at least a debt owed to him by the customer.[80] Unjust enrichment is not wholly engaged by 'wealth' because that concept does not completely align with the concepts of value and exchange.

A third possibility has been suggested by Dr Webb, who argues that 'a sizeable chunk' of unjust enrichment claims can be explained on the basis that the law is concerned with the claimant's exclusive entitlement to the benefit received by the defendant.[81] As he explains:[82]

> The law sets down individuals' entitlements to items and sources of wealth. Sometimes the law allocates such items to a person or group, giving a right to the sole enjoyment of that wealth and with it a right to exclude others from its enjoyment. At other times, the law makes no such allocation. Where no such exclusive entitlement is granted, any person is free to share in it, so far as he is able to, but without any right that others should not similarly benefit. Where, by contrast, the claimant can show that, at the very least *vis-à-vis* the defendant, he was exclusively entitled to the asset or benefit the defendant received, this then gives us a reason to allow the claimant to recover that asset or benefit from the defendant.

The difficulties with this approach mirror those with respect to 'wealth'. Indeed, wealth appears to be an inherent feature of Webb's thesis as set out above. Exclusive entitlement, however, is too narrow a concept. It does not fit with valuable services, which cannot exist in any meaningful sense prior to their performance. It is nonsensical to speak of people having an exclusive entitlement to their own services. The most that can be said is that people have an exclusive entitlement to decide whether or not they perform a service, which is another way of saying they have the freedom to perform or not. If that is correct, however, then it makes more sense to describe the relevant interest engaged in terms of some sort of personal interest or freedom, rather than 'wealth' or 'exclusive entitlement'.

## (1) The Exchange Capacity

The challenge posed by the task of identifying the interest engaged by unjust enrichment is to frame a personal attribute that fits the logic and framework of corrective justice, value, and exchange. To do so, however, we need look no further than the innards of value and exchange. Value, as we have seen, presupposes a system of exchange. A system of exchange requires participants and, importantly, participants free to engage, and capable of engaging, in that system. It follows that the interest protected by unjust enrichment claims is one of exchange; a freedom

[80] See further Penner, 'Value, Property and Unjust Enrichment' (n 34) 311.

[81] Webb, 'Property, Unjust Enrichment, and Defective Transfers' (n 29) 351–52. See also J Gordley, *Foundations of Private Law: Property, Tort, Contract, Unjust Enrichment* (Oxford, Oxford University Press, 2006) 424–26.

[82] Webb, 'Property, Unjust Enrichment, and Defective Transfers' (n 29) 351.

to engage in the systems of exchange that underpin the concept of value.[83] In other words, the interest protected is an exchange freedom or 'exchange capacity'.

This immediately begs two further questions. The first is: exchange of what? The answer lies in recalling the external quality of value and of systems of exchange. Unjust enrichment is engaged by the capacity to exchange those things for which there exists a recognised system of exchange. This is not bootstrap reasoning. It reflects the reality that value is the product of judgements external from the structure of unjust enrichment.[84]

To keep matters simple, we could express the exchange capacity as the freedom to exchange 'assets, liabilities, and services'. But we should not allow that to excite further definitional controversy as to what is and what is not an 'asset', a 'liability', or a 'service'. These are mere labels, and do not provide substantial insight into what is and what is not part of unjust enrichment. What matters is whether a system of exchange exists for the relevant thing in question, not whether that thing can be described as an 'asset', 'liability', or 'service', or something else completely. This, ultimately, is not a legal question but a social and economic one.

A useful example is the time value of money: it is not an 'asset' or even a 'right' in any strict sense of those terms. The highest that can be said is that reflects an incident of the property rights inhering in the principal sum. It is probably *sui generis* in this respect, but that does not mean it cannot be subjected to analysis in unjust enrichment terms. Indeed, it has been so analysed by the House of Lords.[85] This follows the logic of the market: having money for a period of time is something of value in addition to the principal sum. It has a price reflecting a system of exchange, which rests upon the exchange capacity, and engages unjust enrichment analysis. The advantage of conceiving unjust enrichment claims in exchange capacity terms is that it cuts through heterogeneous categories (such as assets, services, and use value) to present a unified picture of the law, which is precisely the point of unjust enrichment scholarship in the first place.[86]

The second question that arises from the identification of the exchange capacity is: what aspects of exchange are engaged by unjust enrichment? Exchange is necessarily a two-sided concept, encompassing both the giving and receipt of the thing exchanged. These two sides conform to the bilateral quality of corrective

[83] Cf J McGhee, 'The Nature of the Enrichment Enquiry' in J Edelman and S Degeling (eds), *Unjust Enrichment in Commercial Law* (Sydney, Thomson Reuters, 2008) 90–92. The exchange capacity also features prominently as a reinforcing concept in the *Third Restatement* (n 73). At various points within the Restatement, the protection that is inherent within unjust enrichment is reinforced by the idea that liability will not extend to cases of 'forced exchange'. See, eg, *Third Restatement* (n 73) §2(4) comment (e), 9 comment (b), §10 comment (a); 50(3). See also *Lumbers v W Cook Builders Pty Ltd (in liquidation)* [2008] HCA 27, (2008) 232 CLR 635, [80] observing the statement by Bowen LJ in *Falcke v Scottish Imperial Insurance Co* (1887) LR 34 Ch D 234 (CA), 248: 'Liabilities are not to be forced upon people behind their backs any more than you can confer a benefit upon a man against his will.'

[84] See above pp 30–35.

[85] *Sempra Metals Ltd (formerly Metallgesellschaft Ltd) v Inland Revenue Commissioners* [2007] UKHL 34, [2008] 1 AC 561 [29] (Lord Hope).

[86] See above pp 1–11.

justice, and unjust enrichment is the concern of both. As we shall see in chapters two and three: 'enrichment' concerns receipt by the defendant, while 'loss' concerns giving by the claimant. Furthermore, many important aspects of unjust enrichment are explicable according to a theory of unjust enrichment based upon the exchange capacity, including: the change of position defence, the quantum of restitution, the correct approach to so-called subjective devaluation and revaluation, and the rejection of the passing on defence. And though it is beyond the stated scope of this book, because the exchange capacity is predicated upon a freedom to exercise that interest, it directs our attention to the necessity of a defect in the exercise of that freedom for a claim to succeed; that is, to the 'unjust factor' inquiry within unjust enrichment.

## (2) Free Will

The exchange capacity is one manifestation of free will, which, as we have observed, has been advanced by Weinrib as the underlying rationale of liability on a corrective justice theory of unjust enrichment based upon Kant's philosophy of right. We have also observed, however, that free will is pitched at too high a level of abstraction and generality to explain the subject matter of claims.[87] The exchange capacity overcomes this problem because it reduces the general rationale to more concise terms that are particular to unjust enrichment, surpassing the limitations inherent in justifying it by free will alone. This is because 'exchange' externalises the analysis of claims and provides substance to the structure of unjust enrichment.

Moreover, that the exchange capacity is one manifestation of the larger freedom of will concept is important to how we situate unjust enrichment relative to other areas of the private law of obligations that are also internally justifiable according to corrective justice. Free will can be manifested in several forms other than the exchange capacity, including personal integrity, proprietary entitlement, and contractual entitlement.[88] But it is only the exchange capacity that engages unjust enrichment as distinct from tort or contract. For example, suppose, on the one hand, that D commits battery by pushing C to the ground. Corrective justice is capable of explaining why D is liable to provide reparation in tort for C's injuries as follows.[89] Prior to D's battery, C's free will was manifested in the form of personal integrity; that personal integrity was the embodiment of C's Kantian right, correlative to a duty upon D not to interfere with it. D's battery violated C's personal integrity and, with the materialisation of injury, the only way left for D to satisfy his obligation of non-interference is to undo its effects.[90] Suppose then,

[87] See above p 24.
[88] See generally Weinrib, *The Idea of Private Law* (n 7) 127–28, 133–44.
[89] ibid 135.
[90] Klimchuk, 'The Normative Foundations of Unjust Enrichment' (n 55) 87.

on the other hand, that rather than C suffering injury from D's battery he was left unscathed by his fall, though D experienced great amusement from the sight of C's falling to the ground and clambering back to his feet. Does C have a claim in unjust enrichment reflective of D's enjoyment? The answer is no: D's amusement is not a benefit in the economic or pecuniary sense required by unjust enrichment. Personal amusement may influence individual utility, and therefore also influence demand for something within a market. But the fact that utility can be derived from something does not mean there is a market for it—as cases involving children, body parts, and illegal substances demonstrate.[91]

The exclusion of non-economic or non-pecuniary benefits from the scope of unjust enrichment is also expressive of a more basal point. If a benefit cannot be expressed in economic or pecuniary terms, then that indicates that there is no system of exchange for that benefit. No system of exchange means no exchange capacity, and without an exchange capacity, unjust enrichment has nothing upon which to bite.

Herein lies a possible basis of theoretical distinction between claims based upon unjust enrichment and those based upon tort or contract. The reason why economic and pecuniary measurement matters so much in unjust enrichment, but less so in contract,[92] and even less so in tort,[93] is that each kind of claim is concerned with a different manifestation of the overarching free will interest: tort with what we might call 'personal and proprietary integrity'; contract with what we might call freedom to contract or contractual entitlement; and unjust enrichment with the exchange capacity.[94] Only in the last case is economic and pecuniary expression essential, that being the means by which we recognise a system of exchange, and with that system the necessary exchange capacity. This does not mean that economic and pecuniary interests are the exclusive domain of unjust enrichment. Harm to the person, damage to property, and loss of contractual entitlement are all regularly measured in economic and pecuniary terms, but each represents the violation of a theoretically different manifestation of free will.

It is not the intention of this book to identify exactly what the theoretical bases of each of contract and tort are, and thereafter neatly and precisely to cordon off the theoretical boundaries of each from the other, as well as from unjust

[91] See above pp 32–35.

[92] Non-pecuniary damages (such as for mental distress, damages to reputation, and loss of enjoyment) are available in contract in limited circumstances. See, eg, *Addis v Gramophone Co* [1909] AC 488 (HL); *Jarvis v Swan's Tours* [1973] QB 233 (CA); *Watts v Morrow* [1991] 1 All ER 937 (CA); *Ruxley Electronics & Construction Ltd v Forsyth* [1996] AC 344 (HL); *Farley v Skinner (No 2)* [2001] UKHL 49, [2002] 2 AC 732. Though these are exceptional, the fact that they are possible is illustrative of the point that the ambit of contractual damages is different from that of liability for unjust enrichment.

[93] Several torts protect non-pecuniary interests, including those for physical, mental, and reputational harm to the person.

[94] See further Weinrib, *The Idea of Private Law* (n 7) 127–29.

enrichment. Nor is it necessarily desirable (or even possible) to do so.[95] The point, instead, is to identify a theoretical and normative framework in which to situate unjust enrichment as a useful legal concept. Understood in this way, there is significant potential for doctrinal overlap between unjust enrichment and other concepts precisely because there is significant theoretical overlap. The recognition and protection of property in tort, for example, includes rights in respect of alienation and exchange. And if contract is conceived, for example, as facilitating the exercise of the exchange capacity, then the boundary between unjust enrichment and contract will be particularly blurred at times. Just as contract facilitates the free engagement of the exchange capacity, unjust enrichment alleviates its defective engagement. Contract and unjust enrichment may, in this way, be two sides of one conceptual coin within private law.[96]

A single act of interference may thus cut across several manifestations of free will.[97] It is, therefore, unsurprising to find cases in which conceptually different claims may be available on the same facts. As Birks explained, restitution is multi-causal,[98] and there is a difference between claims for restitution based upon unjust enrichment and claims for restitution based upon the commission of a wrong.[99] Furthermore, the different claims can arise on one set of facts. *Edwards v Lee's Administrators* was one such case.[100] The claimant's estate was awarded one-third of the profits made by the defendant from exhibiting a cave, one-third of which extended under the claimant's land. This result can be explained as restitution for the wrong of trespass: the defendant's profits embodied the violation of the claimant's proprietary integrity, founding a claim in tort for restitution of the gain.[101] Alternatively, the case is explicable as one of restitution for unjust enrichment: the defendant's profits embodied the violation of the claimant's exchange capacity; that is, the freedom to permit the defendant or someone else to use the cave in

[95] See generally S Waddams, *Dimensions of Private Law: Categories and Concepts in Anglo-American Legal Reasoning* (Cambridge, Cambridge University Press, 2003) Chs 1 and 11; S Waddams, 'Classification of Private Law in Relation to Historical Evidence' (2003) 6 *Current Legal Issues* 265. See also S Hedley, 'The Shock of the Old: Interpretivism in Obligations' in CEF Rickett and RB Grantham (eds), *Structure and Justification in Private Law* (Oxford, Hart 2008) 213; W Gummow, 'Unjust Enrichment, Restitution and Proprietary Remedies' in PD Finn (ed), *Essays on Restitution* (Sydney, Lawbook Co, 1990) 49–52; R Goff, 'Appendix: The Search for Principle' in W Swadling and G Jones (eds), *The Search for Principle: Essays in Honour of Lord of Chieveley* (Oxford, Oxford University Press, 1999) 318.

[96] See further *Third Restatement* (n 73) 479.

[97] Klimchuk, 'The Normative Foundations of Unjust Enrichment' (n 55) 83–84.

[98] Birks, *Unjust Enrichment* (n 39) 25–28.

[99] *Sempra Metals* (n 85) [116] (Lord Nicholls), [230]–[231] (Lord Mance). See also Burrows, *The Law of Restitution* (n 1) 9–12. It should not be forgotten, however, that restitution can follow other events that are neither 'wrong' nor 'unjust enrichment'. As Birks explained, 'If … I ask you to lend me £50, the loan gives you a restitutionary right which is by origin contractual. The contract of loan obliges me to give up value received': Birks, *Unjust Enrichment* (n 39) 25.

[100] *Edwards v Lee's Administrators* 96 SW 2d 1028 (1936) (CA Kent). See further Birks, *Unjust Enrichment* (n 39) 84.

[101] Weinrib, *The Idea of Private Law* (n 7) 142.

exchange for something else (represented in that case by money as the universal medium of exchange).[102]

Proprietary torts, like the trespass in *Edwards v Lee's Administrators*, tend to muddy the relationship between unjust enrichment and other claims precisely because the exchange capacity engaging unjust enrichment is also bound up in notions of proprietary integrity. The problem is an acute one given English law's reluctance to award restitution for wrongs in non-proprietary torts cases.[103] Even if, however, restitution were generally available as a remedy in non-proprietary torts cases (such as for assault, defamation, and false imprisonment) it seems clear, on the approach to unjust enrichment advocated in this book, that dual analysis would not be possible. This is because the kinds of interest protected by those torts and other wrongful conduct are not susceptible to legitimate exchange.[104] An extreme example of this point arose in *Rosenfeldt v Olson*,[105] where a convicted child murderer (of eleven children) had offered to lead the police to the bodies in return for the payment of $100,000 to his wife and child. The police paid the money to a trustee, and the parents of the murdered children subsequently brought a claim in respect of it. The British Columbia Court of Appeal held that no claim was available because the parents had not suffered a 'corresponding deprivation' in respect of the money paid. The parents had suffered the terrible loss of their children, but that did not entail an infringement of their exchange capacity.[106] The most that could be said of the $100,000 is that it was the product of wrongdoing, and therefore should (contrary to the Court's holding) have been paid over to the parents standing in the position of the murdered children's estate.[107]

[102] *Vincent v Lake Erie Transport Company* 109 Minn 456, 124 NW 221 (1910) (SC Minn) is another worthwhile case to consider in this context. The defendant's ship was moored to plaintiff's dock for the purposes of unloading cargo. A violent storm developed and so, despite the unloading being complete, the master maintained the ship's moorings to a dock to preserve her. During the storm the ship was constantly lifted and thrown against the dock, causing damage. *Third Restatement* (n 73) (at §40, illustration 9) suggests that a defence of necessity precluded a finding of tortious liability, thereby limiting restitution to the rental value plus costs of repair. Cf Waddams, *Dimensions of Private Law: Categories and Concepts in Anglo-American Legal Reasoning* (n 95) 86–87.

[103] See generally *Stoke-on-Trent City Council v W&J Wass Ltd* [1988] 1 WLR 1406 (CA); *Halifax Building Society v Thomas* [1996] Ch 217 (CA); *Forsyth-Grant v Allen* [2008] EWCA Civ 505; *Devenish Nutrition Ltd v Sanofi-Aventis SA* [2008] EWCA Civ 1086, [2009] Ch 390.

[104] See above pp 33–35.

[105] *Rosenfeldt v Olson* (1986) 25 DLR (4th) 472 (BCCA).

[106] See also *Brennan v Gardy Estate* [2011] BCSC 1337, where the plaintiff had cohabitated with his friend and provided domestic services prior to the latter's death. In a claim against the friend's estate, the plaintiff argued that he had suffered a 'corresponding deprivation' in the form of harm to his health brought about by living in a mouldy basement and with a furnace that leaked carbon monoxide. The relevance of this harm was rejected by the Court: the corresponding deprivation had to be rooted in an economic analysis, in that case satisfied on the basis of the plaintiff's unremunerated services (at [24]–[26]).

[107] See further G Jones, *Restitution in Public and Private Law* (London, Sweet & Maxwell, 1991) 69–70. Cf *Third Restatement* (n 73) §45, illustration 20, note *i*.

Two important points follow recognition of the potential for overlap. First, the reason why restitution for wrongdoing and restitution for unjust enrichment can be described as 'in the alternative' is that each responds to a different manifestation of the same underlying interest: the claimant's freedom of will as understood within the scheme of private law justified by corrective justice and Kant's philosophy of right. Secondly, the theoretical basis for dual analysis can explain why, in certain cases, dual analysis ought not be possible. *Rosenfeldt v Olson* is a clear (and extreme) example; *Wrotham Park Estate Co Ltd v Parkside Homes Ltd*[108] is another example, perhaps less obviously. The defendant had built houses on its land in breach of a restrictive covenant, and the claimant estate company sought a mandatory injunction that they should be demolished, which was refused on grounds of wastefulness, though damages in lieu were awarded. Those damages were calculated as the sum of money that might reasonably have been demanded by the claimant from the defendant 'as a *quid pro quo* for relaxing the covenant', which Brightman J assessed to be five per cent of the defendant's anticipated profits.[109] The basis of such '*Wrotham Park* damages'—whether they be compensatory or restitutionary—is a matter of ongoing controversy in judicial opinion[110] and academic commentary.[111] Nor is it clear whether, within the restitutionary sphere, the particular award in *Wrotham Park* can explained on an unjust enrichment basis as distinct from a wrongs basis. On the one hand, as the primary judge observed, the claimant owed obligations to existing residents that prevented it from relaxing the covenant.[112] It was not free to exchange the covenant—in the sense of relaxing it in exchange for something else. Without an exchange capacity, there was no possibility of dual analysis in unjust enrichment. On the other hand, adopting what might loosely be described as an 'efficient breach' theory of contract, one could say that the defendant was free to exchange the covenant, albeit with the attendance of certain consequences against their favour *vis-à-vis* the covenant holders.[113] What matters for the purposes of this book is that, whichever view we take, it is on

[108] *Wrotham Park Estate Co Ltd v Parkside Homes Ltd* [1974] 1 WLR 798 (Ch).

[109] ibid 815–816.

[110] See, eg, *Pell Frischmann Engineering Ltd v Bow Valley Iran Ltd* [2009] UKPC 45, [2011] 1 WLR 2370; *Experience Hendrix LLC v PPX Enterprises Inc* [2003] EWCA Civ 323, [2003] 1 All ER (Comm) 830; *WWF World Wide Fund for Nature (formerly World Wildlife Fund) v World Wrestling Federation Entertainment Inc* [2007] EWCA Civ 286, [2008] 1 WLR 445.

[111] See, eg, Burrows, *The Law of Restitution* (n 1) 635–40; T Cutts, '*Wrotham Park* Damages: Compensation, Restitution or a Substitute for the Value of the Infringement of the Right?' [2010] *Lloyd's Maritime and Commercial Law Quarterly* 215; J Edelman, *Gain-Based Damages: Contract, Tort, Equity and Intellectual Property* (Oxford, Hart, 2002) 99–102; R Sharpe and S Waddams, 'Damages for Lost Opportunity to Bargain' (1982) 2 *Oxford Journal of Legal Studies* 290.

[112] *Wrotham Park* (n 108) 815.

[113] This complexity resonates with the earlier observation that factors external to the structure of unjust enrichment claims influence the scope of their application. A further possible argument is that the treatment of breach of contract (and the related intentional tort of inducing breach of contract) as a civil wrong indicates that such a freedom is illegitimate for exchange purposes, and so excludes characterisation of the case as one based upon unjust enrichment.

the analysis of the claimant's exchange capacity that the characterisation of the case as one of unjust enrichment stands or falls.

### (3) Quantification

The exchange capacity is not quantifiable in its own terms. The defendant who is enriched does not have 'more' exchange capacity, and a claimant who suffers a loss does not have 'less' exchange capacity. That is not how the exchange capacity works. Nor has it been the aim of this chapter to suggest that it does. We observed earlier that corrective justice is pitched at too high a level of abstraction to adjudge which situations are within the law of unjust enrichment.[114] The aim of this chapter has been to shift the analysis down a level to the point where that adjudication is possible, and it has been proposed that it is helpful to conceptualise unjust enrichment as consisting of relevantly connected disruptions to each party's exchange capacity.

However, this still tells us nothing about how claims are to be quantified. For that we must shift down a further level in abstraction to 'value'. Value is the quantified expression of exchange systems and so of the exchange capacity. Disruptions to a party's exchange capacity are quantified by value determined according to the relevant system of exchange. In short, quantification follows the logic of exchange, rather than the strict or abstract logic of law.

## (E) The Exchange Capacity and Liability for Unjust Enrichment

If we were to plot the movements in abstraction that have occurred within this chapter, our starting point would be the highly abstract arithmetic equality set out by Aristotle's theory of corrective justice. Relying on the extensive contributions of Weinrib, we could then drop down to the less abstract free will and Kantian self-determining agency. From there we would then drop further to the exchange capacity that is particular to unjust enrichment, and finally to the concept of value according to which claims are actually quantified. The main contribution of this chapter, therefore, has been to identify the exchange capacity as the necessary step in reducing claims from highly abstract concepts such as corrective justice and free will, to the quantifiable concept of value.

As we shall see in chapters two and three, the exchange capacity is, in this way, crucial to correctly defining and quantifying enrichment and loss within unjust enrichment. Enrichment and loss are the relevant disruptions to each of the

[114] See above pp 24–25.

defendant's and the claimant's positions respectively. And while the experiences of enrichment and loss are different (gaining is patently not the same as losing), that does not mean that the two concepts are isolated or independent from each other. They are not; they are closely related because they reflect the same interest: the exchange capacity. Unjust enrichment defendants and claimants are actors within the one system of exchange, and each has an exchange capacity within that system that is engaged when one is enriched at the expense of the other.

As we shall see later, in Part II, this close relationship between enrichment and loss necessitates a broad test for attribution in unjust enrichment that is supported by the case law: the 'but for' counterfactual between enrichment and loss. That the test for attribution in unjust enrichment is broad should not be surprising in the light of the breadth of the exchange capacity and the free will that guides it.

Importantly though, a broad test of attribution in unjust enrichment does *not* equate with (or lead to) a general expansion of liability in unjust enrichment. Attribution in unjust enrichment is not liability in unjust enrichment. As explained in the Introduction to this book, it is one part of a larger methodological scheme for understanding unjust enrichment cases. Neither the exchange capacity nor the rules of attribution are dogmatic formulae that rule the scope of unjust enrichment liability. Indeed, it is a core thesis of this book that there are matters beyond the issue of attribution that qualify liability in unjust enrichment cases. As we shall see in Part III, some of these may be explicable with reference to the exchange capacity, though others may not be. And whatever way they are explained, it may even be that clear and independent recognition of these qualifications—that is, separated from the broad test of attribution—ultimately leads to a general contraction of liability in unjust enrichment as cases are decided with a concern that unjust enrichment not stultify or undermine existing principles of law.

## (F) The Remedy for Unjust Enrichment

As explained in the Introduction, this book is not about the nature of the remedies for unjust enrichment. A great deal has been written elsewhere about that issue and, in particular, the extent to which specific restitution should be available against a defendant who has been enriched at the expense of the claimant.[115] The issue is notoriously difficult, and it may ultimately turn out that the dilemma is incapable of resolution according to a single analytical framework. It would

[115] This book prefers the terminology of 'specific' restitution to that of 'proprietary' restitution because the latter fails to capture the variety of legal relief and mechanisms capable of being understood as restitutionary in character. These include trusts, rescission, rectification, subrogation and equitable liens. See Lodder, *Enrichment in the Law of Unjust Enrichment and Restitution* (n 34) 64. See also E Bant and M Bryan, 'A Model of Proprietary Remedies' in E Bant and M Bryan (eds), *Principles of Proprietary Remedies* (Sydney, Thomson Reuters, 2013) 212.

therefore be naïve for a book of limited size and scope as this to attempt to answer it definitively.

At the same time, however, it is impossible to ignore certain ramifications for the remedy question that follow the approach to attribution advanced by this book. Important consequences follow, in particular, from recognition that the exchange capacity, informed by considerations of corrective justice, provides the normative basis of unjust enrichment. Dr Harding has neatly explained the relationship between the two points:[116]

> [W]hat is required by a norm of corrective justice depends not only on the constituents of that norm—*viz* the specification of an impugned transaction, and the demand to 'allocate back' by subtractive and additive means so as to cancel the transaction—but also on the reasons why the norm has the constituents in question, including the reasons in light of which the transaction is impugned. … Thus, where a norm of corrective justice stipulates restitution of a mistaken payment, whether or not restitution should take the form of a personal order or a constructive trust depends in part on the reasons for worrying about mistaken payments.

## (1) Personal Restitution

Harding goes on to suggest (as though to foreshadow the arguments presented in this chapter) that if the rationale for restitution of mistaken payments is based upon 'the value of people exercising autonomy in respect of money understood, not as an asset in specie, but rather as a medium of exchange' then proprietary or specific restitution may do more than is required by the norm of corrective justice existing at large.[117] Similarly, Edelman J (writing extra-judicially) has remarked that unjust enrichment is not wide enough to countenance the remedy of a constructive trust:[118]

> I had previously held [the view that a trust should be created as a response to unjust enrichment where a person makes a mistaken payment of money to another]. But it is not correct. Whether or not a trust should arise for some other reason, no case has ever yet recognised that such a trust arises as a consequence of unjust enrichment. … [Such an approach] would involve an unjustified re-interpretation of earlier cases to be cases of unjust enrichment. The law of unjust enrichment is not that broad. The rationale of restitution of an unjust enrichment—to reverse a transfer of value—is perfectly satisfied by an order that the recipient repay what was received. The best way to reverse a transfer of money is to order that the recipient repay money.

This is the outlook preferred by this book: personal restitution, being an order that the defendant pay the claimant a sum of money, is the remedy that should

[116] M Harding, 'Constructive Trusts and Distributive Justice' in E Bant and M Bryan (eds), *Principles of Proprietary Remedies* (Sydney, Thomson Reuters, 2013) [2.20], referring also to Gardner, 'What is Tort Law For? Part 1. The Place of Corrective Justice' (n 10).

[117] Harding, 'Constructive Trusts and Distributive Justice' (n 116) [2.20].

[118] J Edelman, 'Restitution of Rights' in E Bant and M Bryan (eds), *Principles of Proprietary Remedies* (Sydney, Thomson Reuters, 2013) [3.90].

generally follow a finding of unjust enrichment.[119] Such an award restores each party's exchange capacity to its pre-unjust enrichment position. As chapter two explains, a defendant is enriched when and insofar as he receives something valuable that he does not have to pay for, and as chapter three explains, a claimant suffers a loss when and insofar as they lose the opportunity to charge for something valuable. Personal restitution eliminates the enrichment and the loss by ordering the defendant to make the missing payment.[120] An order that does more than this is necessarily based upon considerations external to corrective justice, the exchange capacity, and unjust enrichment as explained by this book. So it is with specific restitution: if the underlying unity upon which unjust enrichment cases are based is the exchange capacity, then the analysis which that unity supports runs out before we get to a specific remedy.[121]

## (2) Specific Restitution

It would, however, take matters too far to suggest that specific restitution is *never* possible as a response to unjust enrichment. At least two points weigh against such a hard-line approach. First, though limited unjust enrichment analysis may be incapable of supporting a remedy beyond personal restitution, there is no reason why an expanded analysis, reliant upon further considerations, cannot do so. Secondly, the wholesale rejection of specific remedies for unjust enrichment jars with a number of cases that have explicitly relied upon unjust enrichment to justify such remedies.

### *(a) Additional Considerations*

It has already been observed that unjust enrichment is commonly analysed according to five questions:[122] (1) Was the defendant enriched? (2) Was it at the expense of the claimant? (3) Was there an unjust factor? (4) Is the remedy personal or specific? (5) Are there any defences? The existence of the fourth question in particular leaves analytical space for a consideration of matters that may influence the nature of the appropriate remedy, beyond the inquiry into whether the defendant has been enriched at the expense of the claimant in circumstances that are unjust.[123] It is not the intention of this book to list those matters exhaustively, nor is it to

[119] See further *Bank of Cyprus UK Ltd v Menelaou* [2015] UKSC 66 [55] (Lord Clarke), [81] (Lord Neuberger).

[120] *Benedetti (UKSC)* (n 38) [100] (Lord Reed).

[121] Indeed, if restitution of rights were achieved by the imposition of trust following unjust enrichment, that remedy would exceed the goal of restoring the parties to their pre-unjust enrichment position insofar as the subject matter of the trust would be new rights conditioned upon different obligations to those existing previously. See Edelman, 'Restitution of Rights' (n 118) [3.80].

[122] See above p 2.

[123] See below p 48.

suggest a means of reducing them to a single line of inquiry. Rather, the point is to show that such an outlook has a degree of support, and so the possibility of specific remedies cannot be completely cut off by the exchange capacity view of unjust enrichment.

A key situation to consider is that of a trust arising in respect of money paid by mistake. In *Chase Manhattan*[124] the plaintiff New York bank was instructed to pay two million dollars to another New York bank for the account of the defendant, which carried on business in London. The money was paid, but then a second payment was made in error. The defendant was later wound up. The plaintiff sought a declaration that the defendants received the moneys as trustees, thus entitling the plaintiff to trace the mistaken payment and recover its traceable proceeds. Goulding J held that the plaintiff could, in principle, trace the money in equity on the basis that a party who pays money by mistake retains a continuing proprietary interest in that money and the conscience of the recipient is subjected to a fiduciary duty to respect it.[125] This reasoning was rejected by Lord Browne-Wilkinson in *Westdeutsche Landesbank Girozentrale v Islington LBC*.[126] His Lordship did, however, agree with the *outcome* in *Chase Manhattan* on the basis that the defendant bank knew of the mistake made by the paying bank within two days of the receipt of the moneys, and that the retention of the moneys after that time could well have given rise to a constructive trust.[127] The acquisition of knowledge of the mistake engaged the equitable jurisdiction to award proprietary relief.

Another illustrative case is *Neste Oy v Lloyds Bank plc*.[128] The plaintiffs were the owners of three ships, and from time to time employed a company (PSL) as their agents when one of their vessels entered a UK port. Matters were arranged so that the plaintiffs transferred funds into PSL's account at the defendant bank as an agency fee and to enable it to meet necessary expenses associated with the ships. Over several weeks, the parties entered into six such transactions. Shortly afterwards, the directors of the corporate group to which PSL belonged agreed that the group and its companies could not meet credit as it fell due and should therefore cease trading immediately, and receivers were appointed. The plaintiffs (through their bank) sought to cancel the sixth payment and to get a refund of the amount by which PSL's account had been credited, but it was too late. When the defendant later sought to set-off the money in PSL's account against the debts owed to it, the plaintiffs contended that sums received by PSL into that account were not available for set-off because they were held by PSL on trust. Bingham J held that a trust arose in respect of the sixth payment (and only the sixth payment) because it had been made at a time when the corporate group had already resolved that it and its

[124] *Chase Manhattan NA v Israel-British Bank (London) Ltd* [1981] Ch 105 (Ch).
[125] ibid 119–20.
[126] *Westdeutsche Landesbank Girozentrale v Islington LBC* [1996] AC 669, [1996] 2 WLR 802 (HL) 714 (Lord Browne-Wilkinson).
[127] ibid 715.
[128] *Neste Oy v Lloyds Bank plc* [1983] 2 Lloyd's Rep 658 (QB).

group companies should cease trading immediately, at a time when PSL had not paid for the services for which the sums had been remitted and at a time when in all the circumstances there was no chance that PSL could deliver the services in question. According to Bingham J, PSL could not in good conscience retain the payment and accordingly a constructive trust was to be inferred.[129]

These cases suggest that additional considerations of knowledge and conscience are relevant in granting a specific remedy that goes beyond personal restitution. However, such matters do not seem to fit within a scheme of unjust enrichment premised on strict liability. At the very least, the cases demonstrate that something else is necessary for the award of a specific remedy. Knowledge and conscience are two factors, but they are certainly not mandatory or unique. Other cases involving the award of specific remedies, such as the award of a bailee's possessory lien following the performance of a service with respect to goods,[130] suggest that the range of additional considerations (and the motivations behind them) is broad indeed.

None of this is to suggest that unjust enrichment must completely drop out of the picture where specific remedies are concerned. Quite the contrary: the point is that these additional considerations *complement* a finding of unjust enrichment, and justify a remedy that surpasses the ordinary award of personal restitution. In *Kerr v Baranow*,[131] for example, the award of proprietary remedies following unjust enrichment was described by the Supreme Court of Canada as appropriate in (some) cases when a monetary award is inappropriate or insufficient.[132] By its nature, such a finding cannot be made without first deciding that a monetary award is available as a remedy for an established claim. The nature and function of this complementary relationship is beyond the scope of this book. It may be that certain factors favouring the award of a specific remedy have at their core a concern for the parties' exchange capacities in circumstances where, owing to the unique nature of the case, personal restitution will not suffice to restore them adequately.[133] Other factors may be motivated by historical or policy-based concerns. Whatever the case, the possibility of specific remedies following unjust enrichment cannot be completely dismissed.

### (b) Judicial Reliance

The second reason why specific restitution cannot be completely dismissed as a response to unjust enrichment is that there are cases in which unjust enrichment

[129] ibid 666.

[130] See, eg, *Spencer v S Franses Ltd* [2011] EWHC 1269 (QB).

[131] *Kerr v Baranow, Vanasse v Seguin* (n 64).

[132] ibid [50] (Cromwell J). See further Edelman, 'Restitution of Rights' (n 118) [3.80].

[133] There is much to be said, in this respect, for a comparison between the possible like-justifications for specific restitution of rights and those for the specific performance of obligations under contract. See further Edelman, 'Restitution of Rights' (n 118) [3.80]. See also Bant and Bryan, 'A Model of Proprietary Remedies' (n 115) [12.90]–[12.180].

analysis has been expressly employed to justify remedies in the nature of specific restitution. Rescission, for example, was described by Robert Goff LJ as 'a straightforward remedy in restitution … by which the unjust enrichment of the [defendant] is prevented'.[134] Most notable, however, is the description of subrogation by English Courts as a remedy for unjust enrichment.[135]

In *BFC v Parc (Battersea)*[136] the claimant lent money to Parc for the latter to pay off a debt. That debt was secured by a charge over Parc's property, and the defendant held a second charge over that property. The claimant had not obtained security for its loan to Parc, but was promised that no one in the corporate group to which Parc belonged (which included the defendant) would seek repayment of their loan ahead of it. The defendant, however, was not bound by that promise. Following Parc's insolvency the claimant sought to be subrogated to the initial security that its loan moneys had been used to discharge. Subrogation was granted to prevent the defendant being enriched by the improvement in its position as second chargee. It was also tailored so as to avoid putting the claimant in a better position than that which it might otherwise have then been able to occupy: subrogation to the charge was granted only insofar as it gave the claimant priority over the defendant. The House of Lords explained that subrogation was designed to prevent unjust enrichment.[137] The case is not unique in this respect.[138]

That subrogation has been described in these terms creates a problem for those who argue that restitution for unjust enrichment can only ever be personal. One could attempt to explain away the problem as an instance in which courts are relying upon the pattern of unjust enrichment to reason from one subrogation case to the next; that is, the underlying rationale of subrogation is yet to be explained, but until it is, the structure of unjust enrichment analysis provides a useful yardstick for determining, in the light of previous subrogation cases, if and when subrogation should be an available remedy. That will probably not carry the day: the courts have demonstrated that unjust enrichment analysis is considered to be the rationale of subrogation, rather than a useful pattern of reasoning.

[134] *Whittaker v Campbell* [1984] QB 318 (DC) 327. See generally Lodder, *Enrichment in the Law of Unjust Enrichment and Restitution* (n 34) 119–33; B Häcker, 'Proprietary Restitution After Impaired Consent Transfers: A Generalised Power Model' [2009] *Cambridge Law Journal* 324, 329.

[135] That should be contrasted with the position in Australia, where the description of subrogation as a remedy for unjust enrichment has been disavowed and the utility of unjust enrichment analysis generally in the field of subrogation doubted: see *Bofinger v Kingsway Group Ltd* [2009] HCA 44, (2009) 239 CLR 269 [85]–[98] (Gummow, Hayne, Heydon, Kiefel, and Bell JJ); M Leeming, 'Subrogation, Equity and Unjust Enrichment' in J Glister and P Ridge (eds), *Fault Lines in Equity* (Oxford, Hart, 2012) 28; D Ong, *Ong On Subrogation* (Federation Press, 2014) Ch 4.

[136] *Banque Financière de la Cité SA v Parc (Battersea) Ltd* [1999] 1 AC 221 (HL).

[137] ibid 226–27 (Lord Steyn), 236 (Lord Hoffman), 238 (Lord Clyde), 245–46 (Lord Hutton).

[138] See especially *Bank of Cyprus UK Ltd v Menelaou (UKSC)* (n 119), [50] (Lord Clarke), [91] (Lord Neuberger), but cf [108]–[109] (Lord Carnwath); *Cheltenham & Gloucester plc v Appleyard* [2004] EWCA Civ 291 [31]–[49] (Neuberger LJ). See also *Orakpo v Manson Investments Ltd* [1978] AC 95 (HL) 104 (Lord Diplock); *Boscawen v Bajwa* [1996] 1 WLR 328 (CA) 335 (Millett LJ); *Menelaou v Bank of Cyprus plc* [2013] EWCA Civ 1960 [17]–[21] (Floyd LJ).

The better view is that subrogation, where it is awarded to prevent unjust enrichment, is an example of a specific remedy for unjust enrichment justified by additional considerations of the kind warranting the conclusion that a monetary award is inadequate. In *BFC v Parc (Battersea)*, for example, the defendant's enrichment was described as its 'improved position as chargee' following the payment of Parc's debt with the money loaned to it by the claimant. The relative position of a chargee has an economic significance, and is susceptible to exchange insofar as a chargee may attempt to negotiate an improvement in that position. The chargee's exchange capacity is thus engaged, and the situation therefore susceptible to unjust enrichment analysis. Expressing that capacity in quantifiable terms, however, may be so difficult that a monetary award is incapable of correcting the parties' positions. The improved position of the defendant in *BFC v Parc (Battersea)* could not be reliably reduced to monetary terms, and so a tailored remedy specific to the particular enrichment was necessary and appropriate.

## (G) Enrichment and Loss

This chapter began with the observation that certain everyday beneficial experiences are outside the scope of unjust enrichment. Equipped with the knowledge that it is the exchange capacity that determines that scope, we are now in a position to explain why this is so. The good vibes of a nightclub, the cultural enlightenment of a museum visit, and the affectionate cuddle at the zoo—all of these things may be 'enriching' in a colloquial sense. They influence our individual preferences, utilities, and choices, but they are not susceptible to market analysis in their own right. There is no market for good vibes, cultural enlightenment, or affection. These things cannot be expressed in pecuniary or economic terms because there is no system for their exchange in their own right. No system for exchange means no exchange capacity, and without an exchange capacity, unjust enrichment has nothing upon which to bite.

This does not mean that the proprietors of nightclubs, museums, and zoos have no recourse to unjust enrichment. Society recognises markets for entry to nightclubs, museums, and zoos and the service of entertainment each provides. This is reflected by the fact that each may legitimately charge patrons an entry fee, and it is the saving of that fee that can found an unjust enrichment claim in the case of the patron who fails to pay.[139] The fee reflects the relational value of entry: the comparison and exchange of qualitatively heterogeneous things in quantitatively comparable and equivalent terms, where the relevant 'things' being so compared are entry on the one hand, and money (as a universal medium of exchange) on the other. The relational value of entry is, in turn, derived from the aggregate of

[139] See further below pp 58–60, 85–86.

individuals' preferences, utilities, and choices—and it is within the derivation of those matters that the colloquially 'enriching' character of good vibes, cultural enlightenment, and affection are relevant. Patrons of museums, nightclubs, and zoos demand admission to those places because they derive utility from them, and the proprietors of such places can take advantage of that demand by charging a fee for admission. Demand thus lies between individual utility and the exercise of the exchange capacity. The fee charged does not reflect individual utility in abstract: the benefit we each may (or may not) derive from dancing at nightclub, exploring a museum, or petting an animal at the zoo. Such benefits are relevant to the determination of market price insofar as they reflect individual utility and preference and are therefore a feature of demand and price determination within markets. But utility and preference are not the subject matter of markets in their own right. I may, for example, be especially fond of the vibes experienced at one particular night club, and may therefore be prepared to pay more for entry into that nightclub compared to another. That is a reflection of my personal utility and preference, but it does not mean that the relevant market is one for utility and preference in respect of nightclub vibes. The market is for nightclub entry. There is no market for good vibes: to speak of one is as nonsensical as speaking of a market for love. Likewise the other beneficial experiences: though good vibes, cultural enlightenment, and soft cuddles are inherently good things, we either shirk at, or are confounded by, any attempt to market them in their own right. They are not the subject of systems of exchange and so do not engage unjust enrichment.[140]

Unjust enrichment was described, at the very start of this chapter, as resting upon 'a disruption of both the claimant's and the defendant's position which requires correction'.[141] What this chapter has shown is that these 'disruptions' can be understood at a particular level of normative abstraction as affecting the parties' ability to exchange one thing for another. The challenge that now arises is how to square this theoretical account of unjust enrichment with the doctrinal requirements of claims. In this respect, each disruption has a name: for the defendant, it is 'enrichment'; for the claimant, it is 'loss'. It is to each of these concepts, and their relationship with the parties' underlying exchange capacities, to which this book now turns.

[140] Mitchell, Mitchell, and Watterson, *Goff & Jones* (n 28) para 4.03 has hit upon this same point using further examples: 'The law pays no attention to the cultural, religious, intellectual or emotional value of a benefit, unless they affect its financial value. So, for example, a claim might lie for the monetary value of services, such as psychiatric counselling, which make the defendant happier. But the reason why such services are relevantly valuable is not because of their effect on the defendant's emotional well-being, but because they can be bought and sold on the market. The affection and companionship of family members also make people happier, but these cannot be bought and sold, and the law does not recognise claims for benefits of this kind.'

[141] Burrows, *The Law of Restitution* (n 1) 68.

# 2

# Enrichment

Enrichment is the gist of unjust enrichment.[1] In order to understand attribution in unjust enrichment, we must first understand *what* is being attributed. This becomes particularly important in Part II of this book, when the different connections that can arise between enrichment and loss are set out and considered. Understanding the different forms of enrichment directs us to the different forms of connection. Furthermore, if we subscribe—as this book argues we should—to a theory of unjust enrichment premised upon protection of exchange capacity, then that interest must be accounted for on both sides of unjust enrichment. This chapter considers the enrichment of the defendant. The next chapter considers the loss of the claimant.

## (A) Two Kinds of Enrichment

In his 2009 contribution to *Philosophical Foundations of the Law of Unjust Enrichment*, Professor Chambers identified 'Two Kinds of Enrichment', arguing that enrichment consists of either value or rights.[2] This core idea has since been picked up by others in order to analyse and explain certain difficult issues within the law of unjust enrichment.[3] The most comprehensive work is that of Lodder, who has expanded Chambers' core thesis by advancing a division between 'factual' and 'legal' enrichments. In essence, Lodder explains that:[4]

> [E]nrichment is not a unitary element satisfied by a single test; rather, the same benefit may [sometimes] be understood in two different ways: (i) by the value of the benefit received ('factual enrichment'); or (ii) by the change in the legal relations of the

[1] *Deutsche Morgan Grenfell Group plc v Inland Revenue Commissioners* [2005] EWCA Civ 78, [2006] Ch 243 [294] (Buxton LJ); *Gibb v Maidstone & Tunbridge Wells NHS Trust* [2010] EWCA Civ 678 [32] (Laws LJ).

[2] R Chambers, 'Two Kinds of Enrichment' in R Chambers, C Mitchell, and J Penner (eds), *Philosophical Foundations of the Law of Unjust Enrichment* (Oxford, Oxford University Press, 2009) 277.

[3] See, eg, B McFarlane, 'Unjust Enrichment, Rights and Value' in D Nolan and A Robertson (eds), *Rights and Private Law* (Oxford, Hart, 2012); E Bant, 'Rights and Value in Rescission: Some Implications for Unjust Enrichment' in D Nolan and A Robertson (eds), *Rights and Private Law* (Oxford, Hart, 2012).

[4] AVM Lodder, *Enrichment in the Law of Unjust Enrichment and Restitution* (Oxford, Hart, 2012) 1.

defendant effected by the acquisition of a right or the release of an obligation ('legal enrichment').

Two observations can be made about the Chambers–Lodder thesis. The first is that it suggests a close relationship between the fourth (remedy) and the first (enrichment) question within the five-question organisation of unjust enrichment:[5] the general idea being that remedies of personal restitution respond to factual enrichment, while remedies of specific restitution respond to legal enrichment.[6] Neither Chambers nor Lodder goes so far, however, as to say that the response to unjust enrichment is determined solely by the enrichment inquiry.[7] The number of questions has not been reduced from five to four. As explained above,[8] personal restitution is the usual remedy that should generally follow a finding of unjust enrichment, with specific restitution the unusual exception. Awards of specific restitution against a defendant are subject to legal caveats and considerations beyond the four-question framework of enrichment at the expense of the claimant that is unjust and subject to defences. That is why all five questions are necessary, and why the remedy question is important. As Chambers acknowledges, where specific restitution in the nature of proprietary relief is awarded:[9]

> Unjust enrichment creates the obligation, but there is a general principle at work which confers its proprietary effect. … The right to restitution of a specific asset is created by unjust enrichment and that right is a property right for reasons external to the law of unjust enrichment. This response cannot be justified solely by the law of unjust enrichment, nor can it be justified without it.

Lodder also admits this limitation to his overall thesis, explaining that 'specific restitution is not available where the law does not recognise the existence of a claim for specific restitution of the right in question'.[10] He adds that restitution is subject to the rules of contract, property, and equity that determine the creation and acquisition of rights and obligations.[11] The core point is that specific remedies are only available in a narrow range of circumstances, and switching the focus of enquiry to the nature of the enrichment rather than the nature of the remedy cannot alter this fact.[12]

[5] See above p 2.

[6] See especially Chambers, 'Two Kinds of Enrichment' (n 2) 267–68.

[7] ibid 268–69; Lodder, *Enrichment in the Law of Unjust Enrichment and Restitution* (n 4) 54, 66–67.

[8] See above pp 44–50.

[9] Chambers, 'Two Kinds of Enrichment' (n 2) 268–69.

[10] Lodder, *Enrichment in the Law of Unjust Enrichment and Restitution* (n 4) 66–67. See also Chambers, 'Two Kinds of Enrichment' (n 2) 268.

[11] Lodder, *Enrichment in the Law of Unjust Enrichment and Restitution* (n 4) 67. Moreover, the specific restitution of rights (such as rights to a chattel) may be limited by factual circumstances that make such an order impossible, such as the conveyance or destruction of the subject matter of those rights in advance of a claim being made. And if the defendant cannot rely upon a change of position defence, the claimant will be entitled to personal restitution for the value of those rights. See, eg, *Cressman v Coys of Kensington (Sales) Ltd* [2004] EWCA Civ 47, [2004] 1 WLR 2775.

[12] See further W Gummow, 'Unjust Enrichment, Restitution and Proprietary Remedies' in PD Finn (ed), *Essays on Restitution* (Sydney, Lawbook Co, 1990) 49–52.

The second observation to note about the Chambers–Lodder thesis is that factual and legal enrichment are not mutually exclusive categories. Value, it is to be recalled, is an abstract standard for the comparison and exchange of qualitatively heterogeneous things in quantitatively comparable and equivalent terms.[13] Legal enrichments are capable of having value because they can be measured by reference to that standard. This is why the single enrichment of a defendant who receives a right may be understood in two conceptually distinct ways: the right and its value. This does not mean that a claimant is entitled to restitution twice, once in respect of the right and once in respect of its value. That would generate double recovery: a claimant whose right is restored is thereafter in a position to realise the value of that right. The point is, rather, that whichever way enrichment is conceived, the *single* framework into which it fits is the exchange capacity.

## (B) Enrichment and the Exchange Capacity

In *Ford v Perpetual Trustees Victoria Ltd*[14] the defendant (Mr Ford) signed a loan agreement and mortgage with the claimant (Perpetual) for a loan of $200,000 secured over Mr Ford's residential property. The loaned funds were used to purchase a cleaning business in Mr Ford's name. The business was to be for the benefit of Mr Ford's son, who had persuaded his father to enter the transaction. Only $24,857 of the total loaned funds were actually paid into Mr Ford's own bank account. Mr Ford suffered from a congenital intellectual impairment, was illiterate and had no understanding at all of the transaction. The business subsequently failed and Mr Ford defaulted on the loan agreement. The claimant then commenced proceedings for possession of the property. That action failed at first instance on the basis that the loan and mortgage were void; Mr Ford was able to rely upon a plea of *non est factum*. He was, however, ordered to repay the loan monies paid by the claimant in the mistaken belief that the transaction was valid. That decision was reversed by the NSW Court of Appeal on the basis that (with the exception of the $24,857 actually paid into Mr Ford's bank account) Mr Ford had not been enriched. The question of enrichment was expressed as a matter of 'substance and not form or legal technicality'.[15] The Court explained:[16]

> Mr Ford was a manipulated intermediary with no understanding of any aspect of the overall transaction. In substance, he received no benefit from the loan, beyond the receipt and retention in his account of $24,857. … Looking at the matter as one of substance,

[13] See above p 26.

[14] *Ford (by his Tutor Beatrice Ann Watkinson) v Perpetual Trustees Victoria Ltd* [2009] NSWCA 186, (2009) 75 NSWLR 42.

[15] ibid [123] (Allsop P and Young JA, Sackville AJA agreeing).

[16] ibid [127]. No defence to the claim, such as change of position, had been pleaded by Mr Ford: ibid [119]. See above p 5.

> Mr Ford was the innocent, mentally incapable dupe of his son. Save for the $24,857, in no real or substantive sense did he receive and retain benefits such that it would be unjust for him not to repay the loan.

Following the theoretical account of unjust enrichment claims described in chapter one, enrichment can be understood—at a certain level of abstraction—as an incident of the defendant's exchange capacity. *Ford v Perpetual Trustees Victoria Ltd* provides a stark illustration of this point, and of the result that follows a finding that the exchange capacity is not present. To the extent that Mr Ford was the 'mentally incapable dupe of his son', he was not freely acting on his own behalf in respect of the loan monies;[17] he was not a 'self-determining agent' in the sense required by corrective justice and Kant's philosophy of right. His relevant position—his free will manifested in his exchange capacity—was not engaged in the sense required of unjust enrichment.

Two further points must be made about the relationship between enrichment and the exchange capacity observed in *Ford v Perpetual Trustees Victoria Ltd*. The first is that the assessment of an individual's exchange capacity is a factually nuanced and transaction-specific exercise. Mr Ford lacked the requisite exchange capacity only insofar as he was being used as the 'mentally incapable dupe of his son'. His intellectual impairment did not render him completely invulnerable to a claim in unjust enrichment in all circumstances; indeed, he admitted liability to return the money remaining in his account. Nor would Mr Ford have been unable to claim in unjust enrichment if his son (or someone else) had been enriched at his expense. His impairment did not eliminate his exchange capacity forever and in all circumstances (whether exercised directly by him or through a personal representative or tutor). The point was, rather, that the particular enrichment alleged against him had occurred in circumstances where whatever residual exchange capacity he might have possessed was rendered nugatory by the manipulating acts of his son.

The second point to note about *Ford v Perpetual Trustees Victoria Ltd* is that the analysis of the case must be pitched at the right level. The claim against Mr Ford did not fail because he did not have 'more' exchange capacity. That is not how the exchange capacity works:[18] it is qualitative, not quantitative. The transition from the exchange capacity, to enrichment, and to measurement of value, necessarily proceeds in stages: first, there must be an exchange capacity; secondly, that interest must be engaged by receipt of something susceptible to exchange; and, thirdly, the system according to which the exchange can occur then determines the relevant value of that enrichment. The claim against Mr Ford failed at the first stage.

There are many reasons why the exchange capacity might not be engaged in a given case, and so leave unjust enrichment with nothing on which to bite.

[17] C Mitchell, P Mitchell, and S Watterson (eds), *Goff & Jones: The Law of Unjust Enrichment*, 8th edn (London, Sweet & Maxwell, 2011) para 5.04.

[18] See above p 43.

For example, there may (also for different possible reasons) be no underlying system of exchange—as in the case of illicit substances, or the murdered children in *Rosenfeldt v Olson*.[19] Or, a particular individual may have limited the otherwise legitimate exercise of their exchange capacity—as in the case of covenants binding upon the claimant in *Wrotham Park Estate Co Ltd v Parkside Homes Ltd*.[20] *Ford v Perpetual Trustees Victoria Ltd* illustrates a further possibility: Mr Ford's mental incapacities inhibited him from engaging, in any meaningful way, with the exchange process embodied in the transaction orchestrated by his son. It may have been possible to express the legal effect of this incapacity in terms of a defence to an established claim,[21] or as somehow ameliorating the 'injustice' of any enrichment. Indeed, the latter possibility was identified by the court in its reasoning.[22] Another, however, was to say—as the court did say in the passage extracted above—that the incapacity eliminated a finding of enrichment. This was not based upon the quantification of Mr Ford's exchange capacity, but upon the lack of it in the first place. No exchange capacity meant no unjust enrichment. The case thus provides an illustration of why it is an oversimplification to describe unjust enrichment as concerned with benefits expressible in pecuniary terms, without any regard to the underlying requirement of the exchange capacity.[23] The effect of the court's holding was that the receipt of money did not enrich Mr Ford, precisely because he lacked the necessary exchange capacity.

## (1) Factual Enrichment and the Exchange Capacity

A party who is 'factually enriched' receives something capable of being exchanged in a system of exchange within which they are free to engage. That system of exchange then expresses the enrichment quantitatively via the universal medium of exchange: value in money terms. In this way, the receipt of something valuable engages the exchange capacity, and with it, unjust enrichment. This is ultimately a long-form way of expressing a principle that otherwise seems trite: unjust enrichment responds to the receipt of value. But the long-form is necessary for several reasons. Expressed in its short-form, the principle does not adequately explain unjust enrichment's response to the receipt of services and other cases where what is received cannot be subsequently exchanged. Nor does it have anything to say about how we should account for different assessments of value. The long-form can explain both.

[19] *Rosenfeldt v Olson* (1986) 25 DLR (4th) 472 (BCCA). See above pp 33–35, 41.

[20] *Wrotham Park Estate Co Ltd v Parkside Homes Ltd* [1974] 1 WLR 798 (Ch). See above p 42.

[21] See generally Mitchell, Mitchell, and Watterson, *Goff & Jones* (n 17) Ch 34.

[22] See *Ford v Perpetual Trustees Victoria Ltd* (n 14) [121], [130]–[131].

[23] See above pp 32–35.

### (a) Subsequent Exchangeability

A conceptual difficulty seems to arise when we apply the exchange capacity to receipt of services cases, where the particular service does not generate anything capable of being exchanged in its own right (often referred to as an 'end-product' or a 'marketable residuum'). A possible objection, in these 'pure services' cases, is that the recipient's exchange capacity is unaffected because he is not thereafter in a position to exchange anything received by the service provider. If, for example, A performs a play for B, B afterwards leaves the theatre with nothing more or less tangible than when he entered. Or if, in another example, A cuts B's hair—B may well walk out of the barbershop with less hair, but his exchange capacity appears to be unaffected. And if A paints B's house, he may well increase its market value in doing so, but B's exchange capacity in respect of the house seems unaffected; it was B's house to exchange before A's service, and it remains B's house thereafter. The difficulty, therefore, is how to square the receipt of services with a theory of unjust enrichment built upon exchange.

The status of services within unjust enrichment has been the subject of extensive academic debate.[24] Much has been written, in particular, of the distinction between pure services and those that produce an end product.[25] Lodder, however, has explained why that distinction is irrelevant to the identification of enrichment. Services are susceptible to exchange, and are therefore valuable, irrespective of end product. This fits both theory and case law:[26]

> The performance of a valuable service attracts a fee, whether or not that service results in a tangible end product. It is a trite observation that the market attaches value to the building of houses and the cutting of hair, the mowing of lawns and the performance of live music. The same is true of the law. Defendants have been ordered to pay *quantum meruit* for services as diverse as the making and alteration of clothes, the building of houses, the provision of management and professional services, the making of repairs to property, and the provision of research services. Some of these services saved a necessary expense, some did not; some were designed to produce an end product, others were not. The picture that emerges from the cases is that the law follows the logic of the market: it treats services themselves as transferring value that may enrich a defendant.

All of this is well and good, but it does not address the underlying conceptual difficulty of how the receipt of a valuable service affects the exchange capacity. As Professor Grantham and Professor Rickett have pointed out, the position of

[24] See generally Lodder, *Enrichment in the Law of Unjust Enrichment and Restitution* (n 4) 152–61.

[25] See, eg, A Burrows, *The Law of Restitution*, 3rd edn (Oxford, Oxford University Press, 2011) 46–47, arguing that pure services are received when performance starts; services designed to produce an end product are received when part of the end product is transferred to the recipient. See also G Virgo, *The Principles of the Law of Restitution*, 3rd edn (Oxford, Oxford University Press, 2015) 75–77. Cf J Beatson, 'Benefit, Reliance and the Structure of Unjust Enrichment' in J Beatson (ed), *The Use and Abuse of Unjust Enrichment: Essays on the Law of Restitution* (Oxford, Clarendon Press, 1991) 23.

[26] Lodder, *Enrichment in the Law of Unjust Enrichment and Restitution* (n 4) 87 (footnotes omitted). See further *Benedetti v Sawiris* [2013] UKSC 50, [2013] 3 WLR 351, [14] (Lord Clarke).

someone who receives a pure, albeit valuable, service appears unchanged insofar as they do not thereafter have anything capable of being restored,[27] or of being exchanged for that matter. Indeed, taken at its full, the problem is not limited to pure services, but extends to situations in which a tangible benefit is received but immediately consumed, such as a meal eaten at a restaurant. It is conceptually unclear just how the exchange capacity is engaged in these and similar cases.

The truth about this conceptual difficulty, however, is that it arises from a misunderstanding of the exchange capacity. The reason why pure services are within the scope of unjust enrichment is that they can be (and are regularly) exchanged in their own right. It has nothing to do with whether the service 'increases' the exchange capacity of the recipient because that is not how the exchange capacity works: it is a qualitative, not quantitative, interest. Whether the service leaves a marketable residuum is therefore beside the point. Receipt of a pure service is an enrichment if and insofar as that receipt occurs without payment or other exchange.

Indeed, this point applies to *all* enrichments. Immediate consumables are one example similar to services, but there are others where the comparison is less clear. Where money is received, for example, it may be tempting to explain the enrichment in exchange capacity terms by reference to the fact that the defendant has 'more' exchange capacity in the sense that he is now in a position to realise something that he was not before. But, once again, that is not how the exchange capacity works: it is a qualitative interest, not a quantitative one. The imbalance between claimant and defendant, to which unjust enrichment responds, is a *normative* imbalance. That normative imbalance is *quantified* by the system of exchange. The quantification is not the imbalance itself. Where money is received, it is the fact of its receipt rather than its subsequent exchangeability that is relevant to the recipient's exchange capacity.

Another example arises where the enrichment consists of use value. In *Sempra Metals*,[28] for example, the defendant Revenue had to make restitution to the claimant taxpayer in respect of compound interest accruing on sums of tax prematurely paid during the period between when the tax was paid and when it ought to have been paid. For present purposes, what matters is that a majority of their Lordships assessed liability by reference to what it would have cost the

[27] R Grantham and C Rickett, *Enrichment and Restitution in New Zealand* (Oxford, Hart, 2000) 61. This point should be read, however, in the context of the authors' overall approach to restitution, according to which 'restorability' is centrally important, rather than relational value and exchange. They add the rider (at 61) that: 'This is not to say, however, that pure services are not beneficial to the recipient or that pure services do not have a market value. Nor is it to say that plaintiff who has performed pure services is accordingly without some avenue of legal redress. It is merely, but very importantly, to acknowledge that the law of restorable enrichment does not deal with everything that society might regard as valuable, and that "pure" services is one of those valuable "things" with which the law of restorable enrichment is not concerned.' This book disagrees with that outlook.

[28] *Sempra Metals Ltd (formerly Metallgesellschaft Ltd) v Inland Revenue Commissioners* [2007] UKHL 34, [2008] 1 AC 561.

Revenue to borrow an equivalent sum for that period, rather than by asking what profit the Revenue made or could have made by investing the money.[29] As Lord Nicholls explained:[30]

> In the ordinary course the value of having the use of money, sometimes called the 'use value' or 'time value' of money, is best measured in this restitutionary context by the reasonable cost the defendant would have incurred in borrowing the amount in question for the relevant period. That is the market value of the benefit the defendant acquired by having the use of the money. This means the relevant measure in the present case is the cost the United Kingdom Government would have incurred in borrowing [the tax] for the period of prematurity.

If enrichment were about subsequent exchangeability then *Sempra Metals* would have been decided differently; the relevant enrichment comprised by the use value of the money would have been the actual value derived from investing it. Instead, the enrichment was the saving to the Revenue of having the money for a period of time without having to pay the usual borrowing rate for Government: its exchange capacity was engaged by the receipt of the money, rather than the subsequent use to which that money could be or was put, and the relevant system of exchange was that between Government and lender.[31]

An important consequence of this focus on receipt is that *every* case of factual enrichment can be expressed in 'saved necessary expenditure' terms akin to those in *Sempra Metals*. The receipt of something valuable enriches the defendant because, and insofar as, he does not have to pay for it, which he would otherwise have to do under prevailing market conditions.

This idea resonates with the familiar concept of 'saved necessary expenditure' encountered in the particular context of discharged and released obligations,[32] but it also extends much further. 'Expenditure' does not just mean 'money', but includes all things that may be the subject of exchange—money is simply the universal measure of this susceptibility. And such expenditure is 'necessary' insofar as it reflects what ought to have been (but was not in fact) exchanged by the defendant *vis-à-vis* the claimant for what was received.

What this ultimately means is that while the various kinds of enrichment may be *superficially* distinct, at a higher and appropriate level of abstraction—namely, the exchange capacity—they are all fundamentally the same. Money, services, use value, and property are all capable of forming the subject-matter of an unjust enrichment claim because they are capable of being exchanged and so

[29] ibid [50] (Lord Hope), [103] (Lord Nicholls), [188] (Lord Walker), cf [145] (Lord Scott) and [231] (Lord Mance).

[30] ibid [103] (Lord Nicholls).

[31] See further *Equitas Ltd v Walsham Bros & Co Ltd* [2013] EWHC 3264 (QB) [118], where Males J described the interest award in *Sempra Metals* as 'the interest which a substantial commercial company would have to pay to borrow the amount in question in the market at the relevant time'.

[32] See generally Mitchell, Mitchell, and Watterson, *Goff & Jones* (n 17) paras 4.17–4.26; Lodder, *Enrichment in the Law of Unjust Enrichment and Restitution* (n 4) 312–15.

a defendant who receives them without paying for them is saved the expense of making an exchange.[33]

There are two outstanding matters to consider. First is the particular case of services that either produce a marketable residuum, or enhance the value of property already owned by the defendant. If enrichment arises on receipt of the service, what is the status of that residuum? If A paints B's house, and the value of B's house thereby increases, then B's exchange capacity is manifested twice: first, by the receipt of the valuable painting service; and, secondly, by the gain in value of an asset (B's house) that was susceptible to a system of exchange. We must be careful not to conflate the latter enrichment with subsequent exchangeability or make the error of thinking that B has 'more' exchange capacity. The point is, rather, that improving something that already has value is of itself an incident of the exchange capacity, quantified as the increase in value following the improvement. As we shall see in Part III of this book, however, it does not follow from recognition of this point that all enhancements in marketable residua ultimately give rise to liability in unjust enrichment: the important rider to claims to such residua is that the law may deny them in the interest of protecting a defendant's pre-existing property rights.[34]

Secondly, the focus on receipt of value within the enrichment inquiry does not mean that subsequent exchangeability is completely irrelevant to the larger scheme of unjust enrichment. It is, for example, one important aspect of the change of position defence. That defence too can be expressed in exchange capacity terms that align with the underlying corrective justice foundations of unjust enrichment. Smith has set out that justification as follows:[35]

> One might ask how this defence, invoked by some dealing to which the plaintiff is not a party, can be squared with the bilateral nature of corrective justice. The explanation is that Kantian right requires the plaintiff to recognize the defendant's status as a self-determining agent. Before the defendant has any reason to suspect he is liable to a claim in unjust enrichment, he cannot be faulted for behaving as a self-determining agent, including through consuming that which he reasonably believes to be his own wealth. The plaintiff, whose claim is generally founded on Kantian right, must accept that the logic of Kantian right has implications for the defendant as well. The defendant's reliance expenditures therefore reduce his normative gain and hence his liability.

This justification requires some massaging insofar as it seems to limit the defence to situations of so-called 'reliance expenditure'. Whether the change of position

[33] The receipt of money itself may seem awkward to conceive of in terms of saved necessary expenditure, but the idea holds. If, for example, someone receives a mistaken payment of £100 then what can be said of that person's position is that he has been saved the expense of doing something worth £100, the highest expression of which is the payment of £100. Such a simple benefit as money must, in this way, be subjected to the same conceptual analysis as other, less simple benefits.

[34] See below pp 191–198.

[35] L Smith, 'Restitution: The Heart of Corrective Justice' (2001) 79 *Texas Law Review* 2115, 2148–49. See also J Edelman, 'Change of Position: A Defence of Unjust Disenrichment' (2012) 92 *Boston University Law Review* 1009, 1011.

defence is and ought to be so limited is controversial.[36] On the one hand, it has been held that the defence cannot operate without some form of reliance on the receipt of the benefit by the person whose position has allegedly changed—it not being sufficient that his position changed passively and without his knowledge.[37] On the other hand, the preferable view appears to be that reliance is not a necessary feature of the defence provided there is some sort of 'causal' relationship between the defendant's change of position and their enrichment at the claimant's expense.[38] Were matters otherwise, the defence would not protect a good faith defendant who received a benefit that was subsequently stolen or destroyed for reasons beyond his control. That would be an unsatisfactory state of affairs, but it seems to follow if we subscribe to Smith's version of the defence above because the defendant who is a victim of theft or other misfortune is not acting freely in respect of the event that changes his position.

But this need not be the case. If we examine Smith's explanation of the defence closely, we see that it is the defendant's *status* as a self-determining agent that matters, not the active exercise of that agency. Status is wider than any single manifestation of free will: it encompasses the fact that the defendant is an agent existing in the world, equally capable of exercise self-determining agency as the claimant, and equally susceptible to unintended and unwelcomed intrusions upon that agency and other defects in its exercise.[39] So if the nub of a claimant's case in unjust enrichment is precisely that his own self-determining agency has been exercised defectively or otherwise intruded upon, it would be incongruous to ignore similar shortfalls in the self-determining agency of the defendant.

Indeed, if concern for self-determining agency were limited to the active exercise of free will, then the scope of unjust enrichment generally—and not just the change of position defence—would contract drastically, as unjust factors stemming from the lack of consent (such as ignorance and powerlessness) as opposed to the defective or conditional exercise of consent (such as mistake and duress) would fall outside its scope. There are good reasons for resisting such a contraction,[40] one of the strongest of which is that the practical boundary between a

[36] See generally Mitchell, Mitchell, and Watterson, *Goff & Jones* (n 17) paras 27.27–27.28.

[37] *Streiner v Bank Leumi (UK) plc* Unreported QBD, 31 October 1985.

[38] See, eg, *Scottish Equitable plc v Derby* [2001] EWCA Civ 369, 3 All ER 818 [30]–[31] (Robert Walker LJ). See also *National Bank of New Zealand Limited v Waitaki International Processing Limited (NI) Ltd* [1999] 2 NZLR 211 (NZCA). See further Mitchell, Mitchell, and Watterson, *Goff & Jones* (n 17) para 27.28; Edelman, 'Change of Position: A Defence of Unjust Disenrichment' (n 35) 1014; A Burrows, *A Restatement of the English Law of Unjust Enrichment* (Oxford, Oxford University Press, 2012) 119–120.

[39] Edelman, 'Change of Position: A Defence of Unjust Disenrichment' (n 35) 1011–1014, 1022, and 1026–1027. Justice Edelman limits express consideration of defects in the defendant's intention to situations where it is vitiated or qualified, but tacitly accepts the view that the defence is capable of extending to cases of disenrichment where there was a lack of intention in the first place.

[40] See, eg, Burrows, *A Restatement of the English Law of Unjust Enrichment* (n 38) 13–14, 93–96; Mitchell, Mitchell, and Watterson, *Goff & Jones* (n 17) Ch 8; P Birks, *An Introduction to the Law of Restitution*, revised edn (Oxford, Clarendon Press, 1989) 140–146. Cf W Swadling, 'Ignorance and Unjust Enrichment: The Problem of Title' (2008) 28 *Oxford Journal of Legal Studies* 627.

defective or conditional exercise of consent on the one hand, and a complete lack of consent on the other hand, is very fine and may—in reality—be the product of artificial distinctions.[41] It is incongruous to say, for example, that the state of mind of a claimant who pays money to a defendant by mistake should be susceptible to unjust enrichment analysis, while the state of mind of a claimant whose money is stolen by a defendant should not. The existence of consent may be relevant to the passing of title,[42] but (as we shall see further in chapter four)[43] questions of title do not determine the scope of unjust enrichment—that is, rather, the role of markets and the exchange capacity.

The rationale for the change of position defence is that the defendant's exchange capacity must be accepted by the claimant and respected within the unjust enrichment framework. That rationale is not inherently limited to reliance expenditure or other active manifestations of free will. A final and important point about the relationship between enrichment and the change of position defence follows from recognition of this underlying rationale, though its full and substantial consideration is beyond the scope of this book. That a concern for the exchange capacity arises within both the enrichment inquiry and the change of position defence explains why there is a close theoretical relationship between the two. It is therefore unsurprising to find that the change of position defence been expressed in 'disenrichment' terms,[44] or apparently subsumed in some accounts by the enrichment inquiry itself.[45] But it is not identical: subsequent exchange is relevant to change of position, but not to enrichment. There are, therefore, sound theoretical reasons for treating the two matters conceptually and doctrinally separate.

### *(b) Subjectivity of Value*

Value cannot be forced upon someone. That would be antithetical to free will and the exchange capacity that underlies unjust enrichment and the very idea of value itself. The exchange capacity necessarily includes a freedom *not* to exchange. Equally, however, someone who receives value cannot unreservedly deny it. That too would be antithetical to the concept of value because value presupposes a system of exchange, and one cannot simultaneously benefit from that system yet deny one's participation in it. There is, therefore, an inevitable tension within unjust enrichment between an individual's exchange capacity on the one hand, and the

[41] See further Burrows, *The Law of Restitution* (n 25) 403, where it is said that to deny ignorance as a ground for restitution 'is to reject illogically the simple point that if mistake triggers restitution so, *a fortiori*, must ignorance'.

[42] See, eg, Swadling, 'Ignorance and Unjust Enrichment: The Problem of Title' (n 40).

[43] See below pp 102–103.

[44] See, eg, P Birks, *Unjust Enrichment*, 2nd edn (Oxford, Oxford University Press, 2005) 208–19; Burrows, *The Law of Restitution* (n 25) 526–27, 532.

[45] Chambers, 'Two Kinds of Enrichment' (n 2) 247–49. Cf Edelman, 'Change of Position: A Defence of Unjust Disenrichment' (n 35).

existence of systems of exchange on the other. The law reacts to this tension. As Lord Nicholls observed in *Sempra Metals*:[46]

> A benefit is not always worth its market value to a particular defendant. When it is not it may be unjust to treat the defendant as having received a benefit possessing the value it has to others. In Professor Birks's language, a benefit received by a defendant may sometimes be subject to 'subjective devaluation'.

Much has been written about the subjectivity of value to a defendant, both in decided cases[47] and in academic commentary.[48] It is not the intention of this book to recast that discussion and analysis. The exercise being undertaken here is more basal. The point is that the acknowledgment of subjectivity of value is indicative of the underlying exchange capacity that engages unjust enrichment. Furthermore, that subjectivity of value is not applied absolutely confirms the hypothesis that unjust enrichment is concerned only with a particular manifestation of free will—the exchange capacity—the dimensions of which are necessarily limited and informed by market systems.

### (i) Subjective Devaluation

Lodder has examined subjectivity of value within unjust enrichment according to the two dominant theories: 'subjective devaluation', which permits the defendant to assert that an enrichment was worth less to him than its market value; and 'choice of benefit', which considers the question of whether the defendant chose the benefit, not whether or how the defendant valued it.[49] The former theory holds the defendant's subjective valuations, personal preferences, and spending priorities to be relevant; the latter denies this and holds it to be sufficient that the defendant objectively manifested a choice of the benefit and assumed responsibility to pay for it. Following a careful analysis of judicial decisions, Lodder comes to the conclusion that subjective devaluation is not supported by the case law.[50] He also explains that, on a theoretical level, subjective devaluation is incompatible with the relational concept of value, however it is expressed. Expressed in its

[46] *Sempra Metals* (n 28) [119], referring to Birks, *An Introduction to the Law of Restitution* (n 40).

[47] See, eg, *Benedetti (UKSC)* (n 26); *Chief Constable of Greater Manchester v Wigan Athletic AFC Ltd* [2008] EWCA Civ 1449, [2009] 1 WLR 1580; *Sempra Metals* (n 28); *Cressman* (n 11); *Rowe v Vale of White Horse District Council* [2003] EWHC 388 (Ch), [2003] 1 Lloyd's Rep 418.

[48] See, eg, Mitchell, Mitchell and Watterson, *Goff & Jones* (n 17) paras 4.06–4.33; Lodder, *Enrichment in the Law of Unjust Enrichment and Restitution* (n 4) Ch 5; Burrows, *The Law of Restitution* (n 25) 47–61; 'The Meaning of Loss and Enrichment' in R Chambers, C Mitchell, and J Penner (eds), *Philosophical Foundations of The Law of Unjust Enrichment* (Oxford, Oxford University Press, 2009) 224; G Virgo, *The Principles of the Law of Restitution* (n 25) 64–72; Birks, *Unjust Enrichment* (n 44) 55–62; M Garner, 'The Role of Subjective Benefit in the Law of Unjust Enrichment' (1990) 10 *Oxford Journal of Legal Studies* 42; P Birks, 'In Defence of Free Acceptance' in A Burrows (ed), *Essays on the Law of Restitution* (Oxford, Clarendon Press, 1991); P Birks, *An Introduction to the Law of Restitution* (n 40) Ch 5.

[49] Lodder, *Enrichment in the Law of Unjust Enrichment and Restitution* (n 4) 151–52. See also J McGhee, 'The Nature of the Enrichment Enquiry' in J Edelman and S Degeling (eds), *Unjust Enrichment in Commercial Law* (Sydney, Thomson Reuters, 2008) 90–92.

[50] Lodder, *Enrichment in the Law of Unjust Enrichment and Restitution* (n 4) 155–61.

'strong' form, and taken literally, subjective devaluation relies on an idiosyncratic conception of value—suggesting that the defendant's own valuation of the benefit received is relevant to the award of restitution following unjust enrichment.[51] Expressed in its 'weak' form, subjective devaluation is not concerned with idiosyncratic valuation but with discernment of the parties' subjective intentions as objectively manifested; that is, the objective valuation to a reasonable person in the defendant's position with that person's characteristics, preferences and priorities.[52] Both forms conflict with relational value: the strong form explicitly relies on idiosyncratic over relational value, while the weak form's reliance on objective value to a reasonable person in the defendant's position is a proxy for the idiosyncratic value of a person closely resembling the defendant.[53]

The difficulties afflicting subjective devaluation lead Lodder to favour the second dominant theory of subjectivity of value: choice of benefit. As Professor McInnes has explained, the relevant question is not the defendant's personal valuation of the enrichment, but rather the defendant's personal choice to accept financial responsibility for it.[54] Lodder expresses full agreement with this position and sets about developing a detailed choice of benefit theory that is consistent with the cases and which ensures the protection of the defendant's freedom of choice.[55] In the course of doing so he makes the point that:[56]

> The obligation to make restitution of an enrichment does not arise because of the defendant's freedom of choice; rather, the defendant can object to the obligation to make restitution if his freedom of choice is not respected. However, a defendant who voluntarily assumes the responsibility to pay for a benefit cannot make this objection. If the defendant's choice of a benefit constitutes an assumption of responsibility to pay for that benefit, the defendant cannot refuse to pay market value on the basis that her subjective valuation differs from the market valuation.

The centrality of free will to this choice of benefit approach is self-evident. Importantly, it is by its terms necessarily limited in scope to the exchange capacity identified as central to unjust enrichment in this book. A defendant participates in a system of exchange by receiving a benefit, but he cannot set or alter the terms by which that system of exchange operates: that is, he cannot shun the market value of an enrichment he has received on the basis that his subjective valuation is different from that market value. And it is worthwhile reiterating the point made in chapter one: markets are not limited to large constructs consisting of many participants. A market of two—the claimant and the defendant—will suffice,[57] in which case the market price reflects what a reasonable person in the position of

[51] ibid (n 4) 161.
[52] ibid 161–62.
[53] ibid 162.
[54] M McInnes, 'Enrichment Revisited' in J Neyers, M McInnes, and S Pitel (eds), *Understanding Unjust Enrichment* (Oxford, Hart, 2004) 107–08.
[55] Lodder, *Enrichment in the Law of Unjust Enrichment and Restitution* (n 4) 167–83.
[56] ibid 165–66.
[57] See above p 31.

the defendant would have had to pay the claimant so as to receive the particular enrichment conferred upon him.[58] That is, how the reasonable person in the position of the defendant would have exercised his exchange capacity in the market.

A possible criticism of this approach is that it assumes a defendant's voluntary assumption to pay for a benefit perfectly aligns with the unimpeached exercise of his free will and exchange capacity. In reality, this will rarely be the case.[59] An individual's attitude towards the receipt of a benefit is generally not simply either 'I want it' or 'I don't'—but is adjusted and varies according to different factors, including the price he will have to pay for it, and how this will affect his other spending habits, priorities and desires. This has the difficult consequence of creating feedback between the exchange capacity and market price at the point of deciding whether a defendant has voluntarily assumed the benefit in question. One solution lies in separating out the protection of a defendant's idiosyncrasies and addressing them elsewhere within the unjust enrichment scheme, such as in the change of position defence, rather than at the point of valuing the enrichment from the outset of the claim.[60] This approach is an attractive one because it recognises that not all problems encountered within unjust enrichment need to be resolved at a single stage in the analysis of claims.

This outlook, according to which a fixed approach to subjective devaluation is eschewed in favour of a flexible appreciation for underlying freedom of choice issues, has garnered significant support in the Supreme Court's decision in *Benedetti v Sawiris* (considered in greater detail immediately below).[61] All of their Lordships expressed dissatisfaction with the expression 'subjective devaluation'.[62] As Lord Reed explained, protection of the defendant's autonomy and freedom to assume responsibility to pay for a benefit is central, so analysis is clarified by expressing the relevant principle as one concerned with freedom of choice, rather than subjective devaluation.[63] Moreover, *Benedetti v Sawiris* shows that such a concern can influence more than one stage of analysis within the unjust enrichment framework. Lord Clarke, for example, suggested that a defendant is entitled to argue that he valued an enrichment at less than its proven market value (subject

[58] *Benedetti v Sawiris* [2010] EWCA Civ 1427 [145] (Etherton LJ). See also Lodder, *Enrichment in the Law of Unjust Enrichment and Restitution* (n 4) 160. This hypothetical inquiry will, naturally, be so fact-specific that it is probably impossible (and perhaps naïve) to suppose that broad and universal statements of principle can be formulated any further. Cf American Law Institute, *Restatement of the Law Third: Restitution and Unjust Enrichment* (2012) § 49. It is, for example, by no means universally the case that the price a defendant would have had to pay a claimant will equal the price that might have been paid by others. Different market participants may have different degrees of market power, including that approaching monopolistic, monopsonistic, or oligopolistic power. See below pp 67–70.

[59] See further *Benedetti (UKSC)* (n 26) [115] (Lord Reed).

[60] ibid [118] (Lord Reed). Lodder, *Enrichment in the Law of Unjust Enrichment and Restitution* (n 4) 224. See further *Sempra Metals* (n 28) [119] (Lord Nicholls).

[61] *Benedetti (UKSC)* (n 26).

[62] ibid [26] (Lord Clarke; Lord Kerr and Lord Wilson agreeing), [117], [119] (Lord Reed), [192] (Lord Neuberger).

[63] ibid [117] (Lord Reed). See also at [26] (Lord Clarke; Lord Kerr and Lord Wilson agreeing).

to satisfaction of proof and counter-arguments to the effect that the benefit was incontrovertible, requested, or freely accepted),[64] while Lord Reed suggested that such arguments may more relevantly find expression in deciding whether the enrichment was 'unjust' or subject to a change of position defence.[65] Lord Neuberger added that the exact locus of concern for freedom of choice is unlikely to influence the outcome of cases, though it may have procedural consequences.[66] Whichever way the problem of so-called 'subjective devaluation' is handled, however, it is clear that the defendant's autonomy and freedom of choice with respect to benefits received are central to any analysis. In other words, it is their exchange capacity that matters.

### (ii) Subjective Revaluation

A similar (though, as we shall see, not identical) question to whether a defendant should be able to assert that an enrichment is worth less than its market value to him is whether he should ever be held to a value that is *greater* than the market value. This book takes the view that this question is ultimately an inaccurate one: it is not a matter of valuing an enrichment 'higher' than the market, but of accurately defining the market—with valuation as high (or low) as individuated market conditions make appropriate.

In *Benedetti v Sawiris*[67] the claimant (Benedetti) sought *quantum meruit* for services rendered to the defendant (Sawiris) in promoting and facilitating a large takeover deal. The market value of the claimant's services was €36.3 million,[68] but Patten J awarded the claimant the considerably larger sum of €75.1 million, having particular regard to the fact that this was the amount for which the defendant had offered to settle the claim. This constituted evidence of the value that Sawiris attributed to Benedetti's services.[69] The judge held that regard could be had to post-transaction evidence of the parties' dealings if and so far as that evidence showed (albeit with the benefit of hindsight) the value that Sawiris attributed to the services.[70] This was relevant insofar as it evidenced what was reasonable remuneration for the services Benedetti had provided.[71] The Court of Appeal overturned the decision,[72] and a further appeal to the Supreme Court was dismissed.[73] Though regard could be had to post-transaction evidence, on the facts of the case

[64] ibid [18]–[25] (Lord Clarke; Lord Kerr and Lord Wilson agreeing).

[65] ibid [117]–[119], [138] (Lord Reed).

[66] ibid [189] (Lord Neuberger). His Lordship likely had in mind issues relating to the onus of establishing claims and defences, as well as to burdens of proof. See also [26] (Lord Clarke) and [138] (Lord Reed).

[67] *Benedetti v Sawiris* [2009] EWHC 1330 (Ch).

[68] ibid [566] (Patten J).

[69] ibid [566]–[575].

[70] ibid [568].

[71] ibid [528].

[72] *Benedetti (CA)* (n 58).

[73] *Benedetti (UKSC)* (n 26).

the settlement offer was not good evidence of how Sawiris valued Benedetti's services.[74]

Both the decisions of the Supreme Court and of the Court of Appeal in *Benedetti v Sawiris* confirm the outlook of this book that enrichment is the manifestation of a defendant's exchange capacity, and that the enrichment inquiry follows the logic and operation of markets. The correct question is not whether, as a matter of legal principle, 'subjective devaluation' or 'subjective revaluation' is or is not permissible. Rather, as Etherton LJ explained in the Court of Appeal, the outcome of each case must depend upon how individuated the particular market for the benefit in question was with respect to the defendant:[75]

> What is relevant is the existence of conditions increasing or decreasing the objective value of the benefit to any reasonable person in the same (unusual) position as the defendant.

That such conditions may 'increase' as well as 'decrease' the objective value of an enrichment may appear to suggest that holding a defendant to a value that is *greater* than the market value is a necessary corollary of permitting him to argue that he should have to pay *less* than market value in certain circumstances. That, however, is a mistake based upon confused terminology and a misunderstanding as to the roles of factual analysis and legal principle in this context. As Lord Neuberger rightly observed in *Benedetti v Sawiris*:[76]

> There is a seductive simplicity in the contention that, if a defendant can take advantage of subjective devaluation, then a claimant should be able to take advantage of a subjective revaluation.

It has already been observed that the Supreme Court in *Benedetti* expressed dissatisfaction with the expression 'subjective devaluation' because that term failed to convey the substance of the inquiry as one going to the defendant's freedom of choice.[77] The reason, then, why subjective revaluation is *not* a necessary corollary to permitting a defendant to pay *less* than market value is that the rationales of the two courses are very different. A defendant can argue that he should pay less than market value for a benefit because that preserves the freedom of choice that is basal to his exchange capacity. 'Subjective revaluation', meanwhile, has nothing to do with departing from market value in the interests of free choice: a defendant's free choice is not protected by making him pay more than he would otherwise have.[78] In fact, 'subjective revaluation' has nothing to do with departing from

[74] *Benedetti (CA)* (n 58) [81]–[89] (Arden LJ), [155]–[158] (Etherton LJ); *Benedetti (UKSC)* (n 26) [65]–[67] (Lord Clarke; Lord Kerr and Lord Wilson agreeing), [140]–[149] (Lord Reed), [174], [200] (Lord Neuberger).

[75] *Benedetti (CA)* (n 58) [145] (Etherton LJ).

[76] *Benedetti (UKSC)* (n 26), [194] (Lord Neuberger).

[77] See above pp 65–66.

[78] See C Mitchell, 'Enrichment, Markets, and Spending Decisisions' [2013] *Lloyd's Maritime and Commercial Law Quarterly* 436, 442: '[F]reedom would not be protected by making a defendant pay more than he would have needed to pay to acquire a benefit. Even if he would have been willing to pay more if this had been necessary, he would not have chosen to pay more if this had been unnecessary.'

market value at all: it is an example of determining what the relevant market value actually is. As Lord Reed lucidly explained, 'market value depends critically on the identification of the relevant market',[79] and market operation is necessarily influenced by market participants:[80]

> *Prima facie*, the monetary value of the services can be fairly ascertained by determining what a reasonable person in the position of the defendant would have agreed to pay for them. That will depend on how much it would have cost a reasonable person in the position of the defendant to acquire the services elsewhere in the market (assuming that a relevant market exists, as will normally be the case) … In order to arrive at an award which is just to both parties, it is necessary to take account of circumstances which would affect the value placed upon the services by a reasonable person receiving them. Those are also circumstances which would affect the cost to a reasonable person in that position of acquiring the same services in the market, and the amount which the claimant could have received if he had sold his services to another recipient in the same position. Such circumstances will include in particular the availability and cost of similar services provided by alternative suppliers and prevailing rates and practices in the relevant market. They will include any relevant characteristics of the defendant, such as, in the context of borrowing, its credit rating, or whether it belongs to the public or the private sector. They will include other personal characteristics, such as the defendant's age, gender, occupation or state of health, if they bear on the price at which such a person could obtain the services in question in the market.

Lord Reed's point (echoing that of Etherton LJ in the Court of Appeal) is that valuation is an objective exercise insofar as it follows the logic of the market, but that subjective circumstances are relevant in defining the ambit, scope, and operation of that market.[81] In practice, the exercise of determining the market price relevant to a defendant in a given case may suggest that the Court is engaging in some process of 'devaluation' or 'revaluation' from some fixed or 'ordinary market value'. That is why Etherton LJ referred to 'conditions increasing or decreasing the objective value' of an enrichment, and why Lord Reed indicated that the description of the valuation exercise may vary depending on whether one is a trained economist.[82] That appearance, however, should not obscure the economic substance of the exercise: the concern is to determine the market value of an enrichment to the

[79] *Benedetti (UKSC)* (n 26) [106] (Lord Reed).
[80] ibid [101] (Lord Reed).
[81] See also ibid [15]–[17] (Lord Clarke; Lord Kerr and Lord Wilson agreeing).
[82] ibid (n 26) [108] (Lord Reed): 'There may be room for argument in particular circumstances as to whether the variation in the value of a benefit according to the position of the recipient is more aptly described as an aspect of market value or as a departure from it. The fact that the cost of an annuity may depend on the age, gender, state of health and personal habits of the annuitant would probably be regarded by most people as an aspect of market value: the annuity market differentiates between relatively young female non-smokers in good health and older male smokers in poor health. An economist might take the same view of the more favourable terms on which a film star may be able to buy a designer dress; but most people would probably say that the film star obtained the dress for less than its market value. I shall refer to "ordinary market value" to describe the amount which would be agreed in the market in the absence of some unusual characteristic of the particular purchaser.'

defendant. The only occasion upon which a court can depart from that market value is when a defendant is ordered to pay less than market value to preserve the freedom of choice that is basal to his exchange capacity. On all other occasions—be they cases of apparent 'devaluation' or 'revaluation'—the court is not departing from market value at all, but is merely determining what that market value is.

A simple example exposes this complex (and factually nuanced) reality. Suppose that C mistakenly delivers heating oil to D (rather than to D's neighbour, X) just before Christmas.[83] Suppose further that X was merely topping up his supply, while D was running at a critical shortage and, as a result, would have happily paid double the market rate. The question, 'What is the measure of restitution for the value of the oil?' cannot be answered without the input of further facts about the particular market for oil and the particular circumstances of C, D, and X in that market. If, on the one hand, C were a large retailer operating in a competitive market, and D and X were ordinary retail customers, then D's willingness to pay double would be irrelevant. Retail operators do not ordinarily alter their prices to reflect the demands of individual customers: a McDonald's cheeseburger, for example, costs the same no matter how hungry the particular customer buying it.[84]

If, on the other hand, the market was one in which there was a high degree of individuation in the price of oil, the situation would be different. If, for example, C was able (in the course of its ordinary business operations) to adjust its prices on a customer-by-customer basis to take advantage of the unique demands of each customer, then subjective revaluation would appear to follow. If, however, it were the case that D possessed such a degree of market power that it could ordinarily negotiate more favourable purchase terms for the supply of oil from C or an alternative supplier, then subjective devaluation would appear to follow. In either case, however, the appearance of an adjustment to market price is an illusion: the point is that the value of the benefit to D *is* the market price for D. Expressions such as 'subjective revaluation' and 'subjective devaluation' mask such factually nuanced inquiries with the aurora of legal principle. The issue in these cases is not whether 'subjective revaluation' or 'subjective devaluation' is possible, but what the value of the particular enrichment is to the particular defendant within the context of the particular market.

These conclusions are confirmed by both *Sempra Metals* and *Benedetti*. Speaking in the latter case, Lord Reed observed of the former that the Revenue, as a public body, could purchase the use of money at a lower price than commercial

[83] Burrows, *A Restatement of the English Law of Unjust Enrichment* (n 38) 158. See further *Benedetti (UKSC)* (n 26) [32] (Lord Clarke; Lord Kerr and Lord Wilson agreeing).

[84] See further *Benedetti (UKSC)* (n 26) [197] (Lord Neuberger): 'In many cases where the benefit has a special, higher, value to the defendant, it will by no means be clear that, if the parties had agreed a contractual quantification of the claimant's remuneration, that factor would have been taken into account. That is particularly true given that one is considering cases where the reason the benefits would have a special value to the defendant would not be known to the market or would not be reflected in the market value.'

enterprises, and so the benefit was valued on the basis of the public sector borrowing rate.[85] The relevant market (the identification of which was critical to the determination of market value)[86] was that of public sector borrowing, in which the low risk of default on repayment by governments produces a lower rate of interest as compared to 'ordinary' borrowers.[87] Similarly, Lord Clarke admitted that his initial perception of *Sempra Metals* as a case involving 'subjective devaluation in practice' required reassessment, and that the case may in fact have been an example of 'the objective value of the money to a person in the position of the defendant, namely the Government'.[88]

As to *Benedetti* itself: that case was one in which the relevant controversy centred upon just how the market for Benedetti's services was defined. On the one hand, if his services were unique and his business relationship with Sawiris a highly individuated one, then the market would consist of Benedetti and Sawiris only, so that the objective value of the services in question was determined by the parties' dealings. On the other hand, if Benedetti's services were generic and his relationship with Sawiris a commercially ordinary one, then the market would consist of a many more participants than just the parties to the litigation: the objective value of those services measured accordingly and without the parties' dealings attracting weight. That was the view of the Court of Appeal,[89] and of the Supreme Court.[90]

## (2) Legal Enrichment and the Exchange Capacity

Thus far we have only considered the relevance of the exchange capacity to 'factual enrichments': that is, unjust enrichment claims in which the enrichment consists

[85] ibid (n 26) [107] (Lord Reed).

[86] ibid [106] (Lord Reed) referring to *Sempra Metals* (n 28), [46] (Lord Hope), [103] (Lord Nicholls).

[87] ibid. His Lordship (at [107]) observed further that, if the facts had been such that the recipient of the money presented a higher risk of default, then the relevant market rate would be higher: 'It would still however be an objective value, which had nothing to do with the defendant's personal perception of the value of the money. Indeed, it would be a market value: the defendant in such a case would borrow in a different market from ordinary commercial borrowers, just as public sector borrowers constitute a distinct market.'

[88] *Benedetti (UKSC)* (n 26) [22] (Lord Clarke).

[89] *Benedetti (CA)* (n 58) [77]–[85] (Arden LJ), [146]–[147] (Etherton LJ).

[90] *Benedetti (UKSC)* (n 26) [56] (Lord Clarke; Lord Kerr and Lord Wilson agreeing), [145]–[146] (Lord Reed), [179], [195]–[200] (Lord Neuberger). Another possibility (suggested by Arden LJ in the Court of Appeal at [85]) was that, though the market may have been confined to Benedetti and Sawiris, their dealings and relationship had yet to reach a stage of sufficient certainty to ascribe to Benedetti's services a value within that individuated market; and that being so, defining the market in wider terms would provide the best means of valuing those services. This, in turn, raises the possibility of a further problem: what if a court cannot define the market beyond the incomplete dealings of the parties? On the one hand, it may conclude that it is impossible to value the enrichment, as there is no evidence from which the court could set a price. On the other hand, the very existence of party-dealings (incomplete or not) may indicate that the parties valued the enrichment, albeit in a quantity that is unknown. In such a case, the court may be left with no choice other than to impute a value based upon the incomplete dealings. See generally the discussion of court-based imputation in *Jones v Kernott* [2011] UKSC 53, [2012] 1 AC 776.

of value. That is a relatively straightforward exercise because value is derived from systems of exchange, which presuppose the existence of the exchange capacity. If, however, the exchange capacity is pitched as underlying all of unjust enrichment, then it must also be capable of explaining those situations where the enrichment consists of the acquisition of a right, or the discharge of an obligation, irrespective of value. The relationship between what Lodder has termed 'legal enrichments' and the exchange capacity is not immediately apparent. Nevertheless, Chambers has explained why they must be understood in their own terms:[91]

> It is true that most cases of unjust enrichment involve a transfer of value from claimant to defendant, but ... that is not always true and *in many cases the value of the enrichment is irrelevant*. If unjust enrichment requires a transfer of value, then it is a smaller area of law than many of us suppose. And if enrichment always is value, then specific restitution becomes difficult to justify since it restricts the manner in which the defendant must make restitution of that value.

In other words, the relationship between legal enrichment and the exchange capacity must be understood if the possibility of specific restitution following unjust enrichment (in exceptional circumstances) is left open, as this book has suggested it may be.[92] According to Chambers, the potential scope of specific restitution for unjust enrichment includes certain claims for resulting trusts, rescission, and rectification.[93] Lodder has extended this analysis to include certain cases of subrogation, and equitable liens as examples of specific restitution following the release of obligations.[94]

The key to understanding the relationship between legal enrichment and the exchange capacity lies in appreciating that value is a necessary feature of all rights and obligations that form the subject matter of unjust enrichment. This is not because unjust enrichment responds only to value. Rather, it is because value is the hallmark of the exchange capacity that engages unjust enrichment. Chambers' assertion that 'in many cases the value of the enrichment is irrelevant' thus requires important clarification. Though specific restitution cases are not concerned with the restoration of value to a claimant, and are therefore equally unconcerned with the quantification of value, this does not mean the law is unconcerned by whether a given enrichment has value in the first place. To say that an enrichment has value is to say no more than that it is susceptible to comparison and exchange.

### *(a) Legal Enrichment by Acquisition of a Right*

In the context of legal enrichment by acquisition of right, the proposition that the right is capable of being the subject of a system of comparison and

[91] Chambers, 'Two Kinds of Enrichment' (n 2) 261 (emphasis added).
[92] See above pp 46–50.
[93] Chambers, 'Two Kinds of Enrichment' (n 2) 252. See also Bant, 'Rights and Value in Rescission: Some Implications for Unjust Enrichment' (n 3).
[94] See generally Lodder, *Enrichment in the Law of Unjust Enrichment and Restitution* (n 4) Ch 5.

exchange means that the particular right must be assignable. As Chambers acknowledges:[95]

> [T]he law of unjust enrichment does not include all rights, but only assignable rights. A right which cannot be sold or given to another could not be an unjust enrichment because it could not be transferred to the defendant and back to the claimant again. Rights to the custody of children [for example] are not assignable. They may be surrendered or taken away, but not donated or sold. They remain outside the law of unjust enrichment when enrichment is defined to include both monetary value and assignable rights.

The specific example of children was considered above in chapter one.[96] There it was explained that unjust enrichment does not include the custody of children because there is no market for children: no system of exchange means no unjust enrichment. That children cannot be expressed in economic or pecuniary terms is indicative of this state of affairs. Insofar as rights to custody of children are concerned, the same point holds: they cannot be sold, given to another, or otherwise transferred in the sense required to engage unjust enrichment. To form the subject matter of a claim, a given right must be susceptible to exchange, and this requires its assignability.

Two important distinctions arise here. The first is between the assignability and exchangeability of rights on the one hand, and the actual exchange of rights on the other. Rights cannot be exchanged unless they are assignable, but it does not follow that the only way a right can be assigned is through an exchange transaction. An assignable right can be the subject of a gift, in which case nothing is actually exchanged for that right. This does not mean, however, that the exchange capacity has nothing to do with gifts: a gift is merely the free exercise of the exchange capacity insofar as the donor chooses *not* to seek anything in return for the subject of the gift, which he would otherwise be entitled to do.

The second important distinction is between the existence of value, the exchange capacity and assignability of rights on the one hand, and the need for quantification of value on the other. Insofar as unjust enrichment is concerned with legal enrichments in the form of rights, only the latter is irrelevant in the sense suggested by Chambers. The point, and its significance, can be illustrated by considering assignable rights that are worthless. A child's preschool artwork, for example, may have strong sentimental value to that child's parents (which may influence the parents' idiosyncratic value of the painting), but no one else is likely to pay a single penny for a property right in the painting. In such a case the point is not that this right has no value, but rather that its value is zero. This is a subtle but important distinction. Unlike the right to custody or possession of the child itself, there is nothing inhibiting a system of exchange in respect of the artwork: the child has *no market value* because there is no market for children, while the artwork has a *market value*

[95] Chambers, 'Two Kinds of Enrichment' (n 2) 262. See also at 255.
[96] See above pp 32–33, 41.

*of nothing* because there is a market for artwork in which the value placed on the work of children is negligible (most likely due to the lack of demand). The value of the enrichment is 'irrelevant' in the latter case only in the sense that no claim can lie for restitution of a value of nothing. But a value of nothing is a value nonetheless, and the existence of value—whatever its quantum—is indicative of a system of exchange engaging unjust enrichment. So if, in some far-fetched example, a father were forced under duress to transfer title to his child's artwork under contract to some stranger, the worthlessness of the artwork would not inhibit restitution of those proprietary rights if there were an effective rescission of the contract.[97]

What is true of assets with a value of zero applies equally to assets with a value greater than zero. In *Car & Universal Finance Co Ltd v Caldwell*,[98] for example, Caldwell sold his Jaguar car to a rogue, accepting a cheque in part payment, which was dishonoured. Caldwell therefore asked both the police and the Automobile Association to locate the car. The rogue sold the car to a motor dealer, who then sold it to Car & Universal Finance. The sale to Car & Universal Finance was held to have been ineffective, as title had already been revested in Caldwell. Caldwell thus obtained specific restitution of the right to the car following rescission of the contract of sale with the rogue. As Lodder explains, the quantified value of the right to the car was irrelevant to this result:[99]

> While the right to the car … was undoubtedly a valuable right, there is no reason this must be so. There is no suggestion in the judgments that the outcome turned on the value of the Jaguar or that Caldwell could not have obtained title to the Jaguar by rescission of the contract of sale if the Jaguar had been in an accident and were worth less than the cost of making it roadworthy.

What matters for the purposes of this book is that, although the quantified value of the right to the car was irrelevant, the fact that it had a value was not. That value, whatever the amount, indicated that the right was susceptible to exchange, thus engaging unjust enrichment.

### *(b) Legal Enrichment by Release of an Obligation*

The analysis of the relationship between legal enrichment and the exchange capacity is not confined to the acquisition of rights. As Lodder has explained, legal enrichment can also include the release of obligations:[100]

> The discharge or release of an obligation often involves a transfer of value that may found a factual enrichment claim. However, the award of security interests and rights of

[97] See generally Mitchell, Mitchell, and Watterson, *Goff & Jones* (n 17) paras 40.05–40.24. Indeed, the unique nature of a child's artwork (including its idiosyncratic value to the child and parent) may well be an additional consideration of the kind justifying the award of specific restitution following unjust enrichment in circumstances where a monetary award would not suffice. See above pp 46–48.

[98] *Car & Universal Finance Co Ltd v Caldwell* [1965] 1 QB 525 (CA).

[99] Lodder, *Enrichment in the Law of Unjust Enrichment and Restitution* (n 4) 42.

[100] ibid 141.

> subrogation in unjust enrichment shows that specific restitution is sometimes awarded to reinstate the obligation … Whereas specific restitution of rights involves reversing the acquisition of the right, specific restitution in enrichment by release cases involves reinstating the obligation.

He then argues that the justification and theoretical basis for such reinstatement is restitutionary where it reverses the release of an obligation of the defendant at the claimant's expense by granting the claimant a power formerly held by the defendant (or a third party).[101]

The difficult issue that arises here is not the relationship between the exchange capacity and the value of the obligation discharged. It is relatively uncontroversial that the discharge of a debt can be understood in factual enrichment terms and so subjected to exchange capacity analysis. *Exall v Partridge*,[102] for example, was a straightforward case in which the claimant recovered from the defendants the value of rent paid to the defendants' landlord in order to recover the claimant's carriage, which had been left on the defendants' premises for repair and subsequently seized by the landlord for rent. The discharge of a person's liability engages his exchange capacity because that discharge is a valuable service.[103] Such cases are therefore amenable to the same exchange analysis as services cases.[104]

Lodder suggests, however, that a different analysis is necessary where the discharge or release is conceptualised as a legal enrichment in its own terms. He relies on *Butler v Rice* as an example of this kind of case.[105] Mr Rice asked Butler to lend him £450 to pay off a bank mortgage over a property in his wife's name, but did not inform Butler that the property was not in his name. Butler advanced the loan on a £300 mortgage over the property and a guarantee for the remainder. The bank's mortgage was discharged, but Mrs Rice refused to execute the mortgage in favour of Butler. The judge held that Butler was entitled to be subrogated to the bank's mortgage over the property to secure his right to repayment of the £450 he had advanced. Lodder explains that Mrs Rice was enriched in two ways: payment of the £450 debt (a factual enrichment) *and* discharge of the mortgage (a legal enrichment). His analysis of the outcome with regards to the latter enrichment is as follows:[106]

> To reverse this legal enrichment, Butler was entitled to be subrogated to the bank's charge against Mrs Rice's land, which reinstated the liability and provided Butler with a conditional power to obtain the land if his claim for monetary restitution was not satisfied. The restitutionary character of the subrogation is revealed by the

[101] In all other cases, Lodder argues, the award grant of that power is for prophylactic, and not restitutionary, purposes: ibid 246–47.

[102] *Exall v Partridge* (1799) 8 Term Rep 308 (KB).

[103] Lodder, *Enrichment in the Law of Unjust Enrichment and Restitution* (n 4) 102.

[104] See above pp 57–62.

[105] *Butler v Rice* [1910] 2 Ch 277 (Ch). See Lodder, *Enrichment in the Law of Unjust Enrichment and Restitution* (n 4) 143–44.

[106] Lodder, *Enrichment in the Law of Unjust Enrichment and Restitution* (n 4) 143.

> reinstatement of Mrs Rice's liability under the bank's charge, rather than the £300 mortgage and guarantee that had been agreed by Butler and Mr Rice. Butler's payment had enriched Mrs Rice by the removal of a conditional liability upon the land and subrogating Butler to the mortgage reversed that enrichment.

This book disagrees with Lodder's view as to the distinct nature of discharge or release as legal enrichment, and with his analysis of *Butler v Rice* and similar cases. His approach appears to suggest that specific restitution in the form of subrogation should follow immediately upon a finding of enrichment by discharge from or release of an obligation. But, as this book has already explained, specific restitution (be it in the form of a trust, rescission, lien, or subrogation) should only follow as a response to unjust enrichment (if at all) in exceptional circumstances that complement a finding that would otherwise justify the award of personal restitution only.[107] That being so, one cannot get to a remedy of subrogation without first determining the availability of personal restitution for the value of obligation discharged or released. In other words, it is incorrect to attempt to conceptualise the legal enrichment in its own terms. Instead, one must first consider the value of the legal enrichment. And where that consists of an obligation discharged or release, that value cannot be separated from the correlating right that has been extinguished.

The point is borne out in the analysis of subrogation to extinguished proprietary rights as an instance of unjust enrichment.[108] For subrogation to occur to an extinguished proprietary right, it is essential that a right susceptible to proprietary analysis have existed in the first place, and so we would naturally expect (for the reasons explained in chapter one) that things like children and human tissue would be beyond the purview of subrogation claims and of legal enrichment by release of obligation generally. It is particularly noteworthy that, in considering the limits upon the range of rights that qualify for subrogation, Mitchell and Watterson have observed:[109]

> [W]hatever the extinguished right's origins, an important *prima facie* indicator of whether an equivalent right can be acquired by subrogation is whether it is viewed as non-assignable on grounds of public policy. If the right is assignable, then prima facie an equivalent right can also be acquired by subrogation. Conversely, if the right is considered non-assignable for reasons of public policy, then it should be presumed that an equivalent right cannot be acquired by subrogation.

When we say that a discharged obligation is susceptible to analysis in unjust enrichment, we are really saying nothing more than that the correlating right can be explained in this way, and the litmus test for that conclusion, as we have seen, is the assignability of that right. Legal enrichment by release of an obligation

[107] See above pp 46–50.

[108] *Banque Financiere de la Cite SA v Parc (Battersea) Ltd* [1999] 1 AC 221 (HL) 236 (Lord Hoffmann). See generally C Mitchell and S Watterson, *Subrogation: Law and Practice* (Oxford, Oxford University Press, 2007) para 1.06; Mitchell, Mitchell, and Watterson, *Goff & Jones* (n 17) paras 39.05–39.11.

[109] Mitchell and Watterson, *Subrogation: Law and Practice* (n 108) para 9.45.

therefore fits the underlying exchange capacity analysis propounded by this book because the obligation so released must correlate to an extinguished right that was assignable. Assignability begets value, the exchange capacity, and unjust enrichment. That being so, *Butler v Rice* is best understood as a case in which the value of Mrs Rice's discharged mortgage lay in her improved position following the extinction of the bank's mortgage over her house (a right susceptible to exchange analysis). Just as in *BFC v Parc (Battersea)*,[110] her improved position had an economic significance that was not readily reducible to monetary terms, and so subrogation to the extinguished mortgage was appropriate.

[110] See above p 50.

# 3

# Loss

To understand the meaning and role of loss in unjust enrichment we must distinguish two separate (albeit related) questions. The first is whether a claimant must suffer a loss to establish a claim. The second is whether, if loss is required, restitution is capped by it. This chapter argues that the answer to the first question is 'yes', insofar as the claimant must suffer an *initial* (and not necessarily *persisting*) loss, while the answer to the second question is 'no', insofar as the concept of loss capping obscures the true nature of the relationship between enrichment and loss in unjust enrichment. These arguments align with the statement of Robert Goff J in *BP Exploration Co (Libya) Ltd v Hunt (No 2)* that:[1]

> The plaintiff's expense is a prerequisite of his claim; but it does not limit or control the award of restitution. In assessing an award of restitution, it is the defendant's benefit which has to be identified, in order that restitution may be ordered in respect of that benefit.

The requirement of loss fits the logic and framework of the exchange capacity that underlies unjust enrichment. Just as enrichment reflects the exchange capacity of the defendant, loss reflects that of the claimant.

## (A) Must the Claimant Suffer a Loss?

The statement that loss is a prerequisite to unjust enrichment means nothing unless we first know what loss means in this context. A review of the authorities reveals two points: first, only initial losses matter; and, secondly, loss has a broad meaning that includes pecuniary detriments, the loss of opportunity, and the deprivation of a right. Both points conform to the significance of the claimant's exchange capacity.

[1] *BP Exploration Co (Libya) Ltd v Hunt (No 2)* [1979] 1 WLR 783 (QB) 839–40. See also *Commissioner of State Revenue (Vic) v Royal Insurance Australia Ltd* [1994] HCA 61, 182 CLR 51, 73–74 (Mason CJ).

## (1) Initial, not Persisting, Loss

In *Re BHT (UK) Ltd*[2] the administrative receiver of BHT paid money to NatWest Finance Ltd (NFL) that should have gone to BHT's preferential creditors. A subsequent unjust enrichment claim by the company's liquidator against NFL failed. Kevin Garnett QC (sitting as a deputy High Court judge) held that NFL had not been enriched at BHT's expense because BHT would never have been entitled to the money.[3] The judge explained that 'since anything recovered from NFL would ... go straight to the preferential creditors', BHT had suffered no loss and its balance sheet position was unaffected by what had happened.[4] His Lordship thus insisted on a requirement of loss for the liquidator's claim to succeed.

There is consensus that *Re BHT* was wrongly decided.[5] Notably, it contradicts the Court of Appeal's decision in *Kleinwort Benson Ltd v Birmingham City Council*.[6] That was a swaps case in which the defendant council sought to rely on 'passing on' as a defence to an unjust enrichment claim by the claimant bank, which had allegedly hedged itself against any losses suffered. The court rejected the council's arguments. Saville LJ stated that the expression 'at the expense of the claimant' did not import 'concepts of loss or damage with their attendant concepts of mitigation'.[7] His Lordship was not concerned with whether loss capped the award of restitution, but with whether its very existence was necessary for unjust enrichment to arise in the first place. Morritt and Evans LJJ expressed similar views.[8] All three of their Lordships agreed with Hobhouse J's analysis in the earlier case of *Kleinwort Benson Ltd v South Tyneside MBC*.[9] In that case the judge had rejected loss requirements akin to those arising 'as if one were investigating a right to compensation'.[10] This conformed to Lord Wright's separation of the principles of restitution for unjust enrichment from those of compensation for loss in contract and tort in *Fibrosa Spolka Akcyjna v Fairbairn Lawson Combe Barbour Ltd*.[11] In *Re BHT*, Kevin Garnett QC incorrectly dismissed that distinction as immaterial.[12]

*Re BHT* may be contrasted with *Niru Battery Manufacturing Co v Milestone Trading Ltd (No 1)*.[13] In that case a bank and its customer (Niru) were entitled to maintain claims for restitution of money paid to the defendants under a letter of

[2] *Re BHT (UK) Ltd* [2004] EWHC 201 (Ch), [2004] BCC 301.

[3] ibid [24].

[4] ibid [25].

[5] See, eg, G Jones, *Goff & Jones: The Law of Restitution*, 7th edn (London, Sweet & Maxwell Ltd 2006) [1-044] fn 19; P Birks, *Unjust Enrichment*, 2nd edn (Oxford, Oxford University Press 2005) 80 fn 24; M Rush, *The Defence of Passing On* (Oxford, Hart, 2006) 118.

[6] *Kleinwort Benson Ltd v Birmingham City Council* [1997] QB 380 (CA) 400 (Morritt LJ).

[7] ibid 395 (Saville LJ). See also 393 (Evans LJ), 400–01 (Saville LJ).

[8] ibid 393–94 (Evans LJ), 400 (Morritt LJ).

[9] *Kleinwort Benson Ltd v South Tyneside MBC* [1994] 4 All ER 972 (QB), 984–87.

[10] ibid 984–85.

[11] *Fibrosa Spolka Akcyjna v Fairbairn Lawson Combe Barbour Ltd* [1943] AC 32 (HL).

[12] *Re BHT (UK) Ltd* (n 2) 26.

[13] *Niru Battery Manufacturing Co v Milestone Trading Ltd (No 1)* [2002] EWHC 1425 (Comm), [2002] 2 All ER (Comm) 705.

credit supported by a false bill of lading. This was so despite the fact that, because the bank had reimbursed itself by debiting Niru's account, it would be obliged to account for any sums recovered. The claim was maintainable by the bank despite the fact that 'the only claimant to have suffered a loss [was] Niru'.[14] The relationship between the bank and Niru was analagous to that between the liquidators and preferential creditors in *Re BHT*, but the fact and locus of loss had no bearing on the claims available.

It is tempting to conclude, based on these authorities, that loss is not a necessary feature of unjust enrichment. That, however, would be an overstatement, for the cases only go so far as disclaiming a requirement of *persisting* loss, and do not dismiss the need for some form of *initial* loss. In *Kleinwort Benson Ltd v Birmingham City Council*, for example, whether the claimant bank had suffered a loss was not contentious; nor could it have been, for the bank had paid £353,322 to the defendant council under the void swap.[15] The issue was whether the claim should be defeated because the bank had ultimately mitigated that loss. The court's focus was thus limited to the question of whether the bank's loss needed to persist to sustain its claim. In rejecting the defence of passing on, the court held that it did not. That the court was concerned with persisting rather than initial loss is evident, for example, from Saville LJ's reference to 'concepts of loss or damage *with their attendant concepts of mitigation*'.[16]

Similarly, in *Re BHT*, that BHT had sustained a loss was incontestable because its administrative receiver had paid money to NFL. Kevin Garnett QC held, in effect, that this was not enough to sustain a claim. The money would ultimately go to preferential creditors if repaid, and so BHT could not show it had suffered a persisting loss. The rejection of the passing on defence to unjust enrichment claims in England and other jurisdictions[17] indicates that the persisting quality of a claimant's loss is irrelevant, and that *Re BHT* was therefore wrongly decided.

The issue in these cases has thus been limited to the relevance of the persisting quality of loss: they have not entirely rejected loss as a feature of unjust enrichment. Indeed, as we shall see in chapter four, there are a series of cases involving 'interceptive subtraction' that actively require the claimant to establish loss, his case against a defendant being contingent on his having exhausted a claim (or being unable to claim in the first place) against a third party.[18] A loss requirement also seems to follow from repeated insistence that unjust enrichment is concerned

[14] ibid [145] (Moore-Bick J).

[15] This fact no doubt leads Burrows to observe that the decision is 'inconclusive as to whether one needs an *initial* corresponding loss': A Burrows, *The Law of Restitution*, 3rd edn (Oxford, Oxford University Press, 2011) 65.

[16] *Kleinwort Benson Ltd v Birmingham City Council* (n 6) 395 (emphasis added).

[17] In Australia, see *Roxborough v Rothmans of Pall Mall Australia Ltd* [2001] HCA 68; *Commissioner of State Revenue (Vic)* (n 1); *Mason v New South Wales* [1959] HCA 5, 102 CLR 108. In Canada, see *Kingstreet Investments Ltd v New Brunswick (Finance)* [2007] SCC 1, [2007] 1 SCR 3. Cf *Air Canada v British Columbia* [1989] 1 SCR 1161 (SCC). See further below p 83.

[18] See below pp 116–119, 137–140.

with 'subtractions' from the claimant.[19] As Birks explained, this denotes that 'the plus to the defendant is a minus to the claimant'.[20] Loss has thus been held to be necessary because enrichment and unjustness fail on their own to identify the claimant.[21] This is what their Lordships had in mind in *Kleinwort Benson Ltd v Birmingham City Council* when they held that the rule requiring the defendant's enrichment to have been at the claimant's expense 'identifies the person by or on whose behalf the payment was made and to whom repayment is due', is 'a convenient way of describing the need for the payer to show that his money was used to pay the payee' and captures 'the requirement that the immediate source of the unjust enrichment must be the claimant'.[22]

## (2) Different Kinds of Loss

Identifying loss seems easy in many cases. If D takes C's car and does not return it, loss appears to be a tangible fact. If C pays money to D, or spends it on labour and materials for D, then the loss is similarly uncontroversial. Other cases are less straightforward. If C performs a service for D, and does not spend money doing so, the loss is not readily apparent; likewise if D does no more than occupy or use C's property without permission. If we are to analyse these and similar cases in unjust enrichment terms requiring loss, then we must appreciate the breadth of the concept necessary to do so.

The decision in *Edwards v Lee's Administrators* illustrates this point.[23] As we have seen, the claimant's estate was awarded one-third of the profits made by the defendant from exhibiting a cave, one-third of which extended under the claimant's land—an award that is susceptible to analysis as one of restitution for unjust enrichment.[24] The issue therefore arises as to whether, and if so how, the claimant suffered a loss. One argument is that he did not because his part of the cave was not damaged. The judge, however, observed that the claim was 'very close' to one involving the protection of trade names and trade secrets where 'there may be no tangible loss other than the violation of a right'.[25] Another view is that when the defendant used one-third of the claimant's cave, the claimant lost the opportunity

[19] See, eg, *Sempra Metals Ltd (formerly Metallgesellschaft Ltd) v Inland Revenue Commissioners* [2007] UKHL 34, [2008] 1 AC 561 [231] (Lord Mance); *Foskett v McKeown* [2001] 1 AC 102 (HL) 126 (Lord Hope); Birks, *Unjust Enrichment* (n 5) 74–74; Burrows, *The Law of Restitution* (n 15) 63.

[20] P Birks, *An Introduction to the Law of Restitution*, revised edn (Oxford, Clarendon Press, 1989) 132.

[21] ibid; *Chase Manhattan NA v Israel-British Bank (London) Ltd* [1981] Ch 105 (Ch) 125 (Goulding J).

[22] *Kleinwort Benson v Birmingham City Council* (n 6) 393 (Evans LJ), 395 (Saville LJ), 400 (Morritt LJ).

[23] *Edwards v Lee's Administrators* 96 SW 2d 1028 (1936).

[24] See above pp 40–41.

[25] *Edwards v Lee's Administrators* (n 23) 1031–32 (Stites J).

to use that part of the cave as he saw fit. Yet another is to say that the claimant lost the practical benefit of *dominium* over the cave.[26]

The point is that the loss in *Edwards v Lee's Administrators* (and similar cases)[27] can be identified in a number of different ways. Dr Rush has examined these according to a three-fold division: loss meaning 'detriments'; loss meaning 'opportunities foregone'; and loss meaning 'deprivation of rights'.[28] He ultimately adopts a definition of loss in unjust enrichment meaning 'pecuniary detriment',[29] encompassing six scenarios:[30] (i) loss of money; (ii) loss of something reducible to money; (iii) reductions in value; (iv) loss of use value; (v) depletion of an asset; and (vi) opportunity cost. This book agrees with Rush's analysis of 'pecuniary detriments' but disagrees with his exclusion of 'opportunities foregone' and 'deprivations of rights' from the overall definition of loss in unjust enrichment. That disagreement stems from the substantial overlap between the concepts of 'detriment', 'deprivation', and 'opportunity foregone'. Moreover, as we shall see in the next section, this wide concept of loss fits the theoretical basis of unjust enrichment as responsive to the claimant's exchange capacity.

Three aspects of Rush's own analysis support the wider concept of loss advocated by this book. First, Rush defines 'opportunity cost' as a pecuniary detriment arising 'where a claimant provides a defendant with a service, for no financial reward, when he could have profitably provided it to another person'.[31] But this definition is too narrow, because opportunity costs also arise when a claimant provides one service to a defendant and he could have provided either *that* service or a *different* service to another person: in such a case, the loss of time incurred by providing the particular service to the defendant is part of the claimant's opportunity cost. Rush considers loss of time, however, to be a 'non-pecuniary detriment' distinct from opportunity cost.[32] This achieves little if loss of time is inherent within opportunity cost.

Secondly, Rush asserts that an 'opportunity foregone' is different from an 'opportunity cost'.[33] The reasons why this is so, however, are unclear. Rush argues, for example, that if a defendant watches a movie in the claimant's cinema without permission and without paying, and thus occupies the last seat, then the claimant suffers a loss in the form of an opportunity cost if he turns away a paying patron.[34] He then argues that this loss, an opportunity foregone, requires a real

[26] M McInnes, '*Hambly v Trott* and the Claimant's Expense: Professor Birks' Challenge' in S Degeling and J Edelman (eds), *Unjust Enrichment in Commercial Law* (Sydney, Thomson Reuters, 2008) 128–29.

[27] See, eg, *Hambly v Trott* (1776) 1 Cowp 371 (KB); *Vincent v Lake Erie Transport Company* 109 Minn 456, 124 NW 221 (1910) (SC Minn). See further below pp 84–85.

[28] Rush, *The Defence of Passing On* (n 5) 93–112.

[29] ibid 109.

[30] ibid 93–94.

[31] ibid 94.

[32] ibid 95.

[33] ibid 105.

[34] ibid 94.

opportunity to charge another customer in place of the defendant.[35] Again, the definition is too narrow: it excludes the defendant from the class of person from whom the claimant could have sought payment.[36] There is no reason why the claimant's 'opportunity foregone' does not include the opportunity to charge an entry fee to the defendant, nor is it clear why this is conceptually distinct from an 'opportunity cost'.

Thirdly, in considering loss meaning 'deprivation of a right', Rush considers examples from the law of tort where 'loss' has been conceived as 'the denial' of a right,[37] and draws from them the proposition that the right is 'lost' in the sense of being 'infringed'.[38] If the content of the right, however, includes the opportunity to control the subject-matter of the right, then deprivation of the right is blurred with opportunity cost and opportunity foregone in respect of it. In *The Mediana*, for example, the Earl of Halsbury LC used the example of a defendant taking away a claimant's chair; the defendant could not reduce damages payable by showing that the claimant did not usually sit in the chair.[39] In that example the opportunity to control the chair is coextensive with the right in respect of it.[40] Depriving the claimant of the latter necessarily deprives him of the former. It follows that if opportunity costs are considered losses in unjust enrichment, then so too are opportunities foregone and rights deprived.

## (3) Loss and the Exchange Capacity

That the claimant in an unjust enrichment claim must suffer a loss reflects the underlying necessity of the exchange capacity to unjust enrichment. Loss is the necessary and relevant effect on the claimant's position which, when appropriately connected to the enrichment of the defendant, supports an unjust enrichment analysis. In a theoretical scheme of unjust enrichment based upon restoring normative equality between claimant and defendant, *something* must happen to the claimant's exchange capacity—and that something is called 'loss'.

There are three reasons why this requirement of loss has tended to be obscured within the analysis of unjust enrichment claims. The first is that, in the great

[35] ibid 106.

[36] See, eg, *Tito v Waddell (No 2)* [1977] Ch 106 (Ch) 335 (Sir Robert Megarry VC): 'If the plaintiff has the right to prevent some act being done without his consent, and the defendant does the act without seeking that consent, the plaintiff has suffered a loss in that the defendant has taken without paying for it something for which the plaintiff could have required payment, namely, the right to do the act.'

[37] Rush, *The Defence of Passing On* (n 5) 102 discussing *Owners of the Steamship Mediana v Owners of the Lightship Comet (The Mediana)* [1900] AC 113 (HL) and *Watson Laidlaw & Co Ltd v Pott Cassels & Williamson (A Firm)* (1914) SC (HL) 18 (HL).

[38] Rush, *The Defence of Passing On* (n 5) 104.

[39] *The Mediana* (n 37) 117–18.

[40] McInnes, '*Hambly v Trott* and the Claimant's Expense: Professor Birks' Challenge' (n 26) 118–19 citing J Penner, *The Idea of Property in Law* (Oxford, Oxford University Press, 2000) 71; J Waldron, *The Right to Private Property* (Oxford, Oxford University Press, 1986) 47; T Honoré, 'Ownership' in AG Guest (ed), *Oxford Essays in Jurisprudence* (Oxford, Clarendon Press, 1961) 107.

majority of cases, its existence is so straightforward that it is effectively taken for granted, and therefore under-analysed. In unjust enrichment cases, something has almost always happened to the claimant: he has paid money, lost property, or performed a service. Analysing the position of the claimant is therefore not a priority, and so loss is rarely an active issue on the facts of cases. This ultimately means that it is rarely if ever discussed as a substantive requirement of claims. It does not follow, however, that it is not a substantive requirement of claims.

The second reason why the requirement of loss in unjust enrichment has tended to be obscured is that it has occasionally been elided with the defence of 'passing on' (or 'disimpoverishment'). Rush suggests that there will only be room for the defence if the 'at the expense of the claimant' requirement of claims is interpreted as requiring loss.[41] But it is important to recognise that the opposite does not hold: rejecting the defence does not entail the rejection of any requirement of loss *whatsoever*. Failure to distinguish 'loss' from 'persisting loss' is prone to confuse in this respect. As we have already seen, the leading English case rejecting the defence was limited by virtue of the facts to the relevance of the claimant's persisting losses.[42] Indeed, when that distinction is kept in mind, the rejection of the passing on defence fits the account of unjust enrichment based upon corrective justice and the bilateral equality of the parties' exchange capacities. The reason why the defendant cannot rely upon a mitigation of the claimant's loss (and thereby direct attention to the claimant's persisting loss) is that such mitigation is an incident of the claimant's self-determining agency, which has nothing to do with the defendant. Rejection of the defence is, in this way, a corollary to the acceptance of change of position defence: just as the defendant has the benefit of having his status as a self-determining agent respected following his enrichment,[43] so too must he respect the status of the claimant following the claimant's loss. And just as the emphasis upon the defendant's *status* as a self-determining agent (as opposed to a particular *exercise* of that agency) necessitates applying the change of position defence to detriments regardless of whether they are actively or passively incurred,[44] so too must it necessitate rejecting the passing on defence to mitigation of loss regardless of how that mitigation is achieved. It should make no difference whether the claimant has actively taken steps to mitigate his loss (either before or after it is incurred), or has benefitted from the unsolicited benefaction of a third party. In either case, the point is that the mitigation of the loss from sources external to the bilateral relationship between claimant and defendant is outside the unjust enrichment paradigm, and so no business of the defendant.

[41] Rush, *The Defence of Passing On* (n 5) 89.

[42] *Kleinwort Benson v Birmingham City Council* (n 6). See above pp 78–80. The same point applies *mutatis mutandis* to those cases rejecting the defence in other jurisdictions. See, eg, *Kingstreet Investments* (n 17); *Commissioner of State Revenue (Vic)* (n 1). It is also worthwhile observing that both Birks, *Unjust Enrichment* (n 5) 79, and Burrows, *The Law of Restitution* (n 15) 65, limit the impact of the defence's rejection accordingly.

[43] See above pp 60–62.

[44] ibid.

The third reason why the requirement of loss in unjust enrichment has tended to be obscured is that, where loss does appear to be a contestable issue of fact, its analysis has been limited by attempts to compare and conflate what are superficially distinct species of loss with one another, without reference to their underlying common denominator: the exchange capacity. One example is to be found in treatment of certain dicta of Lord Mansfield in *Hambly v Trott*.[45] The issue in that case was whether a tort victim could 'waive' the tort and bring an *assumpsit* claim against the deceased tortfeasor's executor. In the course of his speech, Lord Mansfield gave the famous example of an *assumpsit* claim for use and hire where one man takes a horse from another, and brings it back again.[46] That example has generated considerable debate. In *Watson Laidlaw & Co Ltd v Pott Cassels & Williamson*, Lord Shaw carried the example further, making the point:[47]

> If A, being a liveryman, keeps his horse standing idle in the stable, and B, against his wish or without his knowledge, rides or drives it out, it is no answer to A for B to say: 'Against what loss do you want to be restored? I restore the horse. There is no loss. The horse is none the worse; it is the better for the exercise.'

According to Birks, this supports the proposition that the English law does not insist upon a claimant suffering a loss in order to bring an unjust enrichment claim.[48] In making this argument, however, he relies upon a narrow definition of loss—one that does not, for example, include the loss of the owner's right to control the horse, or the opportunity lost by the owner of the horse to charge a fee against the person who took it. This might be contrasted with McInnes' argument that the claimant lost the practical benefit of *dominium* in respect of the horse.[49] By *dominium*, McInnes means to convey the core of the common law's conception of property; encompassing the incidents of ownership, including the right to possession, the right to use, and the right to manage.[50] These can be understood in terms of lost opportunity and rights deprived. So, when the horse is taken for a ride but returned, though the horse may be better for the exercise, its owner has suffered a loss in the sense of being deprived of doing with it as he pleased for the period that it was gone.

Underlying these different definitions of loss is a more fundamental issue: is it appropriate to contrast them in the course of a debate over the requirement of loss in unjust enrichment? It is the view of this book that taxonomical debates can only advance our understanding of the law so far before we reach a stalemate, at

[45] *Hambly v Trott* (n 27).
[46] ibid 375.
[47] *Watson Laidlaw* (n 37). See also *Torpey Vander Have Pty Ltd v Mass Constructions Pty Ltd* [2002] NSWCA 263, (2002) 55 IPR 542, discussed in J Edelman and E Bant, *Unjust Enrichment in Australia* (Oxford, Oxford University Press, 2006) 274.
[48] Birks, *Unjust Enrichment* (n 5) 79, 81–82.
[49] McInnes, '*Hambly v Trott* and the Claimant's Expense: Professor Birks' Challenge' (n 26).
[50] ibid 118–19. See further J Edelman, *Gain-Based Damages: Contract, Tort, Equity and Intellectual Property* (Oxford, Hart, 2002) 99–102.

which point pedantry and literalism over the meaning of words takes hold. Birks, for example, insists that the horse owner in Lord Mansfield's example had suffered no loss, but then argues that it stands for the proposition 'from my property, therefore sufficiently from me'.[51] That, however, is a proposition that one who advocates the requirement of loss can equally turn in their favour by equating 'from my property' with an appropriately wide definition of loss. Couching the relevant arguments in terms of a distinction between 'loss' and vague concepts like 'from', or 'from in the weak sense' and 'from in the strong sense' is an equally unhelpful and confusing exercise.[52]

The better approach is to view the different kinds of loss as incidents of the same underlying interest: the claimant's exchange capacity. This mirrors the point made in chapter two about the different kinds of enrichment.[53] When this is done for loss, the differences disappear also. The owner of the horse, for example, suffers a loss because he has been deprived of something that he was free to charge for, as did the cave-owner in *Edwards v Lee's Administrators*.[54] The proposition 'from my property, therefore sufficiently from me' aligns with an exchange capacity conception of loss precisely because the use of property is something that can be exchanged.[55] This also illuminates the analysis of cases in which the identification of loss seems straightforward. If D takes C's car (and does not return it) the loss stems from the fact that the car was something that could be exchanged, and its taking means C no longer has the opportunity to do so. In the simplest case of a payment of money, the loss is not that the payor now has less money but, rather, that money is something we are free to exchange and the loss of the money has deprived the payor of that freedom.

It follows that it is possible to express *all* losses in essentially the same terms: as the lost opportunity to charge or otherwise exercise the exchange capacity. That is the meaning of 'loss' in unjust enrichment according to this book. It aligns with the idea, advanced in chapter two, that all enrichments are expressible in saved expenditure terms,[56] expenditure being 'necessary' insofar as it reflects what ought to have been (but was not in fact) exchanged by the defendant *vis-à-vis* the claimant for what was received. Understood in this way, the identification and valuation of loss performs the important function of confirming that the defendant and claimant exist within the same market, meaning that their exchange capacities are relevantly engaged, and that analysis of their positions according

[51] P Birks, *Unjust Enrichment* (n 5) 79.

[52] See, eg, Burrows, *The Law of Restitution* (n 15) 65; Rush, *The Defence of Passing On* (n 5) 92; Birks, *Unjust Enrichment* (n 5) 74.

[53] See above pp 58–60.

[54] *Edwards v Lee's Administrators* (n 23).

[55] See further C Mitchell, P Mitchell, and S Watterson (eds), *Goff & Jones: The Law of Unjust Enrichment*, 8th edn (London, Sweet & Maxwell, 2011) para 6.71.

[56] See above pp 58–60.

to the law of unjust enrichment is appropriate. Thus, as Lord Reed observed in *Benedetti v Sawiris*, restitution for unjust enrichment requires that:[57]

> [T]he claimant will receive the amount for which he could have sold his services to another recipient in the same position, and the defendant will pay the amount which the services would have cost a reasonable person in his position to acquire from another supplier in the market.

These observations confirm the approach to loss (and enrichment) advanced by this book, subject to two riders: first, they are not limited to services but apply to *all* enrichments; and, secondly, that 'another recipient in the same position' as the defendant necessarily includes the defendant himself (as where the claimant and defendant are the only market participants).[58]

## (4) Loss and Opportunity

The concept of loss advanced by this book is not without detractors. Rush, as we have seen, excludes 'opportunities forgone' from the definition of loss acceptable within the law of unjust enrichment. Whilst acknowledging its attractiveness and potential breadth, he argues that it is nonetheless flawed because it is used 'loosely and inaccurately':[59]

> In order to sustain a 'loss' one must have, possess, or be in a position to realise that which is lost. For example, I may claim that I lost the opportunity to play in the FA Cup final because I was permanently impaired by a debilitating disease when fifteen years old. But if I never possessed any football talent, it is not right to say that playing in the FA Cup was even an opportunity open to me. It was not one I was capable of losing. The same is true of the bicycle example.[60] In theory, because the claimant was the owner of the bicycle, he had the opportunity to sell or hire it. And that opportunity was denied him, for a certain period of time, because the bicycle was in the defendant's possession. But in reality, an opportunity to sell the bicycle was never actually lost or forgone because it was impossible for the claimant to exercise either one of them. The claim that a loss was incurred in this circumstance is fictional. … When a claimant loses an opportunity, one must ascertain whether the opportunity is one that was ever realizable or exercisable. To forgo an opportunity presupposes its actual, and not just theoretical, existence. It follows

[57] See *Benedetti v Sawiris* [2013] UKSC 50, [2013] 3 WLR 351 [100] (Lord Reed). See also at [99]. See further *Tito v Waddell (No 2)* (n 36) and accompanying text.

[58] See above pp 31, 66–70, 81–82.

[59] Rush, *The Defence of Passing On* (n 5) 106.

[60] This is a reference to the following hypothetical example concocted by Birks: 'Suppose that I use your bicycle while you are on holiday. By the time you come back, I have returned it. Let it be that there is no perceptible wear and tear attributable to me. It is clear that I must pay the value of my use. Yet you have suffered no loss. I have taken three weeks' riding "from" you, but I have inflicted no corresponding impoverishment on you.' See P Birks, '"At the Expense of the Claimant": Direct and Indirect Enrichment in English Law' in D Johnston and R Zimmermann (eds), *Unjustified Enrichment: Key Issues in Comparative Perspective* (Cambridge, Cambridge University Press, 2002), 501; P Birks, *The Foundations of Unjust Enrichment: Six Centennial Lectures* (Wellington, Victoria University Press, 2002) 83.

> that 'loss', insofar as it is understood in the broadest sense of an opportunity foregone, should be rejected as the [sic] part of the law of unjust enrichment.

Three responses can be made to this argument. First, there is a difference between having an opportunity that is factually difficult to realise, and not having that opportunity at all. 'Opportunity' in this context is not being used 'loosely and inaccurately' but is limited by the necessity of the claimant's exchange capacity. This point was made in chapter one with respect to those cases in which the claimant's alleged entitlement was not susceptible to exchange,[61] including *Moore v Regents of the University of California*,[62] *Rosenfeldt v Olson*,[63] and *Wrotham Park Estate Co Ltd v Parkside Homes Ltd*.[64] If, however, the claimant's entitlement is something that is susceptible to exchange, then the lost opportunity to exchange is a loss falling within ambit of unjust enrichment. So if D uses C's bicycle while C is away, for example, and C is therefore unable to sell or hire it to D or someone else, it does not follow that C never had such an opportunity in respect of the bicycle, nor indeed that he had it and then lost it when D took the bicycle. The opportunity is coextensive with the exchange capacity in respect of the bicycle (including its use), which is in turn coextensive with the right to the bicycle—and that right is not lost with actual possession.

A useful case to consider in this context is the decision of Lindgren J in Federal Court of Australia in *Re Huntley Management Ltd*.[65] Australian Olives Ltd (AOL) was responsible for managing several olive projects. A contract for the supply of water to those projects (the agreement) was entered into between AOL, Australian Olive Holdings Pty Ltd (AOHL—the water owner) and Collective Olive Groves Ltd (COGL—the land owner). The agreement provided that, should AOL be removed or replaced as manager of the projects, a new regime was to come into operation between AOHL and COGL. It transpired that AOL was replaced by Huntley Management Ltd, after which point AOHL sent invoices to Huntley. Huntley did not pay them, contending that it was not liable to do so. AOHL sought to enforce the agreement against Huntley on the basis the latter had succeeded to AOL's obligations by operation of the Corporations Act 2001 (Cth), an argument that was rejected on the basis that the application of the Act was limited by the agreement's express contemplation of the coming into operation of a new regime. Alternatively AOHL advanced an unjust enrichment claim on the basis that it had conferred a benefit on Huntley in the form of the 'supply of a reliable source of water'. Lindgren J dismissed this benefit as 'elusive'. No water had been supplied.[66] More relevant, however, is that Lindgren J also dismissed AOHL's allegation that

[61] See above pp 32–43.
[62] *Moore v Regents of University of California* 51 Cal 3d 120, 793 P 2d 479 (1990) (SC Calif).
[63] *Rosenfeldt v Olson* (1986) 25 DLR (4th) 472 (BCCA).
[64] *Wrotham Park Estate Co Ltd v Parkside Homes Ltd* [1974] 1 WLR 798 (Ch).
[65] *Re Huntley Management Ltd; Australian Olive Holdings Pty Ltd v Huntley Management Ltd* [2009] FCA 1479, (2009) 76 ACSR 256.
[66] ibid [127].

it had suffered a loss. AOHL alleged that it had lost the opportunity of entering into a contract with Huntley to supply the service of providing a reliable supply of water (or of supplying water) for valuable consideration, and that the loss of this opportunity was an acceptable loss[67] for the purposes of supporting an unjust enrichment claim. Lindgren J rejected this contention shortly on the basis that it had not been shown 'that there would have been a fruitful negotiation between Huntley and AOHL for AOHL to supply Huntley with water' and that, in fact, the evidence suggested the contrary.[68] Moreover, he added: 'AOHL did not lose the opportunity by reason of providing a reliable supply of water.'[69]

The latter point is particularly important because it demonstrates the kinds of lost opportunities unjust enrichment is concerned with. Mere unrealised opportunities to contract are outside the scope of unjust enrichment: they cannot be exchanged in their own right.[70] What *can* be exchanged, however, is the underlying right (or service) in respect of which the contract can be made. In *Re Huntley Management Ltd* the point was that AOHL still had the water: it 'parted with or produced nothing'.[71] It was still free to do with the water as it pleased, including exchanging it. It had not suffered a loss.

The second response to Rush's position on lost opportunities is that his charge that they are 'fictional' is inapt. It is unclear at what point the loss of an opportunity becomes 'fictional' as opposed to being factually difficult to realise or small in value. Indeed, the charge of 'fiction' is an inapt criticism of opportunities because they are, by nature, based upon future, hypothetical, and so non-existent events.[72] Moreover, the charge of 'fiction' in this context reveals that what a lawyer might perceive as disingenuous analysis may in fact turn out to be a genuine and acceptable feature of wider considerations and of extra-legal analysis: the operation of markets, as well as the determination of prices in economic theory, is necessarily premised upon how market participants *might* behave in different circumstances. That being so, a lawyer's complaint that such analysis is 'fictional' misses the point. To the extent that a given opportunity does not align with the claimant's exchange capacity, the point is not that the opportunity is 'fictional', but rather that it either

[67] Neither the judgment or AOHL's pleadings and submissions used the term 'loss'—instead relying on the terminology of 'expense or detriment' and 'expense of the claimant respectively': ibid [129]–[130]. That, however, does not impact upon the overall thrust of the point made in this book, once the arguments about the necessity of loss (and its obscurity in the existing case law) are accepted.

[68] ibid [130].

[69] ibid [130].

[70] This may be one reason why Lindgren J observed (at [130]) that: 'In the absence of contract, the most that can be said is that AOHL had a reliable source of water in proximity to the land the subject of the Projects.' Contractual rights are the realisation of opportunities, and in that sense their loss is the loss of an opportunity relevantly within the law of unjust enrichment.

[71] *Re Huntley Management Ltd* (n 65) [132].

[72] Indeed, the critical charge that a particular legal analysis is 'fictional' loses force if one accepts that a recurring motif within law generally is the use of abstract concepts to give form to things that have no natural existence. See further G Watt, *Equity Stirring: The Story of Justice Beyond Law* (Oxford, Hart, 2009) 135–41.

does not exist or does not fall within the scope of unjust enrichment. In *Re Huntley Management Ltd*, for example, the most that could be said of AOHL was that it had lost the (unrealised) opportunity to contract with Huntley in respect of the supply of water. What it was attempting to do was have the court treat that unrealised opportunity as though it had crystallised into something exchangeable; an argument that Lindgren J rightly dismissed.

The third and final response to Rush's position on lost opportunities is that, to the extent that his 'fictional' criticisms are merely reflective of hardship of realisation or smallness of value, they misplace the role of loss in unjust enrichment. The desire to quantify loss is perhaps an unfortunate by-product of the familiar language of loss in compensation for tort and breach of contract. In those areas loss generally determines the measure of a claimant's award. Limitations of legal taxonomy, however, should not obscure the substance of legal principles. The meaning and role of loss in unjust enrichment are not the same as those in compensation for tort or breach of contract.[73] And as we shall see under the next heading, the claimant's loss—viewed and quantified in isolation—does not determine the quantum of restitution for unjust enrichment.

## (B) Is Restitution 'Capped' by Loss?[74]

In *Sempra Metals Ltd*[75] the claimant company, which was based on the Continent, had been required to pay tax to the UK Revenue earlier than its UK-based counterparts. This was held by the European Court of Justice to be a breach of European Community law. The claimant thereafter sought restitution in the form of interest representing the use value of the prematurely paid tax. One basis of the claim was unjust enrichment. The House of Lords held that the claimant's right to restitution was not determined by the loss it had suffered. Lord Hope held that a claimant in unjust enrichment need not 'have suffered a loss corresponding to the defendant's enrichment'.[76] Lord Mance stated that '[r]estitution of any interest benefit received … is not concerned with loss which a claimant himself actually suffers'.[77] Lord Nicholls directly contrasted the gain-based concern of an award of restitution for unjust enrichment with the loss-based concern of an award of damages.[78] All of their Lordships emphasised that an award of restitution based on

[73] *Commissioner of State Revenue (Vic)* (n 1) 73–74 (Mason CJ).

[74] See generally Burrows, *The Law of Restitution* (n 15) 64–65; Birks, *Unjust Enrichment* (n 5) 78–82. Cf M McInnes, 'Interceptive Subtraction, Unjust Enrichment and Wrongs—A Reply to Professor Birks' (2003) 62 *Cambridge Law Journal* 697.

[75] *Sempra Metals* (n 19).

[76] ibid [30]–[31] (Lord Hope).

[77] ibid [235] (Lord Mance).

[78] ibid [66] (Lord Nicholls).

unjust enrichment was to be measured by reference to the defendant's position.[79] Where their Lordships' opinions diverged was in respect of how to go about determining that position.

The issue in *Sempra Metals* was not whether the claimant needed to have suffered a loss; that was incontestable because Sempra had paid money as tax and had, in doing so, lost not only the money but also the opportunity to use it.[80] Instead, the issue was whether the value of the claimant's loss limited the quantum of restitution. The House of Lords' unanimous opinion was that it did not. Though it is debateable whether this forms part of the *ratio* of the case,[81] the fact remains that *Sempra Metals* at least contains very powerful *dicta* suggesting that the quantum of loss does not affect the quantum of restitution.[82] This is the very point made by Robert Goff J in *BP v Hunt (No 2)*, quoted at the start of this chapter.[83]

## (1) 'Loss Correspondence' and the Exchange Capacity

These issues are often described as ones of 'loss correspondence',[84] though this expression has a tendency to create confusion, for two reasons. The first is that 'correspondence' can be interpreted in different ways, and it is not always clear which interpretation is being used. It may denote a mere qualitative relationship; that is, the existence of an enrichment corresponds to the existence of a loss. Or it may denote a quantitative relationship; that is, the size of an enrichment corresponds to the size of a loss. The cases, and this book, favour the former interpretation.

A second, and more troublesome, source of confusion is the failure to understand loss in unjust enrichment. Loss was defined above as the lost opportunity to charge or otherwise exercise the exchange capacity. It was also observed that such a definition matches that of enrichment as saved necessary expenditure. This is the qualitative correspondence favoured by the case law: the existence of the claimant's lost opportunity to charge corresponds to the existence of the defendant's saved

[79] ibid [45]–[48] (Lord Hope), [103] (Lord Nicholls), [143], [153] (Lord Scott), [178], [188] (Lord Walker), [231], [241] (Lord Mance).

[80] ibid [33] (Lord Hope) [95], [102] (Lord Nicholls), [140] (Lord Scott).

[81] See, eg, C Mitchell, 'Recovery of Compound Interest as Restitution or Damages' (2008) 71 *Modern Law Review* 271, 300. The case was argued on the basis that the loss to the claimants was greater than the gain to the Revenue, so no question of loss capping arose on the facts.

[82] See further *Littlewoods Retail Ltd v Revenue and Customs Commissioners* [2010] EWHC 1071 (Ch) [147] (Vos J); *Equitas Ltd v Walsham Bros & Co Ltd* [2013] EWHC 3264 (QB) [118] (Males J): '*Sempra Metals* was a case where, despite what was said about the need to plead and prove a loss, the damages actually awarded were determined by taking a conventional rate and awarding compound interest. This did not depend on any evidence as to the taxpayer's actual loss, but was simply the interest which a substantial commercial company would have to pay to borrow the amount in question in the market at the relevant time, regardless of what the taxpayer had actually done. Although it may be that this approach was not the subject of specific argument in the House of Lords, it was clearly an approach which the House endorsed.'

[83] See above p 77.

[84] See, eg, Burrows, *The Law of Restitution* (n 15) 64–65; Birks, *Unjust Enrichment* (n 5) 78.

expenditure. Once, however, the correspondence is understood in this way, there also follows a necessary quantitative correspondence: the value of the claimant's lost opportunity necessarily matches the value of the defendant's saved expenditure. The critical point to realise, however, is that this quantitative correspondence has nothing to do with a freestanding 'loss correspondence' requirement. Instead, it follows from the nature of enrichment and loss in unjust enrichment as defined in this book, and from the fact that the defendant and claimant occupy the same market: one party's enrichment *is* the other's loss. Indeed, the futility of a distinct 'loss correspondence' requirement becomes apparent when one realises that, given the market relationship between claimant and defendant, it would be equally plausible to speak in terms of 'enrichment correspondence' according to which the valuation of a claimant's loss matches a defendant's enrichment.

These points are reflected in the Supreme Court of Canada's insistence that a claimant must suffer 'a corresponding deprivation'. In *Peter v Beblow*, Cory J observed that 'once enrichment has been found, the conclusion that the claimant has suffered a corresponding deprivation is virtually automatic'.[85] The concurrently decided cases of *Kerr v Baranow* and *Vanasse v Seguin* confirm this view.[86] Like *Peter v Beblow*, these were cases involving the distribution of assets following the breakdown of a domestic relationship where the court invoked the principle against unjust enrichment. On this occasion the court expressed the principle as requiring that 'the defendant has been enriched by the plaintiff' and that 'the plaintiff has suffered a corresponding deprivation'.[87] There is a subtle difference between this formulation and that in previous cases where the court had stated that there must be 'an enrichment of the defendant' and 'a corresponding deprivation of the plaintiff'.[88] The introduction of 'by the plaintiff' into the first stage of the Canadian inquiry renders the second stage virtually otiose. The court explained that 'the plaintiff's loss is material only if the defendant has gained a benefit or been enriched'.[89] It therefore rightly accepted the gist of the claim to be the enrichment of the defendant, before adding that this was why the plaintiff had to establish that the defendant's gain corresponded to the plaintiff's deprivation.[90] When insistence on a 'corresponding deprivation' is understood in this light, the claimant's loss ceases to have any control over the quantum of restitution for unjust enrichment. This was particularly evident in *Vanasse v Seguin*, where the issue was the connection between Mr Seguin's accumulated wealth and Ms Vanasse's domestic services and how to measure the appropriate pecuniary award. Neither Ms Vanasse's contribution nor the detriment she suffered as a result was

[85] *Peter v Beblow* [1993] 1 SCR 980 (SCC) [79]–[81]. See further Mitchell, Mitchell, and Watterson, *Goff & Jones* (n 55) para 6.66.

[86] *Kerr v Baranow, Vanasse v Seguin* [2011] SCC 10, [2011] 1 SCR 269.

[87] ibid [36].

[88] See, eg, *Garland v Consumers' Gas Co* [2004] SCC 25 [30].

[89] *Kerr v Baranow, Vanasse v Seguin* (n 86) [39] citing *Peel (Regional Municipality) v Canada* [1992] 3 SCR 762 (SCC) 789–90.

[90] *Kerr v Baranow, Vanasse v Seguin* (n 86) [39].

inherently financial.[91] They therefore had to be assigned a value,[92] but no court hearing the matter attempted that exercise independently from the identification of Mr Seguin's gain.[93] 'Corresponding deprivation' added nothing to the determination of the claim—'enrichment by the claimant' was enough.

This is not to say that the cases denying a requirement of loss correspondence in unjust enrichment are in some way wrong or inconsistent with this book. Rather, the point is that the meaning of 'loss correspondence' tends to vary with the task at hand. *Sempra Metals* and *BP v Hunt (No 2)* are authority for the proposition that loss is necessary for unjust enrichment, but does not control the quantum of restitution following. In neither case, however, was it necessary for the court to consider the nature of loss, as that concept is relevant to unjust enrichment and the exchange capacity. For example, viewed in abstract isolation, the premature payment of the money as tax in *Sempra Metals* meant the claimant taxpayers had lost the opportunity to lend or invest their money at the best market rate available to them. But the idea of an abstract and isolated claimant's loss, divorced from the defendant's enrichment, is unsound in the context of a scheme of unjust enrichment underpinned by corrective justice, markets, and the exchange capacity as proposed by this book. The claimants had not temporarily lost their money in a hole;[94] they had paid it to the defendant Revenue, and so their loss was relevantly determined according to the market for Government borrowing.[95] There was a quantitative correspondence following from the nature of enrichment and loss, rather than from some distinct rule of 'loss correspondence'.

It is worthwhile reiterating that the definitions of enrichment and loss proposed by this book mean that valuation is dependent upon market identification and function. In chapter two the point was made that instances of apparent 'subjective devaluation' and 'subjective revaluation' are really just the product of identifying the particular market in which the claimant and defendant exist.[96] A similar point applies here in the context of alternative markets. For example, one might ask why, in *Sempra Metals*, the relevant market was that for Government borrowing, not lending by a Continent-based company. Had it been the latter, the Revenue's enrichment and claimants' loss would have been the amount for which the claimants could have invested the money prematurely paid as tax. Similarly, one could ask why, in *Vanasse v Seguin*, the value of Ms Vanasse's domestic services was determined by reference to Mr Seguin's gain rather than what he might have had to pay (and what Ms Vanasse might have charged) had they been participants in

[91] ibid [147], [152].

[92] ibid [37].

[93] See especially *Vanasse v Seguin* (2008) 168 ACWS (3d) 819 (Ont SC) [110]–[114] (JA Blishen J).

[94] See above pp 22–23. Cf M Doyle, 'Corrective Justice and Unjust Enrichment' (2012) 62 *University of Toronto Law Journal* 229, 240.

[95] See further *Benedetti (UKSC)* (n 57) [106] (Lord Reed), referring to *Sempra Metals* (n 19) [46] (Lord Hope), [103] (Lord Nicholls). See above pp 69–70.

[96] See above pp 66–70.

the retail market for domestic services. In both cases the question reduces to: why pick one market, and not another?

The answer must be that it is a necessary feature of every unjust enrichment case in which there are alternative markets that a finding is made that one party's economic power to determine the applicable market is greater than that of the other party to determine an alternative. Such a finding will be implicit in most cases. In *Sempra Metals* the Revenue's position as a public body was decisive. Not only could it borrow money at a lower price than commercial enterprises, but it also had the economic power to determine the exchange relationship with the claimants in particular. Meanwhile, in *Vanasse v Seguin*, that neither Ms Vanasse's contribution nor the detriment she suffered was considered inherently financial indicates that the Court either did not consider it possible for her to have participated in the retail market for domestic services (indeed, the Court noted that her previous career had been one in national intelligence), or that certain of those contributions (such as parental caring) defied market analysis.[97] And it is arguable that the Court was loathe to impose retail conditions upon what had been a familial relationship. Those things being so, the relevant market could only be that in respect of Mr Seguin's accumulated wealth.

This of course leaves open the possibility that a situation might arise in which the power relationship is reversed, and in a contest between alternative markets the one more favourable to the claimant will prevail. In such a case the onus would be on the claimant to prove its superior power over the defendant, as well as upon the court to make explicit that which has tended to be implicit in the cases: the reasons why one market is preferred over another. But whatever way the particular case is determined, what matters is the centrality of market analysis to the relationship between the parties and their exchange capacity, rather than the application of some distinct rule of 'loss correspondence'.

## (2) 'Capping' and the Exchange Capacity

From time to time various arguments have been advanced as to why restitution should be 'capped' by the claimant's loss. One is that it wastes judicial resources to reallocate a loss or a benefit between claimant and defendant when neither positively deserves it.[98] But that allegation proves too little because, once it is accepted that the claimant in unjust enrichment must first suffer a loss, the criticism that it wastes judicial resources to pursue benefits in excess of that loss has nothing to bite on: those resources will have been expended, in any event, in respect of that loss.[99]

[97] *Kerr v Baranow, Vanasse v Seguin* (n 86) [147], [152].

[98] Mitchell, Mitchell, and Watterson, *Goff & Jones* (n 55) para 6.64; *Roxborough* (n 17) [118] (Kirby J); M McInnes, '"At the Plaintiff's Expense": Quantifying Restitutionary Relief' (1998) 57 *Cambridge Law Journal* 472, 476.

[99] See further Rush, *The Defence of Passing On* (n 5) 151–153.

A more fundamental criticism of the proposition that restitution for unjust enrichment is not capped by loss is that it generates windfalls for claimants without normative justification.[100] McInnes has thus described the situation of a claim in respect of gain exceeding loss as a 'socially neutral' contest between two parties who do not 'positively deserve' the alleged 'windfall', and which ultimately seeks relief 'that is not truly restitutionary'.[101] Unjust enrichment, he argues, is incomprehensible when divorced from material gains and losses: 'It is only by reference to an actual flow of wealth that a court can recognize an unjust enrichment for the defendant and an unjust deprivation for the plaintiff'.[102] This point is made against the background of a three-way distinction between 'compensation', 'disgorgement', and 'restitution'. Compensation is measured exclusively by the plaintiff's loss and without regard to the defendant's corresponding gain, and is an inappropriate response to unjust enrichment because it reaches beyond the scope of the parties' relationship.[103] Disgorgement, on the other hand, is measured exclusively by the defendant's gain, but is likewise an inappropriate response to unjust enrichment because it reaches beyond the scope of the parties' relationship.[104] Restitution, however, does not suffer these failings: it is the only appropriate response to unjust enrichment because it reverses the highest amount common to both the plaintiff's loss and the defendant's gain, and therefore 'does not attempt to capture benefits that the defendant acquired outside of the operative relationship, nor losses that the plaintiff sustained *dehors*'.[105] Grantham and Rickett make a similar point, arguing that the only legitimate objective of unjust enrichment is 'the restoration of the wealth received by the defendant from the claimant'.[106]

This book takes the view that 'loss capping' arguments such as these are actually 'red herrings' based upon a mischaracterisation of enrichment, loss, and the relationship between those two concepts in unjust enrichment. So while 'loss capping' arguments may at first appear attractive insofar as they appear to align with the correspondence points raised in the previous section, they should be disregarded as superficial, inapt, and potentially misleading.

Two complaints can be made of the 'loss capping' arguments. First, they do not align with the underlying proposition advanced in this book that unjust enrichment is concerned with each party's exchange capacity *vis-à-vis* that of the other.

[100] Mitchell, Mitchell, and Watterson, *Goff & Jones* (n 55) para 6.64. See also *Air Canada v British Columbia* (n 17) 1202 (La Forest J).

[101] McInnes, '"At the Plaintiff's Expense": Quantifying Restitutionary Relief' (n 98) 476. See also *Roxborough* (n 17) [118] (Kirby J): '[W]hy should the law intervene at all? Why should it do so, given that the "transfer [of] an unjust enrichment from defendant to plaintiff" would necessarily consume scarce judicial resources towards achieving an outcome that was equally meritless.' See further M McInnes, 'The Measure of Restitution' (2002) 52 *University of Toronto Law Journal* 163, 186–96; R Grantham and C Rickett, 'Disgorgement for Unjust Enrichment?' (2003) 62 *Cambridge Law Journal* 159.

[102] McInnes, 'The Measure of Restitution' (n 101) 195.

[103] ibid 183.

[104] ibid 185.

[105] ibid 181.

[106] Grantham and Rickett, 'Disgorgement for Unjust Enrichment?' (n 101) 160.

The point is that the defendant's enrichment *is* the claimant's loss.[107] The root of the error committed by McInnes, Grantham, and Rickett in this respect lies in the fact that they rely upon an inappropriate definition of loss within unjust enrichment. It is wrong to view the materiality of the claimant's loss in abstract and isolated terms, rather than by reference to their exchange capacity in relation to the defendant. The correspondence between enrichment and loss advanced by this book is not the product of some freestanding principle of 'loss correspondence' or 'loss capping' imposed over the parties' relationship. Rather, the correspondence between enrichment and loss is derived from within that relationship itself: it is the product of the bilateral quality of the parties' exchange capacities as relevantly defined within unjust enrichment. 'Loss capping' and 'loss correspondence' are legal fallacies that mislead and detract from the reality of unjust enrichment.

The second complaint against 'loss capping' arguments is of a more general character. The complaint is that arguments that seek to determine the appropriate size and measure of restitution by reference to the relationship between enrichment and loss, and to some sort of 'loss capping' requirement therein, ultimately present the issue of how to measure restitution for unjust enrichment in misleading terms that are potentially damaging to the correct analysis of cases. One might allege, for example, that if loss is as necessary and as wide a concept in unjust enrichment as this book holds it to be, then it is natural for loss to function as a limiting device upon the quantum of restitution awarded, with the exchange capacity providing the underlying explanation of that limit. Such a function for loss, however, is superfluous within unjust enrichment: the quantum of restitution is determined having regard to the market identified for the relevant enrichment. Once that market is defined, and the enrichment valued accordingly, the only thing that the identification of loss does is confirm that the claimant is relevantly part of that market. Insofar as the value of that loss performs a 'correspondence' or 'capping' function, it really tells us no more than what we already know: the value of the defendant's enrichment in the market to which both claimant and defendant belong. Loss tells us nothing new about the measure of restitution.

Moreover, the reality is that several factors other than the identification of loss may influence the measure of restitution by qualifying the nature and extent of a defendant's liability. Suppose, for example, that a claimant mistakenly transferred certain shares initially worth £100 to the defendant, and that those shares subsequently increased in value to £1,000. Following the result in *Trustee of the Property of FC Jones & Sons v Jones* the claimant would be entitled to £1,000.[108] It may be tempting to herald that conclusion as decisively rejecting a cap on restitution by reference to loss.[109] But that would gloss over the analysis of the case as involving enrichment by the receipt of rights to the shares,[110] the loss being that right as a

[107] See above pp 85–86.

[108] *Trustee of the Property of FC Jones & Sons (A Firm) v Jones* [1997] Ch 159 (CA).

[109] See, eg, Birks, *Unjust Enrichment* (n 5) 82.

[110] See generally AVM Lodder, *Enrichment in the Law of Unjust Enrichment and Restitution* (Oxford, Hart, 2012) 200–01.

manifestation of the claimant's exchange capacity. On that analysis, the value of the claimant's loss (that is, the value of the shares when transferred) is irrelevant because the claim is made in respect of the right to the shares, rather than their value in abstract. On this view, the case has nothing to do with 'capping' restitution according to loss, and attempts to derive principles to this effect are prone to mislead.

Another example of the confusion that can arise from a failure to disentangle the issues surrounding the measure of restitution arises from of Robert Goff J's speech in *BP v Hunt (No 2)*. The facts and reasons in that case are discussed and analysed in greater detail in Part III of this book.[111] The case is raised here because it appears to support *both* sides of the capping debate. On the one hand there is Robert Goff J's explicit statement, quoted at the start of this chapter, that loss 'does not limit or control the award of restitution'.[112] On the other hand, however, it has occasionally been suggested that the outcome of the case actually supports a cap on restitution imposed by loss.[113] This book disagrees with the latter suggestion: not only is the interpretation of the case in that way a contradiction of Robert Goff J's express statement but it also misunderstands the underlying reason as to *why* he made an order for restitution in the quantum that he did. The truth is that *BP v Hunt (No 2)* was not a case about capping restitution according to loss. Rather, and as we shall see in Part III of this book, the case was about the policy that unjust enrichment not undermine a defendant's pre-existing property rights.

What this ultimately means for arguments against awarding restitution in excess of the claimant's loss is that they are couched in terms of the wrong issue. The relevant propositions advanced by this book so far can be summarised as follows. First, unjust enrichment is concerned with the parties' exchange capacity. Secondly, this entails an enrichment to the defendant and a loss to the claimant reflective of how each of those capacities would have been exercised *vis-à-vis* the other within the same market: restitution ensures that the claimant receives from the defendant what the latter ought to have paid for the benefit in question. These propositions say nothing about whether the measure of restitution should thereafter be capped or otherwise qualified. The issues of whether one party is 'deserving' or not of an excess of gain over initial loss, or whether that excess is appropriately described as a normative 'windfall', cannot be answered according to simplified dogmata about loss correspondence or capping. Those issues must be brought to the fore, and dealt with on their own terms—as some are in Part III of this book.

[111] See below pp 193–195.

[112] *BP v Hunt (No 2)* (n 1) 839–40. See above p 77.

[113] See, eg, Mitchell, Mitchell, and Watterson, *Goff & Jones* (n 55) para 6.68; Birks, *Unjust Enrichment* (n 5) 80.

# Part II

# Connecting Enrichment and Loss

Enrichment and loss are the two sides of unjust enrichment, reflecting the exchange capacities of the defendant and claimant respectively within a market framework. The identification of enrichment and loss, however, does not mean that one is attributable to the other: for *this* claimant to recover from *that* defendant requires a connection between the two. Simply because C loses £10 on the same day that D coincidentally finds £10 does not mean C can claim against D. There must be a connection between the defendant's enrichment and the claimant's loss to justify a claim.[1] And merely because the parties' exchange capacities occupy a single market does not mean that connection exists in a given case: C may well have been in a position to exchange his lost £10 with D but, once again, that will not suffice without more for him to enable him to bring a claim against D who happens to find £10. The connection must be specific to the parties, and it must be capable of articulation in a straightforward way.

That is the aim of this Part: to survey the different kinds of case in which a connection has been held to arise, and to generalise that connection for application beyond those cases. That being so, the underlying case-based approach of this Part, starting with chapter four, reflects the necessity of case-sourced principle expounded according to common law methodology.

Before progressing further, however, care must be taken to distinguish the connection between enrichment and loss from another important connection that arises in unjust enrichment; that is, the connection between enrichment and loss on the one hand, and an unjust factor on the other. The distinction between these two connections fits the normative structure of the unjust enrichment claim because the justification of unjust enrichment consists of two limbs: first, a link between the claimant and defendant and, secondly, the need for correction established by a defect.[2] At a high level of abstraction, the two limbs occupy the same exchange capacity framework because the injustice of a connection cannot be adjudged without understanding the qualities to which it ought to conform.[3]

[1] *Banque Financière de la Cité SA v Parc (Battersea) Ltd* [1999] 1 AC 221 (HL) (Lord Clyde); *Uren v First National Home Finance Ltd* [2005] EWHC 2529 (Ch) [22] (Mann J).

[2] J Edelman, 'The Meaning of Loss and Enrichment' in R Chambers, C Mitchell, and J Penner (eds), *Philosophical Foundations of The Law of Unjust Enrichment* (Oxford, Oxford University Press, 2009) 224.

[3] See above p 16.

Nevertheless, a failure to distinguish between the two can generate confusion, an example of which is to be found in the Court of Appeal's decision in *Test Claimants in the FII Group Litigation v Revenue and Customs Commissioners*.[4] The claimants had used tax reliefs to offset their liability to pay a tax that had been unlawfully levied in breach of EU law. Had they not done so, they would have used those reliefs to offset other, lawful, taxes. The Court of Appeal held that any gain to the Revenue was too remote a consequence of the mistake: '[t]he connection between the payment of tax lawfully due … and the mistake … [was] not sufficiently direct to satisfy the requirements of causation in restitution'.[5] The Court held, in effect, that the enrichment was not unjust because it was too remote from the unjust factor; that is, the enrichment was not caused by the mistake. However, the Court then added the difficult postscript that '[t]he *loss* was too remote',[6] suggesting that the actual inquiry was between enrichment and loss. As a result, it is unclear precisely on what basis the Court of Appeal dismissed the claim.[7]

[4] *Test Claimants in the FII Group Litigation v Revenue and Customs Commissioners* [2010] EWCA Civ 103.

[5] ibid [182].

[6] ibid (emphasis added).

[7] ibid [178]. Cf *Test Claimants in the ACT Group Litigation (Class 4) v Revenue and Customs Commissioners* [2010] EWHC 359 (Ch), in which Henderson J appears to frame the relevant question as one of unjustness (albeit—not unreasonably—without reference to *FII* (n 4), decided only three days earlier). See also *Gibb v Maidstone & Tunbridge Wells NHS Trust* [2010] EWCA Civ 678 [32], where Laws LJ appears to mix the 'at the expense of the claimant' inquiry with the 'unjust factor' inquiry under the broader heading of 'causation'. A possible source of confusion may be the appearance of a 'causation' test at several different stages of the unjust enrichment framework of analysis. See generally G Virgo, 'Causation and Remoteness within the Law of Unjust Enrichment' in S Degeling and J Edelman (eds), *Unjust Enrichment in Commercial Law* (Sydney, Thomson Reuters, 2008).

# 4

# Connections

To understand the connection between enrichment and loss we must first examine the cases in which a connection has been held to arise. That exercise reveals that enrichment and loss may be connected in a variety of ways, ranging from single connections involving two parties to multiple connections involving several parties. Once the range of different connections has been surveyed in this chapter, we can then turn our attention, in the next chapter, to generalising them in a manner that transcends the decided case law and is consistent with the exchange capacity analysis of unjust enrichment.

## (A) Single Connections

### (1) Acquisition of a Right

The paradigm case of unjust enrichment is the mistaken payment of money.[1] Money is a store of value,[2] but it is not value in and of itself. Value is an abstract standard for comparison and exchange of qualitatively heterogeneous things in quantitatively comparable and equivalent terms,[3] and because money is 'a universal medium of exchange'[4] its homogeneous quality satisfies that abstract standard in plain terms. A variety of assets fulfil this function.[5] Coins and banknotes are corporeal money,[6] while bank balances, though technically a chose in action, are generically referred to as incorporeal money.[7] In each case, however, money exists via the medium of rights. To have money is to have a right to the store of value it represents. If I possess ten one-pound coins then it is my right of possession that leads us to say that I have ten pounds of money; likewise if I possess a ten-pound

[1] See, eg, *Kelly v Solari* (1841) 9 M & W 54, 152 ER 24 (Exch).
[2] D Fox, *Property Rights in Money* (Oxford, Oxford University Press, 2008) [1.28].
[3] AVM Lodder, *Enrichment in the Law of Unjust Enrichment and Restitution* (Oxford, Hart, 2012) 16.
[4] *BP Exploration Co (Libya) Ltd v Hunt (No 2)* [1979] 1 WLR 783 (QB) 799 (Robert Goff J).
[5] Fox, *Property Rights in Money* (n 2) [1.31]–[1.58].
[6] For the historical position regarding possession of a banknote, see D Fox, 'Bona fide Purchase and the Currency of Money' [1996] *Cambridge Law Journal* 547.
[7] Fox, *Property Rights in Money* (n 2) [1.38].

note. And if I have ten pounds in a bank account the situation is that I have a right against the bank in the amount of ten pounds. Like all personal property, to 'have' money is to have a right in respect of it. The connection in payment of money cases can therefore be stated in broader but no less accurate terms than that of a payer–payee: the claimant is connected to the defendant because the latter has acquired a right from the former. A personal claim for the money is a claim for the value of that right.

This analysis extends to all corporeal and incorporeal assets. It is trite to observe that the law of property is concerned with rights in respect of things, rather than the particular things themselves.[8] The law of unjust enrichment is also uninterested by things insofar as it is concerned with rights in respect of those things and, in turn, the value of those rights. This does not mean, however, that value and rights are the same. In chapter two we observed a central tenet of the Chambers-Lodder thesis to be the difference between factual and legal enrichment, but we also observed that the difference is not a sharp one because rights may themselves be valuable.[9]

*Cressman v Coys of Kensington (Sales) Ltd* is an example of an unjust enrichment claim in which the parties were connected by the acquisition of a right.[10] The executors of Cressman's estate instructed Coys to sell his car without the right to use its personalised number-plate. Coys sold the car to McDonald. Through an administrative error, however, McDonald also acquired the statutory right to use the personalised plate, which he registered in his name. The issue was whether McDonald was liable in unjust enrichment for the value of that right. The estate could not seek the right to use the plate from McDonald because he had transferred it to his partner. All that was left to recover from him was the value of the right to use the plate, a change of position defence being unavailable because he had transferred the right with knowledge of the error.[11] It seems a mundane observation that the estate's loss was connected to McDonald's enrichment because he acquired the right to use the plate 'from' it, in the sense that the estate had held that right prior to McDonald's acquisition of it.

The connection in *Cressman* is simple to explain because the right was acquired under a statutory transfer mechanism.[12] Other cases are less straightforward. There are several ways in which valuable rights can be acquired: transfer by legal assignment is only one example.

A defendant may also acquire a right when the claimant creates one in his favour. This occurred in *Moses v Macferlan*.[13] The claimant (Moses) endorsed

[8] See generally W Swadling, 'Property: General Principles' in A Burrows (ed), *English Private Law*, 3rd edn (Oxford, Oxford University Press, 2013) [4.02].

[9] See above p 54.

[10] *Cressman v Coys of Kensington (Sales) Ltd* [2004] EWCA Civ 47, [2004] 1 WLR 2775.

[11] ibid [41].

[12] ibid [3]–[6].

[13] *Moses v Macferlan* (1760) 2 Burr 1005, 97 ER 676 (KB).

four promissory notes (payable by a third party) to the defendant (Macferlan), who signed an agreement that he would not sue Moses on the notes. Despite that agreement, Macferlan thereafter successfully sued Moses as the endorser of each note. An action for money had and received succeeded. It has been denied that this was based on unjust enrichment. Birks considered the case explicable only as restitution for a wrong, being Macferlan's breach of contract not to sue on the notes.[14] The 'fatal snag' in conceiving the case as one of unjust enrichment was that the claimant's payment to the defendant was compelled by a court judgment.[15] The pressure on the claimant was therefore that of due process of law, which cannot support restitution—at least where the money was due.[16]

The analysis of *Moses v Macferlan* as a case of restitution for wrongdoing is not challenged in this book. What is challenged, however, is its rejection as a case susceptible to unjust enrichment analysis. The problem with Birks's analysis is that it incorrectly identifies the enrichment in the case, and the nature of the connection between the parties. Moses was not connected to Macferlan because he paid money to him under pressure, but because he endorsed the notes for a consideration that subsequently failed (the promise not to sue). Properly understood, Macferlan's enrichment was not the payment of money under the court judgment, but the creation of a right against Moses when he endorsed the notes. That right had a value (the face value of the notes) that was realised into money when Macferlan sued Moses on the notes. When that occurred the consideration for the endorsement failed and Moses's unjust enrichment claim crystallised.

A defendant may also acquire a right by operation of a rule of law, irrespective of the claimant's action, such as the rule that possessory title is acquired with possession of a chattel. This was the foundation of a possible claim identified in *Huyton SA v Peter Cremer GmbH & Co*.[17] The defendant (Cremer) agreed to sell and ship a quantity of wheat to the claimant buyer (Huyton). 'Freight on board' terms were that payment was to follow presentation by Cremer of certain shipping documents and that property in the wheat would only pass to Huyton on payment. Huyton refused to pay because of discrepancies in the documents presented, and a compromise was then agreed to avoid cancellation of the contract, the terms of which were favourable to Huyton. Cremer later claimed that the compromise agreement was the product of illegitimate pressure. One limb of Cremer's case was that Huyton should pay restitution for the value of the wheat received and that

[14] P Birks, *An Introduction to the Law of Restitution*, revised edn (Oxford, Clarendon Press, 1989) 335–36; P Birks, *Unjust Enrichment*, 2nd edn (Oxford, Oxford University Press, 2005) 14–15. See also C Mitchell, 'Unjust Enrichment' in A Burrows (ed), *English Private Law*, 3rd edn (Oxford, Oxford University Press, 2013) [18.262].

[15] Birks, *Unjust Enrichment* (n 14) 233. See further *Phillips v Hunter* (1795) 2 H Bl 402, 126 ER 618 (CP); *Marriot v Hampton* (1797) 7 TR 269 (KB).

[16] Birks, *Unjust Enrichment* (n 14) 14.

[17] *Huyton SA v Peter Cremer GmbH & Co* [1999] 1 Lloyd's Rep 620 (QB).

its failure to do so in the circumstances contributed to the illegitimate pressure.[18] Mance J accepted the possibility of such a claim, explaining:[19]

> [S]ince the property had not passed, [Cremer was] entitled … to recover possession of the goods … Had Cremer shown that Huyton could not return the goods, Cremer could no doubt have acquired a *restitutionary right* or a right in damages; the measure of recovery might then have related to the value of the goods in the Sudan rather than the contract price, although there is in fact no evidence which would enable any positive conclusion as to what, if any, difference, might exist between these two.

As already observed, the law is concerned with rights in respect of things rather than the things themselves. So when Mance J referred to a restitutionary right 'related to the value of the goods' he was referring to the value of Huyton's right to the goods. Property, however, had not passed, and so the only right Huyton had was a right of possession following delivery of the wheat to a silo at its request.[20] The fact that his Lordship was concerned with the value of the goods 'in Sudan' confirms this analysis, as this was the locus of Huyton's possession, and so the relevant market for exchange purposes.[21]

The act of taking possession bestows a right to exclusive possession, good against the whole world save someone with better title.[22] If a defendant takes possession of a claimant's chattel then the claimant continues to have best title to it, while the defendant acquires a right of possession, the value of which can be subject to an unjust enrichment claim.[23] Where corporeal money is concerned, for example, its perfectly liquid quality means there is effectively no difference in the value of legal and possessory title, as there was in the case of the wheat in *Huyton*. The connection between enrichment and loss lies in the fact that the defendant acquires a right from possessing property in respect of which the claimant has title.

It is this final point that Swadling does not appreciate when he attacks the contention that cases analogous to *Holiday v Sigil*[24] can be analysed as unjust enrichment claims.[25] In that case the claimant succeeded in an action for money had and received after the defendant found the banknote which the claimant had lost earlier. Birks and Burrows consider the case susceptible to unjust enrichment analysis.[26] Swadling argues this is incorrect 'for with no title passing … an essential

[18] ibid 630.
[19] ibid 634 (emphasis added).
[20] ibid 624.
[21] See further Lodder, *Enrichment in the Law of Unjust Enrichment and Restitution* (n 3) 93–95. See generally L Smith, 'Unjust Enrichment, Property and the Structure of Trusts' (2000) 116 *Law Quarterly Review* 412, 426.
[22] Swadling, 'Property: General Principles' (n 8) [4.414].
[23] J Edelman and E Bant, *Unjust Enrichment in Australia* (Oxford, Oxford University Press, 2006) 102.
[24] *Holiday v Sigil* (1826) 2 Car & P 176 (Assizes). See also *Moffatt v Kazana* [1969] 2 QB 152 (Assizes).
[25] W Swadling, 'Ignorance and Unjust Enrichment: The Problem of Title' (2008) 28 *Oxford Journal of Legal Studies* 627.
[26] P Birks, *Unjust Enrichment* (n 14) 69, 73; A Burrows, *The Law of Restitution*, 3rd edn (Oxford, Oxford University Press, 2011) 36.

element of a successful claim in unjust enrichment, an enrichment at the claimant's expense, is missing'.[27]

Swadling's argument consists of two limbs. First, he argues that there is no enrichment because the defendant does not obtain legal title, merely possession.[28] This, however, is based upon an unduly narrow conception of enrichment.[29] Swadling's assertion that 'our legal system deals in rights, not things' is correct but incomplete, for as Chambers and Lodder have demonstrated, our legal system is actually concerned with value, rights, *and* value in respect of rights.[30] In cases involving the receipt of money where title does not pass, restitution is concerned with the money so far as it represents a fungible repository of value rather than a specific asset subject to a surviving proprietary interest.[31] The same point applies in cases involving the receipt of property other than money: though the defendant merely acquires a right of possession, and not legal title, that right of possession is valuable. The emphasis on value and the exchange capacity surpasses the need to consider technical rules about the form and passing of title. Enrichment follows the logic of the market, not the strict and abstract logic of the lawyer or legal academic.[32]

The second limb of Swadling's argument is to argue that, even if a defendant is enriched by the acquisition of a valuable right of possession, that enrichment has not come 'at the expense of the claimant' because 'it is an enrichment acquired through his own act, not one conferred on him by his victim'.[33] Burrows's response to this argument is to highlight its unduly narrow view of unjust enrichment as requiring a literal transfer. He explains that just as there is no transfer of a right in the case of services or the discharge of a debt or where the defendant uses the claimant's property, so too is the transfer of a right unnecessary in a case where the defendant receives money from the claimant.[34] The same point underlies the claim suggested in *Huyton*.[35] It also underlies the analysis of *Moses v Macferlan* above. There is no need for a right to have been assigned in these cases, nor in the cases considered below.

## (2) Discharge or Release from an Obligation

Where a defendant is enriched because he is no longer under an obligation to the claimant, it is the release of the obligation that connects the enrichment to the

[27] Swadling, 'Ignorance and Unjust Enrichment: The Problem of Title' (n 25) 658.
[28] ibid 644.
[29] Burrows, *The Law of Restitution* (n 26) 194–98; Lodder, *Enrichment in the Law of Unjust Enrichment and Restitution* (n 3) 170.
[30] See further R Grantham and C Rickett, 'Restitution, Property and Ignorance—A Reply to Mr Swadling' [1996] *Lloyd's Maritime and Commercial Law Quarterly* 463, 465.
[31] Fox, *Property Rights in Money* (n 2) [3.20]–[3.22].
[32] See above pp 37, 68–70.
[33] Swadling, 'Ignorance and Unjust Enrichment: The Problem of Title' (n 25) 650.
[34] Burrows, *The Law of Restitution* (n 26) 196–97.
[35] *Huyton SA v Peter Cremer GmbH & Co* (n 17).

claimant's loss of a corresponding right. Furthermore, and just like acquisition of rights cases, it is important that the enrichment and its connection to loss be correctly identified. In *FII*[36] the claimants would have used tax reliefs to offset their liability to pay lawful tax had they not used them to offset an unlawful tax. The Court of Appeal stated that 'the tax paid in year 2 or subsequent years was lawfully due and so cannot be the subject of recovery'.[37] With respect, this is problematic for the same reason as Birks's analysis of *Moses v Macferlan* above.[38] The relevant enrichment was not the tax paid in year 2, but the benefit to the Revenue resulting from not having to reduce the claimants' future tax liabilities under the tax relief scheme.[39] The claimants were not connected to the Revenue because they had paid tax but, rather, because they had used up their tax reliefs on unlawful taxes, and thereby released the Revenue from an obligation to offset their liability in respect of future taxes if and when those reliefs were used. The value of that obligation was realised the next time the claimants paid taxes to the Revenue and were unable to offset their liability, as they would have done otherwise.[40]

## (3) Use of Property

In *Edwards v Lee's Administrators*[41] the claimant's estate was awarded one-third of the profits made by the defendant from exhibiting a cave, one-third of which extended under the claimant's land. In chapter three we observed how the claimant's loss could be construed in different ways. Now we must consider how that loss was connected to the defendant's enrichment. Though the connection seems obvious, it must be articulated if we are to identify its similarities with other cases. The defendant's enrichment was connected to the claimant's loss because it arose from the use of the claimant's property by the defendant.

There is some overlap between this sort of case and those where the parties are connected by the acquisition of a right. For example, where the defendant obtains possession of personal property in respect of which the claimant continues to have title, he acquires a right of possession that forms the basis of his connection to the claimant.[42] And squatter's rights may arise following the occupation of real

[36] *FII Group Litigation (CA)* (n 4).
[37] ibid [182].
[38] See above pp 100–101.
[39] See further *Investment Trust Companies (In Liquidation) v Revenue and Customs Commissioners* [2012] EWHC 458 (Ch), [2012] STC 1150 [39] (Henderson J).
[40] On this analysis, junior counsel for the claimants need not have accepted the contention that 'there could have been no completed cause of action for unjust enrichment in year 1 because it would have been impossible to say at that point of time if, when and how much more tax would be paid in future years, if the reliefs had not been applied in year 1': *FII Group Litigation (CA)* [180]. The Revenue was enriched in year 1, and a specific claim for restoration of the tax reliefs might have been available at that time. All the contention established was the impossibility of calculating a personal claim based upon the as yet unrealised value of that enrichment.
[41] *Edwards v Lee's Administrators* 96 SW 2d 1028 (1936).
[42] See above pp 102–103.

property for substantial periods. But not every use of property entails the acquisition of a right. Use of real property without permission is generally one example. Another is the claim for restitution following use and occupation of the claimant's land, where the defendant has permission to occupy but no binding agreement has been reached.[43] The defendant's enrichment in these cases is connected to the claimant's loss because it arises from use of the claimant's property.

## (4) Performance of a Service

In *Greenwood v Bennett* Harper spent £226 on labour and materials repairing a stolen car for which he had innocently paid £75.[44] The owner of the car (Bennett) subsequently resumed possession and sold it for £400. Harper was awarded £226 'for the work he did on the car and of which [Bennett] had the benefit'.[45] Bennett's enrichment was connected to Harper's loss because Harper did work to Bennett's property.

This is a straightforward case. The connection in services cases is not, however, limited to tangible encounters with a defendant's property or person. Whether performance of a service connects the claimant and defendant turns upon the construction of the particular service in question, rather than its residuum. So if A performs a play for an audience including B, A will have performed a service for B even if there is no lasting impression on B.

This is most important in cases where, rather than doing work tangibly upon another person (such as a haircut) or their property (such as repairing a car), the service consists of doing something on another person's behalf. Services often consist of both. In *Way v Latilla*,[46] for example, in addition to providing Latilla with information about gold mines and concessions in West Africa, Way also represented him in the course of negotiating and acquiring concessions. If this had been all that Way had done he would still have been entitled to an award in respect of those services because services rendered by an agent not under contract, but nonetheless freely accepted, entitle the agent to a *quantum meruit* award from the principal.[47] Way's negotiations and acquisitions while in West Africa did not tangibly connect him to Latilla. The connection lay in the fact that Way was acting on Latilla's behalf.

As we shall see in section (5) below the connection in most of these cases can equally be explained as the satisfaction of a request, which is a different kind of connection from the performance of a service. It is possible, however, to conceive

43 *Mayor of Thetford v Tyler* (1845) 8 QB 95 (KB) 100 (Lord Denman CJ).
44 *Greenwood v Bennett* [1973] QB 195 (CA).
45 ibid 201 (Lord Denning MR).
46 *Way v Latilla* [1937] 3 All ER 759 (HL).
47 F Reynolds, *Bowstead & Reynolds On Agency*, 19th edn (P G Watts ed, London, Sweet & Maxwell Ltd, 2010) [7-009]; see, eg, *Craven-Ellis v Canons Ltd* [1936] 2 KB 403 (CA).

of performance cases in which there is no request. *Greenwood v Bennett* is one example. And a slight alteration to the facts of *Way v Latilla* provides another. Suppose that no request had actually been made and that Way (acting under a mistake as to this fact) had performed exactly the same negotiation services on Latilla's behalf. The connection between the parties could not be explained on the basis of a request.

The performance of a service can also explain the connection between the parties in difficult cases like *Planché v Colburn*.[48] Planché was contracted by the defendant publishers to write a book that was to be part of a series. When the series was cancelled, Planché terminated the contract for anticipatory breach. He had commenced researching and writing, but never tendered any work to the defendants. A jury award of £50 *quantum meruit* was upheld.[49]

The existence of an enrichment in *Planché v Colburn* (and its relevance to the law of unjust enrichment) is debated.[50] Nevertheless, that there was an enrichment should be accepted on either one of two bases. The first is that Planché's work saved the publishers time and labour which they would have spent in researching and writing the book themselves before the series was cancelled, and the fact that the publishers had contracted with him to do that work meant they could not argue the contrary.[51] The second is that, by analogy with contracts involving the production and delivery of ships,[52] the benefit contracted for in *Planché v Colburn* consisted not only of the end product but also the work of producing it.[53] Both of these conceptions of the enrichment in *Planché v Colburn* are consistent with the underlying definition of enrichment advanced by this book.[54]

The enrichment in *Planché v Colburn* having been identified, we must then explain its connection to Planché's loss. There are actually two explanations. The first is that Planché was researching and writing on behalf of the publishers. The second is that Planché was satisfying a request made by them. The second basis is discussed in section (5) below. Here the concern is with the first, according to which the relationship between the parties was effectively one of agency,[55] in the sense that Planché was doing work on behalf of the publishers. That

[48] *Planché v Colburn* (1831) 5 Car & P 58, 172 ER 876 (Assizes).

[49] ibid 61 (Tindal CJ).

[50] See generally C Mitchell and C Mitchell, '*Planché v Colburn* (1831)' in C Mitchell and P Mitchell (eds), *Landmark Cases in the Law of Restitution* (Oxford, Hart, 2006) especially 91–92.

[51] See further *Brenner v First Artists' Management Pty Ltd* [1993] 2 VR 221 (VSC) (Byrne J).

[52] Lodder, *Enrichment in the Law of Unjust Enrichment and Restitution* (n 3) 85–86 referring to *Hyundai Heavy Industries Co Ltd v Papadopoulos* [1980] 1 WLR 1129 (HL). See further *Menetone v Athawes* (1764) 3 Burr 1592, 97 ER 998 (KB) in which a ship-wright recovered for work and materials provided in repairing a ship which was destroyed in a fire before the work was complete.

[53] See further K Mason, JW Carter, and GJ Tolhurst, *Mason & Carter's Restitution Law in Australia*, 2nd edn (Sydney, LexisNexis Butterworths, 2008) [1168].

[54] See above pp 58–60.

[55] Such a relationship does not require a contract: see F Reynolds, *Bowstead & Reynolds* (n 47) [2-003].

connected his loss to their enrichment. The case is unexceptional in this respect.[56] In *Prickett v Badger*,[57] for example, the claimant estate agent was engaged by the defendant to find a buyer for a parcel of land. The claimant did considerable work and ultimately found a buyer. The defendant did not actually have any interest in the land in question. The claimant successfully sued the defendant for *quantum meruit*. As to the enrichment, the claimant's work saved the defendant the expense of doing it himself, even though it would have served no useful purpose because he had no interest in the land. The connection between the claimant's loss and the defendant's enrichment thus lay in the fact that the defendant had engaged the claimant as his agent.

A final case to consider is *Cobbe v Yeoman's Row Management Ltd*.[58] The claimant, relying on an oral agreement to purchase the defendant's property, spent considerable time and effort in applying for planning permission to erect townhouses on it. The defendant then withdrew from the agreement. The claimant's efforts had substantially increased the value of the property. The claimant was entitled to an award of *quantum meruit* in respect of the money and services he had provided, the basis of the award being unjust enrichment.[59] At first glance this would seem to be a straightforward performance of service case: Cobbe did work for the defendant in the course of obtaining the planning permission. We would therefore expect the case to have been decided in line with *Planché v Colburn* and similar cases. But it was not: the *quantum meruit* award was made contingent on Cobbe's instructing the architects whom he had engaged to permit the defendants to use the plans they had prepared, in respect of which the planning permission had been granted.[60] The House of Lords thus appears to have insisted upon Cobbe's work producing a residuum to the defendant, inconsistently with those cases where merely acting for another, or on another's behalf, was sufficient. Those cases can, however, be reconciled with *Cobbe* by appreciating the nature of Cobbe's services. Both parties had always understood that Cobbe was responsible for obtaining the planning permission at his own expense; that is to say he would take the risk that if no planning permission were obtained he would not recover his expenses. In obtaining the planning permission, therefore, Cobbe was not acting on behalf of the defendant—he was acting for himself. Properly construed, Cobbe's service was not the obtaining of planning permission on the defendant's behalf, but enabling the development of the defendant's land. Obtaining planning permission was a necessary part of that service, but it was not the whole service; the plans also had to be made available.

[56] See also *De Bernardy v Harding* (1853) 8 Ex 822 (Exch); *Menetone v Athawes* (n 52); *Bull v Sibbs* (1799) 8 Term Rep 327, 101 ER 1415 (KB). See further TA Baloch, *Unjust Enrichment and Contract* (Oxford, Hart, 2009) 137–139.

[57] *Prickett v Badger* (1856) 1 CB NS 296, 140 ER 123 (CP).

[58] *Cobbe v Yeoman's Row Management Ltd* [2008] UKHL 55, [2008] 1 WLR 1752.

[59] ibid [40] (Lord Scott; Lord Hoffmann, Lord Brown, and Lord Mance agreeing).

[60] ibid [45] (Lord Scott).

### (5) Satisfaction of a Request

As explained above, many services cases also involve the satisfaction of a request.[61] This is particularly important in older cases based upon the historical form of action for *quantum meruit*, the first two elements of which were (i) that the claimant had done certain work and (ii) that the work was done at the 'special instance and request' of the defendant.[62] Indeed, the request may also be indicative of enrichment.[63]

There are other request cases, however, that do not involve services, such as where satisfaction of the request consists of refraining from action, which turns out to be beneficial to the defendant. In such cases the only connection between the parties is the satisfaction of the defendant's request by the claimant. This occurred in *Gibb v Maidstone and Tunbridge Wells NHS Trust*.[64] The claimant undertook to accept termination of her employment as chief executive of the defendant NHS Trust and not to pursue any grievance or claim against the defendant. In return she was to receive two payments, the second of which the defendant later withheld on grounds that the agreement was *ultra vires*. That was met with the reply that, if the contract were *ultra vires*, then the defendant would have been unjustly enriched at the claimant's expense. The enrichments included the value of the claimant's statutory claim for unfair dismissal and the costs saved from contesting that claim or an internal grievance, and were alleged to have come at the expense of the claimant because she had 'lost her rights' to make a claim for unfair dismissal and to pursue a grievance process internally. The unjust enrichment claim succeeded in *dicta* in the Court of Appeal.[65] Lord Justice Laws emphasised that the case was not one involving the provision of money, goods, or services.[66] Loss and enrichment were connected because the claimant's forbearance in respect of claims against the defendant was done at the latter's request.

## (B) Multiple Connections

In *Investment Trust Companies (In Liquidation) v HMRC*,[67] Henderson J held that the English law of unjust enrichment included a general rule of 'direct enrichment' subject to limited exceptions.[68] While this general rule has come under increasing

[61] See further Baloch, *Unjust Enrichment and Contract* (n 56) 139.

[62] Lodder, *Enrichment in the Law of Unjust Enrichment and Restitution* (n 3) 78–79 citing JH Baker and S Milsom, *Sources of English Legal History: Private Law to 1750* (London, Butterworths, 1986) 474–75.

[63] See above (n 51) and accompanying text.

[64] *Gibb v Maidstone & Tunbridge Wells NHS Trust* (n 7) [32] (Laws LJ).

[65] ibid [36] (Laws LJ), [62] (Rimer LJ).

[66] ibid [37] (Laws LJ).

[67] *Investment Trust Companies (HC)* (n 39).

[68] ibid [67].

judicial scrutiny,[69] and even been doubted,[70] it appears entrenched for now. Judges have been reluctant to express an alternative general rule, preferring instead to deal with the particular facts of cases as they arise in the light of the position set out by Henderson J.[71]

This book challenges the existence of the direct enrichment rule in two stages. First, as we shall see in this section, the authorities do not support the view that unjust enrichment analysis is generally limited to singular connections involving only two parties. Secondly, and as we shall see in Part III, the real work performed by 'directness'—as that term appears in the existing case law—lies in the imposition of qualifications to liability arising despite the connection between enrichment and loss, and not in limiting the connections capable of supporting analysis in unjust enrichment to just one. For now, however, the focus is on the first point: a review of the authorities reveals *many* cases in which unjust enrichment analysis is sustainable beyond the limited situation of a single, 'direct' or 'immediate' connection that Henderson J had in mind. There is, therefore, no general rule of direct enrichment.

## (1) Sequential Connections: C to X to D

A sequential connection case is one in which C confers a benefit on a third party ('X') who then confers it on D.[72] The most common sequential connection cases involve a series of 'transactions', the identification of which involves processes of following or tracing. Transactions are dealt with separately in chapter six because one cannot understand their relevance (and that of tracing in particular) to unjust enrichment without analysing them as a coherent whole.[73]

Other cases do not entail transactions, but many of these, though they at first blush appear to involve sequential connections, can be analysed differently. Suppose C mistakenly pays D via an intermediary bank, X; C pays money to X, which is then transferred to the account of D. There appears to be a sequence of enrichments, but it is an illusion: when X credits D's account it does so as agent for its customer C.[74] C can claim against D because he stands in X's shoes. Such cases actually involve 'concurrent' connections rather than 'sequential' connections.[75]

[69] See, eg, *Investment Trust Companies v Revenue and Customs* [2015] EWCA Civ 82, [46]–[64] (Patten LJ).

[70] See *Bank of Cyprus UK Ltd v Menelaou* [2015] UKSC 66, [27] (Lord Clarke); *Relfo Ltd v Varsani* [2014] EWCA Civ 360, [88] (Arden LJ).

[71] See, eg, *Bank of Cyprus UK Ltd v Menelaou* (*UKSC*) (n 70), [32] (Lord Clarke); *Investment Trust Companies* (*CA*) (n 69), [64]–[68] (Patten LJ); *Relfo Ltd v Varsani* [2014] (*CA*) (n 70), [104] (Gloster LJ), [115] (Floyd LJ).

[72] See, eg, C Mitchell, 'Liability Chains' in S Degeling and J Edelman (eds), *Unjust Enrichment in Commercial Law* (Sydney, Thomson Reuters, 2008).

[73] See, eg, Burrows, *The Law of Restitution* (n 26) 117.

[74] Birks, *Unjust Enrichment* (n 14) 87.

[75] See below pp 114–115.

*BFC v Parc (Battersea)*[76] provides a compelling example of a successful unjust enrichment claim supported by sequential connections. The claimant lent money via a third party (Mr Herzig) to pay off a debt owed by Parc (the loan transaction having been structured in this way to avoid difficulties with Swiss regulatory authorities). The debt was secured by a charge over Parc's property, and the defendant held a second charge over that property. The claimant had not obtained security for its loan to Parc, but was promised that no one in the corporate group to which Parc belonged (which included the defendant) would seek repayment of their loan ahead of it. The defendant, however, was not bound by that promise. Following Parc's insolvency the claimant sought to be subrogated to the initial security that its loan moneys had been used to discharge. Subrogation was granted to prevent the defendant being enriched by the improvement in its position as second chargee. The defendant argued that unjust enrichment could not assist the claimant's case because the interposition of Mr Herzig meant the loan monies received via him were not at the expense of the claimant. Nevertheless, the claimant succeeded. As Lord Steyn explained:[77]

> Stripped to its essentials the argument of counsel for [the defendant] was that the interposition of the loan to Mr Herzig meant that the enrichment of [the defendant] was at the expense of Mr Herzig. The loan to Mr Herzig was a genuine one spurred on by the motive of avoiding Swiss regulatory requirements. But it was nevertheless no more than a formal act designed to allow the transaction to proceed. It does not alter the reality that [the defendant] was enriched by the money advanced by [the claimant] via Mr Herzig to Parc. To allow the interposition of Mr Herzig to alter the substance of the transaction would be pure formalism.

Lord Clyde similarly observed that the structural arrangements made with Mr Herzig in order to avoid a breach of the Swiss banking regulations did not prevent recognition of the reality of the loan transaction.[78] That reality was a connection between claimant and defendant, sufficient for unjust enrichment purposes, and despite the interposition of a third party: the enrichment went from C to X to D.

Along similar lines to *BFC v Parc (Battersea)* is the speech of Henderson J in *Investment Trust Companies*.[79] In that case the claimants had received services from fund managers. They paid money to those managers in the mistaken belief that it was due as Value Added Tax (VAT) on the services. The managers then accounted for this money to the defendant Revenue as output tax (by deducting sums which they had paid on associated supplies as input tax, and paying the defendant the net amount). It transpired that VAT should not have been charged on the services because they were exempt supplies (following a ruling by the European Court of Justice in an unrelated case). The managers recovered some of the money paid to

[76] *Banque Financière de la Cité SA v Parc (Battersea) Ltd* [1999] 1 AC 221 (HL).
[77] ibid 227 (Lord Steyn). See also 234 (Lord Hoffmann).
[78] ibid 238 (Lord Clyde).
[79] *Investment Trust Companies (HC)* (n 39).

the defendant under the applicable statutory scheme, s 80 of the Value Added Tax Act 1994, and passed that over to the claimants. The claimants, however, remained out of pocket because the statutory scheme had rendered some of the managers' statutory claims out of time, and all of them limited to the extent that the managers were prevented from recovering the amount of their input tax credits when claiming money paid as output tax. To recover their shortfall, the claimants brought claims in unjust enrichment against the defendant. Henderson J accepted that such claims could lie but for their exclusion under s 80(7) of the Value Added Tax Act 1994. In doing so, he accepted that the connection between the claimant and the defendant was sufficient for unjust enrichment purposes, despite the interposition of the managers.

Henderson J held that it was 'preferable to think in terms of a general requirement of direct enrichment, to which there are limited exceptions'.[80] He thus adopted a view of unjust enrichment in which sequential connections do not generally suffice. As has already been noted, this book disagrees with that interpretation of the law. Indeed, it will be alleged later in this book that other parts of Henderson J's speech in the case actually undermine his view of the 'general requirement'.[81] Leaving that larger point to one side, however, what is noteworthy about the remainder of Henderson J's speech is the nature of the supposed exception that he relied upon in holding that the general requirement of direct enrichment could be overcome. His Lordship directed attention to the particular qualities of the VAT scheme:[82]

> The scheme of VAT ... is to impose the burden of the tax on the final consumer, and to make the suppliers of the goods or services the collectors of the tax on behalf of the tax authorities. In other words, VAT is a tax on the consumer, collected by the supplier, and paid or accounted for to HMRC. Viewed in this way, the nexus between the consumer and HMRC could hardly be closer or stronger, and in economic terms the person at whose expense unlawful VAT is paid to HMRC is indubitably the consumer. I remind myself at this point that 'at the expense of' is not a statutory requirement, and ... can be satisfied by reference to the underlying commercial reality of a transaction. To recognise that the test is satisfied in the present case would not ... be to dismiss the structure of the VAT legislation as mere formalism, but rather to give due weight to the economic reality which explains and underpins that structure.

On the one hand, it is possible that this reasoning rests on the same sort of agency relationship as that arising between a bank and its customer in the third party payee example considered above: money paid by the customer as VAT to the supplier is collected on behalf of the Revenue.[83] If that is correct, then *Investment Trust Companies* is actually a case involving concurrent connections, and not sequential ones. But the idea that suppliers act as agents of the Revenue for VAT purposes (or

[80] ibid [67]. See further See, eg, *Investment Trust Companies (CA)* (n 69), [66]–[69] (Patten LJ).

[81] See below pp 179–180.

[82] *Investment Trust Companies (HC)* (n 39) [72]. See further *Investment Trust Companies (CA)* (n 69), [44]–[45] (Patten LJ).

[83] ibid [50].

any purpose for that matter) seems a stretch. On the other hand, Henderson J's concluding concern 'to give due weight to the economic reality which explains and underpins that structure' and for 'the common sense proposition that the enrichment of HMRC was indeed at the expense of the claimants'[84] transcends an unrealistic agency-based analysis. The better view is that, just like the House of Lords in *BFC v Parc (Battersea)*, Henderson J was concerned with the substance of what had gone on, rather than the form.

Still more importantly, this reading of *Investment Trust Companies* undermines the very idea of a general rule of direct enrichment. To say that 'reality' and 'common sense' are exceptions to a general rule of law is hard to accept.[85] A simpler view of law conforming to reality and common sense is preferable. On this view, HMRC's enrichment was at the expense of the claimants because the parties were connected sequentially.

Another case in which sequential connections sufficed for unjust enrichment purposes is the Privy Council's decision in *Blue Haven Enterprises Ltd v Tully*.[86] Blue Haven contracted to buy an estate from Tully and then developed it into a mature coffee plantation. Completion of the contract of sale, however, never occurred because the estate had previously been subject to a contract of sale between Tully and a third party, Robinson. Following a dispute over price, Tully had purported to terminate that contract but Robinson had gained an injunction restraining Tully from selling the estate. That injunction was ultimately affirmed. Robinson thereafter obtained possession of the estate from Blue Haven and registered title from Tully. Robinson thus 'became owner and possessor of an established coffee plantation, with all necessary infrastructure, the cost of which had been borne by Blue Haven'.[87] The connection between Blue Haven's loss and Robinson's enrichment was not decisive of the former's unjust enrichment claim, which instead failed at the unjust factor stage.[88]

Sequential connections can explain the connection between Blue Haven and Robinson. Blue Haven developed Tully's land, which was then acquired by Robinson. There were sequential connections between Blue Haven and Robinson: Blue Haven performed a service for Tully in respect of the land, and Robinson then acquired ownership of that land from Tully. The case therefore fits the pattern of an enrichment conferred by C upon X, which is then passed to D.

There is, however, a problem: because of his contract of sale with Tully, Robinson had an equitable interest in the land at the time when Blue Haven improved it. The

[84] ibid.

[85] See, eg, *Menelaou v Bank of Cyprus plc* [2013] EWCA Civ 1960 [62] (Moses LJ): 'There is no need to invoke the somewhat fuzzy concept of economic reality, which, like reliance on common sense … sometimes suggests that the author knows the result he seeks to achieve but is unable to articulate his reasons.' See further below pp 130–134.

[86] *Blue Haven Enterprises Ltd v Tully* [2006] UKPC 17.

[87] ibid [17].

[88] ibid [14], [26]. The critical fact was that shortly after Blue Haven entered into possession it had become aware of Robinson's claim.

case might therefore be analysed as one involving a single connection between Blue Haven and Robinson. Two points, however, warrant attention. First, it is not clear whether their Lordships considered Robinson's equitable interest relevant to Blue Haven's unjust enrichment claim. Secondly, their Lordships described Robinson's enrichment as his having '[become] the owner and in possession of an established coffee plantation, with the necessary infrastructure'.[89] This suggests that the relevant sequence of events was more than just the improvement of land in respect of which Robinson had an equitable interest. Indeed, the transition from equitable interest to possession and legal title required several steps in between.

Sequential connections can also explain recoupment and contribution cases. *Exall v Partridge*,[90] for example, was a recoupment case in which the claimant paid rent to the defendants' landlord in order to recover its carriage, which had been left on the defendants' premises for repair and then seized by the landlord for rent. The claimant recovered in money paid against the defendants.[91] The claimant and defendants were connected sequentially: the landlord acquired a right to the money from the claimant, which was then applied to discharge the defendants' rental debt. Recoupment cases in which the debt discharged was commonly owed, albeit that the claimant's liability was secondary to the defendant's, can be explained in the same way. In *Brook's Wharf & Bull Wharf Ltd v Goodman Bros*,[92] for example, the claimant successfully sought restitution from the defendant for money paid to customs on fur-skins belonging to the defendant. The claimant's payment to customs was applied to the defendant's benefit (the discharge of its tax liability) and so the claimant could sue in respect of the defendant's enrichment.

Likewise contribution cases: where C discharges a liability to X that was commonly owed with D, C's payment connects him with D: the money acquired by X having been applied to the benefit of D. The Civil Liability (Contribution) Act 1978 applies to cases where the common liability is in respect of compensation to pay damages.[93] The Act has been described as an application of the principle against unjust enrichment.[94] The same point has been made about cases outside the Act, such as those involving liability to pay a debt.[95]

A more complex case is *AMP Workers Compensation Services (NSW) Ltd v QBE Insurance Ltd*.[96] The claimant insurer (QBE) satisfied the judgment debt in respect of a claim brought by one employee against another following a negligently caused motor-accident. QBE had paid the money under a motor insurance policy held

[89] ibid [17].

[90] *Exall v Partridge* (1799) 8 Term Rep 308 (KB).

[91] See also *Johnson v Royal Mail Steam Packet Co* (1867) LR 3 CP 38 (CP).

[92] *Brook's Wharf & Bull Wharf Ltd v Goodman Bros* [1937] 1 KB 534 (CA).

[93] Civil Liability (Contribution) Act 1978 s 1.

[94] *Dubai Aluminium Co Ltd v Salaam* [2002] UKHL 48, [2003] 2 AC 366 [76] (Lord Hobouse).

[95] More controversial is whether the Act or the common law covers cases involving liability in respect of mistaken payments and knowing receipt. See generally *Charter plc v City Index* [2007] EWCA Civ 1382, [2008] Ch 313; Burrows, *The Law of Restitution* (n 26) 457.

[96] *AMP Workers Compensation Services (NSW) Ltd v QBE Insurance Ltd* [2001] NSWCA 267, (2001) 53 NSWLR 35.

by the employer that covered the negligent employee. It then sought contribution from the defendant insurer (AMP) with whom the employer had a workers' compensation policy that would have protected the employer if it had been sued by the injured employee. The fact that AMP had not been sued did not inhibit QBE's claim. QBE's payment of the judgment debt had extinguished the liability of the employer and, with it, AMP's liability to indemnify the employer.[97] The case therefore involved several connections in sequence: QBE paid money to the employee, which discharged the employer's obligation, in turn discharging AMP's obligation.

## (2) Concurrent Connections: C to X for D

There is another way to analyse recoupment and contribution cases, *viz* that the claimant and defendant are actually linked by one connection that is concurrent with another: the payment of money to one person in discharge of another's debt constituting an act done on that other's behalf. There are multiple connections, but only one is between the claimant and defendant. So in *Exall v Partridge*,[98] for example, payment of the defendant's debt to the landlord by the claimant was an act done on the former's behalf. *County of Carleton v City of Ottawa* is another example.[99] Carleton was statutorily obliged to provide care for mentally ill residents living within its territory, one of whom was Norah Baker. It fulfilled that duty by sending her to a facility run by the County of Lanark. When county boundaries were redrawn, Ms Baker became a resident of Ottawa and the statutory duty for her care shifted accordingly. Due to an administrative error, however, Carleton continued to pay for her care at the Lanark facility. The Supreme Court of Canada held that Carleton was entitled to restitution from Ottawa of the payments it had made for Ms Baker's care during the period in which Ottawa was responsible for her.[100] Carleton's payments to Lanark were, in effect, on Ottawa's behalf. The single action of paying the money was a benefit to both Lanark (who received the money) and Ottawa (whose statutory duty was discharged).

To a certain extent, whether these cases involve concurrent or sequential connections is an unhelpful digression into metaphysics; determining whether the application of the money for C's benefit occurs simultaneously with or just after payment to X makes no difference. In other cases, however, concurrent connections are the only explanation. One example is where a claimant performs a service or pays money for the benefit of one person under contract with another, such as occurred in *The Trident Beauty*.[101] In that case the claimant (Pan Ocean) had

[97] ibid [15] (Handley JA).
[98] *Exall v Partridge* (n 90).
[99] *County of Carleton v City of Ottawa* [1965] SCR 663 (SCC).
[100] ibid [10].
[101] *Pan Ocean Shipping Co Ltd v Creditcorp Ltd (The Trident Beauty)* [1994] 1 WLR 161 (HL).

time-chartered a ship from Trident, which had assigned its right to hire charges to the defendant (Creditcorp). Pan Ocean paid advance hire directly to Creditcorp for a period when the ship was off-hire and later sought to recover that payment. Pan Ocean's payment thus entailed the acquisition of a right by Creditcorp and an act on Trident's behalf. There were thus two connections, but they were not sequential. Nor did they need to be, for Pan Ocean had paid the money to Creditcorp and was therefore connected to it by that single connection. However, this did not mean that Pan Ocean could claim the payment from Creditcorp in unjust enrichment. As we shall see in Part III, the claim failed for the separate reason that liability was qualified by the contractual regime governing the parties' relationship. Note, however, that the failure of the claim had nothing to do with the absence of a connection between enrichment and loss.

These and other cases,[102] where C confers a benefit on D that constitutes performance of a service or satisfaction of a request for a third party (X), are not on all fours with sequential connection cases. The connections in these cases are concurrent. Cases involving benefits conferred by an agent are also of this kind. In *Stevenson v Mortimer*, Lord Mansfield held that where an agent pays money on behalf of a principal, and that money is not due, either the agent or the principal may bring an action to recover it back, the agent by the authority of the principal and the principal because it was paid by his agent.[103] It was by application of this principle that Moore-Bick J held in *Niru Battery (No 1)* that both the bank and its customer could claim against the defendant.[104] In such a case the principal is connected to the payee because the principal is in a relationship of agency with the payer.[105] *Chief Constable of the Greater Manchester Police v Wigan Athletic AFC Ltd* provides another example.[106] The Chief Constable claimed the unpaid balance for policing services provided to the defendant football club at matches. A large part of the case (and its ultimate failure in the Court of Appeal) turned on the enrichment inquiry. It was accepted, however, that if the club had been enriched, it was at the expense of the Chief Constable: the physical policing services were rendered by individual officers as agents of the Chief Constable.[107]

[102] See also *Hampton v Glamorgan* [1917] AC 13 (HL); *Brown & Davis Ltd v Galbraith* [1972] 1 WLR 997 (CA); *Lloyds Bank plc v Independent Insurance Co Ltd* [2000] QB 110 (CA); *Lumbers v W Cook Builders Pty Ltd (In Liquidation)* [2008] HCA 27, (2008) 232 CLR 635.

[103] *Stevenson v Mortimer* (1778) 2 Cowp 805, 98 ER 1372 (KB) 806.

[104] *Niru Battery Manufacturing Co v Milestone Trading Ltd (No 1)* [2002] EWHC 1425 (Comm), [2002] 2 All ER (Comm) 705 [145].

[105] See further *Hampton v Glamorgan* (n 102), in which the claimant subcontractor carried out work for a school built for the defendant pursuant to a lump-sum contract between the defendant and the main contractor. The main contactor having failed to pay, the House of Lords held that, as the main contractor had not acted as the defendant's agent, the claimant could not recover from the defendant.

[106] *Chief Constable of Greater Manchester v Wigan Athletic AFC Ltd* [2008] EWCA Civ 1449, [2009] 1 WLR 1580.

[107] ibid [49] (Sir Andrew Morritt C).

## (3) Interceptions: X to D, instead of C

Interception involves receipt of a benefit by a defendant that ought to have gone to the claimant.[108] Birks used the expression 'interceptive subtraction' to describe these cases. 'Subtraction' is superfluous, however, once we acknowledge that loss is already a necessary feature of unjust enrichment. The issue is how that loss is connected to the defendant's enrichment. Interception is the answer. In *Re Diplock*,[109] for example, the executors of a will had paid sums of money to charities pursuant to a bequest that was void as a matter of law. The money ought therefore to have gone to the next of kin, who were entitled to a personal remedy against the charities, subject to the exhaustion of their claim against the executors.

Smith is critical of interceptive subtraction. He explains that if D receives a benefit from a third party (X) which ought to have gone to C, then C should not be allowed to recover against D while his rights against X are still intact.[110] This is why, Smith initially argued, the House of Lords in *Re Diplock* insisted that the claimant exhaust its remedies against the executors before proceeding with its claim against the charities.[111] Smith's argument proceeded on a dichotomy between 'general' and 'special' cases. In the general case, C's rights against X remain intact, and so C suffers no loss and therefore cannot bring an unjust enrichment claim against D.[112] In the special case, however, C's rights against X are discharged, and so C does suffer a loss and may therefore bring an unjust enrichment claim against D.[113]

Smith ultimately abandoned this analysis of *Re Diplock*,[114] though he maintained it in respect of other special cases, such as those involving usurpation of office.[115] Nevertheless, it is worthwhile considering his initial treatment of *Re Diplock* as a litmus test for his arguments with respect to interceptions generally. Smith's argument fits the view expressed in this book insofar as loss is a necessary feature of unjust enrichment. That is the first part of the 'at the expense of the claimant' inquiry. The further argument, however, that the special cases involve 'straightforward, direct subtraction'[116] is a gloss on the connection between loss and enrichment. Interception cases are not on all fours with single connection

[108] See generally Birks, *Unjust Enrichment* (n 14) 75; P Birks, *An Introduction to the Law of Restitution* (n 14) 133–38.

[109] *Re Diplock* [1948] Ch 465 (CA), aff'd sub nom *Ministry of Health v Simpson* [1951] AC 251 (HL).

[110] L Smith, 'Three-Party Restitution: A Critique of Birks' Theory of Interceptive Subtraction' (1991) 11 *Oxford Journal of Legal Studies* 481.

[111] ibid 499.

[112] ibid 488.

[113] ibid 493.

[114] Smith, 'Unjust Enrichment, Property and the Structure of Trusts' (n 21), 441–444. Smith's latest view of the case is that the claim was based 'on title, including equity's fault-based rules for the protection of title by personal liability'.

[115] ibid 419.

[116] Smith, 'Three-Party Restitution: A Critique of Birks' Theory of Interceptive Subtraction' (n 110) 493.

cases such as those involving mistaken payment. The charities in *Re Diplock* were paid by the executor, and not by the next of kin.

Further authorities supporting interception as a basis for connection have been collected and thoroughly analysed elsewhere.[117] Chief among them are cases where the defendant usurps the claimant's office, and then receives money from a third party to which the claimant was entitled as the rightful office-holder. The claimant can claim the money from the defendant in these and analogous circumstances, despite the fact that the money has not been paid by the claimant. In *Official Custodian for Charities v Mackey (No 2)* Nourse J explained:[118]

> [I]t is of the essence of all those cases both that there is a contract or some other current obligation between the third party and the plaintiff on which the defendant intervenes and that the third party is indebted to the plaintiff in the precise amount of the sum which he pays to the defendant, so that he cannot claim repayment from the defendant in the face of a claim made against the defendant by the plaintiff. It is that which enables the plaintiff to sue the defendant without joining the third party, who no longer has any interest in the subject matter of the suit.

The principle did not apply in that case. The claimant landlords had leased property to a company, who then sub-let it and raised money on mortgages. The mortgagees appointed joint-receivers who collected rents from sub-lessees. The company forfeited its lease to the claimants following an order for compulsory winding up, but the receivers continued to receive rent from the sub-lessees. The claimants sought to recover this rent from the receivers, and failed. Nourse J held that the sublessees did not owe anything to the claimants and that this was 'probably conclusive of the point'.[119] He added that, even if an obligation had been owed, the extent of that obligation was not necessarily 'the precise equivalent of the sums which they paid to the receivers'.[120]

The issue that tends to arise in interception cases is not whether interception is a valid basis of connection, but whether that which was allegedly intercepted was truly 'on its way' to the claimant. This has been expressed as an issue of certainty.[121] By insisting on a legal obligation between the defendants and claimants in *Mackey*

[117] See, eg, Birks, *An Introduction to the Law of Restitution* (n 14) 133–38. See also G Jones, *Goff & Jones: The Law of Restitution*, 7th edn (London, Sweet & Maxwell Ltd, 2006) [1-044] fn 19 Chs 28–29, where the cases are arranged by the following categories: 'Attornment', 'Cases Where the Defendant Without Right Intervenes Between the Claimant and a Third Party', 'Claims Under a Will or Intestacy or Under an Inter Vivos Trust', and 'Perfection of Imperfect Gifts in Favour of Intended Donees'. Whether these are all true interception is debateable. Peter Birks, for example, considered attornment a 'false interception'. See Birks, *Unjust Enrichment* (n 14) 78. This appears to be the position adopted in Jones, *Goff & Jones* (n 117) itself, where it is stated (at [28-003]): 'Attornment creates a right of property in a specific asset. … The act of attornment is equivalent to a declaration of trust.' See further Smith, 'Three-Party Restitution: A Critique of Birks' Theory of Interceptive Subtraction' (n 110) 506–08.

[118] *Official Custodian for Charities v Mackey (No 2)* [1985] 1 WLR 1308 (Ch) 1314–15.

[119] ibid 1315.

[120] ibid.

[121] See further Birks, *An Introduction to the Law of Restitution* (n 14) 134.

*(No 2)*, Nourse J equated certainty with legal entitlement.[122] That is, the rent from the sublessees must have been subject to an obligation owed to the claimants. The much earlier case of *Boyter v Dodsworth*[123] was decided along subtly different lines. The claimant belfry sexton failed in an action for money had and received against the defendant who had usurped his office and taken money from church visitors. The action failed because the money given to the defendant by visitors was paid as tips for the work he had done in showing them the church. Two matters informed the court's reasoning. First, the money had been paid to the defendant as tips for work he, and not the claimant, had actually done.[124] Secondly, the sums of money, being as they were paid as tips, were not fees.[125] These two points do not sit easily alongside each other if 'fees' are equated with a legal entitlement. It seems reasonably clear, given the court's emphasis on the first point, that if the claimant had actually done the work and had been the intended recipient of the visitor's gratuities, the claim would have succeeded if the defendant had intercepted them, even though their status as gratuities meant they were not paid under legal obligation. 'Fees' were not synonymous with a legal entitlement, but with something closer to factual certainty: whether 'but for' the defendant's usurpation of the claimant's office the latter would have received the money paid by visitors to the church.

The line between factual certainty and legal entitlement is not always clear. The preferable view, however, seems to be that a high threshold of factual certainty is necessary, and that legal entitlement can satisfy this threshold. This underlies Birks's view of *Re Diplock* that '[t]he money which the charities received was, as a matter of law, destined to go to them'.[126] Birks insisted on a test of factual certainty, with a heavy onus resting on the claimant to satisfy that test.[127] In *Re Diplock* that onus was satisfied by the underlying equity against the executor of the estate to give the money to the next of kin. Legal entitlement satisfied the test of factual certainty. Nourse J's dicta in *Mackey (No 2)* about equivalence between the obligation owed to the claimants and the money received by the defendant can also be explained on this basis. The fact that the sums in question were different was contrary to a conclusion that a legal entitlement might otherwise establish. The inquiry was ultimately factual: was the money received by the defendant destined for the claimants? The fact that the sums of money received by the defendant were not the same as those owed to the claimant suggested that it was not.

[122] See further G Virgo, *The Principles of the Law of Restitution*, 3rd edn (Oxford, Oxford University Press, 2015) 112–13.

[123] *Boyter v Dodsworth* (1796) 6 Term Rep 681 (KB).

[124] ibid 772.

[125] Ibid. 'If there had been regular fees due for the duties performed, and the defendant had intruded into the offices, the plaintiff might either have supported an action for money had and received or for disturbing him in his offices' (Lord Kenyon). 'If there were any appropriated fees, the case would be different' (Grose J).

[126] Birks, *Unjust Enrichment* (n 14) 76.

[127] ibid. cf Jones, *Goff & Jones: The Law of Unjust Enrichment*, 8th edn (London, Sweet & Maxwell, 2011) para 6–55.

The Montana case of *Valley County v Thomas* further illustrates how legal entitlement serves a subsidiary role to what is truly a factual inquiry.[128] A state law provided for licensing of motor vehicles by the county in which the vehicle was owned. The claimant (Valley County) alleged that the defendant (McCone County) had unlawfully issued licences and collected licence fees for vehicles owned by Valley County residents, and sought restitution of the fees exacted. The Supreme Court of Montana held that if Valley, not McCone, had been entitled to issue the licences, then Valley was entitled to the fees. The Court held in Valley's favour. This cannot be explained on the basis of legal entitlement. Valley was entitled to issue the licences and, if it did, it would then become entitled to fees in respect of those licences. McCone's issuance of the licences, however, did not entitle Valley to the fees, and so there was no 'current obligation' (to use Nourse J's terminology from *Mackey (No 2)*). What Valley had was a legal entitlement to issue the licences, which would then generate an entitlement to fees, but that entitlement had not crystallised, nor could it following the issue of the licences by McCone: those licences remained valid unless cancelled, and so there was nothing left for Valley to issue. The highest that could be said of Valley's position, therefore, was that it was a factual certainty that if it had exercised its entitlement to issue the licences, it would have collected fees on those licences in accordance with its ensuing legal entitlement.

[128] *Valley County v Thomas, County Treasurer et al* 109 Mont 345 (1939) (SC Mont).

# 5

# Generalisations

For the law of unjust enrichment to develop in accordance with the ordinary method of the common law, its components, including attribution, must be ordered and defined by identifying the relevant characteristics common to new and existing relationships.[1] To do this, the characteristics common to the different connections between enrichment and loss identified in chapter four must be examined and appropriately generalised. That is the aim of this chapter: to extract from the different cases a single test of attribution in unjust enrichment. The two prevailing tests are those of 'transfer' and 'causation', but neither is satisfactory. A third generalisation—the 'but for' counterfactual—is, however, more promising.

## (A) Transfer

The view that the connection between the parties to an unjust enrichment claim is one of transfer is widely accepted. Smith, for example, has explained that the normative justification of restitution of unjust enrichment is the concern of corrective justice to reverse defective transfers.[2] Elaborating on 'transfer', he explains:[3]

> Unjust enrichment includes both a material gain by the defendant and a material loss by the plaintiff. Moreover, the loss and gain do not come together by random chance. They are two sides of the same coin—that coin being a transfer of wealth from plaintiff to defendant. There is a nexus of exchange between the parties. This nexus gives an 'articulated unity' to their bilateral relationship in a transaction which is paradigmatically within Aristotle's conception of corrective justice.

The Supreme Court of Canada echoed this view in *Kingstreet Investments* when it stated that restitution functions to correct a normatively defective transfer.[4]

[1] See above pp 6–11.

[2] L Smith, 'Restitution: The Heart of Corrective Justice' (2001) 79 *Texas Law Review* 2115, 2135. See also A Burrows, *The Law of Restitution*, 3rd edn (Oxford, Oxford University Press, 2011) 36; J Edelman, 'The Meaning of Loss and Enrichment' in R Chambers, C Mitchell, and J Penner (eds), *Philosophical Foundations of The Law of Unjust Enrichment* (Oxford, Oxford University Press, 2009) 224; M Rush, *The Defence of Passing On* (Oxford, Hart, 2006) 144–46.

[3] Smith, 'Restitution: The Heart of Corrective Justice' (n 2) 2141.

[4] *Kingstreet Investments Ltd v New Brunswick (Finance)* [2007] SCC 1, [2007] 1 SCR 3, [32] (Bastarache J, the Court concurring). See also *Benedetti v Sawiris* [2013] UKSC 50, [2013] 3 WLR 351, [97] (Lord Reed).

And in *Commissioner of State Revenue (Vic)* Mason CJ stated that '[r]estitutionary relief … operates to restore to the claimant what has been transferred from the claimant to the defendant whereby the defendant has been unjustly enriched'.[5] And in *Menelaou v Bank of Cyprus UK Ltd*, Floyd LJ in the Court of Appeal and Lord Clarke in the Supreme Court each approved the analysis contained in *Goff & Jones* to the effect that the expression 'at the claimant's expense' reflects the principle that unjust enrichment is concerned with 'the reversal of transfers of value between claimants and defendants'.[6] Despite this widespread acceptance, however, the view that unjust enrichment is concerned with 'transfers' is fraught with difficulties that undermine its utility as a test for connection between enrichment and loss.[7]

## (1) The Limits of Transfer

In chapter four it was observed that there is no 'transfer of a right' in the case of services, discharge of a debt or uses of property.[8] For example, no right in respect of the cave was transferred in *Edwards v Lee's Administrators*. The same is true in cases where a right is acquired by some other mechanism such as the endorsement in *Moses v Macferlan* or taking possession of tangibles in *Huyton*[9] and *Holiday v Sigil*.[10] Nor is there a transfer in cases involving the release from an obligation. And as for the performance of services:[11] if C performs a valuable service for D, it is not the case that C held something of value and then D took possession of it. We do not hold the value of our services in advance, and if we cannot hold that value it makes little sense to speak of transferring it.[12]

The limits of 'transfer of value' are exposed when we recall that value is an abstract standard for comparison and exchange,[13] rather than something that actually moves between people. In the case of things and rights to things, value is

[5] *Commissioner of State Revenue (Vic) v Royal Insurance Australia Ltd* [1994] HCA 61, 182 CLR 51 75. Affirmed in *Roxborough v Rothmans of Pall Mall Australia Ltd* [2001] HCA 68, (2001) 208 CLR 516, [26] (Gleeson CJ, Gaudron and Hayne JJ).

[6] *Menelaou v Bank of Cyprus UK Ltd* [2013] EWCA Civ 1960 [29] (Floyd LJ), and *Bank of Cyprus UK Ltd v Menelaou* [2015] UKSC 66 [23] (Lord Clarke) citing C Mitchell, P Mitchell, and S Watterson (eds), *Goff & Jones: The Law of Unjust Enrichment*, 8th edn (London, Sweet & Maxwell, 2011) para 6.01.

[7] See generally, S Watterson, 'Direct Transfers in the Law of Unjust Enrichment' (2011) *Current Legal Problems* 435.

[8] See above p 103.

[9] *Huyton SA v Peter Cremer GmbH & Co* [1999] 1 Lloyd's Rep 620 (QB).

[10] *Holiday v Sigil* (1826) 2 Car & P 176 (Assizes).

[11] See generally J Penner, 'Value, Property and Unjust Enrichment' in R Chambers, C Mitchell, and J Penner (eds), *Philosophical Foundations of the Law of Unjust Enrichment* (Oxford, Oxford University Press 2009).

[12] See further ibid 310–11. Cf J Edelman and E Bant, *Unjust Enrichment in Australia* (Oxford, Oxford University Press, 2006) 129–30. See also J Harris, 'Doctrine, Justice, and Home-sharing' (1999) 19 *Oxford Journal of Legal Studies* 421, 444.

[13] AVM Lodder, *Enrichment in the Law of Unjust Enrichment and Restitution* (Oxford, Hart, 2012) 44. See above p 26.

a quality they possess. And because rights and things can be legally and literally conveyed, we tend to speak of there being a 'transfer' of value when that occurs.[14] Services, however, cannot be described in this way; they do not transfer value from one person to another.[15] The same applies where the defendant's enrichment is the release of an obligation, or a saving, such as where the claimant abstains from acting at the request of the defendant, like in *Gibb*.[16] There the claimant's forbearance was beneficial to the defendant because it saved the defendant considerable expense. Nothing was actually conveyed between the parties.

Cases involving the discharge of a liability, like *County of Carleton v City of Ottawa*,[17] are more borderline. There is no transfer of right in these cases, but there may be a transfer of value if we conceive of them as involving sequential connections: the value of money paid by the claimant to the third party is transferred to the defendant by its application for the relief of the latter's liability.

Interception cases present a final difficulty. We have already noted Smith's analysis of so-called 'general' and 'special' cases.[18] In the general case the claimant's rights against the third party remain intact; there is no loss, and so the claimant cannot bring an unjust enrichment claim. Instead, the third party can bring a claim. In contrast, in the special case the claimant's rights are discharged, and so there is a loss. There is no transfer, however, between the claimant and defendant. The claimant suffers a loss, but it is a loss against the third party, not against the defendant. And the defendant is enriched, but by the third party, not the claimant. The claimant's loss follows a transfer between the third party and the defendant, but it is a gloss to say that there was a transfer between the claimant and defendant.

## (2) The Taxonomical Role of Transfer

It may be that these criticisms miss the point. Smith, after all, presents 'transfer' as providing an 'articulated unity' to the bilateral relationship between the claimant and defendant in an unjust enrichment claim.[19] He also explains that it is unnecessary for anything to pass from the claimant to the defendant to qualify as a transfer.[20] Understood in this way, 'transfer' is not a test for connection between a claimant and a defendant. The nexus is abstract rather than tangible.[21]

'Transfer' therefore achieves nothing more than the expression 'at the expense of the claimant'. The point has been made that this is not a statutory expression, and should not be interpreted as if it were: the real question is not what those

[14] Smith, 'Restitution: The Heart of Corrective Justice' (n 2) 2142.

[15] See above pp 35–36.

[16] *Gibb v Maidstone & Tunbridge Wells NHS Trust* [2010] EWCA Civ 678 [32] (Laws LJ).

[17] *County of Carleton v City of Ottawa* [1965] SCR 663 (SCC).

[18] L Smith, 'Three-Party Restitution: A Critique of Birks' Theory of Interceptive Subtraction' (1991) 11 *Oxford Journal of Legal Studies* 481. See above p 116.

[19] Smith, 'Restitution: The Heart of Corrective Justice' (n 2) 2141, 2169. See above p 120.

[20] ibid 2142.

[21] ibid. See also Lodder, *Enrichment in the Law of Unjust Enrichment and Restitution* (n 13) 50.

words mean but what constitutes a sufficient connection between the claimant and defendant in an unjust enrichment claim.[22] But it also follows that the question cannot be answered by simply restating it in another form: 'Was there a transfer?' Overgeneralisation does not aid the resolution of substantive legal problems.[23]

'Transfer' is not unique in this respect. Another popular generalisation of the relationship between defendant and claimant in unjust enrichment is that the defendant's enrichment must come 'from' the claimant. 'From', however, is not a straightforward concept.[24] True, we can and do describe certain kinds of benefits as coming 'from' someone else, such as £100 received 'from' a grandparent at Christmas. But when the benefit is the performance of a service, the discharge of an obligation, the use of property, or the satisfaction of a request, 'from' requires stretching. We may, for example, describe the benefit of a service coming 'from' another person in the sense that it comes 'from' their labour, but that really adds nothing to the analysis of *why* each situation is like the other.[25] The 'from' in a simple payment case is different from the 'from' in a discharge, service or other case. If the ultimate goal is to explain why factually different cases are relevantly similar to one another for the purpose of developing the law, then more work needs to be done than sweeping everything under the one intuitive heading (be it 'transfer', 'from', or something else) without further explanation.

To a certain extent, these shortcomings are merely linguistic and terminological. Birks argued that such problems could be overcome by insisting on an enlargement of the everyday usages of words within the limited vocabulary of the English language.[26] Whether this is truly attainable is debatable. Indeed, one of the High Court of Australia's criticisms of 'unjust enrichment as a definitive legal principle according to its own terms' is precisely that legal taxonomy can incorrectly restrict or expand the development of legal principle.[27] That point cuts both ways. On the one hand are cases in which recourse to unjust enrichment has been eschewed on the basis that overgeneralisation may stultify established legal principle.[28] On the other hand, as we have seen in cases involving the retention of title, reliance on the concept of 'transfer' improperly restricts the extension of unjust enrichment analysis.[29] In both instances taxonomy has a substantial effect on the application of principle. This problem reflects a tension between two aims encountered

[22] See above p 1.

[23] *Uren v First National Home Finance Ltd* [2005] EWHC 2529 (Ch) [22] (Mann J). See generally K Mason, JW Carter, and GJ Tolhurst, *Mason & Carter's Restitution Law in Australia*, 2nd edn (Sydney, LexisNexis Butterworths, 2008) Ch 1 [109].

[24] P Birks, *Unjust Enrichment*, 2nd edn (Oxford, Oxford University Press, 2005) 74. See above p 84–85.

[25] See, eg, Harris (n 12) 444.

[26] Birks, *Unjust Enrichment* (n 24) 167–68.

[27] *Roxborough* (n 5) [74] (Gummow J) referring to *David Securities Pty Ltd v Commonwealth Bank of Australia* 378–79 (Mason CJ, Deane, Toohey, Gaudron, and McHugh JJ).

[28] See, eg, *Lumbers v W Cook Builders Pty Ltd (In Liquidation)* [2008] HCA 27, (2008) 232 CLR 635; *Farah Constructions Pty Ltd v Say-Dee Pty Ltd* [2007] HCA 22, (2007) 230 CLR 89; *Pan Ocean Shipping Co Ltd v Creditcorp Ltd (The Trident Beauty)* [1994] 1 WLR 161 (HL). See below Part III.

[29] See above pp 102–103.

throughout law generally: formulating principles in clear terms on the one hand, and ensuring their correct application on the other. To the extent that it is possible to resolve this tension, however, we must also be mindful that clarity will not be achieved by distorting language.[30]

## (B) Causal and Counterfactual Analyses

Various authorities support the view that attribution in unjust enrichment requires a causal relationship between loss and enrichment. In *Uren*, for example, Mann J stated that '[i]t is not enough to say that the defendant has had the benefit of the expenditure by the claimant; there must … be some causal connection or nexus'.[31] Professor Virgo has similarly argued that it is essential to focus on the 'at the claimant's expense' requirement as a causative principle.[32] Mitchell and Watterson have gone further, describing 'at the claimant's expense' as a 'simple causal nexus' and adding that this basic requirement should not be glossed over.[33] Birks's view is more dynamic, arguing that in the particular context of remote recipient cases, a causal relationship rather than direct transfer can satisfy the requirement.[34]

The causal account is not without its detractors. Burrows has suggested that a mere 'but for' causal test is insufficient because it 'would extend the ambit of unjust enrichment too far',[35] while Smith argues that a defendant 'cannot be made liable simply because she has a gain, the claimant has suffered a loss, and there is some kind of causal connection between the two. More is required.'[36] The potency of these criticisms, however, necessarily depends on appreciating the entirety of unjust enrichment analysis. Although this book ultimately rejects 'causation' as the appropriate test of attribution in unjust enrichment, the test proposed in its place

[30] See, eg, P Birks, *An Introduction to the Law of Restitution*, revised edn (Oxford, Clarendon Press, 1989) 21; Birks, *Unjust Enrichment* (n 24) 271–74.

[31] *Uren* (n 23) [23].

[32] G Virgo, *The Principles of the Law of Restitution*, 3rd edn (Oxford, Oxford University Press, 2015) 160–64.

[33] C Mitchell and S Watterson, *Subrogation: Law and Practice* (Oxford, Oxford University Press, 2007) para 5.03; Watterson (n 7); C Mitchell, 'Liability Chains' in S Degeling and J Edelman (eds), *Unjust Enrichment in Commercial Law* (Sydney, Thomson Reuters, 2008). See also M McInnes, '"At the Plaintiff's Expense": Quantifying Restitutionary Relief' (1998) 57 *Cambridge Law Journal* 477 arguing that 'at the expense of the claimant' entails a 'causally related plus and minus'. See further *Pettkus v Becker* [1980] 2 SCR 834 (SCC) [49].

[34] P Birks, '"At the Expense of the Claimant": Direct and Indirect Enrichment in English Law' in D Johnston and R Zimmermann (eds), *Unjustified Enrichment: Key Issues in Comparative Perspective* (Cambridge, Cambridge University Press, 2002), 518–24.

[35] Burrows, *The Law of Restitution* (n 2) 65–66. But see A Burrows, *A Restatement of the English Law of Unjust Enrichment* (Oxford, Oxford University Press, 2012) 44, where it is suggested that 'at the claimant's expense' describes the need for 'causation' between the claimant and the defendant's enrichment.

[36] Smith, 'Restitution: The Heart of Corrective Justice' (n 2) 2174.

functions in a similar way insofar as liability is qualified by matters distinct from attribution. On this approach, Burrows's and Smith's concerns are not dismissed, but merely arise elsewhere in unjust enrichment analysis.

This approach resembles the division of causal analysis in contract and tort between components often expressed as 'factual causation' and 'legal causation'.[37] Hart and Honoré,[38] for example, relied on causation as a means for generalising the attribution of responsibility by reference to factual and moral considerations. Their approach followed a division between fact and policy that consisted of three stages. First were factual issues of causation: (i) 'but for' causation; (ii) tapered by common sense notions of causation (not considerations of policy). Second were considerations of policy or scope: (iii) whether, as a matter of policy, the law ought to enlarge or restrict liability independently of causal connection. Such a division is a continuing feature within causation literature. Professor Stapleton has adopted a similar structure:[39] (i) identifying the purpose of the overall inquiry; (ii) a factual enquiry of 'involvement'; (iii) normative questions of responsibility. Writing extra-judicially, Lord Hoffmann advanced a four-pronged approach with greater emphasis on the legal nature of the causation question:[40] (i) the identification of a prescribed causal connection between a wrongful act and the damage for which one is held liable; (ii) the question of what should count as a sufficient causal connection is a question of law, just as is the question of what makes an act wrongful; (iii) the causal connection, the most commonly prescribed being the standard criteria examined by Hart and Honoré, involving moral notions of what would fairly delimit the responsibility of a defendant; and (iv) reasons to deviate from the standard criteria. These causal analyses have largely developed in the context of liability (be it civil or criminal) for damage or loss based on wrongdoing, but there is no reason why they cannot apply to gains-based liability in unjust enrichment. Indeed, academic literature[41] and decided cases[42] suggest they already have.

Ultimately, however, this book rejects causation as the appropriate test of attribution in unjust enrichment, for two reasons. First, it erroneously conflates a counterfactual relationship with causation. Secondly, the direction of the relationship between enrichment and loss is not uniform across unjust enrichment cases in which a connection between the two has been held to arise. To overcome these difficulties, this book proposes the subtly different generalisation of a counterfactual relationship between enrichment and loss. The counterfactual reflects the

[37] See, eg, P Cane, *Atiyah's Accidents, Compensation and the Law*, 7th edn (Cambridge, Cambridge University Press, 2006) Ch 5.

[38] HLA Hart and T Honoré, *Causation in the Law*, 2nd edn (Oxford, Clarendon Press, 1985).

[39] J Stapleton, 'Choosing What We Mean by "Causation" in the Law' (2008) 73 *Missouri Law Review* 433.

[40] L Hoffmann, 'Causation' (2005) 121 *Law Quarterly Review* 592, 596–97.

[41] See especially E Bant, 'Causation and Scope of Liability in Unjust Enrichment' [2009] *Restitution Law Review* 60.

[42] See, eg, *Gibb* (n 16) [32] (Laws LJ).

underlying unity between enrichment and loss necessary for unjust enrichment analysis based upon corrective justice and the parties' exchange capacities.

## (1) Non-causal Counterfactuals

A counterfactual is a conditional statement, expressing the idea that one event will occur if another event does too. It is expressed in the form 'but for', where the relationship between two events is tested to be true or false.[43] In chapter four we observed that the paradigm unjust enrichment case involves the acquisition of a right.[44] In such cases the defendant's enrichment cannot occur unless the claimant suffers a loss. In *Cressman*, for example, McDonald could not acquire the right to the plate without Cressman's estate losing it. The same logic applies where the defendant acquires a right other than by assignment. In *Moses v Macferlan* the only way Macferlan could acquire a right against Moses was for the latter to take on a liability, and in *Huyton* the only way Huyton could possess the wheat was for Cremer to lose possession. In all these cases the defendant could not gain without the claimant losing. Cases involving the release of an obligation, the use of property, the performance of services and the satisfaction of a request can be explained in a similar fashion. The Revenue in *FII* could not benefit from the exhaustion of the tax reliefs unless the claimant exhausted them. It was the very act of the defendant's use of the claimant's cave in *Edwards v Lee's Administrators* that meant the claimant suffered a loss. And in *Planché v Colburn* the act of performance—like the act of forbearance in *Gibb*—simultaneously produced the benefit to the defendant and the loss to the claimant. One could not occur without the other.

The relationship between loss and enrichment in the single connection cases is thus counterfactual; 'but for' the one, the other would not have occurred. This fits the definition of each according to exchange capacity because, essentially, one *is* the other.[45]

It does not mean, however, that the relationship between the two is causal.[46] That is because counterfactual relationships are not exclusively causal.[47] As Professor Mackie explained, cases in which two events are the collateral effects of a common cause are a limitation of counterfactual-based causal analysis.[48] A simple example illustrates the point (one that resonates with the description of loss and

[43] See generally RN Strassfeld, 'If …: Counterfactuals in the Law' (1992) 60 *George Washington Law Review* 339, 343.

[44] See above pp 99–103.

[45] See above pp 58–60, 84–86, 94–95.

[46] K Barker, 'The Nature of Responsibility for Gain: Gain, Harm and Keeping the Lid on Pandora's Box' in R Chambers, C Mitchell, and J Penner (eds), *Philosophical Foundations of the Law of Unjust Enrichment* (Oxford, Oxford University Press, 2009) 163.

[47] Strassfeld, 'If …: Counterfactuals in the Law' (n 43) 346–48.

[48] JL Mackie, *The Cement of the Universe: A Study of Causation* (Oxford, Clarendon Press, 1980) 33.

enrichment being 'two sides of the same coin').[49] If a coin is tossed and it lands heads up, the fact of its landing tails down is not the cause of its landing heads up; but on a counterfactual analysis one cannot happen 'but for' the other.[50] Equally, in the simplest of cases, where C pays money to D, D is enriched while C suffers a loss, but C's loss is not the cause of D's enrichment: it is the act of payment that has caused both C's loss and D's gain. The connection between enrichment and loss is thus a counterfactual one, indicative of the fact that they are the collateral effects of a common cause.

The same logic applies to multiple connection cases, be they sequential or concurrent. Concurrent connections are susceptible to the same counterfactual analysis as singular connections, the only difference being that 'but for' the claimant's loss several enrichments would not have occurred. So, in *The Trident Beauty*, 'but for' Pan Ocean's payment, Creditcorp would not have been enriched by receipt of the money, nor Trident by payment on its behalf. Likewise with sequential connections. In *Blue Haven*, Blue Haven was connected to Robinson because 'but for' Blue Haven's work, Robinson would not have been enriched. And in *Exall v Partridge*,[51] 'but for' the claimant's payment to the landlord, the defendant's debt would not have been discharged.

## (2) Causal Direction

The second difficulty with a causal analysis of the connection between loss and enrichment is that causation presupposes a particular direction of relationship: one event followed in time by another. Hart and Honoré thus expressed common sense causation as 'cause and effect' or 'providing reasons' or 'providing opportunity or means',[52] and we commonly speak of 'chains' of causation.

These observations are important because the relationship between loss and enrichment in unjust enrichment does not necessarily have a direction and, where it does, it is not uniform across different cases. In a single connection case, such as where C pays money to D, D is enriched and C suffers a loss in the same instant. There is no direction of causation; the coin landing tails down did not precede its landing heads up. This can be contrasted with a multiple connection case. Where C confers a benefit on X, which is then conferred on D, C's loss apparently precedes D's gain. These multiple connection cases seem very different from the single connection cases if causation is used to describe the relationship between enrichment and loss.

[49] Smith, 'Restitution: The Heart of Corrective Justice' (n 2) 2141, 2169.

[50] Mackie, *The Cement of the Universe: A Study of Causation* (n 28) 32. See further MS Moore, *Causation and Responsibility: An Essay in Law, Morals, and Metaphysics* (Oxford, Oxford University Press, 2009) 377–79, 392–425.

[51] *Exall v Partridge* (1799) 8 Term Rep 308 (KB).

[52] Hart and Honoré, *Causation in the Law* (n 38) Ch 2.

Indeed, the same point applies among the multiple connection cases themselves. In *Niru Battery (No 1)*,[53] for example, the claimant bank customer's loss came after the defendant had been enriched, and the bank had passed that loss on by debiting the customer's account. Another situation is where a retailer pays money as VAT to the Revenue before receiving a corresponding VAT payment from a customer. The speech by Henderson J in *Investment Trust Companies* leaves open the possibility that the customer may have an unjust enrichment claim against the Revenue in such circumstances (albeit one that may be precluded by statute),[54] and it does not seem to make any difference in what order the payments are made and collected by the retailer and the Revenue.[55]

Interception cases present a further problem because the direction of the relationship may be reversed. In some cases enrichment and loss may arise in the same instant and so be analogous to the core case of mistaken payment, as in *Valley County v Thomas*, where the moment that McCone County was enriched by the issue and collection of fees on valid licences, Valley County suffered a loss because it was no longer able to collect those fees: the licenses having been issued (and there being no dispute as to their validity), they could not be issued again and so the opportunity to collect fees in respect of them was gone. In other cases, however, enrichment may actually precede loss. This will be so where a defendant is enriched by the receipt of money from a third party that discharges a debt owed by that third party to the claimant, and (exceptionally) the discharge of that debt depends upon an election by the claimant.[56] Another example is where the loss depends on the claimant exhausting his rights against a third party such as in *Re Diplock*.[57] In that case the defendant charities were enriched because they received the money from the executors, but the loss was not sustained until later when the claimant's right against the executors was exhausted.

## (3) Counterfactual Inquiry

Generalising attribution in unjust enrichment as a causal connection between enrichment and loss does not fit the logic of causation, but it does fit the logic of a counterfactual relationship. Thus, stripped of their factual nuances, the one

[53] *Niru Battery Manufacturing Co v Milestone Trading Ltd (No 1)* [2002] EWHC 1425 (Comm), [2002] 2 All ER (Comm) 705.

[54] *Investment Trust Companies (In Liquidation) v Revenue and Customs Commissioners* [2012] EWHC 458 (Ch), [2012] STC 1150, [50], [72]–[73].

[55] Cf *Grantham Cricket Club v Customs and Excise Commissioners* [1998] BVC 2272 (VAT and Duties Tribunal); *R (Building Societies Ombudsman Co Ltd) v Customs and Excise Commissioners* [2000] STC 892 (CA); Value Added Tax Act 1994 ss 80 and 80A. See generally M Chowdry, 'Unjust Enrichment and Section 80(3) of the Value Added Tax Act 1994' [2004] *British Tax Review* 620, 629.

[56] See Mitchell, Mitchell, and Watterson (eds), *Goff & Jones* (n 6) para 6.56.

[57] *Re Diplock* [1948] Ch 465 (CA). Cf Barker, 'The Nature of Responsibility for Gain: Gain, Harm and Keeping the Lid on Pandora's Box' (n 46) 162–63 ff, where it is suggested that in the *Re Diplock* scenario 'harm results in gain'.

thing the different cases in chapter four have in common is that each embodies a non-causal counterfactual relationship between the defendant's enrichment and the claimant's loss. This does not presuppose a particular temporal direction: in some cases there is no direction, in others it runs from loss to enrichment, and in yet others it runs from enrichment to loss. This follows the nature of the exchange capacity analysis.

Though such a counterfactual requirement may seem a low threshold test, there will be cases in which the facts fail to meet it. *Huntley Management Ltd v Australian Olives Ltd* provides a good illustration.[58] AOL had been responsible for managing several olive projects before the investors replaced AOL with Huntley. AOL had been paid management fees in advance[59] and so Huntley claimed from AOL a proportion of the fees referable to the period after which Huntley had taken over. The Court held that the claim could not succeed in principle. Huntley had argued that, while claims for money had and received are generally available to the payer of the funds, there was no reason in principle why a third party who, pursuant to an obligation owed to the payer, has performed the duties to which the payment relates, should not be able to recover the money directly from the recipient.[60] Huntley's claim for a proportion of the fees paid to AOL referable to the time after Huntley took over managing the olive projects was not supported by a counterfactual connection. AOL was enriched by fees from the investors received before it was removed from the relevant projects,[61] and so it was not the case that 'but for' Huntley suffering a loss by performance of management services AOL would not have been enriched. As the Court explained, AOL's enrichment was entirely dependent on its relationship with the investors and had nothing to do with Huntley.[62] Nor was it the case that 'but for' AOL's enrichment, Huntley would not have sustained its loss by performance of management services. The highest that might have been said of the relationship between the parties is that, had the investors not paid AOL the entirety of the relevant management fees, they may have been willing to pay Huntley a proportion and so Huntley would not have been out of pocket in the long run. Though it may have been the case that 'but for' AOL's enrichment Huntley's loss would not have persisted, unjust enrichment is not about persisting losses. Huntley's loss and AOL's enrichment were not in a counterfactual relationship because they were not the collateral effects of a common cause.

The utility of the counterfactual inquiry, as well as the difficulties with the alternative generalisations, is illustrated by *Bank of Cyprus UK Ltd v Menelaou*.[63]

In that case, the Menelaou parents' debts with the Bank of Cyprus ('the Bank') were secured by charges on their home, Rush Green Hall. In 2008 they decided to

58 *Huntley Management Ltd v Australian Olives Ltd* [2010] FCAFC 98.
59 ibid [23]–[26].
60 ibid [41].
61 ibid [23]–[26].
62 ibid [42].
63 *Bank of Cyprus UK Ltd v Menelaou* (n 6); *Menelaou v Bank of Cyprus UK Ltd (CA)* (n 6).

downsize to Great Oak Court—the purchaser of which was their daughter, Melissa (the respondent). Rush Green Hall was sold for a sum inadequate to discharge the parents' debts, but the Bank agreed to release its charges provided that £750,000 was paid to it and a new charge granted over Great Oak Court. That is, rather than call in the proceeds of sale from the Rush Green Hall and then readvance that money to the Menelaous, the Bank 'short-circuited' the process and agreed that the proceeds of sale could be retained for use in the purchase of Great Oak Court.

Rush Green Hall was sold, the money paid, and the new charge registered. Two years later, the Menelaous sought to sell Great Oak Court, and Melissa commenced proceedings to remove the charge from the register. It was agreed at trial that the charge was invalid. The Bank, however, counterclaimed and sought a declaration that it was entitled to an equitable charge arising via subrogation to an unpaid vendor's lien over Great Oak Court. That lien arises by operation of law: as soon as a contract for sale is entered into, the vendor has a lien on the property for the purchase money.[64] Because payment had been made to the vendor in respect of Great Oak Court, and the lien thereby extinguished, the Bank sought subrogation to reverse Melissa's unjust enrichment.[65]

David Donaldson QC (sitting as a deputy judge) rejected the Bank's counterclaim. He held that Melissa's enrichment was not at the Bank's expense because the Bank had released its charges *after* Melissa acquired Great Oak Court. But 'time's arrow' (as Donaldson QC called it) does not control unjust enrichment.[66]

The Court of Appeal rightly allowed an appeal, though in doing so it relied upon the difficult concepts of 'economic reality',[67] 'transfer of value',[68] and 'causal connection'.[69] Counsel for the Bank had argued that to refuse subrogation would embrace formalism over 'economic reality'. He alleged that, by releasing its charges over Rush Green Hall, the Bank had effectively permitted the use of money to buy Great Oak Court which it could have recalled, so it was as if the Bank had provided its own money. Floyd and Tomlinson LJJ accepted this approach but, though it seems attractive, it is not without difficulty. As Moses LJ observed,[70] 'economic reality' is a 'fuzzy concept' which may mask unarticulated reasoning. Moreover, 'economic reality' was used as an exception to a so-called general rule of direct enrichment. As we have seen in chapter four, not only is the authority for that rule questionable,[71] but to start with a general rule and *then* rely upon reality is a difficult pill to swallow.

The Court of Appeal also endorsed the 'transfer of value' generalisation.[72] Floyd LJ held that there was a transfer of value between the Bank and Melissa, 'start[ing]

[64] *Barclays Bank plc v Estates & Commercial Ltd* [1997] 1 WLR 415 (CA) 419 (Millett LJ).
[65] As explained in *Banque Financière de la Cité SA v Parc (Battersea) Ltd* [1999] 1 AC 221 (HL).
[66] See above pp 126–128.
[67] *Menelaou v Bank of Cyprus UK Ltd* (CA) (n 6) [32]–[37] (Floyd LJ).
[68] ibid [38] (Floyd LJ), [57] (Tomlinson LJ).
[69] ibid [42] (Floyd LJ), [61] (Moses LJ).
[70] ibid [61] (Moses LJ).
[71] See above pp 109–114.
[72] *Menelaou v Bank of Cyprus UK Ltd* (CA) (n 6) [29] (Floyd LJ).

with the agreement by the Bank' to release its charges over Rush Green Hall, which released the funds to pay for Great Oak Court.[73] This, however, exposes the difficulties inherent in the 'transfer' concept considered earlier. To say that there was a transfer between the Bank and Melissa is to give the impression that something had gone on between them, and the whole problem in the case was that this was precisely what had not happened. Moreover, it is unclear how an act of agreement fits the transfer concept: the Bank's agreement to release its charges was irrelevant until it was acted upon and the charges actually released. And, in any event, the agreement was between the Bank and Melissa's parents. The mechanism by which that established a connection between the Bank and Melissa herself was glossed over by the 'transfer of value' concept and left largely as a matter of impression.

A further appeal to the Supreme Court was rightly dismissed—though again the reasoning was not without difficulty. Lord Clarke (with whom Lord Kerr and Lord Wilson agreed) agreed with the Court of Appeal's approach and the conclusion that there had been a 'transfer of value' between the Bank and Melissa.[74] His Lordship considered that it would be 'pure formalism' for the Bank to be denied subrogation simply because it had not called-in and then readvanced the proceeds from the sale of Rush Green Hall to the Menelaous.[75] The answer to the question of whether Melissa was enriched at the Bank's expense was 'plainly yes' according to his Lordship because:[76]

> The Bank was central to the scheme from start to finish. It had two charges on Rush Green Hall which secured indebtedness of about £2.2m. It agreed to release £785,000 for the purchase of Great Oak Court in return for a charge on Great Oak Court. It was thus thanks to the Bank that Melissa became owner of Great Oak Court, but only subject to the charge. Unfortunately the charge was void … . In the result Melissa became the owner of Great Oak Court unencumbered by the charge. She was therefore enriched at the expense of the Bank because the value of the property to Melissa was considerably greater than it would have been but for the avoidance of the charge and the Bank was left without the security which was central to the whole arrangement.
>
> As I see it, the two arrangements, namely the sale of Rush Green Hall and the purchase of Great Oak Court, were not separate but part of one scheme, which involved the Bank throughout.

Lord Neuberger (with whom Lord Kerr and Lord Wilson also agreed) said that he agreed with each of Lord Clarke's and Floyd LJ's analysis in respect of whether Melissa had been enriched at the Bank's expense.[77] Like Lord Clarke, Lord Neuberger considered what had gone on was 'one scheme'.[78] His Lordship

[73] ibid [38] (Floyd LJ).
[74] *Bank of Cyprus UK Ltd v Menelaou* (*UKSC*) (n 6) [33] (Lord Clarke).
[75] ibid [26] (Lord Clarke).
[76] ibid [24]–[25] (Lord Clarke).
[77] ibid [61] (Lord Neuberger).
[78] ibid [67] (Lord Neuberger).

added that, on this basis, Melissa could be considered a 'direct recipient' even though her precise characterisation as such did not matter:[79]

> [T]here was in reality a single transaction, and it was from that transaction that Melissa directly benefitted, even though the benefit was affected at the direction of the Menelaou parents. The benefit to Melissa was direct because it arose as the immediate and inevitable result of the very transaction to which she was party and which gave rise to the unjust enrichment … . I should add that, even if Melissa could be characterised as an indirect recipient of any enrichment, I do not consider that that would assist her: she would still properly be liable on the facts of this case, essentially for the same reasons.

Like the approach taken by the Court of Appeal, a significant difficulty with this approach is that it reduces attribution in unjust enrichment to matters of impression and judicial perceptions of 'reality'. Whether (and how) a complex set of facts can be reduced to 'a single scheme' may not be evident in every case. And while it is true (as Lord Clarke observed) that 'whether a particular enrichment is at the expense of the claimant depends upon the facts of the case',[80] there must some principle capable of application across the cases.

The best way to explain *Bank of Cyprus UK Ltd v Menelaou* is through the counterfactual inquiry advocated by this chapter. There was no transfer or other interaction between the Bank and Melissa. The charges that the Bank had released over Rush Green Hall had been in respect of Melissa's parents' debts, not hers. Nor had the Bank's money been used to purchase Great Oak Court; that, instead, came from the sale of Rush Green Hall, which was owned by the parents. The most that could be said of the Bank's position was that 'but for' its release of the charges, Rush Green Hall could not have been sold and the money from that sale used to purchase Great Oak Court for Melissa. This 'but for' relationship was sufficient.

Stripped to its essentials, this is the approach that the Court of Appeal took in allowing the Bank's claim. It held that there was 'a sufficiently close causal connection' between the Bank's agreement and Melissa's enrichment.[81] And while use of the language of 'causation' is problematic for the reasons outlined above,[82] it is clear that the Court of Appeal's decision centred upon the existence of the 'but for' relationship between the Bank's release of its charges and Melissa's acquisition of the house.

The Supreme Court also applied a counterfactual approach. Lord Clarke stated that the test was 'whether there is a sufficient causal connection, in the sense of a sufficient nexus or link, between the loss to the Bank and the benefit received by the defendant, here Melissa'.[83] His Lordship held that it was 'thanks to the Bank

[79] ibid [61] (Lord Neuberger).
[80] ibid [27] (Lord Clarke).
[81] *Menelaou v Bank of Cyprus UK Ltd (CA)* (n 6) [42] (Floyd LJ), [61] (Moses LJ). See also [56]–[57] (Tomlinson LJ).
[82] See above pp 124–128.
[83] *Bank of Cyprus UK Ltd v Menelaou (UKSC)* (n 6) [27] (Lord Clarke).

that Melissa became owner of GOC' and that Melissa was enriched because the value of Great Oak Court 'was considerably greater than it would have been *but for* the avoidance of the charge' (emphasis added).[84] The counterfactual was also key to Lord Neuberger's analysis:[85]

> The Bank had the right to demand the whole of the proceeds of sale of Rush Green Hall, as the Menelaou parents' debt to the Bank, which had been secured on the freehold of Rush Green Hall, exceeded the proceeds of sale. Instead, the Bank agreed that £875,000 of those proceeds of sale could be used to fund the purchase of the freehold of Great Oak Court, but only provided that the Bank was granted a Charge over that freehold at the time of its acquisition. So the Bank would have had the right to prevent the £875,000 being used to purchase the freehold if it had not been provided with a valid Charge. Even assuming … that the Bank had released to the Menelaou parents £875,000 of the proceeds of sale of Rush Green Hall, the release was only on the basis that it would be granted a Charge over Great Oak Court. Therefore, it seems to me clear that the Bank could have prevented the purchase proceeding until it had been granted a Charge.

In other words, 'but for' the Bank's release of its charges, Melissa would not have been enriched.

*Bank of Cyprus UK Ltd v Menelaou* thus illustrates the utility of the counterfactual approach. The relationship between the Bank and Melissa was unique insofar as the facts of the case did not, on their face, appear similar to any other case in which a connection between claimant and defendant has been found sufficient so as to justify an unjust enrichment claim: Melissa did not acquire a right from the Bank; the Bank did not release Melissa from an obligation; and there was no use of property, performance of a service, or satisfaction of a request. Moreover, the interposition of the parents added a further layer of complexity as they first benefitted from the Bank's actions before passing that benefit on to Melissa. A single expression that captures the sequential connection between the parties cannot be arrived at without examining earlier cases and distilling from them a uniform relationship capable of applying to new cases. That uniform relationship is the counterfactual, and it was applied in *Bank of Cyprus UK Ltd v Menelaou* to support an unjust enrichment claim.

Nevertheless, the reasoning deployed in *Bank of Cyprus UK Ltd v Menelaou* is not without difficulty. It is particularly concerning that the counterfactual approach was buried under a needlessly complex approach to attribution. According to Floyd LJ in the Court of Appeal,[86] that approach consists of a 'transfer of value' requirement limited by a direct enrichment rule, a limitation which is then subject to exceptions that conform to 'economic reality' and the need for a 'a close causal connection' (the counterfactual inquiry). All of this is further qualified by the additional conditions listed (non-exhaustively) by Henderson J in *Investment*

[84] ibid [24] (Lord Clarke). See above p 131.
[85] ibid [66] (Lord Neuberger).
[86] See *Menelaou v Bank of Cyprus UK Ltd* (CA) (n 6) [40] (Floyd LJ).

*Trust Companies* including:[87] the need to avoid double recovery; the need to avoid any conflict with contracts between the parties; and the need to confine the remedy to restitution of unjust enrichment, and not to allow it to encroach into the territory of compensation or damages. The Supreme Court endorsed this approach, including the significance of Henderson J's analysis and the considerations set out in *Investment Trust Companies*.[88]

This book takes the view that these considerations have nothing to do with attribution in unjust enrichment, and that the unnecessarily complex approach to attribution evident in *Bank of Cyprus UK Ltd v Menelaou* can and should be simplified. If the counterfactual test underlies the exceptions to 'directness', then that should be *the* test of attribution from the outset. There is no need to fuss about with the difficult concepts of 'transfer of value', 'direct enrichment', 'economic reality' and 'causation'. Moreover, and as explained in Part III of this book, the additional considerations outlined by Henderson J in *Investment Trust Companies v HMRC* (and subsequently endorsed by the Court of Appeal and Supreme Court) have their proper place in unjust enrichment, but that place is not about attributing liability in unjust enrichment; it is about *qualifying* such liability once it has been established. Once a particular defendant's enrichment is attributable to a particular claimant's loss via the satisfaction of the counterfactual inquiry, a completely separate inquiry follows. That inquiry is: are there reasons to deny or otherwise qualify a claim despite the connection between claimant and defendant? That inquiry is the subject of Part III of this book.

## (4) Limiting the Counterfactual

The utility of counterfactual analysis depends upon asking the right question. The events we wish to connect must be confined by legal relevance.[89] The same point has been made in the context of causal analysis.[90] Appreciating the purpose of the counterfactual inquiry in unjust enrichment avoids these 'under-determination' problems.

For example, suppose C pays D £10 by mistake in circumstances in which D knows of the mistake and so is barred from a change of position defence. Suppose further that, upon learning that D has received £10 from C, X decides not to make a gift of £10 to D that he would have made otherwise. Applying a counterfactual analysis: would D have been enriched 'but for' C's payment? The answer is 'yes' because on these facts D can show that had he not received the payment from C he would have received it from X. The result is that C cannot claim the money paid to D.

[87] *Investment Trust Companies (HC)* (n 54). See further below pp 179–180.
[88] *Bank of Cyprus UK Ltd v Menelaou (UKSC)* (n 6) [29]–[33] (Lord Clarke), [61], [77] (Lord Neuberger).
[89] Strassfeld, 'If …: Counterfactuals in the Law' (n 43) 397–407.
[90] Hoffmann, 'Causation' (n 40) 596–97.

Governments are the most likely defendants to have under-determination style arguments available to them. In *Peel* the claimant municipality paid for the support of several delinquent juveniles in homes run by non-government bodies. It had been required to pay by court orders made under empowering legislation that was later declared void. The claimant sought restitution from the Ontario and Federal governments on the basis that it had discharged their liabilities. The claim failed because the defendants were not enriched; no liability was discharged, nor an inevitable expense saved. Justice McLachlin explained that it was neither inevitable nor likely that, in the absence of a scheme that required payment by the municipality, the defendants would have made such payments: 'an entirely different scheme could have been adopted, for example'.[91]

Applying a counterfactual approach, this reasoning could deny claims in otherwise straightforward unjust enrichment cases analogous to the example above. Suppose the facts of *Peel* had been slightly different so that the defendant governments had been under a liability in respect of the juveniles' care. Suppose further that (as hypothesised by McLachlin J) an alternative (and lawful) scheme had been available to cover that liability. On a counterfactual approach, the government would still have been enriched despite the claimant's payment because it would have relied on the alternative lawful scheme. Indeed, such analysis can be applied more widely. In *Sempra Metals*, for example, the government could have argued that an alternative scheme available to it was to ensure that the timing of all taxpayer liabilities was the same. Such an argument depends on further issues of fact, and potentially raises matters concerning the interface between unjust enrichment and public law, including the extent to which courts can engage in counterfactual inquiries requiring them to predict the actions of legislators.[92] The argument seems viable, however, if a counterfactual relationship underpins attribution in unjust enrichment.[93]

Indeed, such an argument was run in *Lady & Kid A/S v Skatteministeriet*.[94] In 1987, the Danish government abolished social security contributions in order to stimulate economic growth and develop employment. To pay for this measure, the government introduced a new tax named the 'employment market contribution', (*arbejdsmarkedsbidrag*, or the 'Ambi' for short). In 1989, the European Court of Justice ruled that the Ambi was incompatible with EU law, and so the Danish government passed legislation laying down the arrangements for reimbursement of the Ambi that had been unlawfully levied. The applicant retailers

[91] *Peel (Regional Municipality) v Canada* [1992] 3 SCR 762 (SCC) [48].

[92] See generally C Mitchell and P Oliver, 'Unjust Enrichment and the Idea of Public Law' in R Chambers, C Mitchell, and J Penner (eds), *Philosophical Foundations of the Law of Unjust Enrichment* (Oxford, Oxford University Press, 2009).

[93] Cf *Re Eurig Estate* [1998] 2 SCR 565 (SCC) where a declaration of invalidity against a provincial government probate fee was suspended on the basis (at [44]) that '[a]n immediate declaration of invalidity would deprive the province of the revenue derived from probate fees, with no opportunity to remedy the legislation or find alternative sources of funding'.

[94] Case C-398/09, *Lady & Kid A/S v Skatteministeriet* [2012] STC 854 (ECJ Grand Chamber).

sought reimbursement of Ambi payments but were refused on the ground that if the government had known that the Ambi was contrary to EU law, it would not have abolished employer social security contributions in the first place, and though the applicant had made Ambi payments, the value of these had been less than the value of the contributions they would otherwise have had to pay. A reference was made to the European Court of Justice to determine (*inter alia*) whether it was open to Denmark to provide that payments of money as tax levied in contravention of EU law could not be recovered if the payer had made a saving as a result of the concomitant abolition of another tax. The European Court of Justice held that the recognition of such a defence by Danish law would be contrary to EU law because the only substantive defence permitted by EU law to so-called *San Giorgio* claims is passing on.[95] For the purposes of this book, however, the case is particularly relevant because the defendant government's argument was that 'but for' the payment of the unlawful tax, the claimant would have paid the government pursuant to a lawful tax—and in a greater amount at that. The European Court of Justice's rejection of this argument according to the particular principles informing *San Giorgio* claims arguably leaves open the possibility that it may succeed in other claims.

That cannot be right. A defendant—government or otherwise—should not escape liability in unjust enrichment simply because it could have exacted benefits in different ways or from alternative sources besides the claimant.

This is why purpose is so important to the counterfactual inquiry. Unjust enrichment is predicated upon corrective justice and the bilateral relationship between defendant and claimant: enrichment and loss, each reflective of the parties' exchange capacities. The definitions of enrichment and loss set out in chapters two and three must not be forgotten; those definitions are crucial to understanding why liability arises in these cases. The contrary view that no liability arises because of under-determination is the result of an incorrect view of enrichment and loss that is inconsistent with this book.

The defendant's enrichment is the saved expenditure in not having to pay the claimant for the benefit received, while the claimant's loss is that of the opportunity to charge the defendant for the same. Each cannot arise 'but for' the other because each is a corollary of the other. The counterfactual inquiry is confined to these *identified* enrichments and losses. Whether someone else *could* have conferred a benefit on the defendant, but did not *in fact* confer such a benefit is irrelevant.[96] Just as the claimant's conduct with third parties 'has nothing to do with the principle of restitution'[97] so too does the hypothetical conduct of the defendant in

[95] ibid [19]–[20], [26]. The popular name for claims for restitution of charges levied in breach of EU law is derived from Case C-199/82, *Amministrazione delle Finanze dello Stato v San Giorgio SpA* [1983] ECR 3595 (ECJ).

[96] This also avoids problems of over-determination, such as the argument that the claimant's loss is equally connected to the fact of his having been born as it is to the fact of the defendant's enrichment.

[97] *Kleinwort Benson Ltd v South Tyneside MBC* [1994] 4 All ER 972 (QB), 985 (Hobhouse J).

acquiring benefits in other ways (whether from the claimant or otherwise).[98] The same is true of loss: it makes no difference to a claim, once there is a connection between enrichment and loss, that the claimant would have suffered the loss in any event. Suppose, for example, C pays D £100 from her purse by mistake, and afterwards is robbed of her purse (and all of its contents) by a thief. D cannot escape liability in unjust enrichment on the basis that C would have suffered the loss in any event. It is sufficient that D's gain of £100 could not have arisen 'but for' C's loss of it: the relationship between C and the thief is irrelevant. The nub of the counterfactual inquiry lies in its application between identified enrichments and losses; that is, between savings and lost opportunities to exchange. Other 'isolated' definitions of enrichment and loss are beside the point.[99]

Under-determination also seems, on first inspection, a problem in interception cases where enrichment precedes loss. This is because, prior to the loss, the position appears to be that the defendant's enrichment would have arisen in any event, and so can have nothing to do with the claimant. A straightforward illustration is *Sergeant and Harris v Stryker*.[100] In that case a sheriff had offered a reward for the apprehension of an escaped prisoner. Stryker captured the prisoner and sought the reward from the sheriff. Sergeant and Harris, however, had already falsely claimed the reward. Stryker's claim against Sergeant and Harris for money had and received was rejected on the basis that the Sergeant and Harris' enrichment had nothing to do with Stryker: the sheriff remained bound to pay Stryker irrespective of the former's dealings with Sergeant and Harris. Hornblower CJ captured matters neatly when he stated that the sheriff remained bound as if he had thrown the money paid into a fire.[101] He may as well have thrown it into a hole so far as Stryker was concerned:[102] the relationship between the sheriff and the two rogues had nothing to do with Stryker. To this extent the facts are analogous to the payment of the fees to AOL in *Australian Olives Ltd*.[103] Stryker had not suffered any loss (his right against the sheriff remained intact)[104] but, even if he had, nothing on the facts indicated a 'but for' relationship between that loss and the enrichment of the two rogues. The latter, it seems, would have arisen in any event.

*Sergeant and Harris v Stryker* is an example of Smith's 'general case':[105] Stryker's right against the sheriff remained intact: hence he suffered no loss and hence he had no claim against the rogues.[106] Had the sheriff, however, been unable to pay

[98] See above pp 86–89.
[99] See below pp 139, 140–142.
[100] *Sergeant and Harris v Stryker* (1838) 32 Am Dec 404 (SC NJ).
[101] ibid 410.
[102] See above p 23.
[103] *Australian Olives* (n 58). See above p 29.
[104] Nothing on the facts or in the speech of Hornblower CJ suggests that Stryker had claimed against or been unable to recover the reward from the sheriff. Indeed, certain aspects of his speech suggest the opposite: *Sergeant and Harris v Stryker* (n 100) 405.
[105] Smith, 'Three-Party Restitution: A Critique of Birks' Theory of Interceptive Subtraction' (n 18) 493. See above p 116.
[106] ibid 488.

Stryker because of the false claim by Sergeant and Harris, the outcome may have been different. If those had been the facts, the case would have transformed into one of Smith's 'special cases'—where the claimant does in fact suffer a loss and so may bring an unjust enrichment claim against the defendant who receives money from a third party.[107] That is what occurred in *Re Diplock*: when the executors of Caleb Diplock's will paid out money to the defendant charities, they remained bound to pay the claimant next-of-kin as if they had thrown the money into the fire. On these facts alone we would expect the case to have been decided as one of Smith's general cases and a claim denied. The additional fact that transformed the case, however, into one of the special kind permitting a claim was the exhaustion of claims against the executor by the next of kin.[108] Immediately before abandoning this account of *Re Diplock*, Smith explained the relevant transformation as follows:[109]

> [W]e need to link the defendant's enrichment with a loss on the part of the plaintiff. If the plaintiff retains its right to have the estate properly administered, it has lost nothing. But if that right is worthless, the plaintiff has suffered a loss. This explanation seems to comprehend the requirement that the plaintiff exhaust its remedies against the executors. It can also comprehend the rule about subsequent deficiencies. If the assets were adequate when the defendant was paid, the plaintiff's loss comes from other errors the executor made. But if the assets were inadequate, then the defendant's gain is more clearly linked to the plaintiff's loss.

This captures the essence of counterfactual analysis within interception cases, including the solution to the apparent under-determination problem where enrichment precedes loss. Smith's account of the two prerequisites to these *Re Diplock*-style claims is particularly important. The first prerequisite—that the claimant exhaust remedies against the executors—has already been explained as consistent with the requirement of loss.[110] Where that is the case (as in *Re Diplock* itself) it would seem that up until the point at which those remedies are in fact exhausted, the situation is on par with *Seargant and Harris v Stryker* or *Australian Olives Ltd*. It is unclear just how a subsequent event (like the exhaustion of remedies) can alter this position. Money burned in a fire cannot be retrieved.

This is why the second pre-requisite is important: the payment to the defendant must have contributed to the deficiency on which the claimant founds his claim.[111] This is borne out by the rule that, if the assets of the estate are originally sufficient to satisfy all the legacies, and one legatee procures payment of his legacy, the remaining legatees cannot claim against the satisfied legatee if the executor thereafter

[107] ibid 493.

[108] Or, at least, transformed it in the sense that the viability of the claim was made dependent upon the claimant first satisfying the requirement.

[109] L Smith, 'Unjust Enrichment, Property and the Structure of Trusts' (2000) 116 *Law Quarterly Review* 412, 426.

[110] See above p 116.

[111] Smith, 'Unjust Enrichment, Property and the Structure of Trusts' (n 109) 439.

wastes the estate so as to render it deficient to meet their legacies.[112] The effect of *Re Diplock* is to extend the availability of such claims—and so this qualifying rule—to defendants who are not legatees.[113] The reason why the payment to the defendant must have contributed to the deficiency on which the claimant founds his claim is that this sets up the counterfactual relationship between enrichment and loss: 'but for' the payment to the defendant, the executor would not have been short of the funds necessary to pay the claimant, and so the claimant would not have suffered its loss.

What this ultimately means for the under-determination problems in interception cases is that they are an illusion. The fact that enrichment and loss may arise at different times is not a basis for denying a connection between between them. Where enrichment precedes loss, it may be that, prior to the loss, the defendant's enrichment is no business of the claimant because it may have arisen in any event and without the loss. But once the loss has arisen, such arguments are beside the point: the counterfactual inquiry is applied between identified enrichments and losses. It is pointless to apply it in the abstract, without first identifying both the enrichment and the loss. Indeed, were matters otherwise, the sequential connection cases detailed in chapter four would be open to the same under-determination criticism: where C pays X who then pays D, C's loss is unconnected with D until D is enriched by the final payment. As we have seen in chapter four, however, such cases can and have been analysed in unjust enrichment terms.[114]

A final issue to consider in this context is *why* Smith abandoned the unjust enrichment explanation of *Re Diplock*, despite it providing such a strong litmus test for interceptive subtraction cases generally. His abandonment was based upon three objections.[115] First is that 'the defendant's enrichment came subtractively from the executors and it is not clear that the fact of their insolvency can change this'.[116] This is a weak objection: the executor's insolvency 'changes' the situation because it establishes a loss to the claimant residuary legatee; and, if the second pre-requisite to such claims is established, the enrichment and loss will be in a counterfactual relationship sufficient for unjust enrichment purposes.

[112] *Re Diplock* (n 57) 494; *Peterson v Peterson* (1866) LR 3 Eq 111 (Ch).

[113] Smith has suggested that this apparent extension can be narrowly construed by reference to the assertion in *Re Diplock* and *Harrison v Kirk* [1904] AC 1 (HL) (at 7 per Lord Davey) that the claim is available against those 'who derive title from the deceased testator or intestate' such that it is *only* available against those who claim under the estate: see Smith, 'Unjust Enrichment, Property and the Structure of Trusts' (n 109) 440. This is open to question. The whole point in *Re Diplock* was that the defendant charities could *not* have claimed under the estate. Lord Simmonds's treatment of the point (at 269) is at best equivocal, while the Court of Appeal in *Re Diplock* (at 502–03) appears to reject the narrow construction of the claim. *In re Lowe's Will Trusts* [1973] 1 WLR 882 (CA) may provide further authority against it. In that case the Court of Appeal (at 887) suggested that an unpaid legatee could rely on *Re Diplock* to claim against the Crown following an escheat to the Crown for want of heirs. But in such a case, the Crown's claim to the estate is based upon the law of escheat (as varied by the Intestates Estate Act 1884), and not under the estate.

[114] See above pp 109–114.

[115] Smith, 'Unjust Enrichment, Property and the Structure of Trusts' (n 109) 441–42.

[116] ibid, 441.

Smith's second objection to the unjust enrichment analysis of *Re Diplock* is that if it were extended by analogy to other cases, it would mean that in any three-party case, the insolvency of the original transferee could allow recovery against remote recipients. This is not so: it would still be necessary to establish a connection between the original transferor's loss of funds and the claimant's own loss (represented by the second pre-requisite in *Re Diplock*-style claims) such that the defendant's enrichment and the claimant's loss are in a counterfactual relationship. Moreover, the objection that *Re Diplock* extends recovery to any three-party case loses force if and when we accept (as this book has argued here and in chapter four) that the interposition of additional parties between claimant and defendant is not a bar in and of itself to unjust enrichment analysis.

This is related to Smith's third objection to the unjust enrichment analysis of *Re Diplock*: it does not explain why such claims are available only against defendants who receive a benefit from an executor purportedly in the administration of an estate. They do not extend to the more general scenario of third party receipt of trust property; in such cases claimants are limited to an action based upon knowing receipt. The relationship between strict liability in unjust enrichment and equitable claims based upon knowing receipt is notoriously difficult, and the reconciliation of the different bases of claim is rife with controversy. It is not the aim of this book to resolve those controversies. Rather, and as we shall see in Part III,[117] this book argues that those controversies must be dealt with separately from the issue of attribution. That being the so, one of the prevailing outlooks towards the relationship between unjust enrichment and knowing receipt has been to see the *Re Diplock*-style claim as a stepping-stone for the application of unjust enrichment principles to other cases involving equitable principles. An alternative view, however, is that the existence of those equitable principles acts as a qualification upon the reach of unjust enrichment analysis despite the existence of a counterfactual connection between enrichment and loss, and that the *Re Diplock*-style claim is—in truth—an exception to that qualification. If that is correct, then Smith's third objection to the unjust enrichment analysis of *Re Diplock* is met by the simple retort that the case is an exceptional one.

## (C) Counterfactual Inquiry and the Exchange Capacity

In Part I of this book it was argued that unjust enrichment responds to disruptions of parties' exchange capacities, as those interests are conceived within the broader context of corrective justice and individual self-determining agency. Within that framework, each of the concepts of 'enrichment' and 'loss' was defined by reference to the other: 'enrichment' being the saving to the defendant of what ought to

[117] See below pp 198–203.

have been paid to the claimant in exchange for what was received, and 'loss' being the lost opportunity of the claimant to charge the defendant in exchange for what was received. Understanding 'enrichment' and 'loss' in this way immediately provides a basis for conceptualising the connection between the two concepts at the level of the exchange capacity because they are, in essence, two sides of the same concept: exchange.

That is all well and good at the particular level of abstraction at which the idea of the exchange capacity is pitched. But for the connection between enrichment and loss to be capable of practical identification in any given case, the abstract concept must be reduced to something more useful and applicable to real-world controversies. It will not always be the case that the connection between a given enrichment and a given loss is as simple to identify or explain as it is in two-party payment cases. If the aim of unjust enrichment scholarship is to enable reasoning by analogy from simple cases to hard cases, then something more than the abstract conceptualisation of the connection between enrichment and loss is necessary.

That has been the aim of this chapter: to propose the counterfactual inquiry as the litmus test for recognising a connection between enrichment and loss capable of grounding analysis of the relationship between two parties in unjust enrichment terms; be those parties connected by a single event (such as the acquisition of a right, the discharge of an obligation, the performance of a service, or the satisfaction of a request), or multiple events (be they sequential, concurrent, or interceptive). The practical essence of the connection between enrichment and loss in all of these cases is that it is possible to say that one cannot arise 'but for' the other, just as is necessary when enrichment and loss are conceived of and defined by reference to each other. This practical relationship provides the best indicator that the parties' disrupted exchange capacities are relevantly connected for unjust enrichment to bite. It fits the exchange capacity analysis of unjust enrichment because, as we have seen, enrichment and loss are two sides of the same coin in that analysis.

Several points follow from these observations. First, because the objective of counterfactual analysis is to connect *identified* enrichments and losses, it is irrelevant to speculate upon how likely it may have been that the parties to a claim might have exercised their exchange capacities. For example, few (if any) taxpayers lend money to the government, and so the notion that the parties in *Sempra Metals* would have ever have actually exercised their exchange capacities so as to enter a loan arrangement on terms that replicated the award made by the court seems far-fetched. But that is beside the point: unjust enrichment is not about mimicking contracts and thereby facilitating the exercise of each parties' exchange capacity.[118]

[118] The old view that unjust enrichment as 'quasi contract' and justified by 'implied contract theory' (see, eg, *Sinclair v Brougham* [1914] AC 398 (HL)) is no longer sound: *Westdeutsche Landesbank Girozentrale v Islington LBC* [1996] AC 669, [1996] 2 WLR 802 (HL) 714 (Lord Browne-Wilkinson). See further Mitchell, Mitchell, and Watterson, *Goff & Jones* (n 6) para 1.06; Burrows, *The Law of Restitution* (n 2) 28–29; Birks, *Unjust Enrichment* (n 24) 267–64. But cf D Priel, 'In Defence of Quasi-Contract' (2012) 75 *Modern Law Review* 54.

That, if anything, is the concern of contract.[119] The concern of unjust enrichment (and, within it, the objective of the counterfactual inquiry) is instead to restore the parties' exchange capacities to the position they would have been had the equality of those interests been maintained.[120] This entails correcting disruptions that have *in fact* occurred: restitution being what the defendant ought to have paid the claimant for what he *in fact* received, but was—as matters transpired—saved from doing so.

The second point is that the existence of a counterfactual relationship between enrichment and loss is not a final test of ultimate liability unjust enrichment. Other factors and considerations may influence and shape the extent of the protection afforded the exchange capacity by the law of unjust enrichment. These qualifications upon liability are considered in Part III. Just as traditional causal analysis has been divided into what may loosely be described as 'factual causation' and 'legal causation' inquiries,[121] so too does this book separate attribution of liability from these qualifications on liability.

The third and final point is that the analysis of the connection between enrichment and loss—including its generalisation into the counterfactual inquiry—is incomplete in one very important respect. It is incomplete because it has yet to explain the relationship between, on the one hand, the connection between enrichment and loss in an unjust enrichment claim, and, on the other hand, the connection defined by the processes of following and tracing. It is to that controversy that this book now turns.

[119] See above pp 39–40.

[120] *Benedetti (UKSC)* (n 44) [100] (Lord Reed); EJ Weinrib, *The Idea of Private Law* (Cambridge, Harvard University Press, 1995) 57.

[121] See above p 125.

# 6

# Transactions

The previous two chapters have explained that attribution in unjust enrichment can be generalised from the existing cases to a counterfactual test between enrichment and loss applicable to new cases. That exercise in generalisation, however, has omitted a particular group of cases from analysis: those in which the connection between claimant and defendant is established by 'transactional links' and, in particular, the process of *following* property and the rights to property, and the process of identifying rights to property as substitutes for rights to other property—a process commonly known as *tracing*.

This chapter explains that transactional links add nothing further to our understanding of attribution in unjust enrichment beyond what has already been established: that is, that there must be a counterfactual relationship between enrichment and loss. The reason transactional links add nothing further to attribution in unjust enrichment is that transactional links are not part of unjust enrichment. Transactional links do not, as has been suggested by others,[1] operate as a supplementary or exceptional basis of attribution in unjust enrichment.

That being so, this whole chapter dedicated to transactional links is necessary because underlying this simple sounding proposition is a certain view of transactions, and of tracing in particular. Though the law of tracing is too big for this book to consider outright, certain observations must first be made about the nature and rationales of tracing before its underwhelming relationship to unjust enrichment can be understood. Specifically, the rationale by which tracing justifies the treatment of one property right as substitute for another must be explained.

This chapter thus carries a risk of disappointment for the reader, for though much of it is dedicated to explaining tracing, the ultimate aim of that discussion is to show that tracing actually has little to do with attribution in unjust enrichment. The legal rules that determine who has rights in what property have nothing to say about the application of unjust enrichment principles in, for example, a mistaken payment case. The distribution and proprietorship of rights, which may constitute the factual substratum of a case, do not affect the principles to be applied as and when those rights are disturbed so that they are susceptible to an unjust enrichment claim; such as when those rights are mistakenly acquired by one person from

[1] See, eg, P Birks, *Unjust Enrichment*, 2nd edn (Oxford, Oxford University Press, 2005) 6–87; A Burrows, *The Law of Restitution*, 3rd edn (Oxford, Oxford University Press, 2011) 75–76.

another. Those rights (including their origin, content, and capacity for transmission) are background facts to which (just like any other facts) unjust enrichment may apply—including the rules of attribution.

This chapter is necessary in order to correct twin errors that pervade much of the existing literature on unjust enrichment and which obscure this reality. Those errors are: (i) the belief that tracing is explicable according to unjust enrichment; and (ii) the assumption that tracing must have something to do with unjust enrichment and, in particular, the 'at the claimant's expense' requirement.[2] This chapter argues otherwise. Tracing cannot be explained by reference to unjust enrichment: it is a multi-stage process with different rationales dependent upon whether it occurs in equity or at common law. While tracing may be relevant to the background facts of an unjust enrichment claim, tracing is not the basis of attribution in unjust enrichment. The test for attribution in unjust enrichment is the counterfactual inquiry—and the counterfactual inquiry alone.

## (A) Following and Tracing

This chapter is mostly about tracing because it is the nature and rationale of tracing that usually cause the most confusion in the context of unjust enrichment. It should not be assumed, however, that tracing is unique in its relevance to unjust enrichment claims involving transactions between claimants and defendants. The term 'transactions' is a superior description of the subject matter discussed in this chapter rather than the term 'tracing' because the former term incorporates the latter as well as the much simpler process of 'following'.

Indeed, following is a useful starting point for the central thesis of this chapter.

Following involves identifying property and the rights to that property as it moves from one person to another. Its simplicity masks its relevance to the connection between enrichment and loss in unjust enrichment. In *Holiday v Sigil*, it is to be recalled, the claimant succeeded in an action for money had and received after the defendant found the claimant's banknote.[3] The connection between enrichment and loss lay in the fact that the defendant acquired a right from possessing property belonging to the claimant: the latter could have charged the former. Following was an inherent feature of the case, but not the unjust enrichment analysis. That property belonging to the claimant could be followed to the hands of the defendant facilitated the conclusion that the latter had acquired a right in respect of it. Following did not establish the claimant's initial right in the banknote, nor was it the basis of recovery (which we would now call unjust enrichment). Rather,

[2] A Burrows, *A Restatement of the English Law of Unjust Enrichment* (Oxford, Oxford University Press, 2012) 57.

[3] *Holiday v Sigil* (1826) 2 Car & P 176 (Assizes). See above pp 102–103.

the process of following the banknote enabled the claimant to show, it being the same banknote, that the defendant's enrichment by receipt of it would not have occurred 'but for' the claimant's loss of it.

This simple idea, stemming from a relatively straightforward following case, provides an important reference point for more complicated analyses of tracing cases and their relationship to unjust enrichment. When considering that relationship it is always helpful to refer back to and analogise with the relevance of following in *Holiday v Sigil*. Further, and as we shall see later in this chapter, the significance of following to unjust enrichment is not limited to such simple cases as *Holiday v Sigil*. It is a key feature of many transaction cases involving tracing that, in addition to being able to trace from an original asset to its substitute, a successful claimant thereafter follows that substitute to the defendant.

Before any of that can be understood, however, we must first have some idea of what tracing is, and why it is possible.

## (B) The Nature and Rationales of Tracing

Attempts to understand tracing typically begin with the recital of certain basal assumptions,[4] chief among which are observations made by Lord Millett in *Foskett v McKeown*.[5] In that case a rogue trustee, Murphy, acting fraudulently and in breach of trust, misappropriated £20,440 from a trust for the development of property in Portugal, and used that money to pay two annual premiums on a life insurance policy previously taken out in his name. He then appointed the benefit of the policy to trustees for the benefit of his children. Following his death by suicide, £1 million was paid by the insurers pursuant to the policy to the trustees. The beneficiaries of the development trust then brought proceedings against the trustees and the children, claiming a proportionate beneficial interest in the policy proceeds in the trustees' hands. The House of Lords held that the beneficiaries had a proprietary right to 40 per cent of the policy proceeds because their equitable interests in the development trust could be traced into the policy moneys. In the course of his judgment, Lord Millett explained that:[6]

> [Tracing and following] … are both exercises in locating assets which are or may be taken to represent an asset belonging to the plaintiffs and to which they assert ownership. The processes of following and tracing are, however, distinct. Following is the process of following the same asset as it moves from hand to hand. Tracing is the process of identifying a new asset as the substitute for the old.

[4] See, eg, *Armstrong DLW GmbH v Winnington Networks Ltd* [2012] EWHC 10 (Ch), [2013] Ch 156, [65]–[66]; Burrows, *A Restatement of the English Law of Unjust Enrichment* (n 2) 56–57.

[5] *Foskett v McKeown* [2001] 1 AC 102 (HL) (Lord Millett). See also *Boscawen v Bajwa* [1996] 1 WLR 328 (CA) 335 (Millett LJ) 334.

[6] *Foskett* (n 5) 127 (Lord Millett).

His Lordship continued, with respect to tracing:[7]

> Tracing is … neither a claim nor a remedy. It is merely the process by which a claimant demonstrates what has happened to his property, identifies its proceeds and the persons who have handled or received them, and justifies his claim that the proceeds can properly be regarded as representing his property. Tracing is also distinct from claiming. It identifies the traceable proceeds of the claimant's property. It enables the claimant to substitute the traceable proceeds for the original asset as the subject matter of his claim. But it does not affect or establish his claim.

Finally, he added that:[8]

> Given its nature, there is nothing inherently legal or equitable about the tracing exercise. There is thus no sense in maintaining different rules for tracing at law and in equity. One set of tracing rules is enough.

These observations can cause substantial confusion about the nature of tracing if they are not properly understood. Moreover, the relationship between tracing and unjust enrichment cannot be made sense of without understanding the distinct rationales that exist for tracing in equity and tracing at common law, the separate existence of which is not inconsistent with the existence of one set of tracing rules.

## (1) The Nature of Tracing

Many of the problems associated with tracing stem as much from linguistic imprecision as conceptual uncertainty. In the above quoted passages, for example, Lord Millett refers to tracing 'assets' and to 'property'. Use of those terms may be criticised, however, because they seem to blur the distinction between rights to property on the one hand, and the physical possession or identification of property on the other. Yet, at the same time, that distinction itself seems to encounter difficulty when used to describe tracing as a singular process when (as we shall see below) it actually consists of two stages. It may be accurate, for example, to say that one traces rights to property insofar as one is concerned, as Lord Millett states, with justifying that substitute property 'can properly be regarded as representing' original property.[9] However, at the point of 'demonstrating what has happened' to property, and of 'identif[ying] its proceeds and the persons who have handled or received them',[10] the rights to that property may not be as relevant as the property itself. One reason, therefore, for using the generic term 'asset' may be that it cuts across these different stages so as to accommodate a necessary degree of contextualism when we use the single term 'tracing' to describe what is actually a two-stage process. For this very reason, however, we must also keep in mind that there are

7 ibid 128 (Lord Millett).
8 ibid.
9 ibid.
10 ibid.

two stages to tracing: 'identification' on the one hand, and 'justification' on the other. Each stage must be understood in its own terms to avoid confusion about the nature of tracing and its relationship to the establishment of claims—be they unjust enrichment or otherwise.

### (a) *Identification and Justification*

According to Lord Millett, tracing is a process that encompasses several steps: demonstrating what has happened to the claimant's asset; identifying the proceeds and the persons who have handled or received that asset; and justifying that the proceeds represent that asset. These several steps can be distilled to the *two* stages of tracing: 'identification' and 'justification'. Each stage is conceptually distinct from the other, as well as from the exercise subsequent to tracing: claiming.

Identification, on the one hand, involves identifying original and substitute property—including the persons who have handled or otherwise received it. It is a factual inquiry about which it is necessary to have legal rules of evidence capable of overcoming factual impasses that may arise in difficult situations, such as where tangible or intangible property is mixed with other property in such a way as to lose its discrete identity, or where a series of substitutions, mixtures and withdrawals occurs with ever-increasing complexity.

Justification, on the other hand, goes beyond factual investigation. It encompasses a legal conclusion: 'justifying' that a substitute property right can 'properly' be regarded as 'representing' the original property right. In other words, justification is a question of law, not of fact. As Smith has explained:[11]

> If a litigant wishes to show that some asset can be traced into some other asset, then she must prove certain facts; and it must be the case that the application to those facts of the rules of tracing leads to the conclusion that the original asset can be traced into the asset which is now the subject matter of the claim. But even though legal rules are inevitably involved, the exercise of tracing is nonetheless just that: an exercise or process which is preliminary to the making of a claim. An analogy may be drawn with a plaintiff who wishes to prove a claim in breach of contract. Such a plaintiff must show that there was a contract. This is done by proving certain facts, such that the application to those facts of the rules of contract formation leads to the conclusion that a contract was formed. Proving that a contract was formed is not a right, nor a remedy … It is just something which one is at liberty to do.

Once again, the difficult term 'asset' features in Smith's explanation. Though the term 'asset' may usefully cut across the different stages of tracing when speaking of it as though it were a single process, it will not do when considering the discrete stages that truly comprise tracing. We must be more accurate in our description of tracing at this point. Identification is about property, while justification is about the rights to that property. Beyond that linguistic correction, however,

[11] L Smith, *The Law of Tracing* (Oxford, Clarendon Press, 2003) 11.

Smith's analogy to contract formation and breach is a particularly useful one. Just as the question 'Was a contract formed?' cannot be accurately answered with one expression (the facts must satisfy a checklist of formation requirements, including offer, acceptance, consideration, certainty, intention, and completeness—each subject to detailed rules and legal principles), neither can the question 'Can C's property right be traced to D's substitute?' One must demonstrate not only that the property and its purported substitute are identifiable (identification), but also that applying the legal principles that explain tracing, C has a right to the substitute (justification).

Understanding that tracing is a process consisting of these two stages is important because it distinguishes the *legal* idea of tracing from mere identification or the *lay* idea of substitution. For example, the *Restatement of the English Law of Unjust Enrichment* gives the following example:[12]

> A gives B £250 as a birthday gift, which B uses to buy a painting which she hangs on her wall. In principle, A can trace the £250 to the painting, but that tracing does not establish a claim against B. On the contrary, A plainly has no right to the painting or its value.

With respect, tracing is not possible here (in principle or otherwise). All A can do is *identify* what happened to the £250: he gave it to B, and B substituted it for the painting. But identification does not conclude the tracing process: A must also *justify* that the right to the painting represents his right to the £250. A cannot do this because he gifted the £250 to B. That fact goes both to the lack of a claim *and also* the inability to trace.

It is also important to appreciate that satisfying the identification and justification requirements of tracing will not conclude a claimant's case. Tracing is not claiming. Just as establishing that a contract exists (by the application of legal rules to the facts) cannot establish a claim for breach of that contract (which entails the application of distinct legal rules to additional facts), so too does the conclusion of the tracing process not entail that a claimant's case is complete. Once an original property right has been traced to a substitute, that *legal* conclusion essentially forms a *fact* upon which a further conclusions can thereafter be built, just as the legal conclusion that there exists a contract forms a fact upon which the further conclusion that contract has been breached can thereafter be made. The description of tracing as 'a process' is thus ultimately a shorthand for conveying its subsidiary yet legal character with respect to the establishment of claims.

### *(b) Justification Distinct from Claiming*

This leads to Lord Millett's second observation about the nature of tracing: it is distinct from claiming. The tracing process—consisting of identification and justification—enables the claimant to show that one property right can be treated in law as a substitute for another. A right, however, is not a claim. To establish a

[12] Burrows, *A Restatement of the English Law of Unjust Enrichment* (n 2) 57.

claim, a claimant must show that the acquisition by the defendant of property in which the claimant has a right violates some legal norm. Simply demonstrating that the right exists, which is all that the process of tracing ultimately does, will not suffice. Rather, tracing can be used within the factual matrix necessary to set up a particular claim. A number of claims can and do rely upon tracing in this way, including: conversion of substitute assets; knowing receipt of substitute trust property; and claims under a trust that vindicate a beneficiary's entitlement to substitute trust property. As we shall see below, tracing may also be relied upon *prior* to an unjust enrichment claim. It is this final category of case with which this chapter is ultimately concerned. Tracing is not unique to unjust enrichment cases, and the unjust enrichment cases are only a small fraction of tracing cases overall.

The reason why the 'tracing distinct from claiming' point tends to create confusion is that both tracing and claiming involve the application of legal rules to property rights. The justification stage of tracing in particular involves the application of legal rules which lead to the *legal* conclusion that a substitute property right represents an original. This legal concept of justification sounds very much like claiming, but it is not. Law, encompassing the development and application of legal rules and principles, is not just about the establishment of claims. To describe tracing as a process, and to say that it is distinct from claiming, is not to deny that tracing has legal substance of its own.

### *(c) Uniform Rules of Identification*

That legal substance is two-fold, reflecting the division within tracing between the identification and justification stages. Though identification is a factual inquiry, it is necessary that legal rules of evidence exist in order to overcome factual impasses that can arise in difficult situations. The rules are familiar ones, including that in *Re Hallett's Estate*[13] and the lowest intermediate balance rule.[14]

One controversy, yet to be definitively resolved,[15] is whether different rules should exist depending on whether one is tracing in equity or at common law. Resolving this controversy is the thrust of Lord Millett's observation that there is 'nothing inherently legal or equitable about the tracing exercise' and that '[o]ne set of tracing rules is enough'.[16] This has a tendency to be misunderstood, with confusing consequences. Lord Millett's point was that there is nothing inherently legal or equitable in the identification stage of tracing, and so it makes no sense to have different evidential rules depending upon the jurisdiction of the court undertaking that exercise. This makes sense because identification is about investigating facts, and the evidential process of investigation is neither legal nor equitable in

[13] *Re Hallett's Estate* (1880) 13 Ch D 696 (CA).

[14] See generally Burrows, *A Restatement of the English Law of Unjust Enrichment* (n 2) s 9(2)–(7).

[15] See, eg, *Foskett* (n 5) 113 (Lord Steyn), 128 (Lord Millett); Burrows, *The Law of Restitution* (n 1) 75–76.

[16] *Foskett* (n 5) 128 (Lord Millett).

nature. That being said, the nature and rationale of the identification stage of tracing is not the concern of this chapter, nor of this book as a whole.

It is important to recognise, however, that the uniformity of evidentiary rules has nothing to do with the justification stage of tracing. The detailed rules regarding mixtures and other factual uncertainties are part of the evidential process of identifying property, and not the legal process of justifying that one right is a substitute for another. That is the core of tracing with which the remainder of this chapter is concerned. To understand tracing we must understand the justification stage of tracing in particular, and to do that we must appreciate that history and principle demonstrate there are in fact two distinct rationales for it: one inherently equitable, and the other inherently legal.

## (2) The Rationales of Tracing

The key to understanding how the law justifies the treatment of one right to property as the substitute for another lies in appreciating two points. The first is that the principled origins of tracing are equitable. The second is that common law tracing (that is, tracing without resort to equitable principle) is the product of an historical error that is today deliberately treated as sound and entrenched legal principle.

In addition to those two points, it is also important to be mindful of a third. That is that, despite numerous attempts to argue a contrary position,[17] the rationale of tracing is *not* unjust enrichment. This book does not present the occasion to explain why this is so in great detail. The lion's share of the work dismissing unjust enrichment as the rationale for tracing has been done elsewhere by others.[18] Nevertheless, in the context of this book, one particularly potent criticism of the unjust enrichment explanation for tracing is that, insofar as the tracing process leads to an entitlement to property, it appears to have the flavour of specific restitution, which is an exceptional response to unjust enrichment.[19] On its face, there is nothing about tracing that warrants such exceptional treatment. A claimant who relies upon unjust enrichment in an effort to trace his original property right to a substitute will have a personal restitution claim in his favour, rather than a specific entitlement to the substitute. That, however, does not atch the reality of tracing. Unjust enrichment cannot explain tracing, nor does it need to.

[17] See, eg, C Mitchell, P Mitchell, and S Watterson (eds), *Goff & Jones: The Law of Unjust Enrichment*, 8th edn (London, Sweet & Maxwell, 2011) 8.30; Burrows, *A Restatement of the English Law of Unjust Enrichment* (n 2) 57–58; Birks, *Unjust Enrichment* (n 1) 36.

[18] See, eg, J Penner, 'Value, Property and Unjust Enrichment' in R Chambers, C Mitchell, and J Penner (eds), *Philosophical Foundations of The Law of Unjust Enrichment* (Oxford, Oxford University Press, 2009); P Millett, 'Proprietary Restitution' in S Degeling and J Edelman (eds), *Equity and Commercial Law* (Sydney, Lawbook, 2005); R Chambers, 'Tracing and Unjust Enrichment' in J Neyers, M McInnes, and S Pitel (eds), *Understanding Unjust Enrichment* (Oxford, Hart, 2004).

[19] See above pp 44–50.

## (a) Tracing in Equity

Writing extra-judicially, Lord Millett has observed that the entitlement of an owner of property to assert ownership of its traceable proceeds is not a rule of natural law.[20] Instead, the justification stage of tracing originates with equity's treatment of property held under trust:[21]

> Equity took the authorised disposition of trust property by the trustee as its starting point. A trust fund is not a res. The beneficiaries' interests in a trust fund are proprietary interests in the assets from time to time comprised in the fund subject to the trustees' overriding powers of managing and alienating the trust assets and substituting others. On an authorised sale of a trust investment, the beneficiaries' proprietary interests in the investment are overreached; that is to say, they are automatically transferred from the investment which is sold to the proceeds of sale and any new investment acquired with them ... The beneficiaries' interests in the new investment are exactly the same as their interest in the old.

As to unauthorised substitutions, he continues:[22]

> The trustee sells a trust investment in breach of trust and uses the proceeds to buy shares for himself. The beneficiaries have a continuing proprietary interest in the original investment but they cannot recover it from the purchaser if he is a *bona fide* purchaser of the legal title without notice of the breach. But they can instead claim a proprietary interest in the shares which the trustee bought for himself. He bought them with trust money, and the beneficiaries are not bound to challenge sale of the trust shares or the purchase of the new shares as a breach of trust. That is a matter for them. They can have the trust account taken on the footing that the sale and purchase were authorised transactions, and the trustee cannot be heard to say they were not. The beneficiaries do not thereby ratify or authorise the trustee's conduct. They simply require the trustee to account for all his dealing with the trust property whether authorised or not; and then decide whether to falsify the account by disallowing the disposal of the trust investments (in which case the trustee must restore them or their value to the trust) or to let the account stand, in which case the new shares are treated as if they were an authorised investment made for the beneficiaries' account. The trustee cannot resist the claim by saying: 'You have got it wrong. I acted in breach of trust. I stole the trust property and used it to buy shares for myself.'

This is what Lord Millett had in mind when, in *Foskett v McKeown*, he stated that the transmission of property rights from one asset to its traceable proceeds 'is part of our law of property, not of the law of unjust enrichment'.[23] The reduction of a complex legal process to a single expression carries a risk of oversimplification, and so we must be careful that the form of expression does not determine the legal substance it represents. 'The law of property' is merely a shorthand expression

[20] Millett (n 18) 314.

[21] ibid 315.

[22] ibid. See further *Foskett* (n 5) 130–31 (Lord Millett), discussing S Williston, 'The Right to Follow Trust Property when Confused with Other Property' (1888) 2 *Harvard Law Review* 28.

[23] *Foskett* (n 5) 127. See above p 3. See also Millett (n 18) 314.

for the rationale of tracing extracted above. The observation that tracing is 'part of the law of property, not … the law of unjust enrichment' merely recognises that the process—dependent on the trust, overreaching, and account—does not fit the structure of unjust enrichment. It does not, as has been suggested,[24] set up a distinction between property and unjust enrichment as competing legal categories in their own right.

Lord Millett's reasoning can also be extended to tracing in respect of fiduciary dispositions. As Penner has explained,[25] like a trustee, any powers a fiduciary has in respect of assets under his charge are derived from the fact that those assets have been so placed with him in his status *as a fiduciary*. So, just as with a trustee, the proceeds of any exchange of that property are clothed with a fiduciary status. *El-Ajou v Dollar Land Holdings plc (No 1)*[26] and *Relfo Ltd (In Liquidation) v Varsani*[27] are examples. In each of those cases, equitable tracing was possible where a fiduciary agent (an investment manager in *El-Ajou*, and a company director in *Relfo*) had disposed of the property of their principal in an unauthorised transaction.

Just how this is achieved has been clarified by Professor Mitchell.[28] He explains that the liability to account (upon which Lord Millett bases equitable tracing, above) is derived from the rule that someone charged with the control and management of property (a 'steward') cannot exceed the terms of his authority when dealing with that property, and that if he does so he will be required to restore the missing property in the same way that a trustee is required to reconstitute a trust fund depleted by unauthorised disposals. The rules that prevent stewards from exceeding their authority are not the same as rules mandating loyalty, which are said to lie at the core of the fiduciary concept in particular.[29] That being so, it is misleading to delimit equitable tracing according to the fiduciary concept. Tracing can instead apply as far as and in respect of anyone charged with the control and management of property not equivalent to ownership. In other words, it is the concept of *stewardship* that is the key to equitable tracing, rather than the trust or other fiduciary relationship. For example, a company director may have powers in relation to that company's bank account, though the legal right in respect of it belongs to the company by virtue of the fact that it is the company's name on the account. Where he exercises his powers, he can only do so within the scope of his authority. Where the transaction is unauthorised, this ultimately means he can only dispose of and receive legal rights to property subject

24 See, eg, Birks, *Unjust Enrichment* (n 1) 36.

25 Penner, 'Value, Property and Unjust Enrichment' (n 18) 328.

26 *El-Ajou v Dollar Land Holdings plc (No 1)* [1993] 3 All ER 717 (Ch).

27 *Relfo Ltd (In Liquidation) v Varsani* [2012] EWHC 2168 (Ch); *Relfo Ltd v Varsani* [2014] EWCA Civ 360. See below pp 165–166.

28 C Mitchell, 'Stewardship of Property and Liability to Account' (Lecture given to the Chancery Bar Association Annual Conference, 17 January 2014) 2–4.

29 See generally M Conaglen, *Fiduciary Loyalty: Protecting the Due Performance of Non-Fiduciary Duties* (Oxford, Hart, 2010).

to an equitable interest of his principal.[30] The equitable interest arises in response to the transaction and to the limits on the steward's authority therein: he was not authorised to dispose of the property, so any disposal or receipt that was nevertheless effective in law is tempered and mitigated in equity. And just like the trustee, the steward cannot resist this conclusion by relying on his wrongful and unauthorised act.[31]

Equitable tracing also extends to third party recipients of property rights subject to *pre-existing* equitable interests. In *Foskett v McKeown*, Lord Millett said that the case of trust property retained by a trustee could not be distinguished from the case of a trust asset given away to a gratuitous donee because the donee cannot obtain a better title than his donor.[32] As Penner has explained:[33]

> The reason why it is just for Equity to extend the trust obligation not only to third parties (not being bona-fide purchasers) but also to proceeds of exchanges is that, in the eyes of Equity, someone whose obligation over the specific asset is such as to deprive him of anything but a trustee's title (the beneficial interest being the beneficiaries') has merely a trustee's title to deal with. When he exercises the powers that go with having legal title, in the eyes of Equity those powers are themselves bound by the trust. In consequence, he can only grant a title that is similarly bound by the trust, and, more importantly, can only receive a title bound by the trust in exchange.

Mitchell reiterates the point that a knowing recipient's power to deal with property is subject to the same constraints as the power to deal with the property that was formerly held by the steward from whom he received it.[34] If the knowing recipient himself deals with the property in an unauthorised fashion (that is, a manner that is inconsistent with the beneficiaries' rights) then he will himself be accountable in the same way as the steward.[35] It also follows, on this view, that any prior equitable interest persists as a power. Someone with a prior equitable interest can, by giving notice of that interest to whomever holds the legal right, transform that right-holder into a trustee, and thereafter compel him to transfer the asset in question.

### *(b) Tracing at Common Law*

In *Taylor v Plumer*,[36] Plumer gave his stockbroker a cheque for £22,000 with instructions that it be used for the purchase of Exchequer bills for Plumer. The stockbroker cashed the cheque and used £6,500 to buy the bills as instructed.

[30] A grant of actual authority to an agent does not include authority to act for the agent's benefit rather than that of his principal: *Hopkins v TL Dallas Group Ltd* [2004] EWHC 1379 (Ch), [2005] 1 BCLC 543.

[31] Millett (n 18) 315. See above p 151.

[32] *Foskett* (n 5) 131.

[33] Penner, 'Value, Property and Unjust Enrichment' (n 18) 326. See *Foskett* (n 5) 130–31 (Lord Millett),

[34] Mitchell, 'Stewardship of Property and Liability to Account' (n 28) 7.

[35] ibid.

[36] *Taylor v Plumer* (1815) 3 M & S 562, 105 ER 721 (KB). See Smith, *The Law of Tracing* (n 11) 162–74.

He misappropriated the rest of the money, using some of it to pay off his debts, and the rest to buy United States government stock and Portuguese gold coins. When he attempted to abscond to the United States, he was apprehended by Plumer's agent, who dispossessed him of the stock and gold. The stockbroker's assignees in bankruptcy then sued Plumer in trover in respect of the stock and gold—arguing that they had become legal owners of it. The claim failed, the received interpretation of the case being that Plumer won because he could invoke common law tracing, and so was the legal owner of the stock and gold.[37] It has now been shown beyond doubt that this is incorrect because,[38] although the King's Bench decided the case, it actually involved the application of equitable principles. The stockbroker held the stock and coins on trust for Plumer, so they did not pass to his assignees in bankruptcy. The correct interpretation of the case is therefore one of equitable tracing. This error has been acknowledged judicially. In *Trustee of the Property of FC Jones & Sons v Jones*, for example, Millett LJ admitted that he had fallen into it previously:[39]

> In *Agip (Africa) Ltd v Jackson* ... I said that the ability of the common law to trace an asset into a changed form in the same hands was established in *Taylor v Plumer* .... In this it appears that I fell into a common error, for it has since been convincingly demonstrated that, although *Taylor v Plumer* was decided by a common law court, the court was in fact applying the rules of equity.

Significantly, however, his Lordship added that this was no reason for concluding that common law tracing was not possible.[40] According to Millett LJ, it was consistent with the doctrine of *stare decisis* to treat tracing in equity as having followed tracing at common law, even though the latter was not declared possible until later cases.[41] There was no indication in *Taylor v Plumer* that tracing was peculiar to equity.[42]

This creates certain difficulties for common law tracing, though they are not insurmountable. The first difficulty is that it is unclear how, if the principled origins of tracing are equitable, the justification stage of tracing is possible at common law and without reliance upon the equitable principles outlined above. Yet, there are cases where this is precisely what has happened. *Banque Belge pour l'Etranger v Hambrouck* is one example.[43] In that case, Hambrouck forged cheques so that £6,000 was debited from his employer's account at the claimant bank and credited to his own account at Farrow's Bank. He then drew cheques on that

[37] Smith, *The Law of Tracing* (n 11) 163.

[38] S Khurshid and P Matthews, 'Tracing Confusion' (1979) 95 *Law Quarterly Review* 78; L Smith, 'Tracing in *Taylor v Plumer*: Equity in the Court of King's Bench' [1995] *Lloyd's Maritime and Commercial Law Quarterly* 240. See also Smith, *The Law of Tracing* (n 11) 168 fn 30.

[39] *Trustee of the Property of FC Jones & Sons (A Firm) v Jones* [1997] Ch 159 (CA).

[40] ibid.

[41] ibid.

[42] ibid. See also Millett (n 18) 314.

[43] *Banque Belge pour l'Etranger v Hambrouck* [1921] 1 KB 321 (CA).

account, and gave them to his mistress, Mlle Spanoghe, without consideration. She paid those cheques into her account at the London Joint City and Midland Bank. The claimant Banque Belge brought an action against Spanoghe and her bankers for a declaration that £315 remaining in her account was theirs. The bankers paid the money into court and so were dismissed from the action. The Court of Appeal held that the claimants were entitled to the declaration and order claimed against Spanoghe. In doing so, it emphasised the legal nature of the case.[44] Spanoghe was not a trustee or other steward. Nor were the claimants beneficiaries or other principals. Equitable principles were not a feature of the case, so it is unclear how Banque Belge could justify the conclusion that the money paid into court could properly be regarded as representing its property.

A second difficulty follows the ability to trace at common law without reliance on equitable principles. It arises by virtue of the fact that the legal right to a substitute asset invariably vests in whoever carries out the substitution, in which case a conflict arises between the ability to trace to the substitute at common law, and the existence of other legal rights in respect of that substitute. This problem led Lord Haldane LC, in *Sinclair v Brougham*, to say that common law tracing into a bank account was impossible because the relationship of debtor and creditor superseded any existing right *in rem*.[45] Yet again, there are cases in which this is precisely what has happened. In *Banque Belge pour l'Etranger v Hambrouck*,[46] for example, prior to the bankers' paying the disputed sum into court, the money was held in an account in Spanoghe's name; in other words, it existed in the form of a debt owed to her by the London Joint City and Midland Bank. The money belonged, at law, to Spanoghe. She was the bank's customer, and her name was on the account. Yet, in order to trace to the money paid into court, Banque Belge must have been able to trace through that account. It is unclear what legal (as opposed to equitable) interest enabled it to do so. Though multiple legal interests in a single asset are possible where that asset is corporeal,[47] one must usually rely upon equity to generate multiple interests in an incorporeal asset.[48]

Another case is *Trustee of the Property of FC Jones*.[49] Mrs Jones received cheques totalling £11,700 drawn by her husband on the bank account of a potato-growing firm in which he was a partner. She used the proceeds of the cheques to invest in potato futures and made a substantial return. She paid the proceeds of her investment into her account at Raphael's Bank. All of this had taken place after the partnership committed an act of bankruptcy, and so its assets were

[44] ibid 326–28 (Bankes LJ), 329–30 (Scrutton LJ), 333–35 (Atkin LJ).

[45] *Sinclair v Brougham* [1914] AC 398 (HL). Cf *Hambrouck* (n 43) 335 (Atkin LJ), referring to *Re Hallett's Estate* (n 13). The problem is not peculiar to inchoate assets such as bank accounts, but arises whenever one person exchanges another's asset for a substitute, and in the process of doing so, acquires good title to that substitute.

[46] *Hambrouck* (n 43).

[47] As in the distinction between rights of ownership and possession, or freehold and leasehold.

[48] D Fox, *Property Rights in Money* (Oxford, Oxford University Press, 2008) [7.52].

[49] *Trustee of the Property of FC Jones & Sons* (n 39).

retrospectively deemed to have vested at law in the trustee in bankruptcy, who brought proceedings against Raphael's, claiming that the partnership was entitled to the balance in Mrs Jones's account. Raphael's interpleaded and paid the money into court. The Court of Appeal held that the trustee was entitled to the money including the profits on Mrs Jones investment. Of Mrs Jones's position, Millett LJ explained:[50]

> If the cheques had passed the legal title to the defendant but not the beneficial ownership, she would have received the money as constructive trustee and be liable to a proprietary restitutionary claim in equity … The defendant would have been obliged, not merely to account for the £11,700 which she had received, but to hand over the £11,700 in specie to the trustee. … But the defendant was not a constructive trustee. She had no legal title to the money. She had no title to it at all. She was merely in possession; that is to say, in a position to deal with it even though it did not belong to her.

The difficulties afflicting *Banque Belge pour l'Etranger v Hambrouck* arise here with greater intensity.[51] In part, this is due to the effect of the Bankruptcy Act 1914 on the case.[52] Section 37 deemed that the firm's bankruptcy related back to its act of bankruptcy, and by section 38 the property of the firm divisible amongst its creditors comprised the property vested in it at that time. The combined effect of these provisions was that the firm's bank account was deemed in law to belong to the trustee in bankruptcy by the doctrine of relation back. This is despite the names on that account being the partners' and not the trustee. This structure was repeated when the money from that account came to Mrs Jones and was paid into her account at Raphael's. In order to trace at common law to the money paid into court, the trustee had to trace through Mrs Jones's account. And that is the point: it was Mrs Jones's account because it represented a debt owed by Raphael's *to her*. The suggestion that Mrs Jones had 'no legal title to the money … [but] was merely in possession' is nonsensical and achieves nothing by way of explanation; not only because the debt was owed to her, but also because a debt is incorporeal and so incapable of possession.[53] The reasoning in the case has thus been described as unsustainable.[54]

The solution to the problems that afflict common law tracing are to be found in its rationale. One possibility is to note that the twin concepts of stewardship and account that are central to the rationalisation of tracing in equity are not distinctly equitable in character, and that they have (or, at least, had) legal

[50] ibid 167.

[51] See generally Fox, *Property Rights in Money* (n 48) [5.96]–[5.106]; Mitchell, Mitchell, and Watterson, *Goff & Jones* (n 17) 8.25–8.29.

[52] Bankruptcy Act 1914.

[53] Nor can it be solved by postulating a distinction, as Lord Millett has (writing extra judicially) between being 'owed' a debt and 'owning' a debt: P Millett, '*Jones v Jones*: Property or Unjust Enrichment?' in A Burrows and Lord Rodger of Earlsferry (eds), *Mapping the Law: Essays in Memory of Peter Birks* (Oxford, Oxford University Press, 2006) 273–74.

[54] Mitchell, Mitchell, and Watterson, *Goff & Jones* (n 17) 8.30.

equivalents. The rules governing account are actually derived from the medieval common law action for account that lay against bailiffs, bailees, scriveners, and agents, but which fell into disuse during the seventeenth century and was taken over by actions in the chancery courts.[55] That being so, it might be argued that common law tracing ought to be explicable in a similar way to equitable tracing. That argument, however, quickly runs into trouble because it is incapable of resolving the conflict between the ability to trace property at common law subject to other legal rights, without resort to the concept of the trust (and, it would seem, a remedial constructive trust at that).[56] In *Trustee of the Property of FC Jones & Sons*, for example, Mrs Jones was more than a steward: the money in the account was hers.

That being so, a different rationale is necessary. This book takes the view that, absent the intervention of equity, the ability to trace property at common law *must* be explicable as an inherent feature of common law property rights. Furthermore, the nature of this 'right to trace' must be such that it survives transmission to substitute property but is subordinate to the rights acquired by others to that substitute. This view is not a novel one. *Trustee of the Property of FC Jones & Sons* has, for example, been described by Mr Fox as involving multiple legal interests arising in respect of a chose in action,[57] while the seminal case of *Lipkin Gorman v Karpnale Ltd*[58] (considered in greater detail below) has been described by the editors of *Goff & Jones* as entailing the existence of some inchoate legal interest enabling tracing.[59]

One possible criticism of this rationale is that it asks too much of property rights.[60] As Chambers rightly points out, ownership of an asset does not entail ownership of its proceeds of sale.[61] Instead, the right to sell property exists because people have both a general property right comprising a power to abandon their property and a power to make binding agreements about their rights—including those to property.[62] This may be true, but it is incomplete insofar as it only describes the underlying rights in respect of sale. The answer to the point made by Chambers, essentially, that a right to property includes a right to the proceeds

[55] SJ Stoljar, 'The Transformation of Account' (1964) 80 *Law Quarterly Review* 203.

[56] A number of decisions, particularly in the Court of Appeal, have set against the idea. See, eg, *Sinclair Investments (UK) Ltd v Versailles Trade Finance Ltd (In Administration)* [2011] EWCA Civ 347, [2012] Ch 453 [37] (Lord Neuberger of Abbotsbury MR); *Re Polly Peck International plc (In Administration) (No 2)* [1998] 3 All ER 812 (CA). See further Smith, *The Law of Tracing* (n 10) 339, where the author suggests that, in those jurisdictions which have accepted a wider availability of remedial trusts, this concern for 'the metaphysics of common law proprietary rights may seem contrived and unnecessary'.

[57] D Fox, 'Relativity of Title at Law and in Equity' (2006) 65 *Cambridge Law Journal* 330, 364.

[58] *Lipkin Gorman v Karpnale Ltd* [1991] 2 AC 548 (HL).

[59] Mitchell, Mitchell and Watterson, *Goff & Jones* (n 17) para 8.25–8.26.

[60] Chambers, 'Tracing and Unjust Enrichment' (n 18) 276–78.

[61] ibid 277.

[62] J Penner, *The Idea of Property in Law* (Oxford, Oxford University Press, 2000).

of its exchange, conditioned on the exchange actually occurring. The theoretical bases of the ability to execute that exchange are therefore beside the point.

A second possible criticism of the 'right to trace' is that it seems artificial and reactionary—fashioned as a reply to common law tracing, rather than a rationale for it. To the extent that this is true, however, it bites just as hard upon common law tracing as it does on nearly any other area of law. The charge that a particular account of property rights is fictional loses force when one realises that property rights are themselves fictional constructs, the definition and content of which is inherently susceptible to manipulation according to choice that defies objective assessment.[63] In a system of law based upon common law reasoning, such manipulation must be kept in check just as much by history as by abstract logic or reason. The recognition of common law tracing may well be an example of precedent and principle outstripping logic, but it is too late to go back.[64] That being so, a solution must be found, and the artificial nature of rights means they are a suitable vehicle for doing so. The right to trace is that solution.

A third possible criticism of the 'right to trace' is that it appears to jar with the rationale of equitable tracing insofar as one might expect that, if the right to trace explains common law tracing, it should also explain equitable tracing: Why does an equitable interest not also include the right to trace to substitutes? The answer, however, is that equitable interests do precisely that, through the relationships of trust and stewardship, and the device of account. An equitable interest is not the same as a common law property right, nor does it need be in order to accommodate tracing. Moreover, to assume that sharing the label 'tracing' means the two processes share the same rationale is to elevate form over substance. Common law tracing and equitable tracing are not substantively identical, which, as we shall see in the next section, holds certain implications for the claims that can follow each.

## (C) Tracing and Unjust Enrichment

The previous section explained that tracing is a legal process that enables an individual to justify the treatment of one property right as a substitute for another. The manner in which this is done (that is, the steps in the process) vary depending upon whether the exercise is distinctively equitable or legal in nature. Equitable

[63] Birks, for example, distinguished property rights from personal rights on the basis of one particular attribute of rights: 'exigibility' ('[a]gainst whom can rights be demanded?'). Importantly, there is nothing inherent in exigibility demanding it be the only quality of rights so mapped. As Birks admitted, rights can be divided by many other criteria—exigibility merely appears to be one important criterion. See Birks, *Unjust Enrichment* (n 1) 28. This leaves open the question whether 'traceability' is another criteria deserving attention in its own respect.

[64] *Trustee of the Property of FC Jones & Sons* (n 39) 169.

tracing, on the one hand, relies upon relationships of trust and stewardship, and the device of account. Common law tracing, on the other hand, relies upon the right to trace that is an inherent feature of property rights. Tracing is neither a uniform nor a singular process.

Importantly, the distinctions that characterise tracing do not end with its rationales. The results of tracing also vary: the treatment of one property right as substitute for another (to use Lord Millett's expression in *Foskett*)[65] is not the same as between tracing in equity and at common law, precisely because each process is different. This means that the claims that are dependent on tracing are not uniform. As Lord Millett observed in *Foskett v McKeown*:[66]

> The successful completion of a tracing exercise may be preliminary to a personal claim (as in *El Ajou v Dollar Land Holdings plc* ...) or a proprietary one, to the enforcement of a legal right (as in *Trustees of the Property of FC Jones & Sons v Jones* ...) or an equitable one.

There is a risk that, in surveying the cases in which tracing has been relevant, one will assume that all such claims are the same, or that, at the very least, they share a uniform rationale. But just because two results are similar does not mean they are based upon the same principles. In this respect, it is regrettable that two different processes—one legal and the other equitable—share the common label, 'tracing', by reason of the similarity of result between the two. The tendency to think the two are the same can generate confusion. Neither *El Ajou* nor *Trustees of the Property of FC Jones & Sons* was an unjust enrichment case. On the one hand, *El Ajou*[67] involved the tracing of money fraudulently invested by the claimant's fiduciary agent, which was subsequently routed around the world before reaching an investment controlled by the defendant. Equitable tracing was relevant, and the (ultimately unsuccessful) claim was an equitable claim for knowing receipt. The fact that an equitable claim followed equitable tracing was not a chance coincidence. Both derived from the fact the claimant's interest in the money as it moved around the world was equitable in nature, meaning its ability to trace was derived from equity and its claim one for knowing receipt of trust property.

*Trustees of the Property of FC Jones & Sons*, on the other hand, involved common law tracing. The common law does not have an equivalent claim to the Roman *vindicatio*, but that does not mean that cases cannot arise in which the right to property is the central claim. As between the trustee and Mrs Jones, the former could not make a proprietary claim against the latter: the trustee's interest in Mrs Jones's bank account was the tracing right that rationalises tracing at common law, and so long as that money existed in the form of Mrs Jones's account, the

[65] *Foskett* (n 5) 127. See above pp 145–146.
[66] ibid 128.
[67] *El Ajou* (n 26).

tracing right was subordinate to her rights as the bank's customer.[68] However, it is important to recognise that that subordinate relationship came to an end when the bank paid the disputed sum of money into court. The fact that the money no longer existed in the form of a bank account in Mrs Jones's name meant she no longer had a competing right in respect of it as against the trustee. The sole right that existed in respect of the money was the trustee's tracing right, and the court ordered that the money be paid to it accordingly.[69]

## (1) Common Law Claims

Common law tracing enables a claimant to maintain that a particular right acquired by the defendant came from him. By reason of the tracing right, a claimant can assert, "That is mine!"—though not as an outright claim. Rather, the assertion is of a fact which, when combined with other facts and subject to unjust enrichment analysis, supports a claim.

That is what occurred in *Lipkin Gorman*.[70] In that case, Mr Cass was a partner at the claimant firm who withdrew money from the firm's client-account and gambled it away at the defendant's casino. The firm succeeded against the defendant in a claim for money had and received, with unjust enrichment expressed as the basis of the claim.[71] The case followed the pattern of sequential connection:[72] the money had gone from C (the claimant firm) to X (Cass) to D (the defendant casino). The claimant was able to establish the connection between it and the money that came to the defendant by tracing that money from its account at the bank to the defendant via Cass. That it could do so had *nothing* to do with unjust enrichment—just like the claimant's ability in *Holiday v Sigil* to follow the dropped banknote. It did not matter that that property had gone through one or even several hands along the way to its receipt by the defendant.[73] So, when the defendant acquired the money through Cass's gambling activities, it was acquiring it from the claimant.

The key to understanding how the claimant in *Lipkin Gorman* was able to do what it did, and how that was relevant to its successful unjust enrichment claim, lies in unpacking the right to trace that defines common law tracing. As Smith has observed, the content of the common law right to trace is closely related to the

[68] cf *Trustee of the Property of FC Jones & Sons* (n 39) 170 (Millett LJ), 171 (Beldham LJ), and 172 (Nourse LJ) where it is suggested, in *dicta*, that the trustee could have demanded the money from the bank directly. That does not seem possible in principle: the money in the bank account was defined by the personal relationship between the bank and Mrs Jones.

[69] The same explanation can be applied *mutatis mutandis* to *Hambrouck* (n 43).

[70] *Lipkin Gorman* (n 58).

[71] ibid 558 (Lord Bridge), 559–60 (Lord Templeman; Lord Griffiths and Lord Ackner agreeing), 572 (Lord Goff, Lord Griffiths, and Lord Ackner agreeing).

[72] See above pp 109–114.

[73] *Lipkin Gorman* (n 58) 573–74 (Lord Goff). See further Birks, *Unjust Enrichment* (n 1) 86–87.

claims it supports.[74] The money that Cass gambled away was not the same money that he had taken from the firm's account: by its nature, the cash was a substitute for the money in the account. As Lord Goff explained, however:[75]

> Before Cass drew upon the solicitors' client account at the bank, there was of course no question of the solicitors having any legal property in any cash lying at the bank. The relationship of the bank with the solicitors was essentially that of debtor and creditor; and since the client account was at all material times in credit, the bank was the debtor and the solicitors were its creditors. Such a debt constitutes a chose in action, which is a species of property; and since the debt was enforceable at common law, the chose in action was legal property belonging to the solicitors at common law. There is in my opinion no reason why the solicitors should not be able to trace their property at common law in that chose in action, or in any part of it, into its product, i.e. cash drawn by Cass from their client account at the bank. Such a claim is consistent with their assertion that the money so obtained by Cass was their property at common law.

Two observations should be made about the role of common law tracing in *Lipkin Gorman*. The first is that, according to the above passage, common law tracing enabled the claimants to treat the money in Cass's hands as their own, so that when the defendant subsequently acquired that money, Cass's loss of the money was *the claimants'* loss of the money. The second point is that tracing was not the final step in the process of establishing the connection between enrichment and loss: the claimant still had to show that the defendant had received the money. In other words, the money had to be *followed* to the defendant so that, in effect, the claimant's assertion 'That is mine!' was coupled with, 'And the defendant has it!'. A counterfactual connection between the defendant's enrichment and the claimant's loss at that point: the firm's loss of money would not have occurred but for the defendant's receipt of it. The tracing exercise having been completed, attribution for unjust enrichment purposes was as simple as in *Holiday v Sigil*.[76]

This analysis clarifies Lord Goff's assertion that the money 'was [the claimants'] property at common law'.[77] Like *Banque Belge pour l'Etranger v Hambrouck* and *Trustee of the Property of FC Jones & Sons*,[78] *Lipkin Gorman* appears to generate a conflict between conflicting legal rights to an asset insofar as Lord Goff held that Cass too had legal property in the cash drawn from the bank account.[79] That conflict disappears, however, if one appreciates the limited nature of the claimants' property right within the tracing process and just what common law tracing achieves. The tracing right is not a full-blown proprietary entitlement, but merely a right to trace—to treat one property right as a substitute for another and to say,

[74] Smith, *The Law of Tracing* (n 11) 338.
[75] *Lipkin Gorman* (n 58) 573–74.
[76] See above p 144–145.
[77] *Lipkin Gorman* (n 58) 573–74.
[78] See above pp 154–156.
[79] *Lipkin Gorman* (n 58) 573, following *Union Bank of Australia Ltd v McClintock* [1922] 1 AC 240 (PC) and *Commercial Banking Co of Sydney Ltd v Mann* [1961] AC 1 (PC).

'That is mine!' without making a claim. That was its substance in *Lipkin Gorman*, and that was how it was relevant to the successful unjust enrichment claim.

One example of the confusion that can result from a failure to appreciate the nature of the tracing right in this way is to be found in *Armstrong DLW GmbH v Winnington Networks Ltd*.[80] In that case, Stephen Morris QC (sitting as a deputy High Court judge) accepted the submission of counsel that the effect of *Trustees of the Property of FC Jones & Sons* and *Foskett v McKeown* was that *Lipkin Gorman* was best understood as involving a proprietary restitution claim.[81] This aligned with Virgo's view of the case as being a proprietary restitution claim concerned with the vindication of the claimants' property right (those rights having been retained because the money was stolen).[82]

That view of *Lipkin Gorman* should not be accepted. It is contrary to the holding in *Lipkin Gorman* that both Cass and the claimant firm had a legal right to the money.[83] It is also contrary to Lord Goff's description of the case as a personal claim, and not a proprietary one.[84] And it is irrelevant insofar as whatever right to the money in its original form (that is, the firm's client-account) the firm might have had, all it subsequently had was a common law tracing right in respect of a substitute asset (the money received by the casino). A claimant cannot 'vindicate' the common law tracing right in the sense meant by Virgo because that right only enables the claimant to treat one property right as a substitute for another. That is not a claim. The claimant must then *follow* the property in which that right subsists to the defendant in order to establish his claim in unjust enrichment. And though the result in *Trustees of the Property of FC Jones & Sons* looks like a vindication of property case dependent on common law tracing, as already explained,[85] that only followed the procedural nuances of the case. If Cass had a right to the money (as it was held he did) then that right was passed to the defendant, and whatever right in the money the defendant had, the point is that the firm's tracing right was incapable of trumping it. The vindication of property rights analysis of *Lipkin Gorman* does not work.

Instead, *Lipkin Gorman* reflects the general position that common law tracing can be a *precursor* to an unjust enrichment claim: establishing the factual matrix to which unjust enrichment analysis can then be applied. That is why unjust enrichment was expressed unanimously to be the underlying basis of the claim,[86] and why the case is generally considered a linchpin in the recognition

[80] *Armstrong DLW GmbH v Winnington Networks Ltd* (n 4).
[81] ibid [75].
[82] G Virgo, *The Principles of the Law of Restitution*, 2nd edn (Oxford, Oxford University Press, 2006) 110.
[83] *Lipkin Gorman* (n 58) 573 (Lord Goff).
[84] ibid 572 (Lord Goff).
[85] See above pp 159–160.
[86] *Lipkin Gorman* (n 58) 558 (Lord Bridge), 559–60 (Lord Templeman; Lord Griffiths and Lord Ackner agreeing), 572 (Lord Goff; Lord Griffiths and Lord Ackner agreeing).

of unjust enrichment in English law.[87] The failure to recognise this stems from a failure to understand the nature of the tracing right at the heart of common law tracing. That right enables the claimant to establish that a substitute acquired by the defendant was acquired from the claimant. That capability is useless for the vindication of property rights in respect of an asset to which a defendant also has a right. Its only use is as a fact thereafter relevant to an unjust enrichment claim.

## (2) Equitable Claims

*Lipkin Gorman* was not mentioned by their Lordships in *Foskett v McKeown*, and for good reason. The two cases are distinct: in the former, common law tracing was part of the background to an unjust enrichment claim, while in the latter tracing in equity was relied on in the course of establishing a claim by trust beneficiaries to vindicate their rights in respect of the traceable proceeds of a trust.

The latter type of claim is not an unjust enrichment claim. As has already been observed, equitable tracing is derived from the entitlement of a beneficiary under a trust to the trust property *vis-à-vis* the trustee.[88] Claims against the trustee in respect of that trust property are based upon the trust itself. The beneficiary can acquire the legal right to an asset held on trust by directing the trustee to transfer it to them, thereby collapsing the trust.[89] Such claims rely upon an existing equitable entitlement, not unjust enrichment.[90] A claimant who relies upon the existence of a trust to claim an asset or its proceeds is not saying that the right to that asset was acquired from him in the sense that a claimant who relies upon common law tracing might do. Rather, he is saying that it is in the nature of the trustee's position that any asset so acquired is held on trust for the claimant. Matters do not change if the trust asset is acquired by a third party, because the beneficiary's interest in that asset continues to exist until it is defeated by operation of law (specifically, the rule relating to *bona fide* purchasers without notice).[91] The claim facilitated by equitable tracing is therefore best understood as one to vindicate the equitable interest upon which equitable tracing is also based. Unlike the common law tracing right, vindication of this equitable interest does not encounter any conflict with a legal right to the asset in question because that legal right is naturally subordinate to the equitable one. Moreover, vindication is a more apt description of what is going on insofar as a claimant who traces in equity thereafter relies upon his equitable entitlement to collapse the trust and compel the transfer of those assets held under it.

[87] Cf Virgo, *The Principles of the Law of Restitution* (n 82) 13–14.
[88] See above pp 151–153.
[89] As in *Saunders v Vautier* (1841) 4 *Beav* 115, 49 ER 282 (Ch).
[90] Millett (n 18) 315. See above p 151.
[91] Penner, 'Value, Property and Unjust Enrichment' (n 18) 326.

This is how the decision in *Foskett v McKeown* should be understood.[92] The beneficiaries in that case had an equitable interest in the money at Murphy's disposal under the trust. When Murphy used that money to pay the insurance premiums, he did so in his capacity as trustee, meaning that the trust thereafter comprised a proportionate share of the insurance policy. It was the beneficiaries' equitable interest under the trust that enabled them to trace into the insurance policy, thereby entitling them to an equitable interest in that policy. This was critically important, as Lord Millett rightly said.[93] Murphy was thereafter incapable of destroying or otherwise altering the beneficiaries' equitable interest in the policy. It did not matter who he settled the policy upon, or how the policy matured to payout upon his death. The equitable interest survived as long as the policy was not acquired by a *bona fide* purchaser for value without notice, which it was not. So, when the policy matured and the money was paid out, the equitable interest was intact. The beneficiaries' proprietary entitlement to the proceeds followed the fact that the money had been paid out under a policy held on trust for them: their right to the money followed the right to payment under the policy. In other words, their claim sought to 'vindicate' their equitable interest in the policy that had existed from the moment that Murphy brought that policy into the trust by his actions, and that equitable interest was the same one that enabled them to trace into the policy in the first place. The final remedy was intimately linked to the basis of tracing from the outset.

It is important to appreciate the point here being made about *Foskett v McKeown*. The decision of the House of Lords was based upon the beneficiaries' pre-existing interest in the insurance policy under the trust. The beneficiaries' claim, and the decision upholding it, were not based upon unjust enrichment, nor did they need to be: the vindication point provided a succinct and orthodox method of claiming the proceeds of the insurance policy. That does not mean, however, that the facts in *Foskett v McKeown* cannot be analysed as giving rise to an alternative claim based upon unjust enrichment. It merely means that such alternate analysis was not necessary for the claimants' case to succeed.

That equitable tracing can be relied upon to support a vindication claim does not mean that equitable interests are irrelevant to unjust enrichment. Consider first the example of *following* an asset in respect of which a claimant has an equitable interest. If the defendant is enriched by receipt of that asset, then there is a counterfactual connection between the claimant's loss and the defendant's enrichment. In line with the exchange capacity analysis advanced by this book, the

[92] See further Mitchell, Mitchell, and Watterson, *Goff & Jones* (n 17) paras 8.88–8.90. However, as to the situation where an unauthorised substitution is made by an innocent third party (though not *bona fide* purchaser for value without notice), who has not assumed the position of trustee or other fiduciary position *vis-à-vis* the assets, see para 8.92. This book takes the view that, in such cases, tracing to substitute property acquired by the third party is possible because his power to exchange the original property is limited by the equitable interest, which has not been extinguished. See above pp 151–153.

[93] *Foskett* (n 5) 134.

defendant's enrichment is the saved expenditure in not having to pay the claimant for receipt of property in respect of which the former had an equitable interest, and the claimant's loss is that of the opportunity to charge the same. Recognition that the loss is not that of the claimant's equitable interest itself is important because it means that the claimant's loss arises irrespective of whether that interest survives the defendant's receipt of the property in question.[94] The characterisation of the interest as personal or proprietary is also irrelevant insofar as it is its susceptibility to exchange and market analysis that matters for unjust enrichment purposes.

That being so, the only role that equitable tracing plays in establishing the connection between enrichment and loss is that it provides the basis for concluding that the claimant had an equitable interest in the asset acquired by the defendant. That is, as with the common law tracing exercise encountered in *Lipkin Gorman*, equitable tracing is not the final step in establishing the connection between enrichment and loss. The asset in question must still be acquired by and *followed* to the defendant.

Equitable tracing was used in this way in *Relfo*.[95] In that case, the liquidator of the claimant company (Relfo) sought to recover monies diverted from that company by its former director (Mr Gorecia) through a complex series of indirect payments to the defendant (Mr Varsani) who held share capital in Relfo. Gorecia had diverted the money after Revenue and Customs began to pursue Relfo for an outstanding tax liability. The liquidators alleged that Gorecia (for a fee) had laundered the money through an overseas bank account for Varsani's benefit. At trial, Sales J held, as a matter of fact, that the liquidator could trace the money despite the evidentiary shortcomings to the claim brought about by the scheme between Gorecia and Varsani.[96] Like *El Ajou v Dollar Land Holdings plc*,[97] the ability to trace was based upon Relfo's equitable interest in the money from the outset:[98]

> Although the court has insufficient information available to be able to map each step in the process by which that result was achieved, it is a fair inference that the [payment to Varsani] was the product of a series of transactions between a number of entities and across a number of bank accounts designed to produce the result that funds [from Relfo] were ... paid on to Bhimji Varsani. Each bank account in the journey of the funds, or

[94] In the same way that questions of legal title are irrelevant to the assessment of enrichment and loss. See above pp 102–103. The highest that might be said of the continued existence of the claimant's equitable interest is that, depending on the terms of the trust and content of that equitable interest, the quantified value of the claim may be affected, just as the locus of possession can affect claims involving legal title to corporeal property (see the discussion of *Huyton SA v Peter Cremer GmbH & Co* [1999] 1 Lloyd's Rep 620 (QB), above pp 101–103). For example, the value of an unjust enrichment claim for the beneficiary of a bare trust is likely to be the same as if he had the legal right to the trust property, but lesser if he was the beneficiary of a special trust (and his equitable interest curtailed accordingly).

[95] *Relfo (High Court)* (n 27).

[96] ibid [76]–[77].

[97] *El Ajou* (n 26).

[98] *Relfo (High Court)* (n 27) [77] (emphasis added).

> each chose in action or obligation assumed by one entity to another to pay on the funds or to account for them and/or reimburse the other for paying them on, *was charged in equity with the obligation to repay the funds to Relfo*, and the funds received by Bhimji Varsani pursuant to the Intertrade payment were similarly so charged.

As the emphasised words make clear, the liquidator's ability to trace was intimately related to Relfo's continuing equitable interest in the funds as they moved between accounts. With each payment into a different account, a substitution occurred. First was a transfer from Relfo's bank account to the Latvian bank account of a company called Mirren. Because Gorecia directed that transfer in his capacity as a director, he was only free to deal with the legal interest in the account proceeds subject to Relfo's equitable interest. That meant that the only interest acquired by Mirren was a legal one subject to Relfo's equitable interest. Mirren, then, could only dispose of the same, and so on through the chain of different accounts. The Court of Appeal upheld Sales J's decision on this point,[99] and the emphasised words in the above passage were described as 'the heart of the process' of tracing.[100]

Deconstructed, each bank transfer took the form, first, of a chose in action assumed by one entity to pay another the funds and then, second, a chose in action at the bank in respect of which the money had been paid. At each stage in process, the payor was only free to dispose of a legal right subject to Relfo's equitable interest. This is why Sales J described the situation as one in which the bank account at each stage was charged in equity with the obligation to repay the funds to Relfo. That being so, though Varsani had a legal right to the funds ultimately paid to him by a company called Intertrade, he held those funds subject to Relfo's equitable interest.

That Relfo had an equitable interest in the money received by Varsani left the liquidator with three possible claims against him. First was a proprietary claim to vindicate its equitable interest in the money held by Varsani in the way that the beneficiaries had done in *Foskett v McKeown*.[101] That was not possible because Varsani no longer retained the funds paid to him.[102] Secondly, the liquidator sought a personal claim based upon knowing receipt of trust property, which succeeded.[103] Thirdly, the liquidator claimed in unjust enrichment. As the liquidator succeeded on the basis of knowing receipt, Sales J considered this third claim in *dicta* only, holding:[104]

> Varsani was clearly enriched by the Intertrade payment at the expense of Relfo. That is so even if the Intertrade payment cannot be identified with the Relfo/Mirren payment

[99] *Relfo (CA)* (n 27) [56]–[68] (Arden LJ, Gloster and Floyd LJJ agreeing).
[100] ibid [44].
[101] See above p 164.
[102] *Relfo (High Court)* (n 27) [68]–[69].
[103] ibid [70]–[84].
[104] ibid [88].

> according to the rules of tracing. Relfo had its funds diverted by Mr Gorecia in breach of his fiduciary duty as a director of Relfo and acting outside the scope of his authority from Relfo. In my judgment, that establishes a proper ground for an in personam claim by Relfo under the law of unjust enrichment against Bhimji Varsani for repayment of a sum equivalent to the extent of his enrichment, namely the amount of the Intertrade payment.

Two observations can be made in respect of the above passage. First, that Sales J was concerned with Varsani's receipt of the money from Intertrade confirms that equitable tracing was relevant only to a point, after which the relevant process was that of following. The money that Intertrade received was traceable in equity, meaning that it was subject to Relfo's equitable interest. There was a counterfactual connection between enrichment and loss: Varsani was enriched by the receipt of the money insofar as he did not have to pay Relfo for it.[105]

The second point is more profound. The fact that Sales J (with whom the Court of Appeal agreed)[106] considered the unjust enrichment claim could be made out even if the money that Intertrade received could not be traced from Relfo confirms the irrelevance of following, tracing, and transactional links to the unjust enrichment analysis of the case. Following, tracing, and transactional links are not part of the test of attribution in unjust enrichment because they are not part of unjust enrichment at all.

## (D) Transactions and the Counterfactual Inquiry

The difficult issue of fact confronting the liquidator in *Relfo* was that the money in respect of which it sought to claim had been diverted through a complex series of payments. That complexity, as regards a possible unjust enrichment claim, made it difficult to say whether Varsani's receipt of the Intertrade payment would have occurred 'but for' Relfo's loss of the money diverted from it by Gorecia. The more complex a series of payments is, the harder it will be to show which initial and intermediate payments were necessary for the final one to occur.

### (1) Transactions are Unnecessary

There are two ways to cut through this complexity in order to establish an unjust enrichment claim. One is to use the process of tracing and then, after that process is complete, to apply an unjust enrichment analysis to the receipt of the traceable

[105] It should be emphasised that (contrary to Sales J's dicta to the contrary *Relfo*) the existence of a connection between enrichment and loss does not mean the overall claim in unjust enrichment will be successful.

[106] *Relfo (CA)* (n 27) [97] (Arden LJ), [103] (Gloster LJ), [122] (Floyd LJ).

substitute by the defendant. Just like following a banknote into the hands of its final recipient, the rules and principles according to which the right in that traceable substitute arises do not form part of the unjust enrichment claim or analysis in respect of that right when the defendant later acquires it. They are just background facts. This was the first basis of unjust enrichment liability in *Relfo*.

The other way to cut through the factual complexity of a series of payments is to simply apply the unjust enrichment analysis (including the counterfactual test of attribution) across the first payment and final receipt. This is what Sales J meant when he said that the unjust enrichment claim was possible 'even if the Intertrade payment [could not] be identified with the Relfo/Mirren payment according to the rules of tracing'.[107] This was the second and alternate basis of unjust enrichment liability in *Relfo*,

Sales J glossed over the exact steps involved in this second alternate basis, but having regard to the relationship between Gorecia and Varsani, the judge considered that the Intertrade payment was the final step in a plan to divert funds from Relfo. The judge found 'that something along the following lines occurred':[108]

> Gorecia felt under considerable pressure in his relationship with the Varsani family … . He therefore decided to divert funds under his control (in the form of the money still held by Relfo, which otherwise would only be lost to the taxman) to the Varsanis in an effort to make some amends … . He used one or other of his contacts in the Ukraine to arrange to transfer the money from Relfo to the Varsanis in a way that disguised its source and the purpose of the payment. The Intertrade payment represented the onward transmission of the Relfo/Mirren payment, effected and disguised using the complex networks which his contacts had at their disposal.

In the Court of Appeal, Floyd LJ was even more dismissive of tracing's relevance to Varsani's liability unjust enrichment. His Lordship considered that the transactions that were a key feature of the tracing analysis were irrelevant to the unjust enrichment analysis (emphasis added):[109]

> I cannot accept the suggestion that *the intervening and meaningless arrangements* orchestrated by Mr Gorecia, which had no other purpose than to disguise the source of the funds diverted from Relfo, changed what would otherwise have been a direct payment into one which the law will not recognise as sufficiently proximate.

The unjust enrichment in *Relfo* thus arose *regardless* of tracing. On the first basis of unjust enrichment liability, Varsani was enriched only after the tracing process was done and complete—when he acquired Relfo's traceable substitute. On the second alternate basis of unjust enrichment, Varsani was enriched following a series of payments, the effect of which was considered independently of any tracing

[107] See also *Relfo (CA)* (n 27) [69] (Arden LJ): 'The point of law is whether, on the facts as found by the judge, Relfo would succeed on a claim for unjust enrichment … *on the hypothesis that Relfo cannot establish any tracing claim to that payment*.' (Emphasis added).

[108] *Relfo (High Court)* (n 27) [59].

[109] *Relfo (CA)* (n 27) [122] (Floyd LJ).

process. Neither basis involved the importation of tracing into the unjust enrichment analysis of the case. *Relfo* thus shows that tracing does not establish attribution in unjust enrichment.[110]

*Filby v Mortgage Express (No 2) Ltd* demonstrates the same point.[111] The defendant, (Mrs Filby) and her husband had bought a property with the assistance of a mortgage from the Halifax Building Society. They later sought to remortgage the property, and to this end a mortgage deed was executed between them and the claimant (Mortgage Express (No 2) Ltd). The husband, however, forged Mrs Filby's signature and so the mortgage was invalid. Nevertheless, and before this fraud was discovered, money was advanced by the claimant and used to discharge the Filbys' debt to Halifax and to reduce a business overdraft with Midland Bank. The Filbys then executed a second charge on the property in favour of Midland. Later, after loan payments to the claimant fell into arrears, the claimant received and (even later) enforced a possession order on the property. It sold the property and the question arose as to what was to be done with the proceeds of sale. The claimant successfully argued that it was entitled to be subrogated to the rights of the Halifax under the original mortgage. It also sought subrogation to the rights of Midland against Mrs Filby to the extent that her joint debt had been discharged by the payment of the monies advanced by the claimant. The Court of Appeal held that the claimant could trace from the money advanced under the invalid mortgage to that applied to the discharge of the Filbys' overdraft with Midland. That money had been paid on trust to solicitors acting for both parties on either side of the fraudulent mortgage transactions. May LJ held:[112]

> [T]he solicitors held the money upon an express trust. The question is not whether the solicitors were in breach of fiduciary duty or breach of trust. … The question is whether the claimants' beneficial interest in the money continued when the money was paid by the solicitors to Midland Bank and until it reached the Midland Bank account in overdraft. In my judgment, it did so continue. … [T]he claimants remained both the legal and beneficial owners of the £60,801 paid to Midland Bank until Midland Bank received it. [Counsel for the claimant] is correct that the tracing requirements … were fulfilled so that Mrs Filby was unjustly enriched at the claimants' expense.

There are a number of difficulties with this reasoning, but they do not impact upon the argument advanced by this chapter regarding the relationship between unjust enrichment and tracing. In particular, the idea that the claimant was *both* legal and beneficial owner of the money paid over to Midland by the solicitors is nonsensical insofar as its having the beneficial interest appears inconsistent with

[110] See also Mitchell, Mitchell, and Watterson, *Goff & Jones* (n 17) para 8.34: '[A]ny [traceable] title which C might have had to the asset has no more than a contingent relevance to his personal claim in unjust enrichment, and there is no need for C to prove that he had title … [A]lthough one way for C to prove that D was enriched at his expense is to show that D received an asset to which C had title, it is not the only way, since C can also establish this by proving "but for" causal links…'

[111] *Filby v Mortgage Express (No 2) Ltd* [2004] EWCA Civ 759.

[112] ibid [29]–[30] (May LJ; Hooper and Kennedy LJJ agreeing).

its also having legal ownership. It is incorrect insofar as the claimant having a legal right to the money is inconsistent with the solicitors holding it on trust. It is also unnecessary insofar as the claimant's ability to trace the money can be explained using the principles of equitable tracing referred to earlier.

Despite these difficulties, *Filby v Mortgage Express (No 2) Ltd* is noteworthy because, *after* tracing the money as far as Midland Bank, the claimant was able to establish that Mrs Filby was enriched at its expense when the money was paid into her overdraft. Importantly, May LJ observed that this could have been established *without* tracing:[113]

> [The claimant] would have no difficulty in establishing the reality that their money was used to reduce the joint Midland Bank loan account, even if, contrary to my view expressed earlier in this judgment, [counsel for the defendant's] submission as to tracing were correct.

The reference to 'reality' resonates strongly with the later case of *Bank of Cyprus plc v Menelaou*,[114] and a comparison of the two decisions usefully demonstrates the irrelevance of tracing to unjust enrichment.[115] On the one hand, tracing was not possible in *Bank of Cyprus plc v Menelaou*, nor was it necessary.[116] None of the Bank's money had been used, traceably or otherwise, to benefit Melissa. Rather, the Bank's loss and Melissa's enrichment were connected for unjust enrichment purposes by reason of the counterfactual relationship between the two: had the Bank not released its charges, Melissa's parents would not have been a position to purchase Great Oak Court in her name. On the other hand, tracing was possible in *Filby v Mortgage Express (No 2) Ltd*, but again it was not necessary. Rather, the relevant point was that Mrs Filby would not have been enriched 'but for' the loss incurred by the claimants insofar as the money held on trust for them was used to discharge her overdraft with Midland. Viewed together, the common denominator between the two cases is the counterfactual relationship between enrichment and loss.

These observations apply as forcefully to common law tracing as they do to equitable tracing. Thus, in *Lipkin Gorman*, the sequence around which the claimant's case was based was one according to which the defendant casino would not have been enriched 'but for' the claimants' loss of money from its account at the direction of Cass. That the sequence could also be analysed as one in which common law tracing was possible provided a precursor to the unjust enrichment analysis of the case and the demonstration of that counterfactual relationship.

[113] ibid (n 111) [50]. Indeed, *Filby v Mortgage Express (No 2) Ltd* was referred to extensively by the Court of Appeal in the later decision.

[114] *Bank of Cyprus UK Ltd v Menelaou* [2015] UKSC 66. See above pp 129–134.

[115] Cf *Relfo (CA)* (n 27) [89]–[98] (Arden LJ).

[116] *Bank of Cyprus UK Ltd v Menelaou* (*UKSC*) (n 114) [84]–[89] (Lord Neuberger). But see also [136]–[140] (Lord Carnwath) where his Lordship suggested that tracing the Bank's beneficial interest in the money was both necessary and possible for subrogation.

The editors of *Goff & Jones* have thus described tracing as 'contingent' to the 'but for' relationship,[117] though even that may be pitching its overall significance too highly. To say that tracing is contingent to a successful unjust enrichment claim suggests that the process is necessary, which it is not. Its role should not be overstated: tracing does not creep into the elements of unjust enrichment, including the relationship between enrichment and loss that is attribution. Tracing may be preliminary, or even coincidental, to that relationship, but it is not the relevant relationship itself and does not belong within unjust enrichment analysis.

This is unsurprising. Tracing and following are, after all, processes and not claims or bases of claims in and of themselves. The conclusion that an asset can be traced, followed, or some combination of both, does not establish a claim in respect of that asset; it forms a fact upon which legal conclusions can be formed by then applying legal analysis—such as unjust enrichment, including the rules of attribution.

## (2) Non-counterfactual Transactions

The idea that transactions are irrelevant to unjust enrichment might be criticised on the basis that there may be cases in which the parties are connected by transactions, unjust enrichment liability is imposed, but the counterfactual between enrichment and loss appears to fail.[118] In the light of a failure in the counterfactual, it seems that transactional links must be doing the work of attribution in unjust enrichment. Smith gives the example of a rogue making a gift to D which the rogue was going to make in any event, but which he happens to make with the traceable product of property taken from C.[119] In such a case it would appear that there is no counterfactual between C's loss and D's enrichment because D would have been enriched in any event. There is a tendency to consider *Foskett v McKeown* along similar lines because the money paid out under the insurance policy in that case would have been so paid even without the premiums contributed by Murphy with the trust money. Indeed, the fact that causal ('counterfactual' according to this book) links could not be established was the basis of the dissenting speeches in that case.[120]

This problem is essentially one of counterfactual under-determination—which, as we have seen, is not unique to transactions. Cases not involving transactions,

[117] Mitchell, Mitchell, and Watterson, *Goff & Jones* (n 17) para 8.34.

[118] I am indebted to Mr Ajay Ratan for his feedback on this point. See further A Ratan, 'Lord Mansfield's Protective Principle and Claims Based on Tracing' (Seminar Paper, Obligations Discussion Group, University of Oxford, 11 February 2014).

[119] L Smith, 'Unjust Enrichment, Property and the Structure of Trusts' (2000) 116 *Law Quarterly Review* 412, 417. See also L Smith, 'Restitution: The Heart of Corrective Justice' (2001) 79 *Texas Law Review* 2115, 2158–59; McFarlane, 'Unjust Enrichment, Property Rights, and Indirect Recipients' [2009] *Restitution Law Review* 37 fn 6.

[120] *Foskett* (n 5) 114–15 (Lord Steyn), 126 (Lord Hope).

where the defendant would apparently have been enriched in any event without the claimant's loss, were considered in chapter five.[121] There it was asserted that it would be nonsensical for a defendant to escape liability in unjust enrichment simply because he could have exacted benefits in different ways or from alternative sources besides the claimant. It was also explained that under-determination is not a real problem because it rests upon an incorrect understanding and definition of enrichment and loss in unjust enrichment. A defendant's enrichment is not the receipt of a benefit in the abstract, but its receipt in circumstances where the claimant could have charged for it. The claimant's loss is that of the opportunity to charge the defendant for the same. It is not to the point that the defendant received a benefit and might have received it in some other way; what matters is that he received the benefit that he did, and that the claimant was entitled to charge him for it.

Explaining why under-determination is not a problem in cases involving transactions proceeds in the same way. That the background facts include the existence of transactions should not obscure the unjust enrichment analysis that follows the end of those transactions.

In *Foskett v McKeown*, the beneficiaries' unjust enrichment claim arose when the insurance proceeds, in which they had an equitable interest, were acquired by Murphy's children. How the beneficiaries came to have an equitable interest in the insurance proceeds had nothing to do with unjust enrichment—just like the origins of the claimant's rights in the banknote in *Holiday v Sigil*. From there, establishing attribution in unjust enrichment proceeds by identifying the relevant enrichment and loss. If Murphy's children had obtained the beneficiaries' share of the policy paid out on his death, then they would have been enriched and the beneficiaries would have suffered a loss—reflecting their lost opportunity to charge in respect of those proceeds in which they had an interest arising because of Murphy's breach of trust. The fact that the policy would have paid out in any event without the payments made in breach of trust was irrelevant because the pay-out was not the relevant enrichment. The enrichment was, instead, the saving that followed the receipt of that payout for which the beneficiaries could have charged for their proportionate share. That enrichment could not arise 'but for' the beneficiaries' lost opportunity to charge.

Of course, that is not how *Foskett v McKeown* was argued, nor how it was decided. So much is plain from the remedy in the case. If the above analysis had been applied then the only appropriate award could have been a personal one for the amount the beneficiaries could have charged in respect of their share in the insurance policy, and that is the amount of that share itself.[122] But the House

[121] See above pp 134–140.

[122] It is also arguable that a change of position defence might have been available to Murphy's children, on the basis that liability in unjust enrichment would have left them worse off than if the trust money had never been paid into the insurance policy in the first place. See Ratan (n 118) 23–29.

of Lords held that the beneficiaries were entitled (at their option) either to claim a proportionate share of the policy or to enforce a lien upon it to secure their claim against Murphy for the amount of the misapplied money. This reflected the proprietary nature of their remedy based upon the vindication of their equitable entitlements established by the tracing process. The account provided of the counterfactual connection in *Foskett v McKeown* is thus an alternative to the analysis according to which the case was actually decided. It does not undermine or contradict how the case was actually decided, nor does it need to.

Returning to Smith's example of a rogue making a gift to D, which he was always going to make but which he makes with the traceable product of property taken from C, the reason that the inevitability of the gift is irrelevant is that the enrichment is not the gift *per se*, but the saved expenditure arising from not having to pay C for the receipt of his traceable product. C was entitled to that traceable product by reason of the rogue's substitution of C's original property, actions which have nothing to do with unjust enrichment.

This does not mean that the non-counterfactual transaction cases are totally uninstructive. There is at least one important lesson that can be derived from them: it is that the second kind of finding made in *Relfo* may not be possible in every unjust enrichment case.

It is to be recalled that in *Relfo* the unjust enrichment claim against Varsani was maintainable on two different bases:[123] first, with respect to Relfo's traceable substitute acquired by Varsani; and, secondly, with respect to the initial payment from Relfo to Mirren and the final payment from Intertrade to Varsani. Sales J and the Court of Appeal considered, in respect of the second basis, that attribution in unjust enrichment was possible irrespective of whatever had transpired in between the bookend payments. The judges may not have been as willing to make this finding, however, had something occurred in between that was analogous to the insurance policy in *Foskett v McKeown*; if Relfo's money had been effectively lost in a transaction out of which Varsani was always going to be paid a defined return regardless of Relfo's contribution, then it seems that no test of attribution—counterfactual, 'reality' or otherwise—could have overcome this. All that would remain was the first basis of unjust enrichment liability, according to which the Relfo's loss of its traceable substitute would not have arisen 'but for' Varsani's acquisition of it.

## (3) Counterfactual Connection is the Test of Attribution

The realisation that the existence of transactions merely precedes or is coincidental to attribution is important because it confirms the existence of a single test of attribution in unjust enrichment. There are not two tests, one general and one

[123] See above pp 167–168.

specific to transactions; the general test of a counterfactual connection between enrichment and loss covers the field and is *the* test.[124] A failure to trace should therefore not be fatal to a claim in unjust enrichment. As Lord Millett explained in *Foskett v McKeown* (emphasis added):[125]

> A plaintiff who brings an action in unjust enrichment must show that the defendant has been enriched at the plaintiff's expense, for he cannot have been unjustly enriched if he has not been enriched at all. *But the plaintiff is not concerned to show that the defendant is in receipt of property belonging beneficially to the plaintiff or its traceable proceeds.*

The pitfalls of failing to realise this point are illustrated by *Agip (Africa) Ltd v Jackson.*[126] In that case, Agip's chief accountant had fraudulently forged payment orders on its account with Banque du Sud in Tunisia, so that payment was directed to be made into the London account of Baker Oil at Lloyd's Bank; Baker Oil being a UK company in respect of which two of the defendants were the sole directors and shareholders. Banque du Sud executed the payment by requesting Lloyds Bank in London to credit Baker Oil's account, and undertaking that it would reimburse Lloyds Bank in New York via its correspondent bank, Citibank in New York. Lloyds Bank complied with the request by crediting Baker Oil's account prior to confirmation of the reimbursement in New York. Baker Oil then directed that the money be paid into the account of a separate firm (Jackson & Co) in respect of which two of the defendants were shareholders and directors, and one an employee. Agip thereafter brought multiple claims against the defendants, one of which was for money had and received by mistake. One response to this claim was the defendant's argument that Agip could not sue, the only proper claimant being Agip's bank, Banque du Sud. The argument was based on the fact that the bank had no right to debit Agip's account on the forged payment orders because it had no mandate do so.[127] Millett J (as his Lordship then was) explained that, though that may well have been the legal rule, as a matter of fact, Agip had been unable to get its bank account recredited.[128] This led his Lordship to conclude, as a matter of fact, that Banque du Sud (whether entitled to do so or not) had paid Agip's money out of its account for the purpose of meeting its undertaking to Lloyds Bank in New York.[129]

The difficult issue in *Agip (Africa) Ltd v Jackson* was the connection between Agip and the defendants. Applying the counterfactual inquiry advocated by this book: was there a counterfactual connection between the former's loss and the

[124] Cf L Smith, 'Tracing and Electronic Funds Transfers' in F Rose (ed), *Restitution and Banking Law* (Oxford, Mansfield Press, 1998).

[125] *Foskett* (n 5) 129 (Lord Millett). See also *Bank of Cyprus UK Ltd v Menelaou* (*UKSC*) (n 114) [38] (Lord Clarke).

[126] *Agip (Africa) Ltd v Jackson* [1990] Ch 265 (Ch); *Agip (Africa) Ltd v Jackson* [1991] Ch 547 (CA).

[127] *Agip (HC)* (n 126) 283.

[128] ibid.

[129] This was affirmed by the Court of Appeal. See *Agip (CA)* 561–63 (Fox LJ).

latters' enrichment? The answer is yes because both resulted from Banque du Sud's execution of the payment orders as agent for Agip. In essence, Banque du Sud 'purchased on credit' a payment to Baker Oil from Lloyds for Agip.[130] This set in motion a sequence of events: the request to Lloyds Bank to credit Baker Oil's account; the undertaking to reimburse Lloyds Bank; the satisfaction of that request and undertaking; and, ultimately, the payment from Baker Oil to the defendants, which would not have occurred 'but for' Banque du Sud's actions and, with it, the loss sustained by Agip by reason of its agency relationship with the bank.

*Agip (Africa) Ltd v Jackson* is relevant to this book in at least two ways. First, it demonstrates the utility of the counterfactual inquiry. Articulating the connection between claimant and defendant in as complex a case as *Agip (Africa) Ltd v Jackson* is not easy if one has only in mind the limited concepts of 'transfer' and 'causation' between loss and enrichment, or simple actions such as 'payment' and 'performance' as the origin of that connection. The counterfactual approach strips these concepts down to their common characteristics, thus enabling the resolution of new and hard cases by analogy to existing and simpler ones. Purchase of payment on credit is not immediately comparable to a simple payment between two parties, but when one considers that both have in common loss and enrichment, neither of which would have occurred 'but for' the happening of a single event, the extension of liabiltiy to one based upon the other becomes a more manageable exercise.

Secondly, *Agip (Africa) Ltd v Jackson* is illustrative of the error that can follow from making too much of tracing's relevance within unjust enrichment. Both Millett J and the Court of Appeal approached the claim for money had and received on the basis that it was necessary for the claimants to show that it was their money that had reached the defendants.[131] That being so, the claim failed because common law tracing through the mixed fund of the New York clearing system for banks was not possible.[132] This book rejects that approach: if the defendant's enrichment would not have arisen 'but for' the claimant's loss, then that should have sufficed for attribution purposes. The ability to trace is not necessary to establish a counterfactual relationship, as demonstrated by the cases subsequent to *Agip (Africa) Ltd v Jackson—Lipkin Gorman*, *Filby v Mortgage Express (No 2)*, *Relfo Ltd (In Liquidation) v Varsani*, and *Bank of Cyprus UK Ltd v Menelaou.*

[130] Smith, *The Law of Tracing* (n 11) 249–52.

[131] *Agip (HC)* (n 126) 285; *Agip (CA)* (n 126) 563.

[132] The claim for knowing receipt did, however, succeed: the mixing of funds was no obstacle to equitable tracing.

## (E) Tracing and Proprietary Restitution

This chapter has argued that transactional links add little further to our understanding of attribution in unjust enrichment beyond what is already known: that is, that attribution requires a counterfactual connection between enrichment and loss. At its highest, a transactional link will be sufficient but not necessary to establish a counterfactual connection. It is merely *coincidental* to the counterfactual connection; it is not the relevant connection itself.

That argument must, however, be subject to a final rider—the complete exploration of which is necessarily beyond the scope of this book. There is potentially one type of unjust enrichment claim in which the existence of a transactional link does appear significant in and of itself, and distinct from the underlying counterfactual connection that link evidences. That is the particular case of an unjust enrichment claim for proprietary restitution. As has already been explained,[133] this book takes the view that such a specific remedy for unjust enrichment is exceptional, and only justifiable in the presence of factors additional to those ordinarily arising within a claim. That being so, if a claimant seeks restitution of specific property on the basis of unjust enrichment, then he will need to show both that the circumstances justify that exceptional remedy, and that it should apply in respect of the particular property he seeks. As the editors of *Goff & Jones* have observed, albeit with reference to the difficult concepts of 'transfer of value' and 'causation':[134]

> [W]here the claimant seeks a proprietary remedy, it is not enough for him to show that there was a transfer of value between the parties: he must also show either that he previously owned the property in which he now claims an ownership or security interest, or else that the defendant acquired this property in exchange for property that was previously owned by the claimant, or else that this property was formerly the subject matter of an interest that was discharged with property that was previously owned by the claimant. This test is more stringent than the causal test used in the context of personal claims, and it serves as a control mechanism to prevent proprietary restitutionary remedies from becoming too freely available.

In such cases, transactional links complement the counterfactual relationship between enrichment and loss. Every unjust enrichment claim requires a 'but for' relationship between enrichment and loss, but (as already explained) proprietary claims require something more.[135] Establishing a transactional link will satisfy both requirements, be it in the form of following, tracing, or a combination of both. If, for example, a claimant mistakenly transfers a unique artwork to the defendant, then he must *follow* it to the defendant before he can seek restitution of it. And if he seeks proprietary restitution in respect of its traceable proceeds (whether at common law or in equity) then he must *trace* to them.

[133] See above pp 44–50.
[134] Mitchell, Mitchell, and Watterson, *Goff & Jones* (n 17) para 7.02.
[135] See above pp 46–48.

The overall picture, however, may yet prove more complicated. Absent a uniform test for specific remedies for unjust enrichment, the possibility of a uniform test of connection within such cases seems moot. Furthermore, there are cases in which transactional links have not been decisive of the success of a claim for specific restitution based upon unjust enrichment.

Subrogation cases are particularly difficult in this respect. In *Boscawen v Bajwa*,[136] for example, Abbey National lent money to the purchasers of Bajwa's house, intending to take a first charge over the property to secure the loan. The funds were paid to the purchasers' solicitors and then to the vendor's solicitors, who discharged Bajwa's mortgage over the property with Halifax Building Society. The sale never took place. Bajwa's judgment creditors later obtained a charging order against the property and sold the house, after which Abbey National claimed that it was entitled to priority over the proceeds of sale by right of subrogation to Halifax's charge over the property. The Court of Appeal held that Abbey National was entitled to be subrogated to the charge. That conclusion cannot be explained by reference to tracing alone because, even if Abbey National's money could be traced to Halifax, it was then lost when it was used to extinguish the debt.[137] No traceable assets were received in exchange for the money, and so the tracing process came to an end. As Millett LJ explained, however, the termination of tracing was not fatal to subrogation (or other specific remedies, for that matter):[138]

> The plaintiff will generally be entitled to a personal remedy; if he seeks a proprietary remedy he must usually prove that the property to which he lays claim is still in the ownership of the defendant. If he succeeds in doing this the court will treat the defendant as holding the property on a constructive trust for the plaintiff and will order the defendant to transfer it *in specie* to the plaintiff. But this is only one of the proprietary remedies which are available to a court of equity. If the plaintiff's money has been applied by the defendant, for example, not in the acquisition of a landed property but in its improvement, then the court may treat the land as charged with the payment to the plaintiff of a sum representing the amount by which the value of the defendant's land has been enhanced by the use of the plaintiff's money. And if the plaintiff's money has been used to discharge a mortgage on the defendant's land, then the court may achieve a similar result by treating the land as subject to a charge by way of subrogation in favour of the plaintiff.

That, as Millett LJ suggests, a number of proprietary remedies are available without reliance on transactional links lessens the general significance of those links within unjust enrichment even further. To claim a proprietary or specific remedy, a claimant must 'usually prove that the property to which he lays claim is still in the ownership of the defendant'—in the language of *Foskett v McKeown*, he must follow or trace that property to the defendant.[139] But he need not do so always,

[136] *Boscawen v Bajwa* (n 5).
[137] ibid 333.
[138] ibid 334–35.
[139] See above pp 145–148.

as subrogation cases like *Boscawen v Bajwa*, *BFC v Parc (Battersea)*, and *Bank of Cyprus UK Ltd v Menelaou* demonstrate.

Cases involving liens illustrate the point further. In *Spencer v S Franses Ltd*,[140] for example, a defendant textile expert was entitled to a possessory lien over embroideries after he had carried out research work establishing their medieval provenance. Transactional links were irrelevant. Instead, the point of principle was that, having done work on the embroideries delivered to him, the defendant was entitled to retain them until he was paid.[141] The embroideries were in his possession already, and his claim did not depend upon following or tracing.

Arguments that seek to raise transactional links to a determinative prominence in cases involving specific remedies must confront the reality that there is, as yet, no uniform test for such remedies on the basis of unjust enrichment. Whether such uniformity is even possible remains to be seen, and is a matter beyond the scope of this book. What *is* within the scope of this book is the larger point that transactional links add nothing to our understanding of attribution in unjust enrichment beyond what is already known: that is, that attribution requires a counterfactual connection between enrichment and loss.

[140] *Spencer v S Franses Ltd* [2011] EWHC 1269 (QB).
[141] ibid [247] (Thirlwall J).

# Part III

# Qualifying Liability

Parts I and II of this book have been concerned with defining enrichment, loss, and the connection that must exist between those two concepts for the attribution requirements of unjust enrichment to be satisfied. This next part, however, involves an important change in emphasis. Rather than focusing on attribution in unjust enrichment, this part is about matters that are actually *irrelevant* to attribution. The concern of this part lies with the separate question of how liability in unjust enrichment can nevertheless be barred, conditioned, or otherwise qualified by reasons extraneous to the definitions of enrichment and loss, and the connection between the two.

This immediately begs the question: Why include this part at all? If this book is about attribution in unjust enrichment, then it appears confusing to include a discussion of matters that have nothing to do with attribution. The substance of this part thus seems to be beside the point.

However, it is precisely to say that these matters are beside the point that the discussion in this part is undertaken. These matters have often tended to be analysed as part of the 'enrichment at the claimant's expense' inquiry, and so mistakenly conflated with the question of whether the claimant and defendant are connected to each other. The aim of this part is to correct that mistake by situating them outside the requirements of attribution—enrichment, loss, and the connection between the two.

This part of the book also differs from the previous two insofar as it comprises only one chapter, chapter seven. Isolating a single chapter within a single part reflects both the structural and substantial significance of the matters under consideration. It has the effect of emphasising that qualifications on liability in unjust enrichment are separate and distinct issues from whether a connection exists between claimant and defendant establishing that liability in the first place. The failure to realise that point can lead to substantial confusion and an inaccurate account of how attribution in unjust enrichment actually works.

An example of such confusion can be found in *Investment Trust Companies v HMRC*.[1] It is to be recalled that Henderson J held in that case that the English

[1] *Investment Trust Companies (In Liquidation) v Revenue and Customs Commissioners* [2012] EWHC 458 (Ch), [2012] STC 1150. See further *Investment Trust Companies v Revenue and Customs* [2015] EWCA Civ 82 [65]–[69] (Patten LJ).

law of unjust enrichment included a general rule of 'direct enrichment' subject to limited exceptions. He then set out how such exceptions should develop:[2]

> [N]o exhaustive list of criteria for the recognition of exceptions has yet been put forward by proponents of the general rule, and I think it is safe to assume that the usual preference of English law for development in a pragmatic and step by step fashion will prevail. Nevertheless, in the search for principle a number of relevant considerations have been identified, including (in no particular order):
>
> (a) the need for a close causal connection between the payment by the claimant and the enrichment of the indirect recipient;
> (b) the need to avoid any risk of double recovery, often coupled with a suggested requirement that the claimant should first be required to exhaust his remedies against the direct recipient;
> (c) the need to avoid any conflict with contracts between the parties, and in particular to prevent 'leapfrogging' over an immediate contractual counterparty in a way which would undermine the contract; and
> (d) the need to confine the remedy to disgorgement of undue enrichment, and not to allow it to encroach into the territory of compensation or damages.

With respect, this approach is flawed. The reality is that there is no general rule of direct enrichment subject to exceptions. If there were, then it would mean that a claimant could not make a claim in unjust enrichment simply because additional parties were interposed between its loss and the defendant's enrichment, and that would contradict the many cases involving sequential and concurrent connections, as well as interceptions, which were considered in chapter four.[3] The perceived existence of the 'direct enrichment' rule is instead the result of a failure to keep the connection and qualification questions separate. Looking closely at Henderson J's list, the only positive requirement is consideration (a), which reflects the need for a connection between enrichment and loss—a 'but for' counterfactual according to this book. This is not an 'exception' unique to indirect recipient cases; it is a general requirement applicable to all cases. The remaining considerations, however, are not 'exceptions' to a direct enrichment rule either; nor are they even suggestive of exceptions. Rather, they are qualifications imposed on liability that arise despite the connection between claimant and defendant. They should not be conflated with attribution in unjust enrichment[4] but should instead be analysed in their own right, as the following chapter aims to do.

[2] ibid [68].

[3] See above pp 108–119.

[4] As Floyd LJ appears to have done in *TFL Management Services Ltd v Lloyds Bank plc* [2013] EWCA Civ 1415, at [57] where his Lordship stated that Henderson J's considerations 'are relevant considerations in deciding the question of whether an indirect benefit was conferred at the claimant's expense'.

# 7

# Qualification

If a counterfactual connection between enrichment and loss, arising in unjust circumstances, were sufficient to establish a claim in unjust enrichment then unjust enrichment claims could extend indeterminately. Suppose, for example, that C and D each own a rare model of car, the only two remaining in the world. Suppose then that C's car is struck by lightning and destroyed. C suffers a loss while the market value of D's now one-of-a-kind car increases significantly, a value that he realises by selling the car. Surely C cannot claim in unjust enrichment in these circumstances despite the counterfactual relationship between loss and enrichment. There is no unjust factor in this example, but that point has its limits insofar as it assumes the connection between loss and enrichment in the first place. A less far-fetched example cannot be explained by the absence of an unjust factor. Suppose C and D are neighbouring landowners and, by mistake, C omits to use some statutory veto power he has to prevent D developing his property into a megalithic block of apartments. The market value of D's land skyrockets, while the market value of C's land plummets (no one wants land in the shadow of D's megalith). There is a counterfactual relationship and an unjust factor, and so something else must prohibit C's claim—if that is to be the conclusion.

Problems of this kind are not unique to unjust enrichment. In chapter five we observed Hart and Honoré's use of 'standard criteria' to limit liability in the context of causation in tort.[1] The issue now is how those 'standard criteria' can be usefully supplemented in the law of unjust enrichment, where legal liability can arise in the absence of conduct, wrongdoing, or fault by the defendant. Lord Hoffmann's approach to causation provides some insight. He explains that common sense principles applied to fault-based liability may not be appropriate to claims based on something other than fault, such as strict liability, in which case the range of situations for which one is liable may be enlarged beyond the standard criteria.[2] President Allsop (as his Honour the Chief Justice then was) has also observed that:[3]

> Hard cases about causation and related topics … are all answered not by common sense or by positing a cause-in-fact/cause-in-law dichotomy, but by selecting for legal policy

[1] See above pp 124–125.

[2] L Hoffmann, 'Causation' (2005) 121 *Law Quarterly Review* 592, 594.

[3] J Allsop, 'Causation in Commercial Law' in S Degeling, J Edelman, and J Goudkamp (eds), *Torts in Commercial Law* (Sydney, Thomson Reuters, 2011).

> reasons different criteria by reference to which to judge liability, that is legal responsibility—being a departure from the usual or standard criteria. These are not intuitive responses based on internalised moral notions of common sense. They are legal rules formulated and explained.

These observations apply as much to unjust enrichment as they do to tort. The relevant legal rules must be found in the cases and articulated for general application. Much like remoteness of liability for tort (or breach of contract), those rules limit the scope of liability in unjust enrichment, rather than inform the nature of the connection that must exist between claimant and defendant for an unjust enrichment claim to arise.

Henderson J's list of relevant considerations in *Investment Trust Companies v HMRC*, extracted at the start of this part, should be understood in this light.[4] Considerations (b), (c), and (d) in that list are different criteria by reference to which the court can judge whether to impose liability despite satisfaction of the standard criteria embodied in consideration (a)—the connection between enrichment and loss. A survey of the cases reveals that there is no exhaustive list of factors and considerations that qualify unjust enrichment in this way. It is not the aim of this chapter to provide one. Rather, the aim is to demonstrate that such qualifications exist, and that they do so independently of attribution in unjust enrichment. The reasons why liability may be so qualified are also generalised—not so that an exhaustive list of qualifications can be ascertained, but so that the list of qualifications can be applied, developed, and understood on a case-by-case basis.

# (A) Contract

The most significant qualification on unjust enrichment evident in the cases arises at its intersection with contract. The relationship between unjust enrichment and contract thus provides a useful starting point for appreciating both the nuance of the qualifications on unjust enrichment, as well as their distinct character (distinct, that is, from attribution). It also provides a foundation for examining the relationship between contract and the normative underpinnings of unjust enrichment according to the exchange capacity explained by this book.

## (1) Contract Bars Recovery

It was observed in chapter four that the claimant in *The Trident Beauty*, Pan Ocean, could not recover money it had paid to the defendant, Creditcorp.[5] Payment meant

[4] *Investment Trust Companies (In Liquidation) v Revenue and Customs Commissioners* [2012] EWHC 458 (Ch), [2012] STC 1150 [39]. See above p 180.

[5] *Pan Ocean Shipping Co Ltd v Creditcorp Ltd (The Trident Beauty)* [1994] 1 WLR 161 (HL). See above pp 114–115.

there was a connection between enrichment and loss but Pan Ocean could not recover because there were contracts between the parties. Lord Goff explained:[6]

> [S]erious difficulties arise if the law seeks to expand the law of restitution to redistribute risks for which provision has been made under an applicable contract. Moreover, it would in any event be unjust to do so in a case such as the present where the defendant, Creditcorp, is not the mere recipient of a windfall but is an assignee who has purchased from Trident the right to receive the contractual debt which the plaintiff, Pan Ocean, is now seeking to recover from Creditcorp in restitution despite the facts that the relevant contract imposes on the assignor (Trident) an obligation of repayment in the circumstances in question, and that there is nothing in the assignment which even contemplates, still less imposes, any additional obligation on the assignee (Creditcorp) to repay.

These comments reflect two different concerns. The first is a concern not to undermine a contract between the claimant and defendant. The second is a concern not to undermine a contract between one of those two parties and a third.

The High Court of Australia expressed the same concerns in *Lumbers v W Cook Builders Pty Ltd (in liquidation)*.[7] The defendant landowner had contracted with a building company (the 'head-contractor') to build a house. The head-contractor engaged the claimant sub-contractor to do the work. The claimant's liquidator later sought money from both the head-contractor and the defendant for the work done. The case against the defendant was based, *inter alia*, on restitution for unjust enrichment. Gleeson CJ explained that the contractual relations among the parties could not be put to one side.[8] The claimant had a viable claim against the head-contractor and there was no reason to interfere with their existing contractual arrangements.[9] The joint judgment approached matters differently; their Honours' concern was to avoid undermining the contractual arrangements between the defendant owner and head-contractor.[10] Despite these differences, however, the overarching concern of both judgments in *Lumbers*, as well as of Lord Goff in *The Trident Beauty*, was the same: to avoid undermining the contractual arrangements and distributions of risk that the parties had constructed.

Cases analogous to *Lumbers*, such as *The Trident Beauty* and others involving the conferral of benefits under contract,[11] were described by Birks as supporting the principle that '[l]eapfrogging out of an initially valid contract is not allowed'.[12] That expression, however, is too limited because 'leapfrogging' really has nothing to do with these cases. Leapfrogging suggests a benefit being passed from one recipient to the next in a series of sequential connections, and that in order to

[6] *The Trident Beauty* (n 5) 166.

[7] *Lumbers v W Cook Builders Pty Ltd (In Liquidation)* [2008] HCA 27, (2008) 232 CLR 635, [83]–[85] (Gummow, Hayne, Crennan, and Kiefel JJ).

[8] ibid [45].

[9] ibid [46]–[47].

[10] ibid [77], [80], [93], [121], [124]–[127] (Gummow, Hayne, Crennan, and Kiefel JJ).

[11] See above p 115.

[12] P Birks, *Unjust Enrichment*, 2nd edn (Oxford, Oxford University Press, 2005) 90.

reach down the line of recipients, the claimant must 'leapfrog' over those earlier in the line. As explained in chapter four,[13] however, cases involving the conferral of a benefit by a claimant on a defendant for a third party actually involve concurrent, not sequential, connections. There is no need to leapfrog anyone: there is a single connection between the claimant and the defendant. What limits recovery is not some principle against leapfrogging, but a principle against liability in unjust enrichment where it would undermine or compete with contract. This is why the joint judgment in *Lumbers* explained that an essential step in considering a claim in *quantum meruit* or for money paid 'is to ask whether and how that claim fits with any particular contract the parties have made'.[14] That step is not limited to cases involving several parties, but applies to two-party cases as well. If a claimant confers a benefit on a defendant under a valid contract then it is not only the absence of an unjust factor that may deny the unjust enrichment claim, but also the very existence of the contract. And as Lord Goff's judgment in *The Trident Beauty* and the different judgments in *Lumbers* demonstrate, it is not only valid contracts between the claimant and the defendant that matter for this purpose, but also those between each of the claimant, defendant, and third parties. The claim is barred because it would be inconsistent with contract as an overriding source of rights and obligations.

These matters were considered by the Court of Appeal in *MacDonald Dickens & Macklin (a firm) v Costello*.[15] The claimant builders performed construction work on land owned by the defendants (the Costellos). Rather than contracting personally with the builders, however, the Costellos had used a company (Oakwood), of which they were the sole shareholders and directors, to engage and pay the builders. The builders knew of this arrangement and had, in fact, been previously engaged in the same way with respect to another development owned by the Costellos. Following a dispute about the standard of the works, £65,038 was outstanding on invoices for work done pursuant to the contract and for additional work outside the terms of the contract. The Court framed the issue in the case as whether the Costellos could be held liable in unjust enrichment when the builder's services from which they had benefited were provided under a contract between the builders and a third party, Oakwood.[16] The Court held them not liable.

Four aspects of the decision are particularly important for this book. First, the builders' loss was not an issue in the case, nor was it discussed in the Court's reasons. Indeed, it was incontestable because the builders had used materials and performed the building services, without payment for which the opportunity to charge would be lost. The case was thus one in which the requirement of loss was not considered in the reasons, but that does not mean it was not a necessary part of the builders' claim.

[13] See above pp 114–115.
[14] *Lumbers* (n 7) [79] citing *Steele v Tardiani* [1946] HCA 21, (1946) 72 CLR 386.
[15] *MacDonald Dickens & Macklin (a firm) v Costello* [2011] EWCA Civ 930, [2012] QB 244.
[16] ibid [4] (Etherton LJ; Pill LJ and Patten LJ agreeing).

Secondly, Etherton LJ described the builders' claim as raising two points of principle. First was whether, 'in terms of causation', the Costellos' enrichment had been at the expense of the builders.[17] He noted that, 'in one sense, of course it was' because the builders had provided services which had benefited the Costellos.[18] On the approach advocated by this book, this 'first point of principle' was the connection between the loss and enrichment—in other words, attribution. Attribution was clearly satisfied, that being the 'one sense' in which the 'at the expense of the claimant' inquiry was 'of course' satisfied. His Lordship added that the next question was whether the builders 'could leapfrog Oakwood' in order to claim against the Costellos.[19] This led to the 'second point of principle': whether the builders' claim 'should be allowed to undermine the contract between Oakwood and Mr and Mrs Costello' and the way in which the parties chose to allocate the risks involved in the transaction.[20] Putting the problematic use of the terms 'causation' and 'leapfrogging' to one side, the approach taken in *Costello* was close to that advocated by this book. After the identification of enrichment, loss, and the connection between the two, a separate question arose as to whether—and despite the connection between enrichment and loss—a reason existed to deny or otherwise qualifying liability in unjust enrichment. It was this latter question that determined the outcome of the case:[21]

> [T]he unjust enrichment claim against Mr and Mrs Costello must fail because it would undermine the contractual arrangements between the parties, that is to say the contract between the respondents and Oakwood and the absence of any contract between the respondents and Mr and Mrs Costello. The *general* rule should be to uphold contractual arrangements by which parties have defined and allocated and, to that extent, restricted their mutual obligations, and, in so doing, have similarly allocated and circumscribed the consequences of non-performance. That general rule reflects a sound legal policy, which acknowledges the parties' autonomy to configure the legal relations between them and provides certainty, and so limits disputes and litigation.

His Lordship relied upon Lord Goff's observations in *The Trident Beauty* as well as those of the joint judgment in *Lumbers* in reaching this conclusion,[22] before adding that the existence of different remedies in unjust enrichment and contract was capable of producing anomalous results and of enabling a claimant to improve on a bad bargain.[23] It would also circumvent the usual consequences of Oakwood's insolvency.[24]

[17] ibid [20].
[18] ibid.
[19] ibid.
[20] ibid [21].
[21] ibid (emphasis added). See also A Burrows, *A Restatement of the English Law of Unjust Enrichment* (Oxford, Oxford University Press, 2012) 53–52.
[22] *Costello* (n 15) [30].
[23] ibid [31].
[24] ibid [21], [32]. See further below at pp 203–204.

Thirdly, it is noteworthy that Etherton LJ's reasoning was not confined to the building services described under the contract, but applied also to additional work outside the terms of the contract. His Lordship thus adopted a broad-brush approach, basing his decision not only on the existence of the contract but upon the totality of the parties' dealings.

This is closely related to a final observation that can be made about the case. His Lordship stated the applicable rule upholding contractual arrangements as only a 'general' rule and then explained that the facts of the case justified its application.[25] That the builders had done work for the Costellos under precisely the same arrangement before (that is, under contract with Oakwood) meant that they had 'gone into the agreement with their eyes open'.[26] On this approach the relationship between unjust enrichment and contract is not strict but subject to nuances of fact. Indeed, as we shall see under the next sub-heading, there are several cases where unjust enrichment claims have intersected with contract, and in which restitution has merely been conditioned rather than completely barred.

## (2) Contract Conditions Recovery

In *Blue Haven*,[27] it is to be recalled, Blue Haven improved land for Tully that was then conveyed under contract of sale to Robinson. In chapter four the case was relied upon as an example of unjust enrichment involving sequential connections between enrichment and loss.[28] But it also seems to come with a catch, for the Privy Council stated that Robinson was enriched at Blue Haven's expense 'only to the extent that recovery by Blue Haven from Mrs Tully [was] not possible'.[29] This seems inconsistent with the position established in chapter three, that unjust enrichment claims are not concerned with a claimant's persisting loss.[30]

It is possible, however, to reconcile that position with *Blue Haven*. The key lies in appreciating the nuances of the relationship between contract and unjust enrichment. The Privy Council's *dictum* that Robinson was enriched at Blue Haven's expense only to the extent that recovery from Tully was impossible was not an endorsement of a persisting loss requirement. Their Lordships were instead concerned not to undermine the contractual regime between Blue Haven and Tully. The existence of that regime meant Tully was liable for substantial damages in contract.[31] Once recovery under contract was deemed impossible, however, that concern evaporated.

[25] ibid [30], [32].
[26] ibid [32].
[27] *Blue Haven Enterprises Ltd v Tully* [2006] UKPC 17.
[28] See above pp 112–113.
[29] *Blue Haven* (n 27) [19].
[30] See, eg, G Jones, *Goff & Jones: The Law of Restitution, First Supplement*, 7th edn (London, Sweet & Maxwell Ltd, 2009) [1-044]. See above pp 78–80.
[31] *Blue Haven* (n 27) [19].

*Blue Haven* is thus an example of the nuances that characterise the qualification of unjust enrichment liability according to contract. In *Costello*, *Lumbers*, and *The Trident Beauty* the unjust enrichment claim had been completely barred. It is noteworthy, however, that in *Costello* Etherton LJ described the rule as a 'general' one, rather than in absolute terms. Furthermore, as the joint judgment explained in *Lumbers*, the 'identification of the rights and obligations of the parties … requires close attention to the particular facts and circumstances of the case'.[32] The claimant sub-contractor in *Lumbers* had contracted with the head-contractor to do work for the benefit of the defendant third party. There was no equivalent in *Blue Haven*. Blue Haven had contracted with Tully without knowledge of Robinson's existence or the benefits he stood to gain from Blue Haven's improvements to the land.[33] Equally as important, Robinson could not have contracted with knowledge of Blue Haven's future improvements. A claim in unjust enrichment would therefore not redistribute any risks for which provision had been made under contract. The parties had not gone into their respective agreements 'with eyes open' as the parties had in *Costello*.[34] In *Blue Haven*, however, liability in unjust enrichment was qualified because it could not stand in the face of recovery under principles of contractual liability, rather than because it might undermine a predetermined distribution of risks. The claim was therefore conditioned upon that contractual liability running out, and was not completely barred by it.

*Blue Haven* is not the only example of such a nuanced approach. In *Niru Battery (No 1)*,[35] for example, Moore-Bick J held that any money recovered by the bank would necessarily be held on trust for its customer because it had already reimbursed itself against the customer's account. Both the bank and its customer had suffered a loss connected to the defendant's enrichment, but permitting the bank to recover unconditionally, if combined with the reimbursement already undertaken pursuant to the contract with its customer, would have the undesired effect of double recovery in the bank's favour.

This analysis also fits the difficult case of *Khan v Permayer*.[36] The claimant (Khan) ran a restaurant that he wanted to sell, along with the lease over the premises, to a third party (Eaves). The defendant landlord (Permayer) agreed to assign the lease on the condition that a debt of £40,000 owed to him by Khan was repaid. Eaves agreed to pay the debt on Khan's behalf, on the condition that Khan and

[32] *Lumbers* (n 7). See further *Roxborough v Rothmans of Pall Mall Australia Ltd* [2001] HCA 68, (2001) 208 CLR 516, in which a retailer successfully reclaimed an *ultra vires* tax which had been contractually paid in advance to a wholesaler, and which had not been remitted to the taxing authority. This was despite the contract between the parties remaining valid.

[33] Blue Haven contracted with Tully on 5 January 1988. It only found out about Robinson in January 1989. See *Blue Haven* (n 27) [5], [14].

[34] *Costello* (n 15) [32].

[35] *Niru Battery Manufacturing Co v Milestone Trading Ltd (No 1)* [2002] EWHC 1425 (Comm), [2002] 2 All ER (Comm) 705. See above pp 78–79.

[36] *Khan v Permayer* [2001] BPIR 95 (CA).

his partner should then pay him £40,000. The agreement was fulfilled: Eaves paid Permayer and Khan reimbursed him. It then emerged that the debt did not exist because it had been discharged in earlier insolvency proceedings. Khan successfully recovered £40,000 from Permayer on the basis of unjust enrichment.

The structure of the claim in *Khan v Permayer* was different from other concurrent connection cases where A confers a benefit on B for C because rather than Eaves (A),[37] it was Khan (C) who pursued Permayer (B) in a claim based upon unjust enrichment. Nevertheless, the existence of concurrent connections between Khan and Eaves on the one hand, and Eaves and Permayer on the other, meant that Khan could claim against Permayer in respect of the latter's enrichment.[38] Two important points then avoided a qualification on Permayer's liability. First, the common mistake between Eaves and Khan as to the existence of the debt meant there was no contract between them; so permitting Khan to pursue Permayer would not undermine a contract between him and Eaves.[39] Secondly, the fact that Khan had reimbursed Eaves meant that no qualification to his claim was necessary as in *Blue Haven* or *Niru Battery (No 1)*. Burrows rightly observes that the effect of the decision was to avoid circuity of action (Eaves suing Permayer and then Khan suing Eaves),[40] but that observation is an incomplete explanation of the case. The circuity of action point would have been equally applicable if a contract between Khan and Eaves was persisting but the contract would have qualified the claim. The larger point is that Khan could claim against Permayer because enrichment was connected to loss, and their contractual arrangements did not qualify the claim.

## (3) Contract and the Exchange Capacity

The cases thus suggest that there is, in effect, a hierachy of norms in which contract sits above unjust enrichment as a source of rights and obligations. The rule appears to be that unjust enrichment is subordinate to the law of contract, in the sense that unjust enrichment claims will not be permitted to undermine those otherwise available in contract. As the *Third Restatement* explains:[41]

> Considerations of both justice and efficiency require that private transfers be made pursuant to contract wherever reasonably possible, and that the parties' own definition of their respective obligations—assuming the validity of their agreement by all pertinent tests—take precedence over the obligations that the law would impose in the absence of

[37] As, for example, in *The Trident Beauty* (n 5) and *Lumbers* (n 7). See generally Birks, *Unjust Enrichment* (n 12) 90–91.

[38] *Khan v Permayer* (n 36) 104. See *Stevenson v Mortimer* (1778) 2 Cowp 805, 98 ER 1372 (KB) 806.

[39] That the contract was void did not, however, undermine the existence of a relationship of agency between Khan and Eaves.

[40] A Burrows, *The Law of Restitution*, 3rd edn (Oxford, Oxford University Press, 2011).

[41] American Law Institute, Restatement of the Law Third: Restitution and Unjust Enrichment (2012) ('*Third Restatement*') § 2(2) comment c.

> agreement. Restitution is accordingly subordinate to contract as an organizing principle of private relationships, and the terms of an enforceable agreement normally displace any claims of unjust enrichment within their reach.

These observations are subject to two important riders. The first is that there is no complete bar to unjust enrichment simply by reason of the fact that a contract is in existence. As the *Third Restatement* acknowledges, the broad statement that there can be no unjust enrichment in contract cases is 'plainly erroneous'.[42] Indeed, as we have seen, there are a number of cases in which contract merely conditions unjust enrichment liability. The second rider is that, as *Costello* suggests, the concern for contract may even prevent an unjust enrichment claim in exceptional circumstances where an agreement has not yet been reached.[43] It is to be recalled, in that case, that some of the barred unjust enrichment claims related to additional work outside the terms of the contract.

Having made the point that the relationship between contract and unjust enrichment works in this way, the question that follows is *why* it should do so. One possibility is that the law adopts a policy against the stultification of different bases of liability. To stultify the law is to undermine or contradict it.[44] 'Stultification' was described by Birks as a diverse defence to unjust enrichment claims,[45] and the relationship between contract and unjust enrichment seems to be an example. The problem with stultification, however, is that it appears to be more of an observation, rather than an explanation. It immediately poses the follow up question of *why* stultification of contract matters in this way. The *Third Restatement* makes inroads into this question insofar as it observes that '[c]onsiderations of both justice and efficiency' determine the superiority of contract, but the challenge is to explain just what those considerations are.[46]

One solution lies in the exchange capacity advanced by this book as the normative basis of unjust enrichment claims. In chapter one it was observed that the exchange capacity is merely one manifestation of the larger freedom of will concept that underpins private law according to corrective justice, and that free will is also the overarching idea behind other principles that inform the law. It was also suggested that contract and unjust enrichment may, in particular, be conceptually similar insofar as contract facilitates the exercise of the exchange capacity, while unjust enrichment alleviates its defective exercise.[47] If that is correct then a relationship between unjust enrichment and contract, of the kind observed in the cases, should be expected. Unjust enrichment is qualified by the existence of contract because the latter indicates the free exercise of the exchange capacity, meaning unjust enrichment has no work to do.

42 ibid.
43 See above p 186.
44 Birks, *Unjust Enrichment* (n 12) 240.
45 ibid 240.
46 See above (n 41) and accompanying text.
47 See above pp 39–40.

This explanation fits important nuances observed in the cases above. First, because unjust enrichment consists of a disruption to each of the defendant's and claimant's exchange capacity, a contract will qualify unjust enrichment liability whether it is between those two parties, or between just one of them and a third. One of either the enrichment or the loss does not arise as defined within unjust enrichment, because it is the product of contract, and so not a defective manifestation of the exchange capacity. That is why, despite the paradigm case of contract qualifying unjust enrichment being that where a contract exists between the claimant and defendant, many of the cases that actually demonstrate that relationship are those in which the relevant contract is between either one of the claimant or the defendant and some other third party—such as between the defendant Creditcorp and Trident (a third party) in *The Trident Beauty*, the claimant builders and Oakwood (a third party) in *Costello*, or the claimant Blue Haven and Tully (a third party) in *Blue Haven.*[48] A defendant who receives a benefit under a contract is not enriched within the meaning of enrichment advanced by this book: he is not saved the expense of having to pay for it because the receipt of it is governed by a contract. Likewise, a claimant who suffers a loss under a contract is not denied the opportunity to charge for the benefit conferred because he has entered into a contract in respect of that benefit, and so exercised that opportunity. This is also why it matters, as demonstrated by the comparison between *Blue Haven* and *Costello*, that parties in respect of whom a contract denies an unjust enrichment claim have gone into their respective agreements 'with eyes open'—this being indicative of a free exercise of their exchange capacities.

Relating the qualification of unjust enrichment according to contract back to the exchange capacity also explains why, in *Costello*, an unjust enrichment claim was barred even in respect of work done outside the contract with Oakwood. If the reason why contract qualifies unjust enrichment is that it indicates the free exercise of the exchange capacity, then it stands to reason that there will be cases in which facts that do not indicate the existence of a fully-formed contract achieve the same result. *Costello* suggests that the performance of work for a third party with whom the claimant has a contract to do related work is sufficient for this purpose. The relationship between the builders and Oakwood only had the effect of barring an unjust enrichment claim by the builders against the Costellos; it did not (and could not) go so far as to impose contractual liability between the builders and Oakwood for work done outside their contract. The ultimate point appears to be that the builders' decision to contract with Oakwood, rather than the Costellos themselves, was a free exercise of their exchange capacity.

[48] See further Burrows, *A Restatement of the English Law of Unjust Enrichment* (n 21) 53.

# (B) Property

A difficult issue commonly arises in unjust enrichment claims where a claimant performs a service that leaves a valuable residuum in the hands of the defendant. That issue is whether restitution should be for the value of the service, or for the increased value of the asset. The view advanced here is that this issue can be resolved having regard to the legal policy not to undermine pre-existing property rights. This is evident in the cases, and can be applied to a range of wider scenarios. Like the relationship between unjust enrichment and contract, it also fits an account of unjust enrichment in which the exchange capacity is of central concern.

## (1) Services and Marketable Residua

The relationship between a particular service and its residuum can vary. Services may preserve the value already inhering in an asset, such as where a herd of cattle is saved from destruction by the construction of the fence.[49] Alternatively, services may generate a new asset, such as where a ship-builder designs and builds a ship.[50] Or services may improve the value of an already existing asset or enable its realisation. In each case, however, it is important to appreciate the true state of affairs as concerns the identification of the enrichment. It is not the case that there is a single enrichment of the defendant, and that the claimant is entitled to a proportion of this. Rather, as was explained in chapter two, there are two separate enrichments, reflecting separate manifestations of the defendant's exchange capacity:[51] the value of the service and the value of the residuum. The value of the service does not merge with the asset's value. Services may contribute to the value of assets in different ways, but they do not thereafter comprise part of that value.

A striking example of this point is provided by *Cobbe*.[52] The claimant successfully sought planning permission in respect of the defendant's property, which substantially increased its value. He was entitled to a *quantum meruit* award for the money and services he had provided. In the course of his judgment, Lord Scott asked '[W]hat is the extent of the unjust enrichment?' It was not the difference in market value between the property without the planning permission

[49] See, eg, R Stevens, 'Three Enrichment Issues' in A Burrows and Lord Rodger of Earlsferry (eds), *Mapping the Law: Essays in Memory of Peter Birks* (Oxford, Oxford University Press, 2006) 53. Cf J Edelman, 'The Meaning of Loss and Enrichment' in R Chambers, C Mitchell, and J Penner (eds), *Philosophical Foundations of The Law of Unjust Enrichment* (Oxford, Oxford University Press, 2009) 224.

[50] See, eg, *Hyundai Heavy Industries Co Ltd v Papadopoulos* [1980] 1 WLR 1129 (HL).

[51] See above p 60.

[52] *Cobbe v Yeoman's Row Management Ltd* [2008] UKHL 55, [2008] 1 WLR 1752.

and the property with it.[53] Instead, the defendant 'was unjustly enriched because it obtained the value of [the claimant's] services without having to pay for them'.[54] His Lordship relied upon the following example:[55]

> An analogy might be drawn with the case of a locked cabinet which is believed to contain valuable treasures but to which there is no key. The cabinet has a high intrinsic value and its owner is unwilling to destroy it in order to ascertain its contents. Instead a locksmith agrees to try to fashion a key. He does so successfully and the cabinet is unlocked. As had been hoped, it is found to contain valuable treasures. The locksmith had hoped to be awarded a share of their value but no agreement to that effect had been concluded and the owner proposes to reward him with no more than sincere gratitude. The owner has been enriched by his work and, many would think, unjustly enriched. For why should a craftsman work for nothing? But surely the extent of the enrichment is no more than the value of the locksmith's services in fashioning the key. Everything else the owner of the cabinet already owned. So here.

This example is not on all fours with *Cobbe*. The locksmith's services enabled the realisation of something valuable that already existed,[56] but in *Cobbe* the property did not increase in value until the claimant performed the development services. Nevertheless, in both cases the defendant's total enrichment was the value of the services plus the value of the residuum. There were two enrichments in *Cobbe*: the value of the claimant's services and the increased value of the property. Lord Scott's point was that the claimant could only claim the former, and not the latter (or any proportion of it).

The locksmith example is important because it illustrates the policy behind the law's position that a claimant is usually only entitled to the value of the services performed, rather than the value of the asset improved. The explanation that '[e]verything else the owner of the cabinet already owned' indicates a preference for the entitlement of a right-holder in respect of the residuum that followed the performance of services. So, in *Cobbe*, the increase in the value of the land lay with the defendant because it was in respect of its property rights, and had merely been 'unlocked' by the claimant. This can be expressed in stultification terms similar

[53] ibid [41].
[54] ibid.
[55] ibid.
[56] Cf *Spencer v S Franses Ltd* [2011] EWHC 1269 (QB), where a textile expert was entitled to a lien over embroideries after he had carried out research work establishing their medieval provenance. Thirlwall J (at [256]–[262]) explained that the work had increased the embroideries' value both culturally and financially and that this constituted an improvement, even though the work had made no physical difference to them. There are two points to consider about the case. First, as it is a case about a bailee's possessory lien and the separate principles developed in that context, its relevance to unjust enrichment is potentially limited. The meaning of 'improvement' in this context is not the same as 'enrichment' in unjust enrichment according to this book. Secondly, and if the case is analogous to Lord Scott's locksmith example in *Cobbe*, then the expert's services only helped to realise or 'unlock' the value already inhering in the embroideries. The embroideries were always medieval, just like the treasures were always in the cabinet.

to those used above with respect to contract. Property rights are a legal regime, just like contract, which unjust enrichment should not undermine. Underlying the choice between these two enrichments (value of the property and value of the services) is a policy to preserve the integrity of property rights. Those rights would be undermined if right-holders could not realise their value, or were made to hand over that value to someone else absent a defect in the acquisition the right itself. So, whereas it is one thing to bring an unjust enrichment claim after the acquisition of a right by the defendant, and to so claim the value of that right (such as in *Cressman*, *Moses v Macferlan* and *Huyton*),[57] it is quite another to claim the value of a right when it was the defendant's to begin with.

This approach to the relationship between property and unjust enrichment can be applied to a range of different circumstances, and is evident in several cases. One example is the difficult speech of Robert Goff J in *BP v Hunt (No 2)*.[58] The defendant (Hunt) had obtained an oil concession from the Libyan government. He and the claimant (BP) entered into a joint venture agreement, according to which BP obtained a half-interest in the concession and began prospecting. BP discovered a giant oilfield in the concession and spent many millions of pounds exploring and developing it before it came online. Expropriation by the Libyan government later frustrated the agreement. BP's share was expropriated first, leaving Hunt to reap a considerable fortune before his share was also expropriated. The case was decided according to section 1(3) of the Law Reform (Frustrated Contracts) Act 1943 ('the Act'), which the judge considered to be a statutory application of the law of unjust enrichment. He accepted $169,902,000 as the amount of Hunt's overall cash-flow benefit. The amount of that benefit obtained by reason of BP's performance of the contract was half that figure ($84,951,000), while the relief awarded to BP was only $35,403,146. He then calculated the just sum to be awarded BP as follows:[59] (a) the costs and expenditure BP incurred for Hunt up until the date on which production came online ($86,180,612); plus (b) BP's 'farm in' payment ($2,000,000); plus (c) the value of BP's 'farm in' oil received by Hunt ($8,801,534); plus (d) the costs and expenditure BP incurred for Hunt after the date on which production came online ($1,123,000). From this total expenditure of (e) $98,105,146, there was deducted (f) the value of the oil reimbursed to BP ($62,702,000), to arrive at (g) the 'just sum' payable to BP under the Act: $35,403,146.

The decision is confusing. It is not clear why, having assessed Hunt's total benefit as $169,902,000, Robert Goff J ultimately awarded BP less than one-fifth of that amount after observing that half of it was due to BP's efforts.[60] Birks considered the decision possible authority for the proposition that restitution for unjust

[57] See above pp 99–103.
[58] *BP Exploration Co (Libya) Ltd v Hunt (No 2)* [1979] 1 WLR 783 (QB) 799.
[59] ibid 826–27.
[60] ibid 816, 821.

enrichment is capped by the claimant's loss.[61] His Lordship, however, expressly stated elsewhere in his judgment that this was not the case.[62] An alternative explanation, advanced by Rush, is to reiterate the two-stage approach adopted by Robert Goff J himself.[63] The first stage values the defendant's benefit. In *BP v Hunt (No 2)* that was $84,951,000. The second stage then calculates a just sum. In *BP v Hunt (No 2)* that was $35,403,146—the eventual relief awarded. The difficulty with that approach, however, is that there is no obvious conjunction between the two stages.

With respect, much of the difficulty surrounding *BP v Hunt (No 2)* disappears once we realise that certain parts of Robert Goff J's reasons do not withstand scrutiny. This follows once we recognise that, just as in *Cobbe*, there were two enrichments accruing to Hunt: the increased value of his concession on the one hand ($169,902,000) and expenditure and oil paid in his favour by BP on the other ($98,105,146). The judge had to decide which of these BP could claim, a point he appears to have appreciated insofar as he accepted that s 1(3) of the Act permitted identification of the defendant's enrichment as either the performance of services or the receipt of their end product in appropriate cases.[64] From this point, Robert Goff J's reasoning runs into trouble, for while he held Hunt's benefit to be the increased value of the concession ($169,902,000) and then calculated what proportion of it was attributable to BP ($84,951,000),[65] he then calculated the just sum on the basis that the relevant enrichment was actually the expenditure and oil paid in Hunt's favour as set out in the calculations above. If his Lordship had stuck to the view that the relevant enrichment was the increased value of the concession, the eventual award would have been $84,951,000 *less* the value of the oil paid to BP ($62,702,000),[66] namely $22,249,000.

The point is not that the result or calculation of the 'just sum' in *BP v Hunt (No 2)* was wrong. The Court of Appeal[67] and the House of Lords[68] upheld this aspect of the decision. Instead, the problem is that Robert Goff J's identification of Hunt's enrichment as the increase in value of the concession was ultimately unnecessary. Having initially identified the enrichment as the increased value of the concession, he in fact awarded restitution on the basis that it was the services that were the relevant enrichment. The reason must be the same as in *Cobbe*: the

61 Birks, *Unjust Enrichment* (n 12) 80.

62 See above p 77.

63 M Rush, *The Defence of Passing On* (Oxford, Hart, 2006) 124–25; *BP v Hunt (No 2)* (n 58) 801–04.

64 *BP v Hunt (No 2)* (n 58) 801.

65 ibid 821.

66 ibid 824.

67 *BP Exploration Co (Libya) Ltd v Hunt (No 2)* [1981] 1 WLR 232 (CA). The Court of Appeal characterised Robert Goff J's award as having been made on 'a reimbursement basis' and identified the benefit provided by the claimant as 'expertise, their capital resources and the services of their staff'. It added that, to the extent Robert Goff J had included the 'farm in payment' within the calculation of a just sum for non-money benefits under s 1(3), that this was an error of form under the Act; the payments being properly recoverable under s 1(2) (at 241).

68 *BP Exploration Co (Libya) Ltd v Hunt (No 2)* [1983] 2 AC 352 (HL).

increased value of the concession was an increase in the value of something that Hunt 'already owned'.

The same approach can be applied to the examples posed at the beginning of this Part. C cannot claim the value of D's car after C's car is destroyed by lightening, nor where the value of D's land increases because of some mistake in allowing D to develop it. Though there is a counterfactual connection between loss and enrichment, a claim cannot lie in respect of the value of D's pre-existing property rights. In the absence of some other enrichment to D (such as the value of some marketable service performed by C) or some other connection between C's loss and the increased value of D's land (such as by the acquisition of a right) C cannot bring a claim.

*Edwards v Lee's Administrators*[69] provides a slightly different illustration of the point. On a counterfactual approach, the claimant would have been entitled to all the defendant's profits from exhibiting the cave but the award of one-third of the defendant's profits made from exhibiting the cave was in proportion to that part of the cave under the claimant's land. The claim was limited by the extent of the claimant's property rights over one-third of the cave, a necessary corollary of which was the defendant's property rights in the other two-thirds.

This approach, according to which liability in an unjust enrichment is qualified by the parties' respective property rights, can also be applied to claims in which the parties have each contributed property to a venture. Suppose D owns a diamond worth £50,000, and he agrees with C, a jeweller, that C will use materials worth £50,000 and labour worth £50,000 to create a necklace for D worth £200,000. After C does the work, they discover that their contract is void, though this does not prevent title to the necklace vesting in D. D is enriched in three ways in this example. First, the £50,000 of labour. Secondly, the £50,000 of materials. Thirdly, the surplus value of the necklace, being £200,000 *less* the cost of producing it (£150,000); that is, £50,000. D did not 'already own' the first two of these enrichments, so C's claim in that respect is unqualified. The third enrichment, however, is more complex. D did not already own the necklace, but he did own the diamond within it. The rest of the materials comprising the necklace belonged to C. In such a case, the amount of the surplus value of the necklace that C can claim should be determined by the proportionate approach evident in *Edwards v Lee's Administrators*; that is, D and C share the surplus in proportion with the property they brought to the venture, a 50:50 split. C can therefore claim half the surplus, £25,000, meaning a total unjust enrichment claim of £125,000.

In practice, whether a claim is actually qualified by the respective property contributions of the claimant and defendant will depend upon factual acknowledgment of the property that each contributes. In *Greenwood v Bennett*, for example, Harper's claim was actually in respect of both labour and materials, though it

[69] *Edwards v Lee's Administrators* 96 SW 2d 1028 (1936) (CA Kent).

appears to have been treated exclusively as a case involving labour,[70] in which case Harper would only have been entitled to the value of the services he performed.[71] No attempt appears to have been made to argue the case in terms of the proportion of materials Harper actually contributed to the car, in which case it would have been open to the Court to apply the proportionate approach described above. Correctly determining the claim relies first upon identifying the defendant's enrichment(s) in a given case.[72]

## (2) Property and the Exchange Capacity

There are several explanations possible for the relationship between property and unjust enrichment evident in the above cases. One is to deny that the increase in value of property following the provision of a service is an 'enrichment' in the first place; the idea being that a defendant's exchange capacity is not relevantly engaged by the increase in value of something he already owns because he has not 'gained' anything susceptible to exchange.[73] That, however, fails to explain what is relevantly meant by 'receipt' in this context. It also jars with common sense: the owner of property that increases in value is better off than he was before, and so it seems odd to deny that he is enriched.

Taking matters slightly further, another possible explanation is that (other factors being equal) property rights are 'just' in their own right,[74] so that no claim lies in respect of them (including their value), absent some defect in their acquisition. On this view, the superiority of property rights ultimately represents a choice made within the law, promoting certainty and security of pre-existing entitlements—similar in form to the priority granted to contractual arrangements. So, though an increase in the value of property rights brought about by the performance of a service is (as an increase in value) an incident of the exchange capacity (and thus susceptible to unjust enrichment analysis), that interest is overridden by the pre-existing proprietary entitlement. In the contest between competing rationales underlying property and unjust enrichment, the former seems to prevail.

It may be possible to carry matters even further, and to explain the relationship between property and unjust enrichment in such cases as not only consistent with, but actually mandated by, corrective justice. The key step to doing so is to have due

[70] *Greenwood v Bennett* [1973] QB 195 (CA) 200 (Lord Denning).

[71] Even though that was also all that he claimed. Cf R Stevens, 'Three Enrichment Issues' in A Burrows and Lord Rodger of Earlsferry (eds), *Mapping the Law: Essays in Memory of Peter Birks* (Oxford, Oxford University Press, 2006) 52.

[72] This was the substance of one of the Court of Appeal's corrections to Robert Goff J's speech in *BP v Hunt (No 2)* with respect to the 'farm in payment'. See above n 67.

[73] See above pp 57–62.

[74] G Watt, *Equity Stirring: The Story of Justice Beyond Law* (Oxford, Hart, 2009) 235, citing C St Germain, *Doctor and Student* (TFT Plucknett and JL Barton trs, London, Selden Society 1974) 5.

regard to the Kantian account of property within the scheme of corrective justice and private law generally. As Weinrib has explained,[75] the existence of property as an institution of positive law within such a scheme is the culmination of three stages of conceptual analysis. In the first stage, Kant's philosophy of right necessitates the existence of an innate right to freedom consisting of the occupation of the human body as the physical organism through which the person expresses his freedom as a self-determining being. That innate right extends to the protection of property interests only insofar as interference with a person's actual physical possession of an external object necessitates interference with their person (such as prying an object from a person's fingers, or removing the person from the land on which they are lying). Property rights surpass the innate right because they treat the person as entitled to an external object even when it is not in their physical possession. Such rights follow, in the second stage of analysis, from 'the postulate of practical reason with regard to rights', under which 'it is possible to have any external object of my choice as mine'.[76] But this leads to a conceptual tension, for while property rights are consistent with the innate right insofar as they allow persons to exercise their freedom, they are inconsistent with it insofar as they do not treat persons as innately equal; property rights have their genesis in a unilateral act of original acquisition, and therefore enable one person to restrict another person's freedom through such unilateral acts.[77] This tension is resolved in the third stage of analysis: Kant introduces the further postulate of 'public right', which holds that '[w]hen you cannot avoid living side by side with all others, you ought to leave the state of nature and proceed with them into a rightful condition'.[78] In this rightful or 'civil' condition the state provides duly authorised institutions of adjudication and enforcement that secure each person's rights by supplementing the need for reciprocal assurances of non-interference between individuals. The equality of innate right is thus satisfied because all individuals are subject to the civil condition, benefitted by security in their property rights, and reciprocally bound to respect the property rights of others.

Herein lies the conceptual consistency between corrective justice and the superiority of pre-existing property rights evident in the services cases. If the law were to award restitution to service providers by reference to the increase in value of property rights consequent upon those services (as distinct from the value of the service itself), then that would be tantamount to the institutional sanctioning of unilateral interference by one person with the property rights of another. The equality of the innate right would fracture, and the civil condition underlying the existence of property rights would fail. There is no relevant difference, in this

[75] EJ Weinrib, *Corrective Justice* (Oxford, Oxford University Press, 2012) 270–80 discussing I Kant, *The Metaphysics of Morals* (Mary Gregor tr, Cambridge, Cambridge University Press, 1996).

[76] Kant, *The Metaphysics of Morals* (n 75) [6:246]–[6:247].

[77] Weinrib, *Corrective Justice* (n 75) 276–77.

[78] Kant, *The Metaphysics of Morals* (n 75) [6:267]. See further Weinrib, *Corrective Justice* (n 75) 277.

context, between D taking C's property by a wrongful act of interference, and D relying on his exchange capacity to claim a proportion of the value of C's property following the provision of a service that increases that value. In both cases, D's action interferes with C's pre-existing entitlement: in the former case to rights of ownership and possession, and in the latter case to the exchange of those rights in the market.

Furthermore, the security promoted by the Kantian account of property rights would be undermined if the legal response to their improvement was the award of a proportion of their value. This is because, if that were the law, a service recipient would be worse off with property than without it. For example, suppose that, in one situation, C services and tunes D's car, while in another situation C services and tunes X's car at the request of D. Suppose also that, in both situations the value of C's service on the market is only £500, while the increase in value of the car after the work is done is £1,000. If C were entitled, in the first situation, to the £1,000 increase in value, then, it would be worse for D (in any subsequent claim against him) to own the car than to not, for in the second situation the only recourse C can possibly have against D is for the value of the service performed at his request. Far from benefitting from security of property rights, D is disadvantaged by them. Limiting claims, in such circumstances, to the value of services avoids both interfering with D's property rights, and effectively penalising D for having those property rights in the first place.

## (C) Equity

The relationship between unjust enrichment and equitable principles is a source of substantial debate, the complete exploration of which lies beyond the scope of this book. One particular issue, however, that neatly reflects the benefits of separating attribution in unjust enrichment from the qualifications imposed on liability is whether an unjust enrichment claim should be available against a third party who receives property misdirected from a trust, or otherwise subject to an equitable interest. There is continuing debate as to whether claims for the equitable wrong of knowing receipt effectively 'cover the field' in this situation, or whether a concurrent claim is available based upon unjust enrichment. The debate is more than semantic, as the two claims are substantially different both in form and substance.[79] Knowing receipt (the so-called 'first limb' of liability in *Barnes v Addy*)[80], on the one hand, is a fault-based claim according to which the recipient

[79] See generally C Mitchell, P Mitchell, and S Watterson (eds), *Goff & Jones: The Law of Unjust Enrichment*, 8th edn (London, Sweet & Maxwell 2011) paras 8.123–8.130. See further C Mitchell and S Watterson, 'Remedies for Knowing Receipt' in C Mitchell (ed), *Constructive and Resulting Trusts* (Oxford, Hart, 2009) 155–158.

[80] *Barnes v Addy* (1874) LR 9 Ch App 244 (CA).

of trust property comes under a core custodial duty to restore it to the trust beneficiary, and against whom remedies for the failure to perform that core duty are the same as those available against an ordinary express trustee—including a personal claim to account.[81] Unjust enrichment, on the other hand, generates strict liability claims for personal restitution of an enrichment received at the expense of the claimant in circumstances that are unjust. The two claims are distinct; one is not merely a sub-species of the other.[82]

It is tempting to consider this issue as one of conflict between unjust enrichment and equitable principles, similar to that which we have observed between unjust enrichment and contract or property above. The reality, however, is that the reasons for denying an unjust enrichment claim in circumstances where a knowing receipt claim would lie do not depend upon a concern for specifically 'equitable' principles against which unjust enrichment undermines. Instead, the apparent conflict is more readily understood as one couched in considerations of policy.

Two different points of view exist as to whether knowing receipt is the only claim that may lie against a recipient of misdirected trust property. First, the argument that such recipients can also be strictly liable in unjust enrichment is supported by some judges (in *dicta* and writing extra-judicially)[83] and commentators.[84] In *Relfo*, Sales J said in *dicta* that an unjust enrichment claim would be available if the payments from Relfo could be traced in equity to Varsani.[85] That is significant insofar as it accepts that unjust enrichment may generate a strict liability personal claim in equity just as it does in analogous cases at common law.[86] Whether it was correct in principle, however, is open to question. For while *Relfo* supports the extension of the counterfactual connection between enrichment and loss to cases involving the receipt of trust property,[87] that does not necessarily mean a claim will ultimately succeed. Recognising that liability in unjust enrichment may be qualified despite that connection is the whole point of this chapter. And in the

[81] See Mitchell and Watterson (n 79) 120–127, 135–138.

[82] See especially P Birks, 'Receipt' in P Birks and A Pretto (eds), *Breach of Trust* (Oxford, Hart, 2002) 223–225.

[83] See, eg, *Twinsectra Ltd v Yardley* [2002] UKHL 12, [2002] 2 AC 164, 194 (Lord Millett); *Dubai Aluminium Co Ltd v Salaam* [2002] UKHL 48, [2003] 2 AC 366 [87] (Lord Millett); P Millett, 'Proprietary Restitution' in S Degeling and J Edelman (eds), *Equity and Commercial Law* (Sydney, Lawbook 2005) 311; D Nicholls, 'Knowing Receipt: The Need for New Landmark' in WR Cornish (ed), *Restitution: Past, Present, and Future* (Oxford, Hart, 1997) 231; R Walker, 'Dishonesty and Unconscionable Conduct in Commercial Life—Some Reflections on Accessory Liability and Knowing Receipt' (2005) 27 *Sydney Law Review* 187, 202.

[84] See, eg, Birks, 'Receipt' (n 82); Burrows, *The Law of Restitution* (n 40) 424–31; Mitchell, Mitchell, and Watterson, *Goff & Jones* (n 79) para 8.63. Cf Mitchell and Watterson (n 79) 156–57, where the authors express a need for caution before English courts accept the possibility of concurrent liability in knowing receipt and unjust enrichment.

[85] *Relfo Ltd (In Liquidation) v Varsani* [2012] EWHC 2168 (Ch) [85]–[88].

[86] See further, T Cutts, 'Untangling Tracing: Rights and Value' (2013) 129 *Law Quarterly Review* 176, 179.

[87] See above p 166–167.

particular context of the debate over concurrent liability in knowing receipt and unjust enrichment, the issue is whether the principles governing the former negate the possibility of the latter.

The argument that they should seems to lie at the core of the opposing view that the recipients of trust property are not susceptible to unjust enrichment claims by the trust beneficiaries. That view was expressed most stridently by the High Court of Australia in *Farah Constructions Pty Ltd v Say-Dee Pty Ltd*.[88] That case involved the development of land as part of a joint venture between two companies: Farah (controlled by Mr Elias) and Say-Dee. The local council required the amalgamation of adjoining land before the development could be approved. A dispute arose as to whether that requirement had been sufficiently disclosed to Say-Dee by Elias, who thereafter arranged for two neighbouring properties to be bought—one by a company he controlled, and the other by himself, his wife, and their daughters. The NSW Court of Appeal held that the disclosure had been insufficient and that Farah had therefore breached its fiduciary duty to Say-Dee. It further held that the wife and daughters were recipients of property transferred in breach of fiduciary duty, and that the guilty knowledge of Elias was imputable to them as their agent. They therefore held the land on constructive trust for Say-Dee. Significantly, however, the Court also held that the wife and daughter were liable in knowing receipt irrespective of any knowledge, because that liability was best viewed as a form of strict liability based upon unjust enrichment.[89]

The High Court of Australia reversed this decision, and described the introduction of unjust enrichment analysis into the case as 'a grave error'.[90] It gave several reasons why the Court of Appeal's decision was wrong in principle,[91] including that it incorrectly treated liability for knowing receipt as a form of liability based upon unjust enrichment. As has already been observed, the two claims are distinct—a position acknowledged by Birks in particular, as the High Court was clear to point out.[92] That being so, it further rejected the possibility of concurrent liability as follows:[93]

> Superficially this does less violence to authority, and does not cut down traditional equitable protection, but in practice it does erode the existing law, because it would tend to nullify the first limb [of *Barnes v Addy*]: for what plaintiff would wish to take on the burden of showing that the defendant had notice under the 'old' first limb if, by reliance on the new doctrine, that burden could be escaped and a contrary and even more onerous burden placed on the defendant?

[88] *Farah Constructions Pty Ltd v Say-Dee Pty Ltd* [2007] HCA 22, (2007) 230 CLR 89.

[89] *Say-Dee Pty Ltd v Farah Constructions Pty Ltd* [2005] NSWCA 309 [216]–[232].

[90] *Farah Constructions Pty Ltd v Say-Dee Pty Ltd* (n 88) [131] (Gleeson CJ, Gummow, Callinan, Heydon, and Crennan JJ).

[91] ibid [147]–[158].

[92] ibid (n 88) [152] citing Birks, 'Receipt' (n 82) 223.

[93] *Farah Constructions Pty Ltd v Say-Dee Pty Ltd* (n 88) [153].

To say that a claimant would never wish to take on the additional burdens of establishing a knowing receipt claim is an exaggeration. As Mitchell and Watterson have explained, once it is recognised that a knowing recipient owes an obligation to restore the property he has received *in specie*, and that he can be ordered to make substitutive performance of that duty if he no longer has the property, then there will be circumstances in which it is advantageous to pursue the more difficult claim of knowing receipt rather than unjust enrichment.[94] Those circumstances include where the value of trust property received but subsequently disposed of has increased, on which facts the knowing receipt claim carries the advantage of establishing liability for the current value of the property, rather than the unjust enrichment liability for the value merely at the date of receipt.

Nevertheless, there is a sting in the High Court's criticism of concurrent liability insofar as the situations envisioned by Mitchell and Watterson appear to be exceptional ones. Concurrent liability in unjust enrichment seems to cut into knowing receipt in the majority of cases. Thus, in *Bank of Credit and Commerce International (Overseas) Ltd v Akindele*,[95] Nourse LJ made the broad observation that concurrent liability appeared 'commercially unworkable' insofar as it would mean (at least in the corporate context) that simply on proof of an internal misapplication of company funds, the burden would shift to the recipient to defend the receipt.[96] Smith has expanded this point, with particular attention to the situation of banks:[97]

> The strict liability approach would contemplate that a plaintiff need only allege that a bank received trust property, not that the bank knew or should have known of the trust; with no more than that, the bank would be required to prove its good faith as a defence, or to account for what it had done with this money. In other words, there is no procedure which a bank, be it ever so honest, can adopt in order to ensure that it is not prima facie liable for the receipt of trust funds. *Prima facie* liability implies potentially extended periods of expense and uncertainty when litigation is pending; and of course it throws on the defendant the risk that even though the elements of some defence are present, they cannot be proved to the satisfaction of the trier of fact.

It follows that, unlike unjust enrichment's relationship to either contract or property, its relationship to knowing receipt is based upon considerations of policy rather than conflicting principles. It is not the aim or intention of this book to resolve the concurrent liability debate by evaluating that policy and weighing it against the arguments in favour of unjust enrichment analysis. Rather, the point is

[94] Mitchell and Watterson (n 79) 158. See also Mitchell, Mitchell, and Watterson, *Goff & Jones* (n 79) para 8.130. Knowing receipt is 'more difficult' in the sense that the claimant must prove the fault of the defendant.

[95] *Bank of Credit and Commerce International (Overseas) Ltd v Akindele* [2001] Ch 437 (CA).

[96] ibid 456.

[97] L Smith, 'Unjust Enrichment, Property and the Structure of Trusts' (2000) 116 *Law Quarterly Review* 412, 433–34.

to demonstrate that the exclusion of unjust enrichment analysis from these cases has nothing to do with the attribution inquiry. It can, therefore, be comfortably observed that the receipt of trust property establishes a counterfactual connection between an enrichment and a loss sufficient for attribution in unjust enrichment, without opening a more difficult debate, which arises only after the attribution inquiry is satisfied. This means, for example, that *Relfo* remains instructive for the purposes of this book,[98] even if Sales J's conclusion that an unjust enrichment claim would have been available may ultimately be incorrect.

Also significant is the status of *Re Diplock*.[99] That case has been important to this book insofar as it is a useful example of interception as a specific basis of connecting enrichment and loss, and of the counterfactual generalisation within unjust enrichment generally.[100] It is also problematic, however, insofar as it is a unique instance of liability arising for the receipt of equitable property.[101] If the case is to be useful for unjust enrichment purposes, then its treatment as an unjust enrichment case must be squared with the exclusion of such claims generally. Absent a resolution of the debate over concurrent liability, the best way forward is to appreciate that the policy arguments excluding unjust enrichment analysis in the equitable property cases do not bite so as to inhibit the *Re Diplock* claim. To understand why this is so requires some historical information about the nature of the claim. As Mr Whittaker (as he then was) explained in detail,[102] the roots of *Re Diplock* lie in the ecclesiastical jurisdiction over the devolution of moveable property. When a legatee was paid under the jurisdiction of those courts, he had to give security for his liability to refund the legacy if unpaid creditors of the deceased should later appear. The requirement was dropped when the jurisdiction passed to Chancery, and in its place an equity was granted to the executor against the legatee to refund the legacy.[103] Smith has described the situation as one establishing a set of priority rules in the administration of estates that effectively put legatees last.[104] The end result, he explains, is that the *Re Diplock* claim is based upon the policy of upholding the correct distribution of estates.[105] Finally, he suggests that the *Re Diplock* claim is maintainable directly by the next of kin as a derivative action from the personal representative of the estate.[106]

This final step may, however, be unnecessary. It is possible to analyse *Re Diplock* according to unjust enrichment, in which case the claim was directly available and without recourse to derivative action. It is also possible to reconcile it with

[98] See above pp 165–169.
[99] *Re Diplock* [1948] Ch 465 (CA).
[100] See above pp 116–118, 138–140.
[101] See generally Mitchell, Mitchell, and Watterson, *Goff & Jones* (n 79) para 8.51–8.58.
[102] SJ Whittaker, 'An Historical Perspective to the "Special Equitable Action" in Re Diplock' (1983) 4 *Journal of Legal History* 3.
[103] ibid 15.
[104] Smith, 'Unjust Enrichment, Property and the Structure of Trusts' (n 97) 440.
[105] ibid 443.
[106] ibid 443–4.

the general restriction upon claims involving equitable property by appreciating where and how matters of policy fit within that analysis. These policy considerations do not obscure the case's significance as one of attribution based upon interception, but instead arise despite attribution. On the one hand, in most equitable property cases, liability in unjust enrichment is qualified by the policy considerations outlined above that resist undercutting liability in knowing receipt. In the *Re Diplock* situation, however, those considerations either do not arise, or are overtaken by other policy considerations peculiar to upholding the correct distribution of estates. In other words, the *Re Diplock* claim is an example of policy considerations cutting against the qualification of liability in unjust enrichment.

## (D) Insolvency

Cases in which an unjust enrichment claim fails on the basis of a third party's insolvency provide a further example both of a qualification upon unjust enrichment liability, and of the erroneous 'direct enrichment' rule that results from failing to keep such qualifications separate from the connection inquiry. In *Uren*,[107] for example, the claimant paid £50,000 to a development company (Arrish) as part payment of the purchase price for two flats in a new development. The defendant bank provided loans to Arrish and, when the latter defaulted, appointed receivers. The development was acquired by a subsidiary of the defendant, which was subsequently purchased by Santa Barbara Ltd. The claimant then paid the remainder of the money due on the flats to the subsidiary in order for the work to be completed. The defendant continued to provide loans for the development. Once the development was complete, the defendant called in its loans and sold the development. The claimant claimed £125,000 from the defendant on the basis of unjust enrichment. Mann J held that any benefits to the defendant were not at the claimant's expense because the relationships involved were not sufficiently 'direct'.[108] The case has thus been identified as an authority for a general rule of 'directness' between the parties to an unjust enrichment claim.[109] As we have already seen, however, such a rule does not really exist. That being so, 'directness' must mean something else in this context. According to this book, 'directness' is really just a gloss over the qualification of liability in unjust enrichment.

[107] *Uren v First National Home Finance Ltd* [2005] EWHC 2529 (Ch).

[108] *Uren* (n 107) [8(c)], [23], [24(v)].

[109] See, eg, Burrows, *The Law of Restitution* (n 40) 71. See generally M McInnes, 'Interceptive Subtraction, Unjust Enrichment and Wrongs—A Reply to Professor Birks' (2003) 62 *Cambridge Law Journal* 697,704; G Virgo, 'Causation and Remoteness within the Law of Unjust Enrichment' in S Degeling and J Edelman (eds), *Unjust Enrichment in Commercial Law* (Sydney, Thomson Reuters, 2008) 160–61.

A close reading of Mann J's speech in *Uren* supports this view. The judge explained that the claimants could not use unjust enrichment 'to overcome the inconveniences of the chain of contracts and incorporation that exist in this case and which have their own consequences'.[110] He had earlier explained that the claimant's first £50,000 was lost when the first development company went into receivership, and the next £75,000 was lost when the second development company became insolvent.[111] The relationship between claimant and defendant was 'indirect' insofar as it touched a series of contracts and insolvency events that could not be ignored. The unjust enrichment claim was barred because it would undermine the ordinary legal consequences of those events.

The Court of Appeal in *Costello* raised the same concern. It explained that, in addition to 'shattering' the 'contractual containment' of risks between the parties, the builders' unjust enrichment claim would also 'alter the usual consequences of Oakwood's insolvency ... since a direct claim against Mr and Mrs Costello would improve the respondents' position over Oakwood's other unsecured creditors'.[112] It added that the builders could have limited their exposure in the event of Oakwood's default or insolvency by taking a guarantee from the Costellos, but had failed to do so. In other words, the court refused relief that the builders could have facilitated by exercising their exchange capacity to obtain a security interest. So, just as the claim could not undermine contractual principles, so too could it not undermine those relating to insolvency.[113]

## (E) Abandonment

The juristic concept of abandonment can be used to explain the denial of restitution in many cases involving incidental gains; the idea being that restitution should be denied to claimants who give up the enrichment received by the defendant.[114]

[110] *Uren* (n 107) [28].

[111] ibid [26].

[112] *Costello* (n 15) [21].

[113] An example of insolvency having this effect on liability in unjust enrichment is to be found in cases involving common law tracing. Smith and Professor Goode have each observed that the common law right to trace appears peculiar insofar as it is capable of generating liability for money had and received against an indirect recipient, but that it will not do so as against a trustee in bankruptcy. See L Smith, *The Law of Tracing* (Oxford, Clarendon Press, 2003) 338 and R Goode, 'The Right to Trace and Its Impact in Commercial Transactions—I' (1976) 92 *Law Quarterly Review* 360 401. As has already been explained in chapter six, however, it is not tracing that justifies the extension of liability to indirect recipients, but the counterfactual inquiry generally. Moreover, the limits observed by Smith and Goode are not inherent to the right to trace, but are reflective of a limitation that exists on unjust enrichment liability generally; such liability will not allow recovery as against a trustee in insolvency because that would undermine the liability regime in insolvency cases.

[114] E Ball, 'Abandonment and the Problem of Incidental Gains in the Law of Restitution of Unjust Enrichment' [2011] *Restitution Law Review* 49. See also *TFL Management Services Ltd v Lloyds Bank plc* [2013] EWCA Civ 1415, [31]–[32] (Floyd LJ) citing Mitchell, Mitchell, and Watterson, *Goff & Jones* (n 79) para 4.53.

So, despite the claimant suffering a loss that is counterfactually connected to the defendant's enrichment, the defendant's liability is curtailed by the abandonment. Abandoned benefits are thus not 'at the expense of the claimant'.[115]

There is no reason in principle to limit such analysis to incidental gains. If C abandons his bicycle and D takes it away, then C has no claim in unjust enrichment to the value of that bicycle for two reasons; not only is there no unjust factor, but also D's enrichment is outside the scope of his liability precisely because C gave it up. The legitimacy of abandonment in this context is based upon analogy to the principled, theoretical, and policy grounds that have legitimised it in other contexts such as personal property and contract.

## (F) Pragmatic Considerations

In *SmithKline Beecham plc v Apotex Europe Ltd*[116] the claimants were a company that manufactured an anti-depressant drug in the UK, and other companies in the same corporate group (collectively, GSK). The defendant was a subsidiary of a Canadian-based company that sought to import a generic form of the drug. GSK commenced infringement proceedings and, pending trial, obtained an interim injunction that included a cross-undertaking as to damages. After the proceedings concluded (in favour of the defendant), the defendant applied to have the cross-undertaking amended so that it extended to cover losses incurred by other Canadian companies in its corporate group that had not been party to the infringement proceedings, and sought to issue a fresh claim form on behalf those companies pleading a claim in unjust enrichment. That claim was based upon the fact that GSK had made more money than it would have done without the interim injunction. That was alleged to be 'at the expense of' the Canadian companies, who had lost profits following the injunction. This argument was apparently based on restitution for unjust enrichment, rather than wrongdoing, expressed as involving the 'transfer' of 'a business opportunity' from the Canadian companies GSK,[117] and raised several issues including whether the enrichment was 'unjust' in the relevant sense, and whether the Court had a general restitutionary power in respect of 'wrongful' injunctions. Noteworthy in the present context, however,

115 Ball (n 114) 54. Cf Burrows, *A Restatement of the English Law of Unjust Enrichment* (n 21) 55.

116 *SmithKline Beecham plc v Apotex Europe Ltd* [2006] EWCA Civ 658, [2007] Ch 71.

117 ibid [35], [61] (Jacob LJ). See further *SmithKline Beecham plc v Apotex Europe Ltd* [2005] EWHC 1655 (Ch), [2006] 1 WLR 872 [76], where Lewison J explained that this loss was insufficient to found a claim in damages (as distinct from restitution for unjust enrichment).

is Jacob LJ's response to the argument that a litigant could be made to disgorge benefits to a third party adversely affected by an injunction:[118]

> I do not see how any rational rule of restitution could. After all when an injunction is granted, there are often non-parties who are affected. Some will benefit, others will lose. Here, for instance, others besides GSK will have benefited. They will include those of GSK's customers who have gained from the higher price which resulted from the injunction, GSK's chemical suppliers and so on. It would be absurd to say that a restitutionary claim would lie against them. Yet if [counsel for the defendant] were right, I can see no reason why it would not.

This illustrates a further possible qualification upon liability in unjust enrichment, one based upon the policy of avoiding potentially indeterminate chains of liability in unjust enrichment. As explained in chapter four, unjust enrichment claims can arise following multiple sequential connections, and so there can be no objection to a claim simply because a loss is connected to an enrichment by a sequence of multiple connections. There are limits, however, to how far a claimant can go in establishing a connection before concerns over indeterminacy arise. Whether a precise test can or should be formulated for what is too long a chain of liability is doubtful but it must be kept in mind that the mere fact of multiple connections cannot of itself qualify recovery. Absent such a test, the reasons for limiting liability despite a connection between loss and enrichment must be articulated in a given case, just like the reasons for departing from the 'standard criteria' of causation in tort.[119] In *SmithKline Beecham* Jacobs LJ did precisely that, articulating the limit as an indeterminacy of 'gainers and losers' following injunctive relief, there being no reason to single out the Canadian companies for special treatment. His Lordship's reasons were thus sound in this respect.

This may be contrasted with the reasons given by the Court of Appeal in *FII*. One of the reasons given by the Court in denying the unjust enrichment claim in that case was that 'the loss was too remote'. Assuming that their Lordships actually intended to distinguish a separate reason for denying liability from that of the connection between enrichment and unjust factor,[120] what they were saying was that, despite the existence of a connection between the claimant's loss and the Revenue's enrichment, the claim should be denied because it was beyond the scope of liability in unjust enrichment. The problem is that the Court did not explain why that was so, beyond suggesting that the loss was sustained in one year, while the enrichment was sustained in another.[121] It is not obvious why this fact limited

[118] *SmithKline Beecham plc v Apotex Europe Ltd* (n 116) [41]. His Lordship later surmised that 'what is really being claimed under the guise of restitution is damages' and concluded that 'there is no possible rational basis for a third party to have a claim in restitution in respect of benefits which accrue to a "wrongful" injunction' (at [42]–[44]).

[119] See above p 125.

[120] See above p 98.

[121] *Test Claimants in the FII Group Litigation v Revenue and Customs Commissioners* [2010] EWCA Civ 103 [182].

the Revenue's liability. Indeed, following observations by the Court of Appeal in *Menelaou v Bank of Cyprus UK Ltd*, it appears that issues of delay between enrichment and loss should not have such an effect.[122] And in any event, on the analysis of *FII* presented in chapter four,[123] it was a gloss on the Revenue's enrichment for the Court to characterise the loss and enrichment as a year apart: the Revenue was enriched when the tax reliefs were exhausted, the only point being that the enrichment was not realised until the payment of tax not subject to relief a year later. The Court's justification for its decision was insufficient; the reasons for denying liability should have been articulated rather than obfuscated by the language of 'remoteness'.

## (G) Generalisation

Other areas of law are familiar with imposing qualifications upon liability despite a connection between claimant and defendant. Such limits on compensation for tort or breach of contract are generally referred to as considerations of 'remoteness', generalised tests for which are standard. So in the law of tort the test for remoteness is foreseeability of the kind of damage,[124] while in contract the test has been variably expressed to limit liability to loss within the reasonable contemplation of the parties when they entered into the contact.[125]

The question therefore arises whether the qualifications upon liability in unjust enrichment outlined in this chapter can (and should) be generalised in a similar fashion. Certainly, there is nothing inherently wrong with describing them, in shorthand, as considerations of 'remoteness'. Indeed, that language has begun to creep into the judicial decisions[126] and academic commentary.[127] Two points, however, should be kept in mind. First, use of the label 'remoteness' must not import into the law of unjust enrichment the considerable baggage that surrounds that term in contract and tort. Remoteness in unjust enrichment is something altogether different. This is closely related to the second point: the meaning of remoteness in unjust enrichment, including the possibility of its generalisation into a uniform test, should not be controlled by taxonomy. The points made in respect of

[122] *Menelaou v Bank of Cyprus UK Ltd* [2013] EWCA Civ 1960 [38]–[39] (Floyd LJ). See further *Bank of Cyprus UK Ltd v Menelaou* [2015] UKSC 66 [25] (Lord Clarke).

[123] See above p 104.

[124] *Overseas Tankship (UK) Ltd v Morts Dock & Engineering Co (The Wagon Mound No 1)* [1961] AC 388 (PC).

[125] *Hadley v Baxendale* (1854) 9 Ex 341 (Exch); *Victoria Laundry (Windsor) v Newman Industries* [1949] 2 KB 528 (CA); Cf *Transfield Shipping Inc v Mercator Shipping Inc (The Achilleas)* [2008] UKHL 48, [2008] 1 AC 61.

[126] See, eg, *FII Group Litigation (CA)* (n 121).

[127] See, eg, Virgo, 'Causation and Remoteness within the Law of Unjust Enrichment' (n 109).

'transfer' in Part II apply equally here: the question is not what 'remoteness' means but what constitutes an acceptable qualification upon liability in unjust enrichment despite the existence of a counterfactual connection between the defendant's enrichment and the claimant's loss.

One possibility is to relate these qualifications back to the exchange capacity. This, as we have seen, can explain the qualifications on unjust enrichment liability relating to contract and property rights. It may also explain those based on insolvency and abandonment. It is not the function of unjust enrichment to facilitate the exercise of the exchange capacity in a manner that avoids the ordinary consequences of insolvency—the onus is on the claimant to protect himself prior to that insolvency occurring. Unjust enrichment corrects the defective exercise of the parties' exchange capacity; it does not facilitate it advantageously on their behalf.[128] Meanwhile, a claimant who abandons a benefit does not suffer a loss:[129] by abandoning that benefit, he is no longer in a position to charge or otherwise exercise his exchange capacity in respect of it. Equally, a defendant who receives an abandoned benefit is not enriched because he is not saved the expense of having to pay for it:[130] that it was abandoned means it was free for him to take without paying anyone for it.

The exchange capacity analysis cannot, however, explain every qualification on unjust enrichment. For example, enrichment and loss arise in cases involving the receipt of property subject to an equitable interest,[131] and so any qualification based upon the relationship between unjust enrichment and equitable principles must be based on some other reason. It was suggested above that the relationship is really one based upon considerations of policy, though another possibility raised by the High Court of Australia's decision in *Farah Constructions Pty Ltd v Say-Dee Pty Ltd* is a concern not to undermine or 'erode' existing law so as to 'nullify' the significance of established principles.[132] This looks substantially like a concern for stultification of the law, which as we observed in relation to contract, lacks explanatory force in its own right. A reason must exist as to why stultification matters so much that it can limit an otherwise acceptable unjust enrichment claim.

The answer may well be that coherence in the law provides a reason in and of itself, or is perhaps tied to broader considerations aimed at the due administration of justice. That is probably the best way to understand the considerations outlined by the Court in *SmithKline Beecham plc v Apotex Europe Ltd*.[133] It also explains the desire to avoid double recovery and encroachment upon compensation, listed

128 See above pp 39–40.
129 See above pp 85–86.
130 See above pp 58–60.
131 See above pp 164–165.
132 *Farah Constructions Pty Ltd v Say-Dee Pty Ltd* (n 88) [153]. See also *Lumbers* (n 7) [75]–[80].
133 See also *Re Eurig Estate* [1998] 2 SCR 565 (SCC).

among Henderson J's considerations in *Investment Trust Companies*.[134] That being so, we must keep in mind that 'coherence' carries a certain degree of subjectivity in its perception and assessment. It is arguable, for example, that a system of liability that denies restitution to claimants in the position of those in *SmithKline Beecham plc v Apotex Europe Ltd* is incoherent because the possibility of indeterminate claims should not undermine actual claims that have arisen for adjudication before a court. And it remains to be seen which scheme of liability as regards the relationship between unjust enrichment and equity is more coherent: one in which concurrent claims in unjust enrichment and knowing receipt are possible (the elements of each having been satisfied), or one in which the existence of one claim necessarily limits the possibility of the other.

These points do not mean, however, that the exchange capacity, stultification, and coherence are unhelpful concepts; they simply mean that the qualifications on liability in unjust enrichment do not necessarily lend themselves to a single expression or generalisation. Nor is the list of qualifications on liability closed. The further development of those qualifications must rely upon the consideration of previous judicial decisions followed by reasoning outwards and incrementally by analogy. This is the ordinary method of the common law, according to which liability is ordered and defined by identifying the relevant characteristics common to new relationships and existing ones, and by explaining, in appropriate cases, relevant considerations that justify imposing new limits on liability. The qualification of unjust enrichment in this way is no less structured than an approach based upon generalised tests of remoteness. In reality the particular qualifications on liability relevant to a given case may be readily apparent and, where they are not, their revelation can be left to a consideration of the facts and the ordinary methodology of the common law.

## (H) Expansion and Contraction

This chapter has sought to clarify attribution in unjust enrichment by separating it from qualifications on liability that have nothing to do with enrichment, loss, and the connection between the two. Those qualifications are situated outside of attribution in unjust enrichment, and should not be conflated with matters that are relevant to attribution.

An inevitable question may arise as to *where* in the analytical scheme of unjust enrichment these qualifications are or should be situated. On the one hand, many textbooks have subsumed some of the qualifications identified above within chapters dedicated to the 'at the claimant's expense' inquiry within the accepted five question scheme of analysis in English law. On the other hand, the editors of the

[134] *Investment Trust Companies (HC)* (n 4) [68]. See above p 181.

latest edition of *Goff & Jones* have sought to recast that scheme by the introduction of a sixth question—whether, despite the analysis of all other questions pointing to liability, there are grounds justifying enrichment so that no liability in unjust enrichment arises.[135] The latter approach is closer to the approach set out in this book. It is advantageous because it avoids the confusion generated by muddying attribution with other issues and considerations that have nothing to do with attribution.

These may not, however, be the only ways to position the qualifications on liability covered by this chapter within unjust enrichment. Indeed, the very idea of a precise analytical location for these and other qualifications on liability is largely beside the point. The Introduction to this book explained both the significance *and* limited utility of precise analytical boundaries to a legal system based on common law reasoning.[136] That early lesson should not be forgotten at the close—particularly when Part II of this book has set out a simple counterfactual test for attribution in unjust enrichment that some might be consider leads to wider-than-desirable liability overall.

The point has already been made that attribution and liability in unjust enrichment are not coextensive.[137] It is a mistake to conclude that the expansion of the former leads to an expansion of the latter. This is because the wider test for attribution proposed in Part II of this book has been accompanied in Part III by the identification and removal of matters that are foreign to attribution, but which may be relevant to the place of unjust enrichment within the wider common law system. Indeed, the clear identification of such matters that qualify liability may ultimately lead to a *contraction* of unjust enrichment liability as the qualifications on liability—freed from confusion with the rules of attribution—are more readily identified and applied on a case-by-case basis.[138] What the qualifications on liability say about the place of unjust enrichment within the common law system may be just as, if not more, significant than precisely locating those qualifications within the formal structure of unjust enrichment itself.

[135] See Mitchell, Mitchell, and Watterson, *Goff & Jones* (n 79) 7 Ch 1 'Justifying Grounds'.
[136] See above pp 1–11.
[137] See above p 142.
[138] See, eg, *Investment Trust Companies v Revenue and Customs* [2015] EWCA Civ 82 [69] (Patten LJ).

# Conclusion

The central contribution of this book to the law of unjust enrichment has been the identification of the rules of attribution and the separation of those rules from other matters which, in truth, have nothing to do with attribution at all.

Attribution in unjust enrichment consists of two requirements: first, the identification of an enrichment to the defendant and a loss to the claimant; and, secondly, the identification of a connection between that enrichment and that loss. This structure fits a normative description of unjust enrichment based upon each party's exchange capacity. A defendant is enriched when he receives something that he has not paid for under prevailing market conditions, and a claimant suffers a loss when he loses the opportunity to charge for something under the same market conditions. A counterfactual test—asking whether each of the enrichment and loss arises 'but for' the other—provides the best generalisation for testing whether enrichment and loss are connected. This fits the logic of the exchange capacity and the definitions of enrichment and loss advanced by this book because enrichment and loss are, in effect, two sides of the same coin.

These rules of attribution should not be confused with matters that in truth have nothing to do with enrichment, loss, and the connection between the two, but which instead qualify unjust enrichment notwithstanding satisfaction of its elements (including the rules of attribution). Those matters include the relationship between unjust enrichment and principles of contract, property, equity, and insolvency. The list of matters is not closed (nor may it ever be), and it at least includes the further juristic concept of abandonment as well as pragmatic considerations of policy. All of these things should be analysed in their own terms, without the unnecessary burden of attempting to rationalise their significance within the general law according to the special regime of unjust enrichment analysis.

The description of attribution in this book, and its separation from non-attribution matters, has the advantage of clarifying the law by eliminating the baggage of a number of unnecessary concepts from the analysis of cases. 'Subjective devaluation', 'subjective revaluation', 'loss correspondence', 'direct enrichment', 'transfers of value', and 'leapfrogging out of contract' have each been shown to be either incorrect or misleading descriptions of how cases are actually decided. Transactional links established by the processes of following and tracing have also been shown to be irrelevant to unjust enrichment analysis. And the relationships between unjust enrichment and each of the matters identified in Part III have been shown to be distinct from the issue of attribution. The law of unjust enrichment is clearer and more coherent when viewed according to the analysis of attribution advanced by this book.

There is, of course, more work to be done. As the Introduction to this book observed, the size and structure of the law of unjust enrichment necessitates limits on the scope of all but the largest treatises, and this book is no exception. Equipped with the analysis contained in this book, however, those limits now provide a ready guide for further work in unjust enrichment and other fields of legal scholarship.

First, the exchange capacity analysis of enrichment and loss advanced by this book provides a stepping-stone for a better understanding of unjust factors within unjust enrichment. As was observed in the Introduction, the unjustness of a relationship cannot be adjudged without understanding that relationship and the qualities to which it ought to conform. The relationship is one of exchange capacity, and so the defects in it justifying restitution ought to be relevant to that capacity.

Secondly, chapter one—though suggesting the exchange capacity analysis advanced by this book naturally limits remedies for unjust enrichment to personal restitution—left open the possibility that specific remedies might be awarded in exceptional cases. Chapter six, meanwhile, suggested that such remedies might provide a limited exception to the underwhelming role of tracing within unjust enrichment claims. Those exceptional cases, and their relationship to the exchange capacity, must be analysed in further detail as part of the continuing controversy about the availability of specific remedies in unjust enrichment cases.

Thirdly, the exchange capacity analysis advanced by this book may provide further insight into the operation and scope of defences to unjust enrichment—as shown in chapters two and three in respect of the change of position and passing on defences. The structured account of attribution in unjust enrichment may also prove useful insofar as the qualifications upon unjust enrichment liability considered in Part III of this book appear to operate as defences. This may indicate a relationship between them, or a more subtle distinction that requires certain established defences to be re-examined to determine whether they truly are defences to claims, or just qualifications upon liability—and what this means for the resolution of cases.

Fourthly, the methodology outlined in the Introduction to this book and the analysis of qualifications on liability considered in Part III tend to show that unjust enrichment analysis cannot be considered an island to itself. There is no reason why difficult legal problems (or, indeed, simple ones for that matter) must be answered by a single principle or conceptual framework—nor is it necessarily desirable that they should be. The fit of unjust enrichment within a system of law based upon the dynamic intersection of history, principle, logic, and policy must be grappled with continuously.

This book began with the observation that attribution in unjust enrichment, reflected by the familiar expression that a defendant 'be enriched at the expense of the claimant', is not a statutory concept and should not be interpreted as if it were. The issue is not what the particular words mean—be those words 'attribution', 'enrichment at the claimant's expense', or something else. The real question is what constitutes a sufficient connection between a claimant and a defendant for unjust enrichment purposes. This book has answered that question in a way that fits the normative basis of unjust enrichment as well as the existing authorities, and which enables the law to develop in a structured yet flexible fashion that acknowledges substantive differences and similarities within the case law.

# BIBLIOGRAPHY

### Texts, Digests, and Restatements


American Law Institute, *Restatement of the Law Third: Restitution and Unjust Enrichment* (2012).

Aristotle, *Nicomachean Ethics* (Brown L ed, Ross D tr, Oxford, Oxford University Press, 2009).

Baker, JH and Milsom S, *Sources of English Legal History: Private Law to 1750* (London, Butterworths, 1986).

Baloch, TA, *Unjust Enrichment and Contract* (Oxford, Hart, 2009).

Birks, P, *The Foundations of Unjust Enrichment: Six Centennial Lectures* (Wellington, Victoria University Press, 2002).

——, *An Introduction to the Law of Restitution*, revised edn (Oxford, Clarendon Press, 1989).

——, *Unjust Enrichment*, 2nd edn (Oxford, Oxford University Press, 2005).

Burrows, A, *The Law of Restitution*, 3rd edn (Oxford, Oxford University Press, 2011).

——, *A Restatement of the English Law of Unjust Enrichment* (Oxford, Oxford University Press, 2012).

Cane, P, *Atiyah's Accidents, Compensation and the Law*, 7th edn (Cambridge, Cambridge University Press, 2006).

Coleman, J, *Risks and Wrongs* (Oxford, Oxford University Press, 2002).

Conaglen, M, *Fiduciary Loyalty: Protecting the Due Performance of Non-Fiduciary Duties* (Oxford, Hart, 2010).

Dagan, H, *The Law and Ethics of Restitution* (Cambridge, Cambridge University Press, 2004).

Edelman, J, *Gain-Based Damages: Contract, Tort, Equity and Intellectual Property* (Oxford, Hart, 2002).

Edelman, J and Bant, E, *Unjust Enrichment in Australia* (Oxford, Oxford University Press, 2006).

Fleming, JG, *The Law of Torts*, 9th edn (Sydney, Lawbook Company 1998).

Fox, D, *Property Rights in Money* (Oxford, Oxford University Press, 2008).

Gordley, J, *Foundations of Private Law: Property, Tort, Contract, Unjust Enrichment* (Oxford, Oxford University Press, 2006).

Grantham, R and Rickett, C, *Enrichment and Restitution in New Zealand* (Oxford, Hart, 2000).

Hardcastle, R, *Law and the Human Body* (Oxford, Hart, 2007).

Hart, HLA and Honoré, T, *Causation in the Law*, 2nd edn (Oxford, Clarendon Press, 1985).

Hawking, S and Mlodinow, L, *The Grand Design* (New York, Bantam Books, 2010).

Jones, G, *Goff & Jones: The Law of Restitution*, 7th edn (London, Sweet & Maxwell Ltd, 2006); First Supplement, 7th edn (London, Sweet & Maxwell Ltd, 2009).

——, *Restitution in Public and Private Law* (London, Sweet & Maxwell, 1991).

Kant, I, *The Metaphysics of Morals* (Gregor M tr, Cambridge, Cambridge University Press, 1996).

Lodder, AVM, *Enrichment in the Law of Unjust Enrichment and Restitution* (Oxford, Hart, 2012).

Mackie, JL, *The Cement of the Universe: A Study of Causation* (Oxford, Clarendon Press, 1980).

Mason, K, Carter JW, and Tolhurst, GJ, *Mason & Carter's Restitution Law in Australia*, 2nd edn (Sydney, LexisNexis Butterworths, 2008).

Mitchell, C, Mitchell, P, and Watterson, S (eds), *Goff & Jones: The Law of Unjust Enrichment*, 8th edn (London, Sweet & Maxwell, 2011).

Mitchell, C and Watterson, S, *Subrogation: Law and Practice* (Oxford, Oxford University Press, 2007).

Moore, MS, *Causation and Responsibility: An Essay in Law, Morals, and Metaphysics* (Oxford, Oxford University Press, 2007).

Ong, D, *Ong on Subrogation* (Federation Press 2014).

Penner, J, *The Idea of Property in Law* (Oxford, Oxford University Press, 2000).

Radin, MJ, *Contested Commodities* (Harvard University Press, 1996).

Reynolds, F, *Bowstead & Reynolds On Agency*, 19th edn (Watts PG, ed, London, Sweet & Maxwell Ltd 2010).

Rush, M, *The Defence of Passing On* (Oxford, Hart, 2006).

Sandel, M, *What Money Can't Buy: The Moral Limits of Markets* (New York, Farrar, Straus and Giroux, 2012).

Satz, D, *Why Some Things Should Not Be for Sale: The Moral Limits of Markets* (Oxford, Oxford University Press, 2010).

Smith, L, *The Law of Tracing* (Oxford, Clarendon Press, 2003).

St Germain, C, *Doctor and Student* (Plucknett TFT and Barton JL trs, London, Selden Society 1974).

Varian, HR, *Intermediate Microeconomics: A Modern Approach* (New York, W W Norton & Company, 2009).

Virgo, G, *The Principles of the Law of Restitution*, 2nd edn (Oxford, Oxford University Press, 2006).

——, *The Principles of the Law of Restitution*, 3rd edn (Oxford, Oxford University Press, 2015).

Waddams, S, *Dimensions of Private Law: Categories and Concepts in Anglo-American Legal Reasoning* (Cambridge, Cambridge University Press, 2003).

Waldron, J, *The Right to Private Property* (Oxford, Oxford University Press, 1986).

Watson, A (ed, tr), *The Digest of Justinian* (Pennsylvania, University of Pennsylvania Press, 1998).

Watt, G, *Equity Stirring: The Story of Justice Beyond Law* (Oxford, Hart, 2009).

Weinrib, EJ, *Corrective Justice* (Oxford, Oxford University Press, 2012).

——, *The Idea of Private Law* (Harvard University Press 1995).

## Journal Articles, Book Chapters, and Conference Papers

Allsop, J, 'Causation in Commercial Law' in Degeling, S, Edelman, J, and Goudkamp, J (eds), *Torts in Commercial Law* (Sydney, Thomson Reuters, 2011).

Ball, E, 'Abandonment and the Problem of Incidental Gains in the Law of Restitution of Unjust Enrichment' [2011] *Restitution Law Review* 49.

Bant, E, 'Causation and Scope of Liability in Unjust Enrichment' [2009] *Restitution Law Review* 60.

——, 'Rights and Value in Rescission: Some Implications for Unjust Enrichment' in Nolan, D and Robertson, A (eds), *Rights and Private Law* (Oxford, Hart, 2012).

Bant, E and Bryan, M, 'A Model of Proprietary Remedies' in Bant E, and Bryan, M (eds), *Principles of Proprietary Remedies* (Sydney, Thomson Reuters, 2013).

Barker K, 'The Nature of Responsibility for Gain: Gain, Harm and Keeping the Lid on Pandora's Box' in Chambers, R, Mitchell C, and Penner, J (eds), *Philosophical Foundations of the Law of Unjust Enrichment* (Oxford, Oxford University Press, 2009).

——, 'Understanding the Unjust Enrichment Principle in Private Law: A Study of the Concept and its Reasons' in Neyers, J, McInnes, M, and Pitel S (eds), *Understanding Unjust Enrichment* (Oxford, Hart, 2004).

Beatson, J, 'Benefit, Reliance and the Structure of Unjust Enrichment' in Beatson, J (ed), *The Use and Abuse of Unjust Enrichment: Essays on the Law of Restitution* (Oxford, Clarendon Press, 1991).

Bell, J, 'Sources of Law' in Burrows, A (ed), *English Private Law*, 2nd edn (Oxford, Oxford University Press, 2007).

Benson, P, 'The Unity of Contract Law' in Benson, P (ed), *The Theory of Contract Law: New Essays* (Cambridge, Cambridge University Press, 2001).

Birks, P, '"At the Expense of the Claimant": Direct and Indirect Enrichment in English Law' in Johnston, D and Zimmermann, R (eds), *Unjustified Enrichment: Key Issues in Comparative Perspective* (Cambridge, Cambridge University Press, 2002).

——, 'In Defence of Free Acceptance' in Burrows, A (ed), *Essays on the Law of Restitution* (Oxford, Clarendon Press, 1991).

——, 'Receipt' in Birks, P and Pretto, A (eds), *Breach of Trust* (Oxford, Hart, 2002).

Bryan M, 'Unjust Enrichment and Unconscionability in Australia: A False Dichotomy?' in Neyers, J, McInnes, M, and Pitel, S (eds), *Understanding Unjust Enrichment* (Oxford, Hart, 2004).

Burrows, A, 'The Australian Law of Restitution: Has the High Court Lost Its Way?' in Bant, E and Harding, M (eds), *Exploring Private Law* (Oxford, Hart, 2010).

Chambers, R, 'Tracing and Unjust Enrichment' in Neyers, J, McInnes, M, and Pitel, S (eds), *Understanding Unjust Enrichment* (Oxford, Hart, 2004).

——, 'Two Kinds of Enrichment' in Chambers, R, Mitchell, C, and Penner J (eds), *Philosophical Foundations of the Law of Unjust Enrichment* (Oxford, Oxford University Press, 2009).

Chowdry, M, 'Unjust Enrichment and Section 80(3) of the Value Added Tax Act 1994' [2004] *British Tax Review* 620.

Cutts, T, 'Untangling Tracing: Rights and Value' (2013) 129 *Law Quarterly Review* 176.

——, '*Wrotham Park* Damages: Compensation, Restitution or a Substitute for the Value of the Infringement of the Right?' [2010] *Lloyd's Maritime and Commercial Law Quarterly* 215.

Dagan, H, 'The Limited Autonomy of Private Law' (2008) 56 *American Journal of Comparative Law* 809.

——, 'Restitution's Realism' in Chambers, R, Mitchell, C, and Penner, J (eds), *Philosophical Foundations of The Law of Unjust Enrichment* (Oxford, Oxford University Press, 2009).

Dietrich, J, 'Unjust Enrichment versus Equitable Principles in England and Australia' in Glister, J and Ridge, P (eds), *Fault Lines in Equity* (Oxford, Hart, 2012).

Doyle, M, 'Corrective Justice and Unjust Enrichment' (2012) 62 *University of Toronto Law Journal* 229.

Edelman, J, 'Change of Position: A Defence of Unjust Disenrichment' (2012) 92 *Boston University Law Review* 1009.

——, 'The Meaning of Loss and Enrichment' in Chambers, R, Mitchell, C, and Penner, J (eds), *Philosophical Foundations of The Law of Unjust Enrichment* (Oxford, Oxford University Press, 2009).

——, 'Restitution of Rights' in Bant, E and Bryan, M (eds), *Principles of Proprietary Remedies* (Sydney, Thomson Reuters 2013).

Fox, D, 'Bona Fide Purchase and the Currency of Money' [1996] *Cambridge Law Journal* 547.

——, 'Relativity of Title at Law and in Equity' (2006) 65 *Cambridge Law Journal* 330.

Gardner, J, 'Corrective Justice, Corrected' (2012) 12 *Diritto & Questioni Pubbliche* 9.

——, 'What is Tort Law For? Part 1. The Place of Corrective Justice' (2011) 30 *Law and Philosophy* 1.

Garner, M, 'The Role of Subjective Benefit in the Law of Unjust Enrichment' (1990) 10 *Oxford Journal of Legal Studies* 42.

Goff, R, '1983 Maccabaean Lecture in Jurisprudence: The Search for Principle' (1983) *LXIX Proceedings of the British Academcy* 169.

——, 'Appendix: The Search for Principle' in Swadling, W and Jones, G (eds), *The Search for Principle: Essays in Honour of Lord of Chieveley* (Oxford, Oxford University Press, 1999).

——, 'The Future of the Common Law' (1997) 46 *International & Comparative Law Quarterly* 745.

Goode, R, 'The Right to Trace and Its Impact in Commercial Transactions—I' (1976) 92 *Law Quarterly Review* 360.

Grantham, R and Rickett, C, 'Disgorgement for Unjust Enrichment?' (2003) 62 *Cambridge Law Journal* 159.

——, 'Restitution, Property and Ignorance—A Reply to Mr Swadling' [1996] *Lloyd's Maritime and Commercial Law Quarterly* 463.

Gummow, W, 'Moses v Macferlan: 250 Years On' (2010) 84 *Australian Law Journal* 756.

—, 'Unjust Enrichment, Restitution and Proprietary Remedies' in Finn, PD (ed), *Essays on Restitution* (Sydney, Lawbook Co, 1990).

Häcker, B, 'Proprietary Restitution After Impaired Consent Transfers: A Generalised Power Model' [2009] *Cambridge Law Journal* 324.

Harding, M, 'Constructive Trusts and Distributive Justice' in Bant, E and Bryan M (eds), *Principles of Proprietary Remedies* (Sydney, Thomson Reuters, 2013).

Harris, J, 'Doctrine, Justice, and Home-sharing' (1999) 19 *Oxford Journal of Legal Studies* 421.

Hedley, S, 'Looking Outward or Looking Inward? Obligations Scholarship in the Early 21st Century' in Robertson, A and Wu, TH (eds), *The Goals of Private Law* (Oxford, Hart, 2009).

—, 'The Shock of the Old: Interpretivism in Obligations' in Rickett, CEF and Grantham, RB (eds), *Structure and Justification in Private Law* (Oxford, Hart, 2008).

Hodgson, G, 'Markets' in Veblen, TB and Mandel, E (eds), *New Palgrave Dictionary of Economics*, 2nd edn (Basingstoke, Macmillan, 2008).

Hoffmann, L, 'Causation' (2005) 121 *Law Quarterly Review* 592.

Honoré, T, 'Ownership' in Guest, AG (ed), *Oxford Essays in Jurisprudence* (Oxford, Clarendon Press, 1961).

Khurshid, S and Matthews, P, 'Tracing Confusion' (1979) 95 *Law Quarterly Review* 78.
Klimchuk, D, 'The Normative Foundations of Unjust Enrichment' in Chambers, R, Mitchell, C, and Penner, J (eds), *Philosophical Foundations of the Law of Unjust Enrichment* (Oxford, Oxford University Press, 2009).
——, 'Unjust Enrichment and Corrective Justice' in Neyers, J, McInnes, M, and Pitel, S (eds), *Understanding Unjust Enrichment* (Oxford, Hart, 2004).
Kremer, B, 'Book Review: Restatement (Third) of Restitution and Unjust Enrichment' (2012) 35 *Melbourne University Law Review* 1197.
Leeming, M, 'Subrogation, Equity and Unjust Enrichment' in Glister, J, and Ridge, P (eds), *Fault Lines in Equity* (Oxford, Hart, 2012).
Mason, K, 'What is Wrong with Top-Down Legal Reasoning?' (2004) 78 *Australian Law Journal* 574.
McFarlane, B, 'Unjust Enrichment, Property Rights, and Indirect Recipients' [2009] *Restitution Law Review* 37.
——, 'Unjust Enrichment, Rights and Value' in Nolan, D and Robertson, A (eds), *Rights and Private Law* (Oxford, Hart, 2012).
McGhee, J, 'The Nature of the Enrichment Enquiry' in Edelman, J and Degeling, S (eds), *Unjust Enrichment in Commercial Law* (Sydney, Thomson Reuters Australia, 2008).
McInnes, M, '"At the Plaintiff's Expense": Quantifying Restitutionary Relief' (1998) 57 *Cambridge Law Journal* 472.
——, 'Enrichment Revisited' in Neyers, J, McInnes, M, and Pitel, S (eds), *Understanding Unjust Enrichment* (Oxford, Hart, 2004).
——, '*Hambly v Trott* and the Claimant's Expense: Professor Birks' Challenge' in Degeling, S and Edelman, J (eds), *Unjust Enrichment in Commercial Law* (Sydney, Thomson Reuters 2008).
——, 'Interceptive Subtraction, Unjust Enrichment and Wrongs—A Reply to Professor Birks' (2003) 62 *Cambridge Law Journal* 697.
——, 'The Measure of Restitution' (2002) 52 *University of Toronto Law Journal* 163.
Millett, P, '*Jones v Jones*: Property or Unjust Enrichment?' in Burrows, A and Rodger, A (eds), *Mapping the Law: Essays in Memory of Peter Birks* (Oxford, Oxford University Press, 2006).
——, 'Proprietary Restitution' in Degeling, S and Edelman, J (eds), *Equity and Commercial Law* (Sydney, Lawbook 2005).
Mitchell, C, 'Enrichment, Markets, and Spending Decisisions' [2013] *Lloyd's Maritime and Commercial Law Quarterly* 436.
——, 'Liability Chains' in Degeling, S and Edelman, J (eds), *Unjust Enrichment in Commercial Law* (Sydney, Thomson Reuters, 2008).
——, 'Recovery of Compound Interest as Restitution or Damages' (2008) 71 *Modern Law Review* 271.
——, 'Stewardship of Property and Liability to Account' (Lecture given to the Chancery Bar Association Annual Conference, 17 January 2014).
——, 'Unjust Enrichment' in Burrows, A (ed), *English Private Law*, 3rd edn (Oxford, Oxford University Press, 2013).
Mitchell, C, and Mitchell, C, '*Planché v Colburn* (1831)' in Mitchell, C and Mitchell, P (eds), *Landmark Cases in the Law of Restitution* (Oxford, Hart, 2006).
Mitchell, C, and Oliver, P, 'Unjust Enrichment and the Idea of Public Law' in Chambers, R, Mitchell, C, and Penner, J (eds), *Philosophical Foundations of the Law of Unjust Enrichment* (Oxford, Oxford University Press, 2009).

Mitchell, C, and Watterson, S, 'Remedies for Knowing Receipt' in Mitchell, C (ed), *Constructive and Resulting Trusts* (Oxford, Hart, 2009).

Nadler, JM, 'What Right Does Unjust Enrichment Law Protect?' (2008) 28 *Oxford Journal of Legal Studies* 245.

Nicholls, D, 'Knowing Receipt: The Need for New Landmark' in Cornish, WR (ed), *Restitution: Past, Present, and Future* (Oxford, Hart, 1997).

Nolan, D and Davies, J, 'Torts and Equitable Wrongs' in Burrows, A (ed), *English Private Law*, 3rd edn (Oxford, Oxford University Press, 2013).

Penner, J, 'Value, Property and Unjust Enrichment' in Chambers, R, Mitchell, C, and Penner, J (eds), *Philosophical Foundations of The Law of Unjust Enrichment* (Oxford, Oxford University Press, 2009).

Posner, RA, 'Legal Reasoning from the Top Down and from the Bottom Up: The Question of Unenumerated Constitutional Rights' (1992) 59 *University of Chicago Law Review* 433.

Priel, D, 'In Defence of Quasi-Contract' (2012) 75 *Modern Law Review* 54.

Ratan, A, 'Lord Mansfield's Protective Principle and Claims Based on Tracing' (Seminar Paper, Obligations Discussion Group, Univeristy of Oxford, 11 February 2014).

Rudden, B, 'Things as Thing and Things as Wealth' (1994) 14 *Oxford Journal of Legal Studies* 81.

Sharpe, R and Waddams, S, 'Damages for Lost Opportunity to Bargain' (1982) 2 *Oxford Journal of Legal Studies* 290.

Skene, L, 'Proprietary Rights in Human Bodies, Body Parts and Tissue' (2002) 22 *Legal Studies* 102.

Smith, L, 'Legal Epistemology in the Restatement (Third) of Restitution And Unjust Enrichment' (2012) 92 *Boston University Law Review* 899.

—, 'Restitution: The Heart of Corrective Justice' (2001) 79 *Texas Law Review* 2115.

—, 'Three-Party Restitution: A Critique of Birks' Theory of Interceptive Subtraction' (1991) 11 *Oxford Journal of Legal Studies* 481.

—, 'Tracing and Electronic Funds Transfers' in Rose, F (ed), *Restitution and Banking Law* (London, Mansfield Press, 1998).

—, 'Tracing in Taylor v Plumer: Equity in the Court of King's Bench' [1995] *Lloyd's Maritime and Commercial Law Quarterly* 240.

—, 'Unjust Enrichment, Property and the Structure of Trusts' (2000) 116 *Law Quarterly Review* 412.

Smith, S, 'Justifying the Law of Unjust Enrichment' (2001) 29 *Texas Law Review* 2177.

Stapleton, J, 'Choosing What We Mean by "Causation" in the Law' (2008) 73 *Missouri Law Review* 433.

Stevens, R, 'Three Enrichment Issues' in Burrows, A and Rodger, A (eds), *Mapping the Law: Essays in Memory of Peter Birks* (Oxford, Oxford University Press, 2006).

Stoljar, SJ, 'The Transformation of Account' (1964) 80 *Law Quarterly Review* 203.

Strassfeld, RN, 'If …: Counterfactuals in the Law' (1992) 60 *George Washington Law Review* 339.

Swadling, W, 'Ignorance and Unjust Enrichment: The Problem of Title' (2008) 28 *Oxford Journal of Legal Studies* 627.

—, 'Property: General Principles' in Burrows A (ed), *English Private Law*, 3rd edn (Oxford, Oxford University Press, 2013).

Traynor, M, 'The Unjust Enrichment Claim in Moore v Regents' (1990) 9 *Biotechnology Law Report* 240.

Virgo, G, 'Causation and Remoteness within the Law of Unjust Enrichment' in Degeling, S and Edelman, J (eds), *Unjust Enrichment in Commercial Law* (Sydney, Thomson Reuters, 2008).

Waddams, S, 'Classification of Private Law in Relation to Historical Evidence' (2003) 6 *Current Legal Issues* 265.

Walker, R, 'Dishonesty and Unconscionable Conduct in Commercial Life—Some Reflections on Accessory Liability and Knowing Receipt' (2005) 27 *Sydney Law Review* 187.

Watterson, S, 'Direct Transfers in the Law of Unjust Enrichment' (2011) *Current Legal Problems* 435.

Webb, C, 'Property, Unjust Enrichment, and Defective Transfers' in Chambers, R, Mitchell C, and Penner J (eds), *Philosophical Foundations of the Law of Unjust Enrichment* (Oxford, Oxford University Press, 2009).

——, 'Treating Like Cases Alike: Principle and Classification in Private Law' in Robertson, A and Wu, TH (eds), *The Goals of Private Law* (Oxford, Hart, 2009).

Weinrib, EJ, 'Correctively Unjust Enrichment' in Chambers, R, Mitchell, C, and Penner, J (eds), *Philosophical Foundations of the Law of Unjust Enrichment* (Oxford, Oxford University Press, 2009).

——, 'The Normative Structure of Unjust Enrichment' in Rickett, C, and Grantham, R (eds), *Structure and Justification in Private Law* (Oxford, Hart, 2008).

——, 'Restoring Restitution' (2005) 91 *Virginia Law Review* 861.

——, 'The Structure of Unjustness' (2012) 92 *Boston University Law Review* 1067.

Whittaker, SJ, 'An Historical Perspective to the "Special Equitable Action" in Re Diplock' (1983) 4 *Journal of Legal History* 3.

Williston, S, 'The Right to Follow Trust Property when Confused with Other Property' (1888) 2 *Harvard Law Review* 28.

# INDEX

**Introductory Note**

References such as '178–9' indicate (not necessarily continuous) discussion of a topic across a range of pages. Wherever possible in the case of topics with many references, these have either been divided into sub-topics or only the most significant discussions of the topic are listed. Because the entire work is about 'unjust enrichment', the use of this term (and certain others which occur constantly throughout the book) as an entry point has been minimised. Information will be found under the corresponding detailed topics.

www.ingramcontent.com/pod-product-compliance
Ingram Content Group UK Ltd.
Pitfield, Milton Keynes, MK11 3LW, UK
UKHW020138290926
15471UKWH00003B/572

9 781509 928880